STRATEGIES FOR
HELPING STUDENTS

STRATEGIES FOR
HELPING STUDENTS

By

CALVIN D. CATTERALL
Director
Staff Development Consultants
Columbus, Ohio
Former Associate Professor
School Psychology Training Program
The Ohio State University

and

GEORGE M. GAZDA
Research Professor of Education
University of Georgia
Athens, Georgia
Consulting Professor of Psychiatry
Department of Psychiatry
Medical College of Georgia
Augusta, Georgia

CHARLES C THOMAS • PUBLISHER
Springfield • Illinois • U.S.A.

Published and Distributed Throughout the World by
CHARLES C THOMAS • PUBLISHER
BANNERSTONE HOUSE
301-327 East Lawrence Avenue, Springfield, Illinois, U.S.A.

With THOMAS BOOKS *careful attention is given to all details of
manufacturing and design. It is the Publisher's desire to present
books that are satisfactory as to their physical qualities and artistic
possibilities and appropriate for their particular use.* THOMAS
BOOKS *will be true to those laws of quality that assure a good
name and good will.*

Printed in the United States of America
N-11

Library of Congress Cataloging in Publication Data

Catterall, Calvin D
    Strategies for helping students.

    Bibliography: p.
    Includes index.
    1. Remedial teaching. I. Gazda, George Michael, 1931-   joint
author. II. Title.
LB1029.R4C36   371.3   77-8218
ISBN 0-398-03686-1

To our wives
Gretchen B. Catterall
and
Barbara E. Gazda

PREFACE

T HIS BOOK ATTEMPTS to organize and briefly describe all of the *strategies for helping students* which are available to school personnel. People working in the schools tend to use only a limited number of helping procedures. There has long been a need for a system which helps us to organize and to broaden the ways in which we can help students. We all need to work to create a delivery system in education that is developmentally based, thereby preventing many major problems from occurring. The system also should have a corrective/remedial component ready to assist the students as their unique needs and problems are identified. If education is to approximate its ultimate goal of helping students to develop to their maximum, we must not only be sensitive to problems as they arise, but we must all be actively involved in the process of finding and perfecting helping strategies.

Before describing the strategies, however, a basic approach to establishing helping relationships is described in Part I that creates the climate in which these strategies can be most effectively utilized. The characteristics that are most facilitative in the helping person are described in Chapter 2 and concrete suggestions are given on how these characteristics can be developed and utilized. This approach should permeate all of education but will be found especially useful in helping students with more complex problems. Chapter 3 shows why it is important to view students and the helping process along five broad developmental dimensions: psychosocial, physiological-sexual, cognitive, vocational, and moral.

In Part II the specific strategies are described in four chapters each of which represents a major focus or approach to helping students. Whereas any categorization of these techniques tends to become artificial, it has been found helpful to distinguish between strategies that are used essentially for developmental/preventive purposes in contrast to those interventions which are used primarily in a corrective/remedial way. Another helpful analysis indicates that two approaches focus on strategies which are primarily academic/intellectual in nature and that two are directed more toward the humanistic/life skills.

The major part of the book briefly describes all of the helping strategies available to students as follows:

Developing Academic/Intellectual Skills (Chapter 4)—these are the strategies that can be done *around* the student to help him or her to progress effectively through the broadly defined academic areas of the curriculum.

Corrective/Remedial Interventions (Chapter 5)—those interventions that can be done *for* the student when the developmental program has not met his or her academic/intellectual needs.

Developing Humanistic/Life Skills (Chapter 6)—those strategies that can be carried out *with* the student which will help him or her to develop along six broad strands of a humanistic/life skills curriculum.

Corrective/Therapeutic Interventions (Chapter 7)—those interventions which can be taken *in behalf of* the student with specialized personal-social needs to help him or her to learn to use more effectively appropriate life skills.

Strategies for Helping Students is *not* a cookbook, i.e. "with a student who has this problem you should use such-and-such a strategy." The state of the art does not support the use of such ready-made prescriptions. At the same time some strategies have proven to be more helpful than others. Chapter 8 describes the process of systematically choosing strategies which have the best chance of being effective. A series of questions is raised which attempts to determine whether or not everyone is working toward the utilization of a process which develops and corrects the academic/intellectual and life-skill needs found in students.

This book has been written for the following groups:

Teachers, who have the most frequent (and certainly the most important) contacts with students.

Administrators, who must provide the necessary support to the teachers to enable them to be better able to help the students.

Specialists, whose expertise is urgently needed especially in providing the corrective/remedial/therapeutic interventions needed by students.

All educators who desire to improve their skills in helping students by developing a higher level of expertise in using a wide spectrum of services and people to help meet students' needs.

A book such as this cannot be the sole product of its authors. We would like to thank all of those professional colleagues and students, too numerous to mention, who over the years have interacted with us to help identify, sharpen, and use the complete series of helping strategies. We would also like to recognize and express our sincere thanks to Gretchen Catterall, Barbara Gazda, and Kathy Pattison without whose countless hours of critical feedback and strong secretarial support this book would not have been possible.

CALVIN D. CATTERALL
GEORGE M. GAZDA

CONTENTS

STRATEGIES FOR
HELPING STUDENTS

PART I

INTRODUCTION

PART I CONSISTS of three chapters: Chapter 1 includes a description of the evolution of the book and the rationale for its development in this current form.

Chapter 2 contains a description of a model for helpers (interventionists) to guide them in relationship building and problem solving. This model provides the users of this text with the basic conditions of a helping relationship which, if they are followed, would go a long way toward ensuring the successful application of the interventions and strategies described in Chapters 4 through 8. In other words, Chapter 2 provides a blueprint of a proven model which, if followed, will maximize the value of the interventions/strategies outlined in this text. The action phase of this model can only be implemented if the users have a repertoire of proven interventions or strategies to call upon, once the student is ready to change but needs help with specific things to do that will increase his/her chances for success.

Chapter 3 provides an example for implementing the model outlined in Chapter 2. A program involving several interventions and strategies is developed to illustrate the need to consider the various strengths and deficits of the whole person when developing a program to assist him/her. A step-by-step process leading toward a comprehensive plan of action for the student is outlined in Chapter 3.

It is the wish of the authors that the users of this text will appreciate both the necessity for a model in which various interventions/strategies can be implemented and the need for a compendium of interventions/strategies to apply to the varying needs/deficits of a given student. The model and the interventions/strategies are interdependent. The action phase of the model requires the application of strategies.

Chapter 1

THE NEED FOR AND THE PURPOSES OF
INTERVENTIONS AND STRATEGIES

In this book the authors attempt to organize and briefly to describe *the strategies for helping students* which are available to school personnel. Education has needed a classification system which would systematically classify and extend the use of the full range of services needed by students. School personnel tend to develop a limited number of strategies for helping the students with whom they come in contact, i.e. teachers teach, counselors counsel, and psychologists test. Educators need to increase the number of ways in which they work with students. Perhaps most important, educators need to create a social and psychological climate in which they can all work together to develop and to use a broader spectrum of helping strategies.

Not only is it necessary for educators to have a broad repertoire of responses (intervention strategies) to draw upon for preventative as well as remedial purposes, but perhaps even more important, these strategies must be employed within the context of a proven model. In Chapter 2 this model is described. Chapter 3 contains an illustration of the application of a series of interventions and strategies within the context of the model to complete a *program of intervention.*

All of the programs and procedures listed in this book which are designed to help students are strategies because they do the following:

1. Represent an attempt to focus on and to organize the known principles of helping students;
2. Reflect an action-oriented program applicable to the broad spectrum of student needs typically found in the school;
3. Are practical insofar as they describe techniques that can be used in the school setting (although some may also be used

5

in other agencies) using factors over which the schools have control;

4. Set in motion the interaction of a number of strategists with varying backgrounds and skills to bring the maximum amount of expertise to the task of helping students;

5. Stress the need for selecting and using several strategies in stereo for helping a specific student; and

6. Describe a full range of services starting with the basic developmental curriculum (which has a strong preventative component) through all of the corrective/remedial therapeutic activities.

Educators have been trying for years to find ways to categorize and to organize the helping strategies. The early contributions by David Kiersey are recognized; unfortunately little of his creative thinking has been published and so it has not been widely utilized. In 1967 Catterall authored a monograph entitled *Strategies for Prescriptive Interventions* (now out of print) to help students with problems. This monograph set forth three major types of interventions: environmental (indirect attempts to help students through a broadly based curriculum); installed (direct approaches to helping students through working on their personal problems); and transactional (direct ways of working with students through a broadly defined counseling approach). The model set forth in this monograph was later summarized in a brief article, "The Taxonomy of Prescriptive Interventions" (Catterall, 1970).

Blanco approached the task of categorizing helping strategies from a different direction. He took the list of pathological symptoms published by the Group for the Advancement of Psychiatry (1966) and asked a large group of practicing school psychologists to submit prescriptions they had found successful in working with children with those symptoms. Blanco's (1970) first publication on this work was an article entitled "Fifty Recommendations to Aid Exceptional Children." This was followed by a book, *Prescriptions for Children with Learning and Adjustment Problems* (Blanco, 1972). Both of these publications emphasized the following: "If you have a student with certain symptoms, here are some prescriptions which have been found helpful by practitioners in the field."

Recently Swift and Spivak (1975) authored a book for teachers and psychologists to assist them in their work with behaviorally troubled, elementary school-age children. In the same year, Catterall revised his earlier monograph under the title, *Strategies for Helping Students* (1975). The four-way structure in the revised publication included the following areas: Developing Academic/ Intellectual Skills, Corrective/Remedial Interventions, Developing Humanistic Skills, and Corrective/Therapeutic Interventions.

In the first edition of *Human Relations Development: A Manual for Educators,* Gazda et al. (1973) indicated that there was a need for *action strategies* and problem-solving procedures to complete more fully the facilitative dimensions stressed in that edition. The revised edition of Gazda et al. (1977) has a more complete rationale for problem-solving interventions. This rationale is outlined in Chapters 2 and 3 of this text. It should be obvious from these chapters that a compendium of intervention strategies such as contained within this text completes the developmental model outlined by Gazda et al. (1977).

Although these earlier works provide a start, there is still a need for an expanded listing of ways to help all students, not just those in trouble. An approach is needed which would provide the classroom teacher as well as other educators with a structure around which they could organize and develop the strategies needed by the students with whom they are working. In the past, more attention had been given to helping students in academic/intellectual learning areas. There is currently a need to organize and to extend the many ways that schools can help students develop appropriate *life-coping skills* (Gazda, 1977). There is a need for a listing of the full spectrum of strategies, from those which are developmental in nature and should be available for all students, to those that are corrective or remedial in nature for students who have special needs. Rather than being restricted primarily to younger children, such a taxonomy should list all of the ways to help students across the full range of student ages, from preschool through high school.

Previous efforts to find simple solutions to the problem of students have overemphasized assessment. Nevertheless, there is still a place for it (described in Chapter 8 in this text). Even though some problems go unrecognized in students, a much more pressing concern is the ability to know what to do with the problems that have already been identified. In general, teachers know which students need special help, but often they do not know *how* to help them. Assessment is too often aimed at the process of trying to label the problem of the student rather than in trying to identify specific strategies for helping the student. In some instances the very process of labeling students, e.g. "emotionally disturbed," tends to block more services than it brings to them. Although one cannot avoid labels completely, in this book the authors have tried to deemphasize many of the negative labels which have caused so much trouble, and to emphasize those which will help to identify the strategies and interventions needed by the student.

In some ways it would be desirable to have a book which could specify that for a given kind of problem, one should try a certain kind of strategy. Unfortunately, the state of the art at this time does not support this kind of approach, if indeed it ever will. This approach implies that specialists can agree that they are describing the same kinds of behavior when they apply a certain label to a child. It also suggests that there is a "best" strategy for all students with a given problem. To the best of the authors' knowledge, neither of these assumptions have been verified.

It is obvious that strategies gain their meaning from the complex social situation in which they are found. For the sake of emphasis, strategies in this book will be singled out and described one at a time. They only have meaning, however, when used in the context of the total social environment of the school setting.

The emphasis in this book is, therefore, the classification and categorization of all available strategies for helping students. Rather than singling out those strategies that are innovative or those which seem to have greatest promise, an attempt has been made (within reasonable limits) to include *all* such strategies. Some strategies have been included that continue to be used frequently even though there is evidence that they are not very effective. They still represent part of the total range of strategies available to school personnel. The fact that they have not worked well may simply reflect the fact that educators have not learned to use them well or that they have used them separately when they should have been used in stereo.

The emphasis in this work has been to stretch the conceptual framework of the educator to become aware of a much broader spectrum of strategies that can be employed. It is hoped that this book will also help educators to find some common frames of reference as attempts are made to define the various strategies. Educators will then be in a better position to begin the process of identifying the conditions under which these strategies are most likely to be successful. References to the literature, whenever possible, have been made, and the "hunches" of the authors about which strategies work for which students have sometimes been included. In general, educators and others are at a very primitive stage in the process of trying to identify which strategy to use for a particular deficit. Suggestions for selecting strategies will be provided in Chapter 8, but the process is currently much more of an art than it is a science. To facilitate the process of selecting strategies, the establishment of a *Learning Facilitation Team* is suggested. This team utilizes the expertise of several people with different points of view—a team that evaluates the individual student as well as the total school environment.

The assumption upon which this book has been developed is that everyone in education must be involved in both the identification of causes of problems and the possible solutions of those problems. The older model of taking the "problem" student out of the class, subjecting him or her to study by specialists in an isolated situation, and waiting for the list of "recommendations" which would solve the problems is not effective. There are too many of these students with specialized needs. Their needs change from day to day and from one period of life to another. It should also be recognized that student problems often originate from the educational procedures rather than from the student. The cure is increasingly being found in bringing a broader range of services to bear to help the student as well as revising educational practices. This is often made possible by increased knowledge and technology. It is the wish of the authors that the brief descriptions of the strategies provided in this book will trigger a whole new spectrum of as-yet-undreamed-of ways for helping students.

Educators are being pushed in several directions at once:

(1) They are being asked to *become more professional.* They are urged to take additional course work, to participate in programs of continuing education, to become actively engaged in professional organizations, to "stand up and be counted," and to negotiate for what they think is best for the profession. At the same time, they are asked to set aside their professional identity and to think primarily of the effect of the "total team." They are asked to *involve* a wide group of *volunteers, aides, and paraprofessionals* in helping to meet student needs.

(2) Educators are strongly encouraged to be more precise, to be more efficient, to be accountable, to use more powerful techniques, to develop the skills needed for correcting or remediating deficits. They are urged to attend meetings and to contribute to the new educational technology. At the same time, they are asked to *be more humane,* to improve their interpersonal communication, to make education more relevant, and to pay more attention to the rights of students and parents.

(3) Educators are under pressure from the courts to help all students to both enroll and stay in school and to receive a relevant education in a normal setting. At the same time some teachers and administrators want to expel students with serious problems.

Strategies for Helping Students was written to provide a framework within which the seemingly opposing pressures on education can be brought into focus and which will help all educators to—

BECOME MORE PROFESSIONAL. It points the way to a variety of things everyone can do to become more professional as they use a wider selection of strategies and as they learn to make their unique professional contributions to the team that is working to help students.

INVOLVE MORE PARAPROFESSIONALS. The book offers guidelines and examples of a variety of ways of involving a great number of other people in the task of helping. These paraprofessionals include teacher aides, parents, community workers, and students, among others.

DEVELOP A MORE EFFICIENT TECHNOLOGY. The book should help educators become more critical and precise in their thinking as they first identify needs and then set out to provide developmental and corrective programs to meet those needs.

HELP TO MAKE EDUCATION MORE HUMANE AND PERSONALLY RELEVANT. The book directs attention to how educators can use themselves to model and to teach good life-skills development and to make the process of education more relevant and personally meaningful for all.

Strategies for Helping Students has been written for the following: *Teachers,* who have the most frequent (and certainly the most important) contacts with the students; *Administrators,* who must provide the necessary support to the teachers, enabling them to help the students; *Specialists,* whose expertise is urgently needed to provide the Corrective/Remedial/Therapeutic services needed by students; *All educators,* who contribute to the learning facilitation team to use as a guideline for involving a wide spectrum of services and people to meet students' needs.

REFERENCES

Blanco, R. F. Fifty recommendations to aid exceptional children. *Psychology in the Schools,* 1970, *7,* 29-37.

Blanco, R. F. *Prescriptions for children with learning and behavior adjustment problems.* Springfield, Ill.: Charles C Thomas, 1972.

Catterall, C. D. *Strategies for prescriptive interventions.* Santa Clara, Calif.: Santa Clara Unified School District, 1967 (out of print).

Catterall, C. D. Taxonomy of prescriptive interventions. *Journal of School Psychology,* 1970, *8,* 5-12.

Catterall, C. D. *Strategies for helping students.* Columbus, Ohio: Author, 1975.

Gazda, G. M. Developmental education: The conceptual components of a comprehensive counseling and guidance program. In C. D. Johnson (Ed.), *Guidance Personnel 1984: Models for the Future.* Fullerton, Calif.: California Personnel and Guidance Association, 1977, 8-22.

Gazda, G. M., Asbury, F. A., Balzer, F. J., Childers, W. C., Desselle, R. E., & Walters, R. P. *Human relations development: A manual for educators.* Boston: Allyn & Bacon, 1973.

Gazda, G. M., Asbury, F. A., Balzer, F. J., Childers, W. C., & Walters, R. P. *Human relations development: A manual for educators* (2nd ed.), Boston: Allyn & Bacon, 1977.

Group for the Advancement of Psychiatry. *Psychopathological disorders in childhood: Theoretical considerations and a proposed classification* (Rept. no. 62). New York: Author, 1966.

Swift, M. S. & Spivak, G. *Alternative teaching strategies: Helping behaviorally troubled children achieve.* Champaign, Ill.: Research Press, 1975.

Chapter 2

A MODEL FOR A PREFERRED MODE OF HELPING*

T HE MODEL WHICH WILL BE DESCRIBED in this chapter has evolved from hundreds of studies based on the research of numerous counselors and psychotherapists. From the many studies of divergent theories and therapies, a common thread has been discovered. Truax and Carkhuff (1967) have carefully traced this thread, and they have described it as consisting of certain particular characteristics of the therapist. The characteristics first described were termed *accurate empathy, nonpossessive warmth,* and *genuineness.* Rogers (1957) served as the impetus to focus renewed interest on these and similar characteristics.

Working with Rogers at the University of Wisconsin, Truax, Carkhuff, and many others began to investigate the effect of the presence of the "common thread" in the therapist-client relationship. They discovered that certain conditions or dimensions offered by the therapist, when present in high levels, led to growth on the part of the client, and when absent, or only present in low levels, led to deterioration of the client. The accumulated evidence of the validity of the "core" conditions, or dimensions, as they were to be called, can be found in several volumes, especially in Rogers, Gendlin, Kiesler, and Truax (1967), Truax and Carkhuff (1967), Berenson and Carkhuff (1967), Carkhuff and Berenson (1967), Carkhuff (1969a, 1969b, 1971a), and Berenson and Mitchell (1974).

As the research progressed, several new dimensions were discovered and scales for rating these dimensions were developed (Carkhuff, 1969a, 1969b; Carkhuff and Berenson, 1967; Truax and

---

*A significant part of this chapter is reproduced from Gazda, G. M., Asbury, F. A., Balzer, F. J., Childers, W. C., and Walters, R. P. *Human relations development: A manual for educators* (2nd ed.). Boston: Allyn & Bacon, 1977. Reproduced by permission.

13

Carkhuff, 1967). Eventually Carkhuff (1969a, 1969b) refined, re-
named, and standardized the scales of the core dimensions and
added a rationale which seemed to complete the model for a helping relationship. Although further refinement of existing dimensions and scales and the search for new dimensions continues, there
is now available a substantial body of research and knowledge to
support a preferred mode of helping. The authors know of no
other model for human relations training which has been so thor-
oughly researched and so carefully developed, and therefore it is
offered with considerable confidence in its validity.

THE GOALS OF HELPING

Generally speaking, the universally accepted goal of helping is
to generate more appropriate behavior. The specific goals for a
given helpee† will be determined by the helper and helpee collab-
oratively as they interact in the helping relationship. The nature
of the interaction must be controlled by the helper. The educator
who is acting in the role of helper is the expert on the conditions
necessary for change to occur; therefore he/she must control his/
her own behavior and create an atmosphere of security and trust
that are prerequisites for the first step or goal in helping. The
conditions necessary for healthy, productive interpersonal relationships can be systematically taught, practiced, and incorporated
into one's life-style.

Carkhuff (1971a) has outlined (and the authors have adapted)
the three goals of helping as follows:

---

†Helpee(s) is used throughout this chapter and the next to designate the person(s)
seeking some kind of assistance. The authors do not wish to imply that the
helpee is the kind of person who is continuously in a state of emotional turmoil
or some other difficulty. The authors have simply chosen this term as a suc-
cinct means of referring to a person on the help-seeking or help-receiving end
of a continuum at a given moment. In other words, the helpee may be showing
a very positive behavior in actively seeking assistance and understanding that in
every respect is prevention oriented, whereas at other times the helpee may, in
fact, be the passive recipient of the helper's action. Whether the helpee is the
seeker or passive recipient of help, the goal of the model is the same—to provide
the conditions that enable the helpee to be actively involved in the solution of
his/her problems in such a manner that he/she may also be willing to accept
responsibility for his/her actions.

HELPEE SELF-EXPLORATION. The first goal of helping is to facilitate helpee self-exploration. Before helpers can be of any assistance to a helpee, they must understand the helpee's problem in depth. Likewise, helpees must know their own problems in all their ramifications if they are to be fully involved in their solution.

Untrained lay "helpers" frequently miss their first opportunity to help by being too willing to accept the helpees' initial statement of their problems as the primary concern. The helper then often gives advice on how the helpee should handle the problem. This is what is called "cheap and dirty" advice because frequently it is "off the top of the head" of the helper and based on too little information. It is typically the kind of advice that the helpee has already considered and probably even tried, unsuccessfully.

HELPEE UNDERSTANDING AND COMMITMENT. When helpees are permitted to explore or are helped to explore their problems in depth, they are likely to understand them and themselves better. The role of helpers is to assist helpees in making some kind of sense out of the many pieces of their puzzle. Typically, helpees have thought about their problems a great deal, but because they did not have the necessary skills or responses or could not put them together in the proper combination, they were unable to change their behavior and so remained problem ridden.

Although self-understanding is generally considered to be a prerequisite condition for most types of problem solving, it is a well-accepted fact among professional helpers that understanding alone is frequently insufficient in changing behavior: witness, for example, the many people who know (cognitively) that smoking is harmful to their physical health and yet persist in smoking. What is missing from the persons who know what is best for them and do not act to change in that direction is *commitment*. Therefore, during the second phase of helping, the helpee must not only understand their problem(s) in depth but must also make a cognitive *and* visceral decision to follow through with a plan or program designed to correct their deficits.

HELPPEE ACTION. Often the most difficult step in problem solving is taking the necessary action to correct the identified

problem.   The helper and helpee must devise a plan of action
helpees can follow to resolve their problems.   It must be a plan
that is possible to complete.   That is, helpees have to be capable
of taking a series of successful steps or actions that will ensure the
success of the next step and ultimately the successful resolution of
the problem.   In the process of arriving at a given course of action, helper and helpee consider alternate plans and the possible
consequences of different plans before selecting one (see Chapter
3 for a more complete description of program planning) .

It is important to understand here that not all teachers and
educators will always be able to develop a sequence of action that
will lead to a desired outcome.   Often, the educator-helper will be
just one link in the chain of life of a helpee.   The helper may
simply be the person who assists in developing a few key responses
in the helpee's total repertoire of responses that he/she can use in
the future to help solve his/her problems or enrich his/her life.

THE CYCLE OF HELPING

If helpees will *self-explore,* this usually leads to a better understanding of their concerns and a commitment to change, which,
in turn, makes possible a more successful course of action.   The
action itself provides the ultimate feedback to helpees.   Often
they will need to refine or alter their responses to arrive at the preferred behavioral outcome.   Helpees repeat the cycle as often as
necessary to lead them toward their goals.

Carkhuff has outlined, and the authors have adapted, a three-
phase cycle for problem solving: *self-exploration* → *better self-
understanding and a commitment to change* → *more appropriate
action or direction.*   This cycle works for most people; however,
there are exceptions.   With individuals who are not in good contact with reality, it is usually necessary to reverse the cycle and
first do something to get them back in contact with reality before
understanding can occur.   The authors, at this point, are generally describing the severely emotional and mentally disturbed,
and since educators are not expected to deal extensively with this
population, this type of helping will not be emphasized in this
text.

THE PROCESS OF HELPING

Table 2-I contains the key concepts in the helping model developed by Carkhuff (1969a,b; 1971a; 1972) and adapted by Balzer (in Gazda, Walters, and Childers, 1975). The first phase of helping is directed toward establishing a base or building a good relationship with the helpee. It might entail verbal expression, nonverbal expression, direct physical action, or a combination of all of these modes depending upon the age, intelligence, and degree of contact with reality of the helpee.

Preparing for a space shot and firing the rocket is analogous to the two *basic* phases of helping: facilitation and action. Before a rocket can be fired many preparations must be made. First, a very strong base must be built under the rocket to hold it and to sustain the backward thrust when it is fired. Similarly, in a helping relationship, the helper must first use the less threatening (facilitative) dimensions to prepare and sustain the helpee for the more threatening but often necessary action or initiative dimensions. If helpers will carefully build their base with helpees, they will help ensure their success when they become judgmental (conditional) with helpees at a later action period. Carkhuff (1971b) succinctly stated the importance of the facilitation phase of helping when he said, "Even if you have just fifteen minutes to help, you must use five minutes or so responding (facilitating) to the helpee in order to find out for sure where the helpee is before starting to put the picture together initiating and acting upon that picture" (p. 22).

FACILITATION DIMENSIONS

Helpers begin to build their base with helpees by first responding with *empathy, respect,* and *warmth.* Table 2-I shows how this leads to increased helpee exploration (the first goal of helping).

To achieve success in the first goal of helping, helpers must be able to refrain from acting on their value judgments about helpees. Virtually no one can refrain from making evaluations or judgments about others, but helpers can refrain from *acting* prematurely on their judgments. This is especially important if their early evaluations or judgments are negative. For example, helpers

TABLE 2-I. PHASES OF THE HELPING RELATIONSHIP

Dimensions	Facilitation	Transition	Action
Empathy	Level 3 (reflective interchangeable affect/meaning)	Level 4 (interpretation of underlying feelings/meaning)	Level 4 (emphasizes periodic feedback)
Respect	Level 3 (belief in helpee's worth and potential)	Level 4 (deep valuing and commitment to helpee's growth)	Level 4 (deep valuing and commitment to helpee's growth)
Warmth	Level 3 (shows attention and interest clearly)	Level 4 (wholly, intensely attentive and supportive)	Level 4 (wholly, intensely attentive and supportive)
Concreteness	Level 3 (specific, concrete expressions)	Level 4 (Concreteness may be de-emphasized; abstract exploration is sometimes necessary)	Level 4 (specificity plus solicitation of specificity for plans and programs of action)
Genuineness	Level 3 (controlled expression of feelings; absence of phoniness)	Level 3 (controlled expression of feeling; absence of phoniness) and Level 4 (congruence between verbal and nonverbal messages; spontaneity)	Level 4 (congruence between verbal and nonverbal messages; spontaneity)
Self-Disclosure		Level 3 (volunteers own general material) and Level 4 (volunteers own specific material)	Level 4 (volunteers own specific material, and may risk exposing own fear; hang-ups, etc.)
Confrontation		Level 3 (tentative expression of discrepancy)	Level 4 (explicit expression of discrepancy)
Immediacy		Level 3 (discusses relationship in a general way)	Level 4 (discusses relationship in a specific way)

Self-Exploration → Self-Understanding and Commitment → Action

The helper's communication, having these dimensions, serves as a stimulus and elicits → these behaviors from the helpee in response

Helper-offered levels of the core dimensions and helpee behaviors in the phases of helping. (This represents an extension of the figure by Carkhuff, 1969b, p 101. Prepared by Fred J. Balzer.) Adapted from G. M. Gazda, R. P. Walters, and W. C. Childers, *Human Relations Development: A Manual for Health Sciences* (Boston: Allyn and Bacon, 1975.) Reproduced by permission.

may initially be repulsed by helpees for a number of good reasons; nevertheless, if they can suspend acting on these feelings, they can usually discover something good or likeable about the helpees and at that point begin to invest in the helpees and build a base from which to work.

"Putting oneself in the shoes of another" and "seeing through the eyes of another" are ways of describing *empathy*. Empathy appears to be the most important dimension in the helping process (Carkhuff 1969a, p. 202). If one cannot understand (empathize with) the helpee, one cannot help him/her.

Another facilitative dimension is *respect*. Helpers cannot help helpees if they have no faith in the helpees ability to solve their own problems. Respect develops as helpers learn about the uniqueness and the capabilities of helpees. It grows as helpers observe helpees' efforts in many aspects of their lives. Respect can usually be demonstrated by good helpers' attending behavior and a belief in the capacity of helpees to help themselves, as exemplified by not doing something for them when they can do it for themselves, but rather supporting them in their efforts.

Warmth or caring is closely related to empathy and respect. People tend to love or have concern for those they know (understand) and believe in (respect). It is difficult to conceive of a helper being able to help anyone for whom he/she does not care. ("Help" here means to "make a significant investment in.") In this model, warmth is communicated primarily through nonverbal means, such as a smile, caress, touch, or hug.

FACILITATION-ACTION DIMENSIONS—
HELPER-ORIENTED

As the helper begins to develop a base with the helpee by responding with empathy, respect, and warmth, the helpee self-explores in greater and greater depth. In fact, the clue to whether or not the helper is being successful in the early phase of helping is based on the degree to which the helpee uses helper responses to make deeper and more thorough self-explorations.

With repeated interchangeable helper responses—responses that give back to helpees essentially that which they have given to helpers—helpees often begin to repeat themselves and "spin their wheels" or reach a plateau of self-exploration and understanding. Before helpees reach a plateau the dimensions of *concreteness, genuineness,* and *self-disclosure* are next carefully implemented. When helpers press for greater concreteness or specificity on the part of the helpees, however, they introduce a certain degree of threat. The same thing occurs when helpers become more genuine and set the stage (model) for the helpees to become more genuine. Helpers' self-disclosure encourages greater intimacy in the relationship, which can lead to increased threat to the helpees. In other words, these three dimensions increase the threat level for the helpee, and they are thus *action oriented* as well as facilitative. In addition to the relationship between level of threat and the action phase, these three dimensions are also involved in the problem-solving or planning stages of the action phase.

Specifically, *concreteness* refers to the helpees pinpointing or accurately labeling feelings and experiences. Helpers facilitate this by being specific themselves, or at least as specific as the helpees have been. When helpers are more specific than helpees, they are going beyond where the helpees are or they are *additive.* If helpers' *timing* of their use of additive concreteness is correct, the helpees can achieve greater understanding because their concerns were made more explicit.

Genuineness refers to the ability of helpers to be real or honest with the helpees. Their verbalizations are congruent with their inner feeilngs. Whether or not the helpers' genuineness is useful to helpees will often depend upon the helpers' ability to time their level of honesty so as to lead to greater trust and understanding. As Carkhuff (1971b, p. 21) has said, "Helping is for the helpee." If the helpee cannot utilize the helper genuineness, it may be useless or even hurtful. The saying, "Honesty is the best policy," is not always correct, especially if brutal honesty is employed and the recipients are not capable of dealing with it to improve themselves. To illustrate, encounter groups are often harmful to certain persons, especially when, as is sometimes the case, frankness precedes the establishment of a solid base or relationship.

Self-disclosure by helpers can lead to greater closeness between helpers and helpees *if it is appropriate* or relevant to the helpee's problem. If the helper has had a concern similar to that of the helpee and has found a solution to the problem, this can be reassuring to the helpee. Furthermore, the helpee's solution may even be similar to the one employed by the helper. The success of Alcoholics Anonymous and other self-help groups is related to this dimension. Drinking alcoholics, for example, look to "dry alcoholics" of AA for the solution to their own problems. The "speaker" phase of AA thus uses the self-disclosure dimension.

When helper self-disclosure is premature or irrelevant to the helpee's problem, it tends to confuse the helpee or put the focus on the helper. There is a danger of stealing the spotlight when the helper self-discloses prematurely.

FACILITATION-ACTION DIMENSIONS— HELPEE-ORIENTED

The facilitation-action dimensions of concreteness, genuineness, and self-disclosure can be used to predict the degree of success of the *helpee's help-seeking.* The degree to which helpees can be concrete about their problems (can label them accurately, for instance), can be honest and open with helpers, and can self-disclose at high levels will determine whether or not the helpees will, in fact, receive help. Of course, the other important factor in the help-seeking equation is the helpers. If helpees choose to be concrete, genuine, and to self-disclose to persons who are incapable of helping them, helpees may become disillusioned or, worse still, hurt. (Truax and Carkhuff, 1967, p. 143).

Prospective helpers (educators) can predict the relative success that they might achieve with a given student-helpee. For example, helper-educators can rate student-helpees on the Helpee Help-Seeking Scale, e.g. their willingness to seek help actively; on the Helpee Self-Exploration Scale, based on the extent they will volunteer personally relevant material; and on the Helpee Action-Implementing Scale, based on the helpee's effort to follow an accepted course of action. These dimensions and others for rating helpees' potential for receiving help are described in Table 2-II.

TABLE 2-II
SCALES FOR RATING THE HELPEE*

The three scales to be presented are Helpee Help-Seeking Scale, Helpee Self-Exploration Scale, and Helpee Action-Implementing Scale. These scales are designed to ensure that helpees are at high levels on the Help-Seeking Scale before they can move on to high levels on the Self-Exploration Scale and, likewise, they must be high on the Self-Exploration Scale before they can be high on the Action-Implementing Scale. Thus, the three scales roughly form a continuum of helpees' commitment to the process of their own problem resolution or personal growth.

The three helpee rating scales are outlined in the following section and the levels are defined.

Helpee Help-Seeking Scale

The Help-Seeking Scale is a measure of whether or not the helpee wants to be involved in a helper-helpee relationship. Helpees are rated on this scale according to the strength of their desire for help.

Level 5   Helpee actively seeks help.

Level 4   Helpee accepts help when provided.

Level 3   Helpee is open to being helped, will consider entering a helping relationship.

Level 2   Helpee admits need for help but avoids entering a helping relationship.

Level 1   Helpee overtly refuses available help, or the helpee participates in helper-helpee relationships in order to qualify for benefits extrinsic to the aims of the helping relationship.

Helpee Self-Exploration Scale

The Helpee Self-Exploration Scale is a measure of the extent to which the helpee is actively searching for new feelings and

*From Gazda, G. M., Walters, R. P., and Childers, W. C. *Human relations development: A manual for health sciences.* Boston: Allyn & Bacon, 1975. Reproduced by permission.

understandings. Helpees are rated on this scale according to the strength of their desire to self-explore.

Level 5   Helpee actively searches for new feelings and under-standings (even if they arouse anxiety) .

Level 4   Helpee volunteers personally relevant material with spontaneity and emotional proximity.

Level 3   Helpee volunteers personally relevant material but mechanically and with no feeling.

Level 2   Helpee responds mechanically and with no feeling to personally relevant material introduced by the helper.

Level 1   Helpee avoids all self-expression, is defensive, and pro-vides no opportunity to discuss personally relevant material.

Helpee Action-Implementing Scale

The Implementing Scale is a measure of the degree to which the helpee participates in the determination and practice of prob-lem-solving or growth-directed behaviors. The course of action is defined as the steps helpees take toward solving their problems and includes training, counseling, socialization, education, resti-tution, physical exercise, relaxation, or other efforts.

Level 5   Helpee follows the course of action to the extent that it exists. He/she does everything known to be done for that situation at that time.

Level 4   Helpee accepts part of the course of action.

Level 3   Helpee considers following the course of action as it is evolving.

Level 2   Helpee is accepting of helper communication that is high on action dimensions.

Level 1   Helpee rejects or avoids helper communication.

By using the scale, helpers may observe the degree to which helpees employ the basic defense mechanisms and may predict whether or not helpees are amenable to receiving help.

If prospective helpees are reluctant to seek out helpers, if helpees talk about their concerns in vague and general terms (not concrete), are observed to be playing a role or relate in a superficial or phony manner (not genuine), do not make personally relevant disclosures, and do not follow courses of action that they agreed upon, helpers are relatively safe in predicting that these helpees will be difficult to help. Also, the process might require a relatively long period of time in developing the base—the first phase of helping—before any positive action may occur.

ACTION DIMENSIONS

The action or initiative phase of helping may be considered as the most important phase. It is in this phase that tough decisions are made and the hard work must be done. It is the ultimate test of whether or not the helper is, in fact, the "more knowing" individual and is tough and confident enough to believe both in his/her own and his/her helpee's ability to come up with a plan of action or program (a series of interventions) and follow through on it when the going gets difficult. The helper must be capable of helping to develop a program or series of interrelated interventions for the helpee that will lead to the successful resolution of the helpee's current problem and, at the same time, provide the helpee with a method for attacking future problems. Since teachers usually do not have the time or perhaps the special training in behavior problem solving, they should not expect to carry the primary burden of developing strategies for behavioral problem solving, but instead be partners in the Learning Facilitation Team, composed of other educational specialists as well as teachers (see Chapter 8).

If helpers themselves have not resolved the particular problem or concern of the helpee in question, it is highly unlikely that they can assist their helpees with the problem. That "you cannot help someone else solve a problem you have not resolved yourself" is a maxim every helper must use to guide all helping attempts.

If helpers know themselves they will be unlikely to enter into a helping relationship in a problem area that remains unresolved for themselves.

There is another cardinal rule in helping: One does not confront nor emphasize the action dimensions until one has earned the right, that is, has built the base. One often hears, especially from young people, "Tell it like it is." Telling it like it is often is tantamount to confronting someone. It must be emphasized once more that one can be most punitive or harmful when one is being brutally honest and confronting. *Confrontation,* a key action dimension, can be helpful when the helpee has learned, from earlier experience, that the helper is concerned about his/her welfare and cares enough even to risk the relationship to "level" with him/her.

Frequently, confrontation refers to dealing with a discrepancy between what helpees have been saying about themselves and what they have, in fact, been doing. A common confrontation is assisting helpees to face the reality of a situation. The most threatening type of confrontation is one that does not allow helpees to "save face." This is the type of confrontation that deals with the here and now. When helpees are caught behaving contrary to the way they claim to behave and they are confronted directly with it, it is difficult for them to deny it. They have few good means of defense and may use denial and other inappropriate short-term mechanisms that have long-term disadvantages. For example, if a mother catches her son in the cookie jar and accuses him of stealing cookies, the child may actually deny that he was taking a cookie. This often happens; the child often denies reality when the external threat is great enough. Parents and teachers often unknowingly teach children to lie and to deny reality by the use of threats.

Berenson and Mitchell's (1974) extensive research on the effects of the use of confrontation is quite sobering. They contend that confrontation is never necessary, but that it can be effective and efficient when used by highly functioning persons. Jacobs (1975) reported that in a series of eleven studies on verbal feedback in groups, no evidence was found where negative feedback (one might consider this a form of confrontation of deficits) was advantageous to the group or recipient. Positive feedback (confrontation of one's potential) was rated as more believable, desirable, and of greater impact by recipients and donors with various populations of participants, types of leaders, manners and styles of delivery, and types and amounts of information exchanged. Jacobs furthermore contends that believability of information seems likely to be a necessary, although perhaps not always a sufficient condition for attitudinal and behavioral change. In other words, the evidence is beginning to suggest that confrontation of one's deficits (negative feedback) must only be used by highly functioning, sensitive helpers. Even then, the evidence suggests that the risk may be too great for potential benefits to be derived.

The last dimension, *immediacy*, is often related to confrontation. It refers to what is really going on between helper and helpee. When helpees are unaware of their reactions toward helpers, helpers may need to describe or explain them. It includes "telling it like it is" between helper and helpee in the here and now. Helpees can gain a better understanding of themselves, especially how they affect others (in this case the helper), when helpers appropriately use the immediacy dimension. Once again, the helper must carefully time the employment of immediacy if the helpee is to be able to use it productively.

The productive use of the action dimensions of confrontation and immediacy can be guaranteed by taking the position that "the customer (helpee) is always right." By this we simply mean that regardless of how brilliant and creative the responses of a helper may appear to be, if helpees cannot use them in solving their problems they are worthless—if not harmful—to them.

Implementing a Course of Action

The courses of action that may be developed for helpees to achieve their goals or to give them direction may be many and varied. They may involve the physical, psychosocial, cognitive, vocational, or moral domains, or for some, all five of them.

The principles involved in implementing a course of action recommended by Carkhuff (1969a, p. 243) are summarized as follows: (1) the helper must check with the helpee at all stages of development and implementation to be sure that what is planned or performed is relevant to the helpee's functioning; (2) the focus of change should usually be on the helpee first and only second-arily on the helpee's relationships with others; (3) only those measures or procedures that ensure the highest probability of con-structive change are employed; (4) the emphasis is on outcomes and the achievement of attainable goals. The helper and helpee must be shaped by the feedback that they receive.

Often the real test of helpers, as stated earlier in this chapter, will be whether or not they can develop appropriate plans of ac-tion for their helpees. Frequently helpees will be unable to de-velop their own courses of action and will require help in structur-ing their programs. When helpees cannot participate fully in the program planning, Carkhuff (1969a) cautions helpers to develop programs that will "enable the helpee to carry some of the burden of responsibility for his own life" (p. 243).

If teachers and other educators can master the basic dimensions of the helping relationship that have been outlined in this chapter, they will prevent the development of many potential problem children and problem adults. Even with higher-level-functioning teachers in the classroom, other external factors such as the home, school, and community environment will produce child casualties. The teacher will need the assistance of educational experts, such as school counselors and school psychologists, reading experts, and special education experts, who can work as a Learning Facilitation Team for the prevention and resolution of problems.

Helping Involves Teaching and Learning

As helpers show empathy, respect, and warmth, helpees explore themselves and their problems. As helpers continue to show em-pathy, respect, and warmth, while displaying appropriate levels of concreteness, genuineness, and confrontation, helpees begin to un-derstand themselves and their problems and make a commitment to change. After the base is built, helpers may carefully and selec-tively use confrontation and immediacy to help the helpees take action or find direction. This description (as shown in Table 2-I) is oversimplified, but generally, this is the pattern of helping: reinforcing certain behaviors and extinguishing others. Showing empathy, respect, and warmth generally reinforces whatever helpees say or do, which increases the probability of self-exploration and problem exploration.

Responding with appropriate levels of concreteness, genuineness, and confrontation results in more selective reinforcement. Helpers are no longer speaking strictly from the helpees' point of view. They begin to focus on aspects of helpee behavior that they think will be more productive, they begin to relate more of their own feelings which reinforce in a certain direction, and they point out discrepancies in helpee behavior. This emphasis increases the probability that helpees will understand themselves and their problems.

If an adequate relationship has been established, effective levels of confrontation clearly reinforce certain kinds of behavior and extinguish others. These helper responses increase the probability that helpees will act on their problems and try to find some direction to follow which may solve their problems.

The art of helping includes first knowing *how* to respond helpfully and then knowing *when* to seek higher levels on various dimensions or *when* to use interchangeable responses. Many beginning helpers learn to show interchangeable empathy, respect, and warmth, but never become capable of displaying other more action-oriented dimensions. They often say, "I don't want to be responsible if he/she makes the wrong decision so I always make sure it's his/her decision"; or "I don't want him/her to become dependent on others to make his/her decisions." These are legitimate concerns, but they must be kept in perspective.

Helpers who display only interchangeable levels of empathy, respect, and warmth are not very selective in what they reinforce. This often results in helpees accepting their problems as a permanent part of themselves instead of solving them. If helpees are rewarded for discussing their problems over and over without moving toward some goal, they become desensitized to the problem and begin to think it is acceptable to have that problem.

It is extremely important for helpers to be aware of what behaviors they are reinforcing. The art of helping, therefore, includes knowing what behaviors to reinforce at a given time and how to do it. The next chapter provides the theoretical rationale for assisting the helper attend to, and focus on, helpee behavior and respond appropriately to it with a program of action interventions and strategies.

REFERENCES

Berenson, B. G., & Carkhuff, R. R. *Sources of gain in counseling and psychotherapy: Readings and commentary.* New York: Holt, Rinehart & Winston, 1967.

Berenson, B. G., & Mitchell, K. M. *Confrontation: For better or worse!* Amherst, Mass.: Human Resources Development Press, 1974.

Carkhuff, R. R. *Helping and human relations: A primer for lay and professional helpers.* Vol. 1: *Selection and training.* New York: Holt, Rinehart & Winston, 1969a.

Carkhuff, R. R. *Helping and human relations: A primer for lay and professional helpers.* Vol. 2: *Practice and research.* New York: Holt, Rinehart & Winston, 1969b.

Carkhuff, R. R. *The development of human resources: Education, psychology, and social change.* New York: Holt, Rinehart & Winston, 1971a.

Carkhuff, R. R. Helping and human relations: A brief guide for training lay helpers. *Journal of Research and Development in Education,* 1971b, *4,* 17-27.

Carkhuff, R. R. *The art of helping.* Amherst, Mass.: Human Resources Development Press, 1972.

Carkhuff, R. R., & Berenson, B. G. *Beyond counseling and therapy.* New York: Holt, Rinehart & Winston, 1967.

Gazda, G. M., Asbury, F. A., Balzer, F. J., Childers, W. C., & Walters, R. P. *Human relations development: A manual for educators* (2nd ed.) Boston: Allyn & Bacon, 1977.

Gazda, G. M., Walters, R. P., & Childers, W. C. *Human relations development: A manual for health sciences.* Boston: Allyn & Bacon, 1975.

Jacobs, A. *Research on methods of social intervention: The study of the exchange of personal information in brief personal growth groups.* Paper presented at the Invited Conference on Small Group Research, Indiana University, Bloomington, April, 1975.

Rogers, C. R. The necessary and sufficient conditions of therapeutic personality change. *Journal of Consulting Psychology,* 1957, *21,* 95-103.

Rogers, C. R., Gendlin, E. T., Kiesler, D. J., & Truax, C. B. *The therapeutic relationship and its impact: A study of psychotherapy with schizophrenics.* Madison: University of Wisconsin Press, 1967.

Truax, C. G., & Carkhuff, R. R. *Toward effective counseling and psychotherapy: Training and practice.* Chicago: Aldine, 1967.

Chapter 3

THE APPLICATION OF INTERVENTION STRATEGIES WITHIN A DEVELOPMENTAL MODEL*

In Chapter 2 the rationale for a model which described the element of a helping relationship was presented. In this chapter a student with a school conduct problem is used to illustrate how the Learning Facilitation Team, the Human Relations Training model (Gazda et al., 1977) in conjunction with Gazda's Developmental Model (Gazda, 1971, 1978), and selected strategies are combined in the action phase of helping to develop a complete *program* of facilitative intervention.

The procedure begins with an interaction between a student helpee (David) and his teacher in the illustration outlined in this chapter, but it might begin with a concern expressed by the student to any other member of the Learning Facilitation Team or vice versa. The teacher worked at the facilitation phase of helping with David and through this was able to prepare him for the action stage, at which time she referred David to the counselor who was able to move through the action (problem-solving) stage. The counselor utilized the system of profiling David's strengths and deficits within the five basic developmental human processes recommended by Gazda (1978) (see Table 3-I).

In order to consider the *whole* individual when appraising his/her total development, one needs to be cognizant of the developmental processes that each person experiences. Gazda (1978) has abstracted five of these developmental processes. They include the psychosocial (as outlined by Havighurst and by Erickson), the

---

*A significant part of this chapter is reproduced from Gazda, G. M., Asbury, F. A., Balzer, F. J., Childers, W. C., and Walters, R. P. *Human relations development: A manual for educators* (2nd ed.). Boston: Allyn & Bacon, 1977. Reproduced by permission. (John O'Connell coauthored this chapter.)

physical-sexual (of Gesell and colleagues), the cognitive (according to Piaget's model), the vocational (based on the work of Super and associates), and the moral (of Kohlberg). Tables of these developmental processes containing each age grouping with coping behaviors/developmental tasks which are appropriate for each age level will be available in Gazda's *Group Counseling: A Developmental Approach,* 2nd Edition (1978).

Following David's and the counselor's development of David's strengths and deficits with suggested possible interventions or strategies, David had to establish priorities, i.e. which actions he would employ to initiate the program. This was accomplished through the use of a matrix wherein David considered his values along with potential courses of action (see Table 3-II). Figure 3-1 represents the implementation process of David's choice of initiating actions. These actions are combinations of interventions and strategies that are the emphasis of Chapters 4 through 8 in this text.

The application of this model is, of course, most applicable to preadolescents, adolescents, and adults. Major changes would be necessary for use with children from approximately kindergarten to age nine. With preschool and early school children, the profiling would reside primarily with the Learning Facilitation Team.

DESCRIPTION OF THE STUDENT-HELPEE

David, the helpee in the protocol, is a fourteen-year-old eighth grader with above average intellectual ability. Academically he does poorly and often disrupts classroom activity by misbehavior, which usually leads to losing his temper after being reprimanded.

The helpee sees himself as an underachiever: intellectually, emotionally, and physically. In order to counteract his low self-image, he allows himself to be coerced and manipulated through peer acceptance needs, usually ending with the helpee receiving most of the blame for disruption, much to the satifsaction of his "friends." Attempts at denial and excuse generally lead to an explosive temper outbreak and a heated verbal battle with the teacher.

TEACHER-STUDENT INTERACTION

The protocol that follows (a portion of a longer series of sessions) was one of several held with the student during the school year. The helper (interviewer) was one of the student's classroom teachers who knew the student very well and had established a good base with him, as the protocol segment illustrates.

The problem area to be illustrated in the protocol and the program that follows deal with the student's maladaptive behavior in the classroom. Since the student (David) and teacher-helper (Mrs. Harris) are both prepared to move toward the action phase of problem solving, that segment of the interaction focusing on the action phase is presented below:

Student: You know, it seems that every time there is trouble in the classroom you always look at me as if I'm the one who starts it all the time.

Teacher: David, you get pretty upset at me when there's a disturbance in the classroom and I automatically look in your direction, or even accuse you of causing it.

Student: Mm-mm. Sometimes it makes me mad so I want to get back at you, especially when I wasn't even doing anything.

Teacher: You feel it's really unfair when I do this to you, so much so, that sometimes you just want to get even with me.

Student: Yeah . . . (pause), I know a lot of the times I do deserve it since I goof around so much. I guess you think it's me all the time because everyone says that I'm the worst kid in the class.

Teacher: You get mad when I always think you're the cause of the trouble, yet you seem to realize that a lot of the time, you are, and maybe this is why I do it. You may also be wondering if being labeled "the worst kid in the class" doesn't have something to do with all of this.

Student: Yeah, I don't know why it is, I mean, even last year in the seventh grade the teacher gave me an award at the end of the year for the one who caused her to get the most gray hairs. I didn't know whether to bring it home or throw it away.

Teacher: You don't know why people think of you this way, but you feel by goofing off in class, this is maybe what they expect of you anyway — so why not do it.

Student: That's kind of the way it is. Even the kids who never get in trouble and always make real good grades try to get me to do things that *I'll* get in trouble for, but they're the ones who told me to do it.

Teacher: A lot of the times you find yourself doing things that you don't really want to do, and which usually gets you in trouble, but you feel afraid of disappointing the fellas. And then when you get in trouble, you get angry and lose your temper with me. And David, it just seems like you and I can never get it together.

Student: (Pause) . . . Yeah, you're right about losing my temper at you. I do that a lot.

Teacher: And that just makes matters worse because you feel so angry with yourself that maybe you take it out on me, which . . . .

Student: Which just gets me in more hot water, right? I guess I kinda' see what's been happening. I really need to do something about it.

Teacher: You seem to feel that this type of behavior doesn't really get you anywhere, and perhaps there is something you can do about it. Would you be willing to look at some possibilities and maybe try some things that might work better for you?

Student: Yeah, I think I'd do almost anything if it would keep me from getting in trouble so much.

At this point the teacher met with the school counselor, school psychologist, and David's other teachers (the Learning Facilitation Team) to initiate a potential program for David. During this case conference it was decided that the school counselor would meet with David and assist him in developing a profile of his strengths and deficits.

GENERATING A DEVELOPMENTAL PROFILE

In order to develop a thorough profile of the helpee's strengths and deficits, it becomes necessary to develop a scheme into which will fit diverse problem areas. One such scheme takes into account five separate modalities. These modalities are psychosocial, physical-sexual, cognitive, vocational, and moral (see Gazda, 1978).

By including a helpee's strengths as well as deficits in the profile and considering combinations of the modalities, a *total* program for problem resolution can be developed. This profile allows the helper and helpee to set priorities and begin dealing with the most urgent concern first. Of course, improvement in one modality might very well have an effect on other modalities, so that the scheme is constantly subject to revision.

The following interaction will serve to illustrate the *Develop-*

mental approach. Keep in mind that helper (school counselor) and helpee are in the *action phase* of helping; thus, the helper has earned the right to be more directive and judgmental.

Counselor: Okay, David, when we finished up last week I heard you say that you were going to be thinking of things to put in your profile.

Student: Yeah, I've been thinking about it. I understand it better now, especially after I looked at the sample you gave me.

Counselor: David, I guess you have been pretty busy thinking of things in the different areas that you would like to see changed, that is, specific things that you want to *stop* doing, and others that you want to *start* doing.

Student: Yeah, I have been. You know, like in the first area, the psychosocial one, well, I was thinking that I should stop giving Mrs. Harris such a hard time in the classroom. I mean, you know, act right and not lose my temper when I get caught doing something.

Counselor: Okay, good, David. I get the feeling that you would really like to see some changes in this area.

Student: Yeah, I would. We also talked a few weeks back about me doing something about, I think you called it self-image. Would that come under this area?

Counselor: I think it might. Could you be a little more specific David?

Student: Well, you know, like we were talking about last week. I wish I wasn't afraid to try new things. Like sports, I would really like to be able to play and forget about thinking that I won't be good at it, or feel embarrassed because people are looking at me. I know I run like I have two left feet but I still want to play.

Counselor: Trying something new is hard for you, especially in sports. You realize that you have some limitations, but you would like to participate anyway, and just enjoy the sport and maybe even get good at it.

Student: Yeah. If I played enough I probably could get good, or a lot better, anyway.

Counselor: Let's record it this way. Write down "losing temper," and "classroom misbehavior" in the psychosocial column, and under the physical-sexual column put, "feels clumsy and awkward in sports." David, you seem to be saying that to be good at something it takes practice and work.

Student: Yeah. Like Mrs. Harris says, I could do much better in school work if I tried harder. You know, do my homework and study, and things like that.

Counselor: I sense from the way you said that that you sort of agree with Mrs. Harris.

Student: Yeah, I don't do much in school, anyway. Goof around, mostly.

Counselor: The problem with school work would seem to fit the cognitive area, David. It's not an easy thing to talk about our own faults, even among friends.

Student: Well, I was thinking about the vocational area and how it may tie in with my paper route job.

Counselor: Mm-mm.

Student: Well, Mr. Mead, he's my paper route manager, he told me that unless I become more responsible, he'll have to take my route away from me. I suppose that could fit into this area.

Counselor: David, sounds like there's more to the story.

Student: "Well, a couple of times I didn't get my papers delivered, or I was late delivering them, and my customers called Mr. Mead on the phone. Boy, was he mad!

Counselor: Something must have come up to take priority those times you didn't get your papers delivered.

Student: Not really. Actually, one time I forgot, and the other times I just didn't feel like it.

Counselor: It sounds like you would like to be more responsible.

Student: Yeah. And another thing, Mrs. Harris always saves last period on Fridays to talk about careers and jobs and all that stuff. She always wants us to talk about what we want to do some day. I think it's stupid. I can never think of anything, anyway.

Counselor: You feel this weekly activity is of no real importance, and it's frustrating, too, because you never know what to say.

Student: Exactly.

Counselor: Okay, why don't we write down, "shows little interest in thinking about future vocational choices," and put that under, "lacks responsibility" in the vocational column. David, you look a little puzzled.

Student: Well, I think we've covered all the areas except the moral area, and I'm not sure what to put for this one.

Counselor: Okay, let's take a minute to go over the moral area. I think this will help you understand what we mean by moral. Moral principles are principles of choice for resolving conflicts of obligation. "Moral" is not simply a tag to be attached to actions we approve of, but a means for deciding what one should or should not do in situations involving competing moral values. Does that clear some things up at all?

Student: I'm still not sure what to put down on my profile under this area.

Counselor: It might help if we go over the handout I gave you on Kohlberg's stages of moral development. At one of these stages we learn to conform to the personal expectations of others and to social rules.

Student: Lots of times in class I don't do what Mrs. Harris expects me

to do. It really gets me in trouble sometimes.
Counselor: Sounds like you don't measure up to Mrs. Harris's expectations of you. Seems like you're getting pretty good at doing this self-profiling. Well, we've gone over our time, let's stop for today.

As the counseling with David continued, David and the counselor constructed David's Developmental Profile (Table 3-I). which illustrates that David's problems (like most other persons) are not the result of a single developmental deficit but rather are intertwined; to change David will involve a program that attacks his deficits (supported by also focusing on his strengths) from many directions (developmental areas).

LISTING/RANKING STUDENT'S VALUES

Having completed the developmental profile, it became necessary for David to establish priorities in his program, i.e. just where in the program he wished to begin. This system involves a systematic way of choosing the preferred course of action from among several alternatives. The helpee's value system is considered concurrently with the proposed courses of action. The helpee is asked to list his values (those that pertain to the problem(s), and then label them with any unit from 1 to 5, with the value of the greatest importance being given the greatest weight. (These are arbitrary units and some other unit could work equally well.) It is not necessary to use all weights, and some values may be weighted equally.

IDENTIFYING POSSIBLE COURSES OF ACTION

In addition to the values, the helpee and helper generate reasonable alternatives to pursue in order to solve the problem. These may be labeled "potential course of action." These alternatives are also ranked by the helpee from a negative to a plus, i.e. −2, −1, 0, +1, +2 to indicate the degree to which that alternative will enhance or decrease movement toward the particular value in that row of the matrix. The numerical weight assigned to the value is then multiplied by the rating assigned to the alternative and the product is recorded in the appropriate cell. The helper and helpee under consideration here worked out the matrix system in Table 3-II.

TABLE 3-I
DEVELOPMENTAL PROFILE

Strengths	Problems (Deficits)	Proposed Treatment
PSYCHO-SOCIAL DEVELOPMENT		
Able to achieve an appropriate dependence-independence pattern, e.g. saves money from paper route to help pay for summer camp	Rebellious attitude; frequently causes disruption in classroom and loses temper when reprimanded; low self- image	Group counseling: behavior contract with teacher and parents regarding disruptive and aggressive acting-out
Strong identification with one's sex mates, also with male hero identity figures, e.g. athletes, movie actors	Low image of parents; mother seen as nagging and punishing, father as cowardly and uncaring	Counselor develops Positive Characteristics Chart — a list of David's positive traits Counselor appointment with family to discuss family counseling possibilities
PHYSICAL-SEXUAL DEVELOPMENT		
Good physical health, strong and large in size, onset of puberty and normal development of prominent secondary sexual characteristics	Feels clumsy and uncoordinated in physical activities; afraid to participate in organized sports fearing embarassment or failure	"Time Projective Technique" (Gazda, Walters, and Childers, 1975) — learning to enjoy activities, especially athletics, for their own sake, by imagining realistically the good things that could happen in the future as a result of athletic participation Physical fitness remediation program
Able to understand his future role in heterosexual relationships; normal interest in, and search for understanding of, his sexual ability	Feels uneasy around girls his own age; wishes he didn't have to "show off" to get their attention	"People Happenings Technique" (Simon, Hartnell, and Hawkins, 1973) — presentation of events without the pressures of reality; goal is to explore alternative responses as well as own thoughts, feelings, and behaviors; facilitates counselee to become better prepared for dealing with real situations which involve other people

TABLE 3-I — (Continued)

Strengths	Problems (Deficits)	Proposed Treatment
COGNITIVE DEVELOPMENT		
Above average intellectual ability (full-scale IQ of 115 on WISC)	Skill deficiency: particular weakness in general information and vocabulary development	Tutoring, remediation, proper educational placement by grade and class
Particular strength in motor and simple assembly skills	Visual perception and spatial conceptualization	Wood Shop Program: individualized work using geometric forms, Cuisenaire rods™, jigsaw puzzles, maps and graphs
VOCATIONAL DEVELOPMENT		
Likes to undertake cooperative enterprises, e.g. supplements allowance with a paper route	Often lacks responsibility; negligent, e.g. plays with friends and may forget to deliver newspapers	"Life Careers Game" (Catterall and Gazda, this text) — small group interaction using role-playing techniques simulating decision making and work situations
Ability to concentrate over long periods of time, especially on tasks of special interest	Has no interest in cognitively developing ideas about occupations and possible career aspirations	"Life Style Assessment" (Catterall and Gazda, this text) — technique using vocation of family breadwinner to show total effects on family; counselee learns that vocational choice is more than just a way to earn money
		"Projected Life Plan Line" (Gysbers, Miller, and Moore, 1973) — technique that brings planning out of the purely thinking realm and puts it into a visual, graphic form; a simple way of "trying on the future" or of seeing more clearly the relationship between decision making, planning, and their resultant consequences

TABLE 3-I — (Continued)

Strengths	Problems (Deficits)	Proposed Treatment
	MORAL DEVELOPMENT	
Able to define right action as that which satisfies his own needs and occasionally the needs of others	Minimal ability to see the world as made up of social relationships, consequently fails to conform to the personal expectations of others and to social rules (Kohlberg's Conventional Level of Moral Reasoning)	"Moral Dilemmas Discussion Technique" (A New Rationale for Guidance, 1974) (a) counselee comes to see certain inadequacies in his reasoning as a result of interacting with more complex arguments made by other people; (b) counselee is placed in the roles of various parties in the dilemma and examines his reasoning from these several perspectives

DEVELOPING A PROGRAM OF ACTION

One course of action emerged as David's first choice to pursue, and related courses of action were not far behind. The helpee and helper agreed that the reason alternative 1 (improve self-image) received the highest weight was because of its close interrelationship with several other alternatives. In other words, an improved self-image might affect classroom behavior, which could reduce temper outbreaks and, subsequently, increased academic achievement might result. Thus, of immediate concern was alternative 1 which involved preparing the helpee to work on and to improve his self-image. The helper and helpee then decided to develop a self-image enhancement program for the helpee as the first phase of solving his classroom-related problem. Since this area of deficit was most closely related to the psychosocial area of development, David and his counselor were able to initiate David's corrective program with emphasis on this area of human development.

A sample of the self-image enhancement program which David and the counselor developed together is outlined in Figure 3-1. Note that David's total program would involve an integration of strategies built around each of the five basic areas of human development.

TABLE 3-II

MATRIX SYSTEM FOR SELECTING COURSE OF ACTION[1]

Counselee's Values Hierarchy		Counselee's (David's) Potential Courses of Action						
		Improve Self-image	Modify Classroom Behavior	Explore Dynamics of Group Pressure	Improve Interpersonal Skills	Control Temper	Improve Academic Achievement	Change Schools
1. Self-image	(5)	(+2) 10	(+2) 10	(+1) 5	(+2) 10	(+1) 5	(+1) 5	(−2) −10
2. Family	(4)	(+1) 4	(+1) 4	(0) 0	(+1) 4	(+1) 4	(+1) 4	(0) 0
3. School	(3)	(+2) 6	(+2) 6	(+1) 3	(+1) 3	(+2) 6	(+2) 6	(−1) −3
4. Other students	(3)	(+2) 6	(+1) 3	(+1) 3	(+1) 3	(+1) 3	(0) 0	(0) 0
TOTAL		26	23	11	20	18	15	−13

[1]This matrix was adapted from the system developed by Dr. Robert R. Carkhuff and described in *The Art of Problem Solving*, Amherst, Mass.: Human Resource Development Press, 1973.

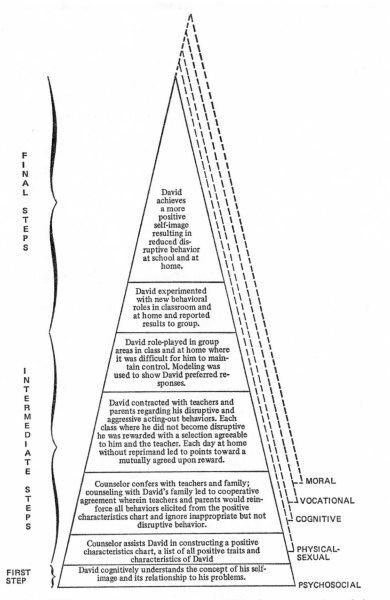

Figure 3-1. Self-image enhancement program. This figure was adapted from Gazda, G. M., Asbury, F. A., Balzar, F. J., Childers, W. C., & Walters, R. P. HUMAN RELATIONS DEVELOPMENT: A MANUAL FOR EDUCATORS. 2nd Ed.) Boston: Allyn & Bacon, 1977. Reproduced by permission.

CONCLUSIONS

Figure 3-1 illustrates the first part of a more complete program that can be completed from the student's developmental profile. It is important to remember here that the learning facilitation team collaborated in the development of the student's developmental profile. If students are to receive more than simply an education in the cognitive domain, it will become necessary to involve Learning Facilitation Teams, plus the student and parents in planning a total program of life-coping skills, utilizing the five basic human developmental processes. "Profiling" all students along the basic developmental processes will involve both preventative and remedial strategies for helping, which is the subject of the remainder of this book.

REFERENCES

A new rationale for guidance. *Focus on Guidance.* Denver: Love Publishing Co., 1974.

Carkhuff, R.R. *The art of problem solving.* Amherst, Mass.: Human Resource Development Press, 1973.

Gazda, G. M. *Group counseling: A developmental approach.* Boston: Allyn & Bacon, 1971.

Gazda, G. M. *Group counseling: A developmental approach* (2nd ed.), Boston: Allyn & Bacon, 1978.

Gazda, G. M., Asbury, F. A., Balzer, F. J., Childers, W. C., & Walters, R. P. *Human relations development: A manual for educators* (2nd ed.). Boston: Allyn & Bacon, 1977.

Gazda, G. M., Walters, R. P., & Childers, W. C. *Human relations development: A manual for health sciences.* Boston: Allyn & Bacon, 1975.

Gysbers, N., Miller, W., & Moore, E. J. (Eds.) *Developing careers in the elementary school.* Columbus, Oh.: Charles E. Merrill, 1973.

Simon, S., Hartnell, M. R., & Hawkins, L. A. *Values clarification: Friends and other people.* Arlington Heights, Ill.: PAXCOM — A Division of Modular Communications, Inc., 1973.

PART II

INTRODUCTION

Part II is organized under four major processes around which all of the strategies for helping students can be grouped (see Table II-I).

1. *Strategies around the student.* These are the strategies designed to affect the curriculum and the total school environment to direct the growth of the normally developing student in broadly defined academic areas. If carried out effectively, these ways of helping students will prevent many other problems from developing. In Chapter 4 these strategies will be described under the heading of "Developing Academic/Intellectual Skills."

2. *Interventions for the student.* These are the interventions which can be used when the normal developmental program was not able to meet the specific academic/intellectual needs of the student. In Chapter 5 these will be referred to as "corrective/remedial interventions."

3. *Strategies with the student.* These include the developmental strategies designed to help all students grow along six broad strands of a humanistic/life-skills curriculum. If they are used systematically and efficiently, they will prevent the development of a large number of major personal/social problems. In Chapter 6 strategies have been brought together under the heading of "Developing Humanistic/Life Skills."

4. *Interventions in behalf of the student.* This section brings together those interventions designed to provide certain students with specialized help for their personal/social, life-skill problems. In Chapter 7 these interventions have been described under the heading of "Corrective/Therapeutic Interventions."

Part II closes with Chapter 8. This chapter provides the reader with a system for selecting strategies. When Chapter 8 is combined with Chapters 2 and 3, the reader has a rather complete model for conceptualizing and implementing strategies/interventions for helping students.

TABLE II-I

THE FOUR MAJOR STRATEGIES FOR HELPING STUDENTS

Types of Strategies

	Developmental/ Preventative	Corrective/ Remedial
Academic/ Intellectual Skills	*Developing Academic/ Intellectual Skills* Strategies *around* the Student	*Corrective/Remedial Interventions* Interventions *for* the Student
Humanistic/ Life Skills	*Developing Humanistic/ Life Skills* Strategies *with* the Student	*Corrective/Therapeutic Interventions* Interventions *in behalf of* the student

Focus of Strategies

Chapter 4

STRATEGIES FOR DEVELOPING
ACADEMIC/INTELLECTUAL SKILLS

THE STRATEGIES DESCRIBED in this chapter deal primarily with those curricular programs and adjustments which are designed to help the young child and student to develop the basic skills and understanding of the culture. The goal of all of these techniques is as follows:

> To help all students develop those cognitive and intellectual skills which are appropriate to their age level, which have been adapted to their learning style, and which are relevant to the changing world in which they live.

The strategies in this chapter deal with the broad-based development programs which should be available for all students. These programs are designed to help the majority of students to become adequately prepared for life. As used in this context, the developmental program is broader than the information usually organized into the formal school curriculum. It includes all of those school-related activities, including many so-called extracurricular activities, which are part of the total school program. Such a program is essentially developmental rather than remedial in nature, but should have built within it a system for identifying those students who need special corrective and remedial work. It will tend to stress large group and small group activities (but not exclusively), as opposed to the one-to-one programs.

Tables 4-I and 4-II provide an overview for the reader of the basic thrust (Table 4-I) and organization (Table 4-II) of this chapter.

Although there has been general acceptance of the importance of a good, extensive curriculum for the typically developing student, we are only now beginning to appreciate the tremendous

TABLE 4-I

STRATEGIES THAT CAN BE DONE AROUND THE STUDENT

	Developmental/ *Preventative*	*Corrective/* *Remedial*
Academic/ *Intellectual* *Skills*	*Strategies For Developing* *Academic/Intellectual* *Skills* Things that can be done *around* the student	
Life *Skills*		

power of this approach both in preventing failures and, if used properly, in correcting identified learning and behavior problems. Although simple environmental manipulations were long ridiculed and looked down upon by the therapeutic community, it is now being recognized that an appropriate placement in the broad curricular offerings of a school can produce dramatic and lasting effects.

Any attempt to catalogue all of the *strategies for helping students* must start with a consideration of helping students find the most appropriate place to address the curriculum (taking into consideration their social as well as their academic level of development). If a student's needs can be met and he/she can be helped to find success day after day in the school situation, education will be performing a preventive function because the student will be much less likely to require corrective/remedial services.

It is the purpose of this book to provide the broad spectrum of strategies, rather than to attempt to go into any great detail on

TABLE 4-II

ORGANIZATION OF STRATEGIES FOR
DEVELOPING ACADEMIC/INTELLECTUAL SKILLS

Determining Who Shall Be Educated	*Individualizing the Curriculum*
A. Infant stimulation programs	A. Developmental Adjustment
B. Preschool Programs	B. Learning Uniqueness
C. Preschool Screening	C. Interest/Involvement
D. Early Admission to School	D. Relevancy
E. Exclusions	E. Goal Oriented
F. Compulsory Attendance	F. Pacing
G. Life-long Education	G. Aiding Conceptual Development

Grouping Placement	H. Knowledge of results
	  1. Self-assessment
	  2. Peer Feedback
	  3. Teacher Assessment

A. Adjustments Within the Local School
  1. Preselecting the environment
  2. Adjustments within the Classroom
  3. Organizational Adjustments
  4. Resource/Media Centers
  5. Special Groupings
  6. Retention
  7. Acceleration
  8. Suspension or Expulsion	

	Structuring

B. Grouping/Placement Adjustments Between Schools
  1. Cooperation Between Feeder Schools
  2. Another School
  3. The Voucher System
  4. Dual Eligibility
  5. Regional Vocational Centers
  6. Alternate Schools
  7. Special Education Classes
	A. Clarifying the Rules for New Students
	B. Involving Students in Making the Rules
	C. Providing Consistency in Enforcing the Rules
	D. Providing Additional Structure
	E. Providing Less Structure

C. Placement Outside the Regular School
  1. Special Programs for the Severely Handicapped
  2. Youth in Correctional Programs
  3. Children Not in Any Program	

how each one should be implemented. Since this book is not intended to be essentially a list of innovations in the process of helping students, many of the techniques listed are already well known to the educational community. When a given strategy is less well known, specific references to the literature will be made. In addition, lists of references will be provided for the reader seeking a broader understanding of the suggested strategies.

The techniques listed in this chapter are directed at improving the *process* of education and have been organized into four sections. "Determining Who Shall be Educated" discusses the issues of the age at which formal education should begin and for how long the compulsory attendance laws should be enforced. "Grouping/Placement" procedures are those strategies which have to do with the group or program in which the learner is placed. "Individualizing the Curriculum" describes those strategies which have to do with the organizational and programmed aspects of a child's curriculum, i.e. where it should begin, how it should be introduced, how fast it should move, etc. *"Structuring"* refers to the various ways in which a child or student can be helped to meet the requirements of the curriculum through variations in the amount and type of structure provided for him/her. These four sections represent the major focal points of helping strategies for things that can be done *around* the student.

DETERMINING WHO SHALL BE EDUCATED

Although this book is essentially about those *strategies* designed to assist young people while they are in school, it would be relevant to start with a brief look at the larger picture of who is and who is not being accepted into the basic educational programs of our culture. This is important because so many of the standard educational practices are currently under "fire" and because a whole new spectrum of helping strategies is being brought to bear on those who are not normally considered to be part of the larger educational "system." As does any large institution, schools have to establish "gates" which determine who can get in, under what conditions they can stay, and when they must leave.

INFANT STIMULATION PROGRAMS. Although we have long held

that children who are profoundly hard-of-hearing need early and systematic use of auditory stimulation, it is only relatively recently that we have found evidence to support the idea that early intellectual stimulation of those who are retarded has been helpful. The strategy of identifying children with special needs very early and providing a home-based training program for the child and for his/her parents as early as possible has proven to be very effective (Nurturing Intelligence, 1972). This has been found to be true even when the parents presented a learning problem themselves. When parents are given specific instructions on how to help their handicapped child, i.e. what specifically the next developmental step is and how they can help him/her to achieve that step, the parents have been found to be very effective in helping their child (Chilman, 1972; Hoffman, Jordan and McCormick, 1971; Knitzer, 1972; McFadden, 1972). This work has been done with children with identified handicaps, but it seems likely that equally dramatic results can be seen in helping parents of normally developing children to identify and to use strategies for helping their young children.

PRESCHOOL PROGRAMS. Although a variety of nursery and preschool programs have been available for a number of years, they were seen by many as a relatively ineffective strategy for helping students and of little concern to the main educational program. Many educators held the belief that it did not make much difference what happened to the child before he/she came to school. Many programs were developed under the sponsorship of state and local adult education departments. In general they appealed to middle and upper class families, that basically had children of normal development. The programs were typically quite free-flowing in nature; were aimed at helping the child enhance his/her self-concept; and were structured to help the child develop through simple preacademic exercises. In general they were not highly structured and were designed to provide a climate in which the child could "unfold." While this was the prevalent theory in preschool education, many professional educators held the belief that it did not make much difference if the child had this kind of experience before coming to school. This kind of thinking was

reinforced by the general lack of resources and technology to provide services to the preschool child. It should also be remembered
that in many states there are still no provisions for publicly supported kindergartens, and, that in an even larger percentage of
states, attendance at kindergarten is still not mandatory (Weber,
1970).

There is also currently a growing interest in the value of play
on the part of those who are trying to identify strategies for helping students. The first approach (Kephart and Radler, 1960)
pointed out that children's play was in essence their "work" and
that it provided a means for them to grow both physically and intellectually. Play has continued to be refined as a means of helping young children and it is now considered to be a method of
helping parents assist their preschool children to develop language
and visual skills, motor coordination, number concepts, and self-
concept (Hartman, 1976).

When the federal government decided to declare "War on
Poverty" in the 1960s, it began to fund Head Start programs as a
means of helping a large number of children from culturally different and culturally deprived homes. The battle raged between
the "free flowing" philosophy and the approach which utilized
much greater amounts of structure. Although the gains shown in
these children while they were in Head Start programs did not
always seem to continue into the later grades in the traditional
educational program, it became accepted that children could be
helped if a specific assessment of their needs was made and if
fairly structured educational procedures were used. This does not
mean, however, that they will not need to receive continued help
once they enter the regular school program.

Closely associated with the Head Start movement was the development of a series of strategies to help disadvantaged youth
when, in March of 1968 "Sesame Street" and later "The Electric
Company" were first introduced (Gibbon and Palmer, 1975). These
daily, hour-long television programs were designed to provide a
useful educational experience for three-, four-, and five-year-olds
and give special attention to the language and cognitive development of the disadvantaged. Using a highly motivating "TV"

assigned task for a longer period of time, and the ability to make meaningful discriminations in the learning task as well as to follow instructions. Preschoolers are helped to learn to relate to other children in groups and, if they have appropriate success, it is hoped that they will develop an acceptable self-image in a learning-type situation (Weber, 1970). Schools situated in areas where there is no such program should consider the strategy of helping to bring together the necessary community support to begin such a preschool program.

PRESCHOOL SCREENING. Although the age at which formal schooling begins varies, every state has some provision for determining the age at which a child can enter school (typically at or near the age of five). Since it is obvious that all children of the same age are not equally ready for school, efforts have been made over a number of years to identify other factors which would help to predict success or failure in the early years of school. One factor which has been studied over a long period of time is the use of the child's "bone age" as a possible indicator of physiological readiness for school (Olson, 1947). Since boys have traditionally had more difficulty in the early years of school than girls, many people have suggested that girls should enter school earlier than boys. This sex difference has been noted in almost every culture with the possible exception of Germany (Preston, 1962). The differences between boys and girls have been blamed on a variety of factors, i.e. boys tend to be more active than girls and are penalized by the way the schools require them to learn; boys tend to be less fluent verbally than girls; boys listen and attend less adequately than girls; and much of the instructional material used in schools is of less interest to boys than girls. Several attempts have been made with apparent success (McNeil, 1964; Wyatt, 1966) to change the curriculum to meet the needs of boys more adequately.

Another area of great interest has been in the perceptual problems of children as they have entered school. Although some of these studies have been primarily aimed at kindergarten children (McBeath, 1966), others have tried to find ways to test children for hidden handicaps or perceptual problems before they are ready to enroll in kindergarten. As usual, testing done on these young children is associated with excessive variability which, in turn, takes away from the test's ability to predict which children are going to have difficulty. There seems to be little question that children vary in their ability to perform visual-motor types of tasks. That children can also be helped to develop perceptual-motor skills also seems well established (Lowder, 1956). There is increasing doubt, however, about whether or not improving perceptual skills in-and-of-itself does much to enhance formal academic learning (Goodman and Hammill, 1973; Hammill, Goodman, and Wiederhold, 1974; Newcomer and Hammill, 1973). While waiting for further research evidence on this topic, educators interested in helping "high risk" children to learn to read should adopt the following program: the implementation of perceptual-motor training should be used more widely in the pre-school level than for kindergarten and school-age children. For school-age children it should be essentially a remedial program which should accompany (but not serve as a substitute for) formal teaching in reading, language, or arithmetic skills (Hammill and Bartel, 1975, 229-230).

The search for other variables which would help to identify and to predict school success continues (Mardell and Goldenberg, 1972). In most states screening programs are a hit-or-miss affair which come as the result of an interested teacher, principal, or school psychologist. However, in other states, such as New York, there is a more systematic approach to early screening which would affect all children either just before or soon after they have entered school. The current pressures to identify all handicapped children at an early age will continue to provide momentum for this movement. Because of the problems in this area, it would be wise for the strategist to insist that screening be carried out only when there are specific programs for helping the students identified as being in need. They should also do everything possible to minimize the use of labels which might have a negative effect on the child and help to make certain that the prescribed program be carried out in as normal an educational setting as possible.

The earlier preschool programs frequently had as their spoken or unspoken goal the process of identifying the "high risk" child and asking him or her (more often "him" than "her") to stay home for a period of time (usually a school year) before entering school. This was done on the assumption that the child would mature more while staying home and would fit in better with other children who were chronologically a year younger. Although there is some obvious truth to these assumptions, the state of the art of helping these children has progressed to the point where keeping a child out of a school program is rarely indicated. The modern strategist works on the assumption that every child should have a carefully planned educational program. Whereas maturation does take care of some problems, the much more useful strategy is to provide the child with a program of help (which, of course, does not always have to take place in a regular school program). The fact that a child has reached the age of entrance into school with an identifiable deficit almost always indicates a need for a positive, planned program of action rather than a passive "go home and you will outgrow it" approach.

Although the material thus far presented in this chapter has described programs which are largely taking place outside the traditional school program and therefore are not directly applicable to the classroom teacher, they are included in this section of the book to remind the reader that one of the best strategies for helping students is to get to them early and to provide them with the additional help they need. Although major advances are being made in providing services for special and regular preschool children, there is much that still needs to be done. As professional educators we have taken on a responsibility (albeit somewhat limited) for *all* children and youth. Active support for preschool programs which help students with specialized needs to become more ready to enter school is definitely indicated at this time.

EARLY ADMISSION TO SCHOOL. All of the previous discussion about individual differences as they relate to school readiness suggests that the following strategy should be considered, i.e. allowing some children early entrance into the traditional program. Educators traditionally have been much less willing to consider this strategy than they have the idea of having some children stay home for a year. Most states have some sort of a provision for either allowing children to come to school early or to progress from kindergarten to the first grade in a very short period of time. There was at one time a great deal of suspicion that if the restrictions were made too easy, many (if not most) parents would want their children admitted to school early, but this does not seem to be as prevalent a feeling as it once was. The strategy will be less needed as we continue to develop better and better preschool programs. Since this strategy has the same effect as an acceleration or a double promotion, the reader is referred to a discussion of the problems connected with that later in this chapter. In general it is safe to say that it is not extensively used and that the commonly used procedure of curricular enrichment (perhaps combined with having the child seek out a reading or academic achievement group for a short time each day) seems to be the preferred strategy.

EXCLUSIONS. To the extent that an exclusion comes after the child has entered school, it should and will be discussed as a form of grouping placement strategies in the next section. There is a growing amount of attention being paid to the large numbers of children who are never in school or who are there for very brief periods of time. The average American assumes that "all" children are in school. Recent news releases by the Children's Defense Fund (1974), based on an extensive eighteen-month study, estimates that there are conservatively 2,000,000 children between the ages of seven and seventeen who are out of school. This does not include those out of school for disciplinary reasons, those who are truant, or those who are handicapped. As would be expected these children come most frequently from low income or unemployed families, from minority families, and from rural families with low levels of education (American Children Out of School, 1975). It would appear that we have defined the "gates" of education in such a narrow way that a fairly sizeable part of the population either cannot or does not take advantage of a formal education.

COMPULSORY ATTENDANCE. Just as every state sets a time when children can start school (or must start school), so too every state professing compulsory education must set an age through which all children must attend school. It is, of course, one thing to establish compulsory attendance in school, but it is quite another thing to enforce it. Some states are currently reducing the age of compulsory attendance for school; others are trying to raise it. Although most people would agree that the state has the right to demand students attend school since there is a need for an informed citizenry in order for a liberal democracy to operate, some people (Bereiter, 1974) are questioning whether compulsory attendance should go through the age of eighteen. The pressures on the school to rethink this problem are being created by the lowering of the age at which young people are considered adults in many states and the Supreme Court's decisions in favor of Amish parents who had previously been forced to send their children to high school. The school has an undeniable "baby-sitting" function. Many people who are the most willing to enforce the compulsory attendance laws are the last to ask the question, "What is the school program doing to help the student?" As a general strategy, it would appear desirable for many educators to begin to identify people and resources in the community who could become part of the student's ongoing educational experience for which he/she would receive school credit, i.e. through the use of work experience programs, career exploration activities, etc. and that this would tend to help bridge the gap for many students who are for one reason or another "turned off" to school.

LIFE-LONG EDUCATION. As in many issues, there appear to be two opposing forces operating. Some of those who are in school want to get out while some who are out want to get back in. There are few who would argue that learning should be a life-long venture; how this dream can be made operational is a very complex matter. Many schools have developed a wide range of evening courses which are helpful but somehow or other do not seem to have a very good holding power, and many who sign up for the courses never complete them. Perhaps the emphasis within the period of formal schooling which stresses that learning is a life-long activity would be another strategy for helping students, young and old.

GROUPING/PLACEMENT

Once the decision has been made about who will be educated (who will be allowed in and who will be required to stay), basic grouping/placement decisions must be made to decide how the system will best be able to meet a student's individual needs. Since society does not support the teaching of students on a one-to-one basis (and indeed, for the normally developing student, such a system would probably be less productive than would be education in a group), one way to help a child to learn is to place him/her with a group which will provide the maximum intellectual support and interaction for that individual's learning. It is extremely difficult to decide what the best placement is for many students, but the *right* placement (or group) represents an extremely powerful strategy for helping a student grow.

Included among the grouping/placement procedures would be the total organizational pattern of the district, i.e. which students would go to the elementary, intermediate or junior high, and the high schools, over which the individual educator has very little control. It would also include a variety of adjustments within the local school (over which the teacher can and should have considerable control), as well as those made between schools. In the traditional school, lines between these placement programs were relatively rigid and well defined. Once a student was placed, it was difficult to get him/her changed. In the modern school, the distinction between what has been referred to as individualizing the curriculum (described in the next section) and grouping/placement strategies is (fortunately) increasingly hard to make. In categorizing all of the strategies designed to help students, however, a meaningful distinction can be made between the programatic/curricular offerings provided for students and the placement procedures used to put them into groups.

Grouping and placement strategies have been used for a long time; dissatisfaction with them has led to a continued process of change. It would appear altogether too often that whatever system of grouping or organizational structure is in use, another one tends to be in favor. The hard reality is that no grouping/placement procedure fits all of the needs of any one individual, let alone all the members of a group. In brief, the stance for an individual teacher to take is to work for and to demand as much flexibility as possible within the grouping procedure being used; to help make sure that the systems for providing this flexibility are followed fairly and in the best interests of the student; and not to spend too much time hunting for the perfect solution. The goal is to find a learning environment which will enable a particular student to learn as efficiently as possible while, at the same time, providing a social environment conducive to maintaining good feelings of self-worth.

We continue to hear the argument about whether grouping should be basically homogeneous or heterogeneous. A word should be said about grouping on a so-called ability level, using scores from intelligence tests. This practice is under increasing attack from the courts because of actions which have been initiated by the parents of minority students and also increasingly from other groups. It was originally based on the assumption that, other things being equal, the Intelligence Quotient is constant over time. Although over large groups of students IQs probably do remain fairly stable, this is probably more closely related to the fact that their homes, neighborhoods, and school environments do not change radically than it is to any inherent level of ability.

The circular reasoning of taking all students who score low on IQ tests out of the mainstream, i.e. the regular program, and putting them into slower-moving classes (where they are *more* likely to score low on later testing) becomes more and more obvious. Although there is a great deal of overlap between so-called "ability" and so-called "achievement," it is still a little more acceptable to group students on differing levels of their actual achievement. The focus should be, "Here is where you work best at this time. We are not implying that you will stay at this level for any length of time. We cannot and will not try to predict where you will be in the future. You are at a certain level of achievement; we will help you while you are at that level move on to the next level." Since students learn different subjects at different speeds, there will always be some who are, by definition, "below average" (which is arbitrarily defined as that point at which

50 percent of the students fall below and 50 percent are above).
The less the emphasis is on the fact that there is a "slow" or
"dumb" (or whatever name we think up for hiding it, it's *low)*
group, and the more emphasis on "this is where we are working at
this time," the better (Birch, 1974; Grzynkowicz, 1975; Hobbs,
1974a; Hoffman, 1962; Neff and Pilch, 1975) .

Research has found that no matter how much effort has been
made to group on any one factor, you do not significantly reduce
the tremendous variations in individual differences, even on the
variable that was used for originally grouping the students.   At
the same time, variations in other subjects will probably be wide.
Much of the justification for this effort has been to try to reduce
the range to make it easier to teach.   If grouping is done on actual
achievement, it is somewhat more dependable than if it is done on
some other variables.   There is more and more evidence that students learn a great deal from the differences that they see in each
other, making it even more desirable not to try to group too
closely.

No matter what the plan, the real problem comes in handling
the slower-moving students.   There has been an increasing use of
the courts on the part of parents of minority groups against any
type of grouping based on an "arbitrary" use of IQs *(Hobson v.
Hanson,* 1967; *Smuck v. Hobson,* 1969) .   They felt, with some
justification, that no matter how their children were grouped,
they always ended up on the bottom of the "pile."   Court decisions and, more recently, legislative enactments are prohibiting
schools from making any major change in the student's basic educational program without the parent's signed, informed consent.
It is becoming increasingly difficult to keep students in any group
if they or their parents object.   Although school personnel can
still advise, they are going to have to spend more time educating
the parents and students regarding their options and letting them
use their best judgment.   Some grouping is inevitable; one cannot
work with all of the students in a district in a single group.   Being
aware of some of the arguments surrounding grouping today,
teachers will be more sensitive when suggesting changes in a
student's placement and less certain that any one placement is

best. As battles over grouping are waged, educational technology is fortunately increasing so that there is a better chance to place students more on the basis of their social needs than on their academic levels. It would be well, however, for teachers to be aware of and to help to develop a broader spectrum of grouping placement procedures in the schools they serve and to take an active part in constantly evaluating whether or not the placement of their students is the best one possible.

Adjustments Within the Local School

It is quite clear, in light of all the factors to be considered, that the closer students are to their normal school program and yet are provided with the services they need the better. (This is referred to as the "least restrictive environment" in the new legislation on this topic.) This cannot be stressed too much; in this day of specialization there is a strong tendency to try to find a special group for almost every unique kind of learner. It has been humorously (and somewhat ironically) said that if this trend continues, the only student who will be left in the classroom will be the quiet, conforming, rapid-learning, long-haired, blue-eyed girl. Special groups would have been found for all the rest of the class. Much of this is done with good intentions; we could argue, at one level, that every student would profit from a smaller class with a specially trained teacher and a curriculum designed specifically for his/her particular needs. Evidence is pointing to the fact, however, that a well-designed regular program, with the addition of some needed specialized services brought to the child in the regular class, has a tremendous potential for helping the majority of students with special needs.

PRESELECTING THE ENVIRONMENT. If several classes are available at a given level in a school, it is important to *try* to identify which students will progress most satisfactorily with specific teachers and specific groups of children. There is not a great deal of evidence to predict whether or not a student will get along well in a certain class. There is, very likely, a relationship between the learning style of certain teachers, the curriculum to be covered at that grade, and the learning-behavior style of the student. These interrelationships need to be studied more. The preselection that has been done by principals and teachers at the elementary school level traditionally takes on the dimensions of separating certain youngsters from each other, typically the hyperactive boys. At the secondary school, counselors have been trying to do this for years. As computers are used more and more for programming, this will be much more difficult to do, although some programs permit the counselor to place specific students on the first "pass" through the computer, before all the rest are scheduled. It is difficult to predict when putting a class together what the social climate will be when all of the students and the teacher begin to interact (McNeil, 1972).

Another preselection technique, which has not yet been perfected, would be the process whereby students who move into a school during the year would be interviewed and assigned to specific classrooms on the basis of strengths or weaknesses identified in the interview. It is obvious that many students could learn much more effectively if this process were done well. In exceptional instances, sensitive principals in the elementary school have allowed children to visit classes and to select the teacher or class where they felt that they could work best.

ADJUSTMENTS WITHIN THE CLASSROOM. Once the student has been placed in a class, teachers have at their disposal a variety of grouping/placement techniques which will facilitate learning. Decisions must be made as to how to structure the classroom, where each student will sit, and how to group them for best learning. The classroom climate will strongly influence the way that students will interact with the teacher and with each other (Barclay, 1971). Some teachers use sociometric techniques which indicate how the students would like to relate to each other as the basis for the seating arrangement. Fortunately, seating classes alphabetically is not done much any more; although research evidence on this point is lacking, it would seem logical to assume that constantly being placed in the back of a room because their name starts with z would have an effect on the student's learning. Techniques which bring teachers out from behind the desk and get them to move around in a classroom tend to increase the involvement of all and to eliminate the "dead spot" frequently seen in the back of the room.   If space permits, various centers in different parts of the room should suggest the appropriate learning activities that go on there.   Grouping in most classes can range from all students working in one group, to a totally individualized program, depending on the learning required.

A system of helping students is needed that would bring them required instructional materials as efficiently as possible.   Each teacher's classroom will usually have only a limited amount of materials, just as he/she will have only a limited number of teaching techniques available at any one time.   Special materials for students with special problems are readily available on the market; much that has been purchased is not well used and remains on the shelf.   Teachers working with students at the same level should learn to share equipment and materials with each other in some sort of a systematic way.

There has been a strong trend toward individualized instruction in recent years.   When students learn individually, they should have an opportunity to bring back that information to a large or small group and to relate it to the social learning going on in the classroom.   The power that the total classroom environment/interaction has over purely individualized learning comes in this kind of social interaction and in the reinforcement of the learning that is taking place.

ORGANIZATIONAL ADJUSTMENTS.   There are a great many ways for schools to organize to try to get more flexible groupings.   Although the list below is not exhaustive, several ways of bringing this about will be mentioned to show how staffs have worked together to provide more flexibility.   In addition to the traditional before-and-after-school time period, high school teachers have set up evening seminars on specific topics for invited and/or volunteer students, in some cases at the teacher's home and sometimes at the school.

No discussion of organizational strategies for helping young students in this day would be complete without at least a comment on the much-talked-about British Infant School.   Although any truly "open" system is hard to define, the main characteristics of these schools are as follows: Learning tends to be a very active process, i.e. the five-, six-, and seven-year-olds are expected to learn things but more through a sense of inquiry than through "being told." The rigid structure of bells and class periods is gone; structure comes from the students and the teachers working together on subjects around interest centers, and the net effect is a more integrated day. Children are grouped in "family groups" with students from several age spans placed in the same group. The goal is to treat each child as an individual and for the teacher to learn to use a much wider series of resources both in the school and in the community. In this type of setting children accept the responsibility of teaching other children as needed (Heyman, 1972; Weber, 1971).

Some elementary schools have organized a process called "staggered reading" in which typically the primary grades are split into two groups; half of the students (usually the ones who are making the least progress) come either a half hour early or at the regular time. They would again subdivide and one-half would work with the teacher (in many cases augmented by older students who would volunteer to come early or would miss the first part of their own class) and the other group would do independent seat work; then they would switch at mid-period. The rest of the children would come one hour after the first group had arrived, and the major middle portion of the day would be devoted to all of the other subjects. At either thirty minutes before, or at the usual dismissal time, the group that had come early would go home and the rest would remain for one more hour, again working in two groups. In this way, all of the children are at the school the usual length of time, but the teacher (who has to put in an extra hour) will have been able to give more intensive supervision to the smaller groups of children. This plan could be worked within one classroom, but usually involves the total primary grades in a school.

Some schools for older students (junior high or high school) have developed a "floating period" which has somewhat the same effect as the above plan. A six-period day (for example) would be scheduled but the student would only take five classes. On

Monday, the first period would be the floating period; on Tuesday, the second period, and so on through the week. During the floating period, students would be allowed to seek out whatever help they needed or they could get involved in any project that they wished. Since the whole school had a separate period at the same time, every teacher would be available to every student who sought their help. The floating period could, of course, also be used for school-wide assemblies.

Variations on team teaching at all levels of education have been tried in which a team of teachers (usually three or more with some aides) assumes the responsibility of working with a large group of students. Learning tasks are broken down into those requiring small group instruction (where everyone would have a group) and those permitting or profiting from large group instruction (thereby permitting some free time for small, special-interest or remedial groups) (Trump and Baynham, 1962).

A very creative principal in an elementary school initiated what he called "share teaching." One of the teachers (who had volunteered to be the "share" coordinator) put up a list asking all staff members to volunteer to share one or more specific, short-term skills or units; the help of parents in the community was also enlisted (they represent what is probably the major source of untapped educational resources available today). Almost everyone has at least one topic or skill which he/she would be willing to share with other teachers. The next step was for teachers to sign up for the short-term units which had been offered by other staff members or people from the community. When another staff member was going to share with a specific class, instead of just having the two teachers exchange classes (the administratively easy way), arrangements were made to cover the class of the teacher who was sharing (often the principal would take over) and both the regular and the "sharing" teacher would work with the class together. In this way, the regular teacher could see the sharing teacher doing what he/she most liked to do. This enabled the receiving teacher to observe good teaching (How often does one teacher in a typical school get to observe someone else teaching?), who was then better able to provide the necessary follow-up on the shared topic.

The use of the "mini-course" is growing in popularity. Teachers volunteer to teach a brief course. The duration of these mini-courses can be half of the traditional semester (which usually prevents district personnel from participating). With this model the students typically receive academic credit. In other instances, courses are much shorter; one organizational structure takes a week out of the regular schedule; others plan one full day or several two-hour mini-courses in any given day. These courses typically have no assignments, no quizzes, and no credit when they are this brief. The plan provides a welcome change of pace to both students and faculty and enhances the concept (which frequently gets lost) of the fun of learning. Some colleges are using a similar model called an "intercession," often lasting for about a month between the two regular semesters.

Some elementary schools use a variation called an "interest club" period. For the six or eight weeks before Open House, as soon as the primary children are released to go home, the fourth, fifth, and sixth graders go to the interest group of their "choice" (since some remedial subjects are given, students who especially need that kind of help are strongly encouraged to sign up for one of these needed subjects which again is taught as more of an activity than a formal subject). Other groups are organized for enrichment activities such as putting on plays, doing advanced art work, etc. One group of aggressive boys "worked" on a unit on dinosaurs with great glee and were able to work off some of their hyperactivity in that way.

A series of approaches called "modular scheduling," again used primarily at the junior and senior high school level, questions the value of every class taking the traditional fifty- to sixty-minute period, five days a week, for one or two semesters. The principle is to break up the day into small units (modules of twenty to forty minutes) and assign to class subjects the number of units required for the material which is to be taught. Lab periods and group discussions on large topics might be scheduled for two or three hours, once or twice a week. Subjects such as foreign language would have daily, short-term, concentrated practice (possibly with the use of language labs) and would be scheduled for a single module each day.   (For a much more complete discussion of scheduling in the secondary schools see Trump and Baynham, 1962.)   Modular scheduling can also be worked out with the "open space" schools; openness is much more a state of mind than a condition of where the walls are placed.

In some schools, modular scheduling has been taken further and called "demand scheduling."   Each day the faculty puts in requests for "single occurring events" which could be special interest groups, outside speakers, large-group activities, e.g. "model United Nations," etc.   Each day as the students arrive at school, they are given a list of the single occurring events of that day. Certain basic classes, such as freshman English, could be taken at any period of the day when they were being offered.   The students would work out a daily schedule based on the single occurring events that they wanted or were required to take, and then work in the other daily routine classes at any time and with any teacher they wanted.   This means that freshman English teachers have to coordinate their programs and that students have to integrate all subjects that they take from several teachers.   It also means that students have a great deal of free time (just as they do in college) which in some instances leads to discipline problems.

Although this last example may be more flexibility than is needed or desired in the typical secondary school, these examples illustrate how school staffs can work together to provide for special interests in special groups.   The point is that every student has unique needs; the creativity to build a plan to meet most of those needs lies within every faculty if they choose to use it.

RESOURCE/MEDIA CENTERS.   An increasingly large number of schools are trying to solve the distribution problem of cataloging, storing, and distributing the increasing amount of printed and audiovisual material by organizing some sort of a resource media center.   This is logical because much that would otherwise be stored in the classroom would only be used occasionally, and much of what is remedial at one level is enrichment at another.   These centers can be school wide, or located in grade-level or departmental sections of the school.   These are generally more useful for average or above-average students (especially in the lower grades) who are already relatively independent learners, and not so helpful for students who are unable to find the material they need in order to work on their own. Some centers are staffed by student or parent volunteers. The goal of a good resource media center is to bring the most appropriate material to the place where the students who need it the most can use it most effectively. In many secondary schools, this type of program is fortunately replacing the older concept of study halls, a concept designed more to help put together a schedule than it was to assist true learning. The Resources Center will become even more important as many students previously placed in special classes are integrated into the mainstream. Much of the material that has been needed and used in special programs will have to be made available in the regular class through resource centers. There are already state and regional instructional centers for the handicapped which are well organized and well equipped. Because of their experience at working with children with learning problems, many of the teachers who have been serving these classes would make excellent personnel to staff resource centers. In secondary schools, many of these resource media centers become highly specialized in specific subject areas such as science or mathematics (Davis, 1968; Klinge, 1974; Sabatino, 1971).

SPECIAL GROUPINGS. Most schools have woven into their regular curricular offering a series of special groups which are variations of the grouping/placement strategies. In the elementary school these would include groups working with the remedial reading and speech correction teachers. There is also some increasing interest in corrective physical education classes. These are set up both for the child who has been traditionally thought of as physically handicapped and for the less obvious child with poor coordination, a condition often associated in young children with poor reading and writing. Some of these are designed basically as developmental programs where all children are taught a variety of techniques designed to develop better body integration. Whereas most children make good progress in the area of physical integration with only a small amount of help, others need more specialized assistance, often in small group situations.

RETENTION. One of the oldest ways used by schools to group or change the placement of students was through retention. It was originally used when a student, for any reason, did not meet the standard set for a given grade level. It was often more an indication of the failure of the instructional program than it was the failure of the student. Some "experts" have indicated that as many as 90 percent of the students in the first grade should be retained; this even more dramatically points to the need for programmatic curriculum changes. If a program does not fit the needs of as high as 90 percent of the students, it should be changed rather than retaining the students.

Most of the research on the value of retention is quite old (Goodlad, 1952). At one time the nonpromotion rate often reached 75 percent. In more recent days it still affects from 2 to 10 percent, with boys being retained approximately three times as often as girls, and the youngest children in each class are most likely to be retained. A larger percentage of children coming from lower socioeconomic homes are retained. Currently retentions are typically carried out in the primary grades and there is rarely an occasion when a child is retained more than once. Many studies have found teachers to be frequently in favor of retention; parents of students who have been retained, although more ambivalent, have also been found to be in agreement with the decision. Academic gains following the retention do not generally support the procedure, although again results fluctuate (Goodlad, 1952; Kowitz and Armstrong, 1961). Social problems are often found in children who have been retained (Goodlad, 1954), but it is difficult to know whether this was related to the cause for the retention or is a result of it. Overage students are much less likely to ever finish school (Holmes and Finley, 1957). There is a growing feeling that retention should be used only sparingly and then only after careful study involving a school psychologist or other objective person. If there is any one person—the teacher, a parent, or the child, who is strongly against the retention, it is usually not indicated.

It is best to start to help children who might need to be retained as early as possible either before they enter school, in kindergarten, or in the first grade (see the earlier section of this chapter). Many of the other strategies listed in other sections of this book can be used to help individualize and strengthen children's education, thereby reducing the chances of their ever having to be retained. A form of retention formerly used by schools, although it was never called that, was withholding some children (whom school personnel felt could not make it through the first year of school) or sending them home "to mature." It is obviously quite true that not all children are ready for the school program at the same time; however leaving the immature, slow children in the same home and neighborhood seldom prepares them for the next year. There should be a structured preschool program for such children, involving both systematic training of the parents to help the child, as well as a good program in the school. Otherwise, the most effective strategy for help is to provide this kind of child with a modified experience in the regular first year of school.

About ten years ago there was much emphasis on building into the curriculum "transitional grades" such as "junior first grades" or "preparation second grades." Traditionally, remedial services could not (and still in many cases cannot) be provided for a child until he/she has already failed a grade. These transitional classes were often a part of a "zero reject" concept, i.e. no child should fail. This concept is worth holding on to as an organizing strategy for helping children. In some ways these models were the forerunners of the continuous progress concept, which is being used more of late (Hillson and Bongo, 1971), and of the open concept school, which, to a large degree, came into being to avoid the use of retention and its potential damage to the child's self-concept because of its association with failure (Department of Elementary School Principals, 1968; Otto, 1969; Purdom,1970). It is generally agreed that this approach to organizing the school takes additional time on the part of teachers. If, however, it helps students come out of the experience with a better image of self, it would be well worth it.

ACCELERATION. Another placement procedure previously used

for children who were able to move more rapidly than the others in the "lock step" of the curriculum was to have a child "skip a grade." It has always been an interesting phenomenon that not as many teachers felt that a child should be put ahead as there were teachers who felt that certain children should be held back.

This brings up the whole topic of what to do with the gifted in our educational system. Special schools have been used and generally found not very satisfactory (although some research supported them) and so very few exist today. Special classes have been and are still being tried. One of the authors once studied the advantages of a full-time special class for fourth to sixth grade high achievers as compared to leaving a similar group in the regular class and bringing them into a special center one day a week. Although the evidence pointed to the value of the more integrated program, the administration (under some pressure from parents) moved in the direction of the special class, which had to be abandoned several years later.

There is little question that many high achievers at all levels are not stimulated by the regular pace of the curriculum. Obviously, a specialized curriculum can be devised where these students can move more rapidly. Rather than just giving these students more of the same kind of problems because they can do them faster, a good program actually stresses the higher cognitive levels of analysis and application. The problem comes with taking these students out of their regular class (or, worse still, their regular school), since they lose out on their normal social relationships and become even more socially isolated than their high ability would normally make them.

Once again the strategy that seems to be preferable (and which is surely most often used) is to place rapid learners/high achievers into the fastest moving group in the school and to provide them with enrichment activities in the regular classroom that they can do while maintaining normal social contacts. This is quite different than just leaving them in the regular class and not providing them with any special opportunities. A helping strategy for these students is to reach out into the community and, for example, organize a science club which would bring in scientists from the area. In other locations, parents have organized Saturday morning programs in which a variety of speakers and experiences are planned for the high achievers. The development of such groups should be encouraged and, once established, they should be left open to any who want to come, rather than limited to the older concept of the "gifted." A student may be very poor in mathematics, average in science, but need enrichment activities in English and social studies. The approach of one creative teacher should be applauded: She formed interest-activities, usually involving a Saturday trip, and took the eight most interested students (all who could fit into a station wagon) out for a first-hand experience.

At the secondary school, the faculty in every department should systematically appraise all of the students that come through their department and identify those who need special enrichment activities (as indeed they should identify children that need special remedial activities). They should then attempt to identify a wide spectrum of ways to provide the necessary enrichment; this could include such things as special individualized extracurricular activities, projects, special duties, e.g. lab assistantships, special opportunities, e.g. submission of art work to regional art shows, and advanced placement for one or more subjects in college as well as in high school. Some regular courses are almost by definition enrichment courses for the rapidly moving student. Physics would, for example, be typically classified in such a category.

One word of warning seems in order: Educators should stop trying to recreate the world in the classroom. They should make a cooperative effort to bring the real business and professional world in to work with the school and to send the student out to the real world. This should be true for all students, but especially for those moving too slowly or too rapidly for the regular curriculum. There is an increased sense of excitement and involvement in getting away from the "artificialness" imposed by the limits of the regular school and getting out into the real world. The modern school should be using a wide variety of "professional exploration" opportunities which assign older students to professional people in the community, where they can get first-hand information about a specific career field.

Another word about grouping/placement activities for the gifted: Do not think of giftedness in too narrow a sense. For too long, giftedness has been a term reserved for the "book worm" or "math whiz." Special activities should be available for outstanding achievement in all areas. In some very traditional secondary schools the only really "gifted" program is for the super-athletes who are specially trained, provided with expensive equipment and facilities, and rewarded for their unique type of giftedness. Let us not take it away from the athlete, but rather let us try to get some of that recognition to the gifted in other areas. It is another powerful strategy to help probably as many as the top 15 to 20 percent of the students in each academic area.

In addition to thinking of many different kinds of gifted students, educators should probably also be thinking of the different degrees of giftedness, i.e. the student who is one in 1,000 may need a very different program than one who is less gifted. Chamberlin and Catterall (1963) suggest an acceleration program for potential dropouts.

SUSPENSIONS OR EXPULSIONS. Although it has already been discussed (and it will be discussed again), a special case of placement, i.e. taking the student *out* of a group that is available in the school, is that of putting students out of school for either short or long periods of time. This is a technique which has been used extensively for years, especially in the secondary school. As a strategy for helping the suspended or expelled student learn, it leaves much to be desired; but it is difficult to argue against its usefulness as a way of helping to maintain the peace and quiet of the total school so that learning can continue for other students.

As in many other areas, the conflict between the rights of the student and the rights of the school authorities is being brought under sharp attack by the courts. The hard facts are that suspension is used most frequently with the minority student and with those from lower socioeconomic backgrounds. While it is true that there are many factors in the environment and life-style of these students which complicate the matter, it is equally evident that many schools have not, for a variety of reasons, made a concentrated effort to meet the needs of these students. It is also becoming obvious that such activities seriously reduce the student's ability to complete his/her education and take advantage of the social rewards of the culture. Such activities have often not followed appropriate "due process" procedures and have not adequately protected the student's rights. The education code in some states permits classroom teachers to expel students; in the current litigious climate, it is extremely unwise for such a major decision to be made by any one person. This is true for an individual teacher, but even to some extent, for the principal or vice-principal, the traditional persons "authorized by the school board" to do this. Such a decision should be made by a group, with carefully documented reasons, and with careful attention to the process of informing the student and his or her parents of the reasons for such an action and of their rights to appeal. Such time-consuming (although essential) procedures will probably make this expedient strategy less useful. Schools will have to find other ways of helping these students while, at the same time, safeguarding the peace.

Two strategies which are being tried in some schools to remedy the problem of school suspensions are probation and in-school suspension (Iowa Department of Public Instruction, 1975). Used in this context, probation refers to a process of granting to an individual the right of conditional attendance during a trial period. In this procedure the principal (or his/her agent), after careful investigation of the charges against the student, informs the student of those charges and that he/she is being granted probationary status for a period not longer than ten school days with the conditions which would permit continued attendance. In addition, written notice of the probation and the reasons for it are sent to the student's parents or legal guardians and to the superintendent of schools and the president of the school board. In-school suspension refers to a temporary period of isolating students for one or more classes while they are under appropriate administrative supervision. It will ordinarily not be imposed for a period of longer than five days. As above, it would only be administered after a careful investigation had been made, the student was able to clearly understand the charges made against him/her, and a notice of such an action had been sent to the parents, the superintendent, and the president of the board (Iowa Department of Public Instruction, 1975).

The wording describing such strategies as probation and in-school suspension must of necessity become more legal and more exact because of the Supreme Court decision (*Goss v. Lopez,* 1975) which much more carefully describes the responsibilities of the school in informing students of the charges against them, informing the parents of the school's decisions, and of informing the students and/or their parents of their right to appeal. The situation is getting more complicated for those students who are over eighteen and who, in many states, have recently been held to be no longer minors. Fortunately, many of those who are still in school over the compulsory age of attendance have not in the past been the ones who have needed this kind of intervention strategy.

Grouping/Placement Adjustments Between Schools

Individual schools cannot hope to offer all of the programs needed to meet all of the grouping/placement needs of all of the students. They should work cooperatively with other schools to bring about more opportunities and ways to help students learn. These adjustments can be a simple exchange between two schools in the same district or can involve much more complex systems including total districts, counties, and (increasingly) cooperative educational districts, stretching over large areas. The following is a partial list of arrangements which provide additional strategies for helping students.

COOPERATION BETWEEN FEEDER SCHOOLS. A few schools have moved to the "educational park" concept where all students from kindergarten through high school (and sometimes even college) are on one campus. Almost all schools have at their disposal the opportunity (although few really use it) to work cooperatively with the other schools serving the same attendance areas. As the momentum for using students to help other students increases, there is a new-felt emphasis on cooperation between feeder schools in a given area.

Principals and faculties of intermediate and high schools have tended to "look down their noses" at schools serving younger students. They would be less inclined to do this if they realized that freeing older students to help younger ones is quite defensible, both for the student tutor and for the one being helped. Transporting students across long distances is often difficult to arrange. Having older students take the first or last period of their day (or any other mutually convenient time) to apply what they know about a subject by teaching it, under supervision, to another student does much to increase the credibility of education and, at the same time, reduces the forgetting taking place in the older student. Such an exchange can involve either average or above-average students, but there is also increasingly abundant evidence that older students who have had difficulty in learning to read, for example, make some of the best tutors with children who are having difficulty in this subject (and they probably also get more out of it personally than do students who have never had difficulty).

There is often an experimental program in one school that needs more students in order to operate at its maximum potential, and encouraging an exchange of students between cooperating schools is likely to improve the educational program of both. One seldom hears of elementary children being invited to high schools to watch such things as music or dramatic productions; even less frequently does one hear of young students being used by high schools or colleges in courses in psychology (high school psychology is one of the fastest growing courses in the curriculum today), home economics, education, etc.

Cooperation between feeder schools can take other forms. There is often the student who, for one reason or another, should be promoted sooner than would normally be the case, i.e. the faster moving student, the overage, overly mature, etc. To be an effective strategy for helping the latter type of student, there has to be a joint process of intelligent problem solving and cooperation, not just the old, "We can't handle him here; let's send him on; he won't be much of a problem where there are older students to control him." Because too much of this kind of behavior has taken place in the past, the true strength of this strategy is seldom realized.

Although high schools struggle with the problem of helping their students make appropriate life-career choices, not many have encouraged the development of a Future Teacher's Club. Such a model also works very well by having college students volunteer to tutor younger students. This can involve a formal course in tutoring (which is probably best) or can leave the tutors to their own devices to get some help from the teacher of the child with whom they are working. Lack of formal training should not, in most instances, rule out such a program. It can be given for credit (at either the high school or college level) or be considered a volunteer service activity. In one county in California, there were over 5,000 college students (most of whom had been trained) who had volunteered to help tutor. How much longer can education continue to struggle to meet so many individual needs without making use of all resources available to it (Mastors, 1975)?

ANOTHER SCHOOL. Another placement strategy involves sending a student from one school to another, either in the same district or another one. When this involves disruptive students, as it frequently does, one district labels it a "lend lease" program. Although for some students it produces desirable results, for most it might well have been called the "last chance" strategy. For younger students who have "gotten in over their heads" in a given situation (after appropriate efforts have been made on the part of the faculty and students of the first school), a new environment might be called for, and, if properly utilized, can be helpful.

A variation of the use of another school is the long-standing procedure of allowing some students to attend school outside of their normal district boundary. This usually involves some sort of formal interdistrict agreement between the two districts. It can be done as an accommodation to working parents, for example, or to help a child or student find a new or different program. Although this procedure has been used for many years, it has not tended to be popular among educators, even when the same

number of students want to exchange between two districts and
their parents are willing to arrange for transportation. As the
school-age population decreases, especially at the elementary level,
one may see more willingness on the part of schools and districts
to work out such plans.

THE VOUCHER SYSTEM. A variation of the use of another
school which is getting a lot of attention these days is the system of
giving the parents "vouchers" which enable them to take the child
to any school that they think will provide the best education. It
is being used for exceptional children with major educational
needs where the solution is usually to take the child to a private
school or institution where the tuition is paid in full or in part by
the public schools. On the assumption that it will provide more
parental involvement in the educational decision-making process,
it is also being used with students within the mainstream of education, often between one or more public schools in an area,
where the payment of money is not an issue. Many educators are
afraid that this will turn the selection of an educational program
into a "popularity contest." Others counter that this would be
better than thinking of school as a "straightjacket," which students
have to attend whether they want to or not, or whether they are
geting anything out of it or not. Of course parents with money
have almost always had this opportunity by simply enrolling their
children in private schools. There has been a major growth of the
"private school" (which is hard to justify when one looks at their
programs) in areas where racial desegregation has been mandated.
Although the voucher system could, if abused, probably do a great
deal of damage to public education, it could, if properly used,
also inaugurate a new period of innovation and reform in American schools (Cohodes, 1970; Noue, 1972). If it is to make this
kind of a contribution to American education it must have a
blending of tradition and innovation, action and caution, energy
and patience, theory and practice (Haden and King, 1971).

DUAL ELIGIBILITY. A slight variation on the above-mentioned
strategies is where, usually at the secondary level, students are allowed to attend their regular school half-time (to get the basic
educational subjects and to maintain contact with their friends)

and another school for the rest of the time. This can be done for a variety of reasons, usually to provide students with a specialized course or program, especially in the industrial or technical areas. These technical programs are usually very expensive to equip and there are often too few students to make it financially practical to start such a program in every school. It is consistent with the rule of providing specialized services for students as close to their normal learning situation as possible. This type of program is more typical for the last two years of high school and usually an arrangement is made whereby students graduate with their regular class rather than from the school with the specialized program. If there are enough interested students, most high schools should develop a component of trade and technical classes and specialized programs.   In addition, there should be cooperatively planned programs which can be filled by the students from two or more schools, placed where facilities and staff permit.   Students will also use dual eligibility to enrich superior education, especially if they can, at the same time, hold onto their identity and social contacts with their regular school.

REGIONAL VOCATIONAL CENTERS. These centers will normally serve a still larger geographic area than the cooperative lend-lease programs.   They often require even larger facilities and more specialized staffing. The programs they offer will tend to attract a smaller percentage of all secondary students. Over the last few years there has been a tremendous, nationwide increase in interest in vocational education. It has suffered in the past from a variety of factors including the following: too little equipment and staff, not enough students to take the courses, and the stigma that only students who could not "hack it" anywhere else would attend. This has been fostered by a great many factors, but these problems seem to be lessening.

The overemphasis on academic work by both the American public and its high schools, together with a tendency on the part of the culture to extend childhood (partly to keep students off the labor market which cannot support them), have made it extremely difficult to get older students to look realistically at the tremendously important career development aspects of their lives. The majority of people have to work (with women's "lib," an increasing number of women will probably be employed) and the total life-style dictated by one's vocational choice makes it clearly one of the major decisions that a person must make. At the same time, speaking conservatively, less than 5 percent of the teaching/ learning effort in high school is even remotely related to the career decisions that the student must eventually make. Too many people blindly assume that (1) all students will finish high school (obviously this is not true, since we consistently have about a 17 percent dropout rate) ; (2) most people will go on to college (nationwide, less than half even start a postsecondary education and probably less than 25 percent finish either a two-year or longer educational program) ; and (3) those that do not go to college will be readily absorbed into the labor market, even though they have no saleable skills (which is another absurdity). Few would advocate the system, common in Europe and various countries of the world, where educational/vocational decisions are made (sometimes irrevocably) at an early age. It is hard to deny that these factors contribute heavily to the aimlessness and the lack of relevancy seen by many students in the modern secondary school. There seems to be a shift to work-related education on the part of the postsecondary students and on the part of some educators, but the real power of the strategy of helping students direct what they are doing in the school to the real world remains to be felt (Gibson, 1972; Ginsberg, 1971; Keiser and Wampler, 1974; Pucinski and Hirsch, 1971; Reardon and Burck, 1975; Rhodes, 1971; Wampler, 1973).

ALTERNATE SCHOOLS. There is a growing amount of interest and effort being expended in the direction of building alternate schools, frequently (but not exclusively) for older secondary students. An increasing number of students, even though they still want a high school diploma, are finding the traditional secondary curriculum and social climate too impersonal, too sterile, or too irrelevant, and are seeking alternative programs (Silberman, 1970). Some, but by no means all, of these students have academic difficulties and a few have been behavior problems. A large number, however, fit neither of those stereotypes and are seeking a smaller, more personal and more individualized educational program in which they can do "more of their own thing." Some are the "push-outs" (as distinct from the "dropouts") of the system, the troublemakers (often including the students who are caught smoking on campus), the pregnant girls, etc. In some cases they either need to or prefer to work; there are still many secondary schools that will not permit students to attend unless they do so full-time (which seems hard to justify).

Alternate schools are given various names; in some places they are called "continuation schools," in others (usually low-income, urban settings) they are called "store-front schools." They are usually on a separate campus where different teaching/learning strategies can be used and where different rules of conduct can be maintained. Most involve a more personal teacher/pupil relationship; many try to relate the activity in the alternative school more directly to the world into which the student will move.

There are also some alternate schools for younger children which adopt different teaching programs or life-styles, but these to date have not played a major role in American education. Schools that "march to a different drummer" represent another major strategy for helping particular students, some of whom "failed" *in* the regular system, and others who were "failed" or let down *by* the system (Spodek, 1973).

SPECIAL EDUCATION CLASSES. Most of the discussion about special classes and special education in general belongs in Chapter 5 where these classes are discussed as Corrective/Remedial Interventions. They also belong to a discussion of grouping/placement procedures designed to teach basic academic/intellectual skills. Such classes can be held at the student's school, of course, but they are listed here because they usually involve a between-school arrangement. At one time it would have been much easier to list them as separate interventions which were, by definition, special, and which were not part of the regular curriculum. One of the current changes and challenges to education is the need to maintain or reintegrate into the mainstream of education many children who would previously have been screened out of the regular class and put into these special groups. This change is being forced on the schools as the result of a great deal of litigation which has been brought against special education (Birch, 1974; Grzynkowicz, 1975; Hobbs, 1974a; Jones, 1971; Neff and Pilch, 1975; Reger, Schroeder and Uschold, 1968; Telford and Sawrey, 1972).

Placements Outside the Regular School

Whereas an extensive discussion of placements outside the school is to some extent outside the pupose of this book, any complete listing of strategies for helping students should at least recognize that there are large numbers of children and youth who are outside the regular school programs, both public and private (see Chapter 7).

SPECIAL PROGRAMS FOR THE SEVERELY HANDICAPPED CHILD. There are, as one would expect, large numbers of children and youth in institutions for the physically and mentally handicapped. One would think that all of these young people were more severely handicapped than those who are in special classes in the public and private school but this is not necessarily the case. Although the general level of handicap is probably more severe, there are a great many other factors which cause certain young people to be placed in these institutions, i.e. lack of home supervision, lack of educational facilities close to home, the amount of emotional disturbance, multiply-handicapping conditions, etc. Many of the same pressures which are forcing schools to find programs for educating the students in the "least restrictive environment" are causing these institutions to release those who can get along (often with a great deal of help) in the regular community. Although some, upon release, will be able to profit from a fairly normal school program, many of them will be asked to get into special programs within the public schools. Parents of these children are approaching the schools with a great deal more sophistication about their rights than they had when the children were first refused programming (Abeson, Bolick, and Hess, 1975; Coordinating Council for Handicapped Children, 1974). It would appear that one of the strategies educators could use to assist many of these young people is to help other students, parents, and the community at large to be more accepting of the handicapped. The fact that an individual has been in an institution, no matter what the circumstances, tends to label the child or young person in the minds of many and they are unwilling to try to find an appropriate place for them either in the community or school situation (Hobbs, 1974a,b).

YOUTH IN CORRECTIONAL PROGRAMS. Although many of the school-age youngsters in institutions of a correctional type are technically in "schools," they are certainly not in "the mainstream" of education. Many of them come from backgrounds which make it extremely difficult to take advantage of the school situations that they have had; it is undoubtedly equally true that some of them have had school programs which, at best, have been unresponsive to their needs, or at worst, have sorely aggravated the problem. Whatever the cause, most of these institutions are overcrowded. Those who make the decisions about adding new facilities can see the futility of constantly building more and larger institutions of this nature. They are aware that no matter how devoted a staff or how good a program an institution may have, in many instances the peer culture is highly conducive to creating people who function outside the law once they have been released. We need to help those who are released come back into society with the necessary skills to move into a positive life or a feeling of self-worth which will enable them to handle the additional social and economic pressures outside the institution. Those persons who have been trying to help the youths while they are in the correctional programs are also trying to help them get back into regular society as rapidly as possible with as much chance for success as possible. The questions that arise are the following: How able and willing are the educators in the regular programs to accept these youngsters? Do they consider that these young people have just as much of a handicapping condition as many of those who are labeled as being "exceptional"? Can educators put into effect all of the strategies and resources to give the student a real chance to succeed? All of these questions are factors which must be considered. As in the case with the institutionalized exceptional child, these youths and their parents are becoming more skillful in identifying and demanding the services to which they are entitled. Some of the correctional agencies are developing strategies for sending a diagnostic teacher or an ombudsman with students to try to ensure that they get into the best possible program and to monitor their progress. These strategies show a great deal of promise. (For a more complete discussion, see Chapter 7.)

CHILDREN NOT IN A PROGRAM. As mentioned in the earlier section of this chapter, there is a growing concern for the estimated two million children and youth of school age who are not in a program (American Children Out of School, 1975; Children's Defense Fund, 1974). Many of the factors discussed in the earlier section are applicable here. There is more and more legal and legislative authority to support any student's (or his/her parents') claim to his/her right to an education (*Mills v. Board of Education,* 1972; *Pennsylvania Association for Retarded Children, v. Commonwealth of Pennsylvania* 1971).

INDIVIDUALIZING THE CURRICULUM

After it is decided who should be educated and the kind of group in which they are to be placed, there is also a need to decide what programs are most suitable. Programs refer to the various strategies which have to do with adaptations in the curriculum. Within each school there are certain levels and approaches to the achievement areas which are better for a given child or student, taking into consideration his/her age, social maturity, ability, and previous school experience. Part of the strategy for helping a child, therefore, should be directed to the problem of whether or not he or she can meet the demands of schools, i.e. whether or not the child has the necessary prerequisites to do what is asked of him/her. The decision must be made as to whether or not the response which is desired from a child is already in his/her repertoire of response patterns but is not being brought out, or whether the response has to be initially developed. A student who *can* do something but is not doing it will require one strategy. If a student *cannot* do it, one would ordinarily have to devise a plan whereby one would help to provide the child with the necessary prerequisites to enable him/her to make the desired response. A more detailed presentation of this approach will be found later in this chapter. (For a good description of three systems of individualization, see Talmage, 1975.)

It is the responsibility of each educator to work continually toward the goal of increasing the school's ability to be flexible in the curricular demands that it makes on students. It becomes evident that the vast majority of the behavioral problems that are seen in schools are either caused by (or seriously aggravated by) the school's inability to manage properly the broad curriculum offered to the students, i.e. to be flexible enough to meet their individual needs.

Developmental Adjustment

This category refers to those adjustments made in the level at which the child is presented academic material. This approach can be most clearly seen at the preschool level where programs are rapidly increasing, especially for the so-called culturally deprived and the handicapped. There is a great deal of power in the process of identifying all of the developmental "milestones," sequencing them, observing or testing the child through various developmental stages until he/she can no longer perform a task at a specific level, and then initiating steps to help the child attain the next developmental stage (Stock, Wnek, Newborg, Schenck, Gabel, Spurgeon, and Ray, 1976). It has become even more apparent from this work that many young children who have come to school in the past have not had the prerequisite developmental skills to make satisfactory progress in the traditional curriculum. At the early childhood level, educators are building a total readiness curriculum on the sequence of a normally developing child and are creating a whole new educational technology for helping students attain these developmental tasks (Alpern and Boll, 1972; Frankenburg, Dodds, and Fandel, 1970; Quick, Little, and Campbell, 1973b).

During the primary years (and indeed to some extent throughout the whole school experience), the majority of labels which describe students as "immature," "can't learn," "short attention span," "hyperactive," etc., can best be understood as age-appropriate behavior for a younger child. One of the typical developmental adjustments requires the presentation of material in a more concrete fashion for the child who is not yet able to make the necessary abstractions. In planning a program for a specific child, either academic or behavioral, one of the first decisions that the strategist must make is where to "insert" a given child into the curriculum.

At the secondary level, a great deal of emphasis is placed on the use of "prerequisites" to bring about a more homogeneous group. In subjects where it is possible to develop a scope and sequence within a course, such as in mathematics, this procedure can be partially justified if it is used intelligently. It is certainly more difficult to justify in connection with such subjects as language arts and social studies, where it is more difficult to build such a carefully graduated sequence. Many secondary school faculty members become so involved with the content that they are attempting to teach that they lose sight of the students they are trying to help. At all educational levels, the problem exists for both the slow learner and the more able student. The main problem, of course, is to provide the necessary academic program in a normal social emotional climate which will facilitate maximum growth. Teaching machines and programmed texts, although still relatively primitive, show promise of helping to bridge this gap. These and a variety of other well-known techniques all have in common the fact that they make an adjustment in the developmental program presented to the student (Bulletin of the National Association of Secondary School Principals, 1970; Calvin, 1969; Thiagarajan, 1971).

Educators have long since learned that even though a ninth grade student, for example, is working at a primer level in reading, the student cannot simply be taken back and put into a first or second grade class because of what it would do to his/her feelings of self-worth. Probably most classes which are heterogeneously grouped, i.e. which do *not* make an attempt to group on the basis of either ability or achievement, should be prepared to handle four levels of reading: an above-average enrichment level in which students can often work independently; an average level; and at least two levels below average (Miller, 1974).

Learning Uniqueness

In addition to an adjustment in the academic level of a student, observations and testing often indicate that an adjustment is needed corresponding to the child's unique learning pattern. Such a strategy starts with the concept of a learning abilities profile. A program is then provided for the student designed to "teach to his/her strengths" while, at the same time, "training to his/her weaknesses," thereby building up strengths and reducing deficits so that they do not continue to represent major breaks in his/her development. Each person has a unique or preferred style of learning. When an instructional pattern rigidly approaches a sensory weakness or where the weaknesses become seriously damaging to the total learning pattern, educators should intervene with a special program. When a student has previously met failure, a new approach can often produce success. A common mistake is to give a student the same approach, i.e. a phonetic approach to reading, merely at a different level (a developmental adjustment strategy) instead of providing a different instructional program, i.e one based more on an activity approach, which would help the student master the material through different sense modalities. Children with perceptual deficits are often difficult to detect; they too will often need a strategy involving a unique learning adjustment. There is a great deal of instructional material now available which is designed to help students with these kinds of special needs. In the opinion of many, there is too much effort spent in education to find *the* way to teach reading (research reports on this topic could easily fill the Washington Monument). The tremendously conflicting research results should point clearly to the fact that there is no one best way to teach this important skill (Arena, 1969; Frostig, Maslow, Lefever, and Whittlesey, 1964; Humphrey, 1975; Larsen and Hammill, 1975; Markoff, 1976; Oakland and Williams, 1971; Wedell, 1973).

Interest/Involvement

A tried-and-true strategy (that is nevertheless often forgotten in this day of advanced educational technology) is that of relating learning in one area with another subject in which the student has particular interest. An example would be the special interest of a group of young boys for studying dinosaurs or of a group of girls (who are slightly older) for horses. Again, with still older students, teaching mathematics through the development of a construction project, or teaching students reading by having them read the vehicle code in order to get their driver's license, would double their interest. Taking advantage of an interest stimulated by a movie or a television show would be another example. For almost anything that takes place either in the world outside or in the classroom, some students will get "turned on" (Ogle and Menuey, n.d.). A creative teacher will either teach basic reading, writing, and computation skills through a subject in which the student is interested, or he/she will help the student get additional information about the topic through using an academic skill. At the secondary level, this strategy often takes the form of having students do special projects, write term papers, or work on such things as student-run newspapers (Swift and Spivak, 1975; Wadsworth, 1971).

Even when students do not have a natural interest in given topics, in some cases this interest can be sparked by helping students choose what they are going to study or the order in which they wish to study a topic. Teachers who have learned to conduct effective classroom discussions can help their students to become more involved in what they are studying by means of relating it to their own life. This strategy is especially helpful for the young, distractable children who often are preoccupied with thoughts, ideas, interests, and activities which keep them from focusing their attention on the events in the classroom (Swift and Spivak, 1975). Some people have felt that the main advantage of the use of games and simulations is that they tend to increase the involvement on the part of the student because the game is essentially a "simplified slice of reality" (Gordon, 1972).

Relevancy

In addition to determining the appropriate developmental/instructional level of material, the teacher (especially of older students) should certainly use the yardstick of relevancy. To borrow from legal terminology, would a "reasonably prudent man" judge that which is being taught as important and necessary in leading a useful life for *some* students (which can probably usually be answered "yes") or for *most* students (a *much* more stringent criterion)? In performing their function of passing on the facts of a culture in order to provide the cohesion that helps a group of people form a society, schools are often asked to teach information which may (or may not) have been useful in times gone by, but which is no longer necessary. It has been said somewhat cynically that teachers are hired to tell "little white lies" to children.

There is always a discrepancy between the goals of a culture, i.e. "all men are created equal," and its actions, i.e. those actions which are screaming evidence that all men are not *treated* equally. Whether or not something is relevant certainly varies with the kinds of students and the changing times, making a solution difficult. Are students being trained to live in the world as it *is*, as it *will be* when they graduate, or as it *should be?* No one of these choices is completely adequate; therefore compromises must be made. Students must be helped to maintain one foot in the past to be able to survive in the present and to be able to move stridently into the future. Students must be able to see both the strengths and weaknesses of the present to be able to make good decisions on how they will attempt to shape their futures (Monson, 1970; Postman and Weingartner, 1969).

What is "needed" in life, and therefore relevant by one definition, is complicated by the entrance requirements of institutions of higher education. Something which is useless and trivial in the "real world" may help students pass the entrance test hurdles of the college or university, and thereby help them to become more functional in life. As educators become more concerned about teaching values, the issue becomes further complicated by the following considerations: Is it better to teach a fact (even a highly useful one) which could be readily retrieved from "storage," i.e. a book, computer, etc., or a value which cannot be retrieved and almost has to be internalized if it is ever to be useful?

Although no culture has ever left to the classroom teacher the complete power over what should be taught, in the final analysis it is almost impossible to monitor what actually goes on in the classroom. Censure of teachers for what they teach is extremely rare. The individual teacher, therefore, has a great deal of power to use the "relevancy" test. One suggestion is that teachers should discipline themselves by asking, "Is what I am teaching really relevant in this day and age?"

The next question must be, "Can I inform, convey, convince, persuade, i.e. educate, my students to accept the fact that it is important?" In the context of developing strategies for improving learning, it does little good (although there may be some subtle, nonverbal clues given by the teacher who is convinced that something is important for the student) for the learners until they can see the importance, value, and relevance of a subject. One speaker once dismissed (perhaps too lightly) this topic by saying, "To solve that problem requires effective education; as professional educators we are the experts, hence there really is no problem." Suffice it to say that one of the main individualization strategies is to determine that what is being taught *is* relevant and to help the student understand *why* it is relevant.

Goal Oriented

Research demonstrates that learning takes place most effectively when it is goal oriented (Rendfrey, 1971). The school has great difficulty in building a curriculum which meets the needs of students from all different kinds of backgrounds. Another strategy, therefore, is to help students to identify existing goals, or to develop new ones, and to begin to relate what they are doing today in school to what they want to build toward tomorrow. This is an increasingly difficult task in a culture which, for example, provides very few opportunities for vocational and life-goal orientation in a period of rather constant vocational change (Reardon and Burck, 1975). By and large, the position of American education seems to be to provide students with a comprehensive, liberal arts program to meet the varying changes and pressures. Educators, however, are beginning to see that, for many, this plan is too narrow because it requires some students to delay immediate rewards much too long. Assisting students to develop short- and long-range goals, therefore, can be a powerful way of helping them.

With some students a "contract approach" can be used wherein an agreement is made that a student will finish a specific unit of work which frequently has been shortened or otherwise adapted to his/her individual needs. The contract appears to be yet another way of allowing students to take up projects which have a unique value to them, to give them guidelines to do some independent study, and to bring the work back into the credit-granting format upon which the school is built. The concept of the teacher (or for that matter someone out in the community) serving as a "mentor" for the student in this and other types of projects is being utilized. At the secondary level, there is a steadily increasing interest in vocational or technical education and a somewhat diminishing interest in the "rah-rah" spirit which has been traditionally associated with our high schools. There has, for instance, been a reduction of the number of students attending the small, liberal arts college and an increase in the number of students in community colleges and vocational-technical schools. This, together with the decrease in applications in many colleges and universities for on-campus housing, is probably related to the fact that older students are seeking a higher degree of relationship between what they are studying in school and the goals they have established for their lives.

Pacing

The appropriate speed at which educational material should be presented to the learner should also be given careful consideration. For preschool children, the pace at which the material should be presented will depend upon the child's changing level of maturation, although more and more attention is being given to stimulus-induced maturation, i.e. experiences which are so well paced and at such an appropriate developmental level that the child is helped to advance academically, intellectually, and socially. Recent efforts to put material into programmed texts and to develop various types of programmed instruction have provided educators with a great deal more information. For example, educators now know more about what the most appropriately sized steps should be in teaching students, how often old material should be reinforced, and how rapidly the learner can absorb new material. For most children (and again, there are individual differences), the pace should be slow enough so that approximately 90 percent of the student's responses are correct, while new material is simultaneously introduced fast enough to keep the student challenged and interested.

Another dimension closely related to the pace at which the material is presented is the factor of the speed and complexity with which directions are given to the learner. The instructions given in many workbooks and in other kinds of educational material are illustrative of what students can absorb. Instructions which are typically given for assembling toys and other articles by the purchaser (they always seem detailed, yet lacking vital information) are also illustrative of what can be absorbed through printed instructions. The student in the classroom has the additional problem of following instructions that he/she is receiving auditorily. The student has little or no opportunity to retrieve details that he/she has missed. For the inattentive child, this is the most critical point of the learning assignment. Many teachers have not paid enough attention to the fact that the way they give the instructions has a vital impact on the child's ability to work successfully. Verbal instructions should be short and free of excess verbiage. The essential information should be given slowly and clearly. Furthermore, the instructions should not be repeated so many times that the students are discouraged from listening. (Swift and Spivak, 1975).

Aiding Conceptual Development

One area of concern associated with introducing educational material at an appropriate pace is the teaching of concepts. In a sense, most of the teaching in schools should be directed to the task of conceptual development. With the information "explosion," there is an ever-increasing number of facts at one's disposal. With the increase in information storage and retrieval systems (most dramatically, but not restricted to the use of computer technology), educators need to question continually where the information should be stored. What information does a student need to have internalized and ready for instant response? Most people would agree that simple computation facts such as 2×2 should be ready for instant retrieval. Other information, on the other hand, should more properly be stored in a variety of places (books, files, computer, encyclopedias, etc.) The task of the school is to help students know when they need certain information, where it is, and how most effectively to get it and to use it. There are other facts which probably fall somewhere in between these two extremes. For each concept, the child must be given certain basic information that contributes to the development of that concept; when does the child develop a concept of "cat" out of all the soft fur, sharp claws, meowing, purring, etc. that separates cats from other animals?

Much teaching should be directed to helping students learn to integrate and to synthesize isolated bits of information and experience into meaningful concepts. A careful assessment should be made to be certain that all of the necesssary concepts are provided for the child and that they are introduced at an appropriate rate. These are important considerations for the teacher, whether he/ she is teaching the concept of "cat" or the much more complex concept of "infinity squared." The sensitive teacher will look for clues (often very subtle) in the student's response pattern which will tell whether or not the pace has been appropriate. The child's *mistakes,* when viewed in this light, will often *point to inadequacies in the pacing/teaching process* as much, if not more, than the child's inability. Once again, new information coming from the field of programmed instruction is helping educators to pay more attention to the factors associated with the pacing of learning (Haden and King, 1971).

Knowledge of Results

To make maximum progress in learning, the student needs to have precise knowledge of results. A dramatic example of this is seen in deaf persons who, because of their hearing condition, are never able to know whether the sounds they make (if indeed they know that they make sounds) have any relationship to the sounds other people make. This begins a whole spiraling effect of poor language development, poor reading, and poor conceptual development (for a dramatic illustration of this problem see Levine, *Lisa and Her Soundless World,* 1974). In general, the more immediate the feedback, the better it is for helping the learning to progress. The tremendously dramatic results which have been seen in the use of behavior modification technology in recent years have been at least partially associated with the fact that the learner often gets immediate knowledge of whether or not his/her response is right (Haring and Phillips, 1972). Although there are questions about the ethical use of this technology (which will be discussed in more detail in the next chapter), there can be little question that these techniques are extremely powerful, especially in learning small, relatively discrete bits of information. Part of this improved learning can be attributed to the fact that students are provided with appropriate feedback. For many students, the semester grade (which has served as the traditional feedback system) is relatively meaningless. A major strategy for helping students learn is, therefore, found in using some of the following ways of helping students get immediate, meaningful feedback on their learning progress.

SELF-ASSESSMENT. In general, feedback is best when students can check their own progress. When appropriate, the students should first be asked to make an attempt to solve a problem before being given the answer. The now seldom-used technique of providing the answers in the back of the book gave immediate feedback, but unfortunately many students did not make the appropriate prior effort, and so maximum learning was not achieved.

Some creative teachers have provided a "Bureau of Standards," a file or place where correct answers (for use with subjects like arithmetic) or standards against which students can compare their progress (as in subjects like handwriting, social studies, etc.). Involving the students in establishing the standards can be a very valuable process. One technique for establishing standards is to have a class of fifth graders take anonymous handwriting samples from another fifth grade classroom and sort them (usually into five piles), from the best to the worst. The most typical sample would be selected from each pile and these would then be used as "standards" against which individuals could judge themselves and watch their progress. Unquestionably, many students have difficulty performing in a way approved by the teacher, because they do not know exactly what is expected of them. Helping to provide a student with an answer (or even with appropriate guidelines for subjects where there is not a "right" answer) would clearly be a strategy in helping students to learn. In order to be able to give the amount of instant feedback needed by a class full of students, teachers will need to find a system which does not make too many demands on their time (Randolph and Catterall, 1964).

Another strategy is to try to help students begin to make what can be called a "positive use of error." Typically, when graded papers are returned, students will take a quick look at the total score, maybe count the number of checks, and then put away or throw away the paper. There is little or no use of the check marks to guide the student's future learning efforts. The following approach should help to overcome this: The teacher begins by stressing that everyone should make some errors; if they do not make any mistakes it is a sign that either the material or the test is too easy. (Of course, a teacher may, on occasion, want to give a test for primarily motivational purposes, on which many students would get almost all of the items correct.) On carefully constructed, nationally standardized achievement tests the items should sample the whole academic area and no student should "go off the top." (If a student does, the educator does not know how much more the student really knows that the test did not measure.) In one sense there is nothing so imperfect as never taking a risk, i.e. never pushing oneself up to, and slightly beyond, one's limit.

In the "positive use of error" the student would be helped to see that the check mark stands as an arrow pointing to the most profitable place for him/her to continue learning. Far from being a sign of rejection and failure, the check mark should be thought of as a road sign pointing to things still waiting to be learned. (Pain in the body to signal problems is analogous to the "positive use of error.") The "positive use of error" would be further helped by two things: Students should feel that there are no "trick" or trivial questions, and each unit or test should lead toward some larger, more important concept. If teachers also use their own errors constructively, it will help to increase the acceptance of error on the part of students (Swift and Spivak, 1975).

The ability to remember facts that have been learned is traditionally encouraged by the use of frequent quizzes and the traditional end-of-the-year exams which must be passed in order to move on to the next level. The return to these tests, which in many schools have been abandoned, is not being advocated because they create many other problems. However they illustrate the fact that all too often the curriculum is compartmentalized so much that students do not see the relationship between Unit A and Unit B. Once students have passed the Unit A test they can "forget it." (Sometimes the forgetting proceeds passively, but sometimes there appears to be a conscious effort to forget the earlier material.) There is truth to the fact that in order to survive in a noisy world, one has to learn to ignore much of the meaningless "static" that one hears. There may also be truth to the fact that in order to survive in this day of exploding information, one has to put out of his/her mind some things that he/she has learned in order to master new material.

Another aspect of self-assessment is to have all students evaluate themselves in writing at periodic intervals, using a form consisting of factors that the whole class considers to be important. For very young children (or older students who are having difficulties) this might have to be done daily. More mature students could move to a weekly, monthly, or semester schedule.

PEER FEEDBACK. Fellow students are another source of assistance to give feedback needed to maximize learning. One of the great recent breakthroughs in education is the use of students to help other students in a variety of ways. Some teachers prefer to use students who are as nearly equally matched as possible on the theory that this will assist both the student who is helping and the student who receives help in the original learning process.

It would be an interesting experiment to involve a total school in what might be labeled as "cycle teaching." The greatest amount of learning would likely take place if students who had already developed a skill were used to help other students to gain that skill. Cycle teaching would be based on the theory that for every fact learned, a process of forgetting begins rapidly, especially if the fact is never used. There is some evidence to support the hypothesis that so-called "slow" students learn about as fast as average students, but forget faster. Therefore, the "slow" students have to take more time to relearn everything and consequently have less time to learn new material. This, in turn, is more difficult to learn because "slow" students do not have the correct prerequisites and thus get farther and farther behind. It is a little like the old question of, "How long will it take a frog to get out of a twenty-foot well if he jumps up three feet each day and falls back two?" Educators might be able to get more students out of the "hole" if as much attention were given to the problems of forgetting as to the problems of learning.

Cycle teaching would stress the concept that everyone who has the privilege of learning something (and there are many who never get that privilege), should also assume the right, the responsibility, the pleasure (or the mixture thereof) of passing that knowledge on to someone else. The emphasis would be clearly on the value to both the person receiving the feedback necessary for the initial learning and the person serving as "mentor" or tutor, who, through the process of using what they know will tend to remember it longer. This would help each student feel more involved in the teaching-learning process instead of having "teaching" the sole responsibility of the teacher and learning passively resisted by the student. By this approach, the schools could help students feel that there was more of a reason for learning the required subject matter. Some would object that such a process would take too much time away from original learning, but if educators would slow down the pace of "pouring new ideas into the heads of students" and would build systematic ways of using or reinforcing what has been learned, they would have developed a major strategy for improving learning (Harris, 1971).

TEACHER ASSESSMENT. As previously indicated, teachers should try to free themselves as much as possible from the necessity of providing feedback. There is, however, an expectation on the part of the public that the teacher must ultimately determine whether or not the student has acquired the necessary skills, and through this process, evaluate the student's progress. If properly done, the teacher's assessment is very valuable because of the teacher's "ultimate authority" role. The most productive ways to do this depend upon the following: the maturity level of the student, the subject matter being evaluated, and the personality and teaching style of the teacher. In general, the more there can be two-way communication between the teacher and learner, preferably in a one-to-one conversation, the better. There are several reasons why such two-way communication would be helpful: It would help the teacher to clarify to the learner the basis for the assessment, usually involving many direct observations of the student, his/her attitude, his/her effort, etc., as well as "objective" grades. It would also give students an opportunity to explain how important the topic is to them. As adults we are not "cut down" by doing poorly in something in which we have no interest; why should we expect the student to be equally interested or proficient in everything? The students could also indicate how much effort they had put into their studies, and the teacher could inform each student about directions for continued growth in the subject, if the student felt it to be important.

Clarifying a student's assessment takes time, which is all too precious especially at the end of a semester or year. Methods for implementing effective assessment policies might involve the following: (1) students setting their own goals and writing notes of self-evaluation to the teacher, together with the grade they feel they deserve; (2) the teacher writing a note to the student (one teacher ordered cassette recorders and took them home each night to record messages for each student) ; (3) the teacher encouraging students who want to "talk about" their progress to come in for personal conferences (it is relatively easy to give feedback to those doing well; few people who are doing poorly like to be told so, yet they probably need appropriate feedback the most).

An additional note should be made about "charting," the process of having someone count the behaviors that teacher and student are trying to increase and decrease and display them on some sort of graph. Lindsley (1967) was one of the early advocates of this system. There is evidence that just paying attention to specific behaviors and plotting them on the chart has brought about highly desirable results. The charting could be done by the student, a peer, or by the teacher. It would be a specific case of helping learners to get knowledge of their results and would fit under the general strategy of helping students.

STRUCTURING

In addition to determining who shall be educated, how they will be grouped or where they will be placed, or what techniques will be used to individualize the curriculum to meet the learner's needs, another major strategy can be used by the teacher which involves the amount of *structure* needed to facilitate maximum learning. Structuring, as used in this sense, refers to the amount of "ground rules" that need to be made, the amount of stability or routine required in a certain situation, how clearly and precisely the instructions have to be given in order for students to begin to work on their own, etc. This will vary tremendously from group to group and individual to individual. The good teacher adapts, more or less instinctively, to the need for different amounts of structure. In general, the more immature and/or less academicly inclined the students, the more the need for structure. A similar condition prevails when new topics are introduced. For example, no matter how well the instructions are given or how much order there is in the classroom, there will often be one or two students who need special help with the rules. Sensitive teachers will be sure that they have the attention of these students; they will speak directly to them; and they will maintain eye contact with them while giving instructions to the entire class. When total classrooms begin to have difficulty at any age level, but especially with younger children, attention should be given to the amount of preparation and structure being given to the class. Need for structure will vary considerably; some students need to have a lot, others very little. In general, the rule of thumb is to provide as little structure as is needed to keep the students learning.

Clarifying the Rules for New Students

A busy school is a very complex place; thought needs to be given for ways of "orienting" new students, both when a new group arrives at the beginning of the year, and when children enroll sporadically during the year. The variation in the amount of rules or structure in schools cannot be appreciated by the average teacher who does not have the opportunity to see many different schools in action. The need for rules seems to reflect the need for structuring on the part of the staff more than it does within the student body. Educators still do not know how long it takes to integrate a new student into a school. Some learn better through their movements; others are confused by the verbal concepts in which the rules are embedded. Both of these kinds of students might better be helped by "walking through the rules" with them. Certainly the "buzzing activity" of most secondary schools must be difficult for a new student to understand. It must take quite a while to learn that you cannot walk on the Senior Lawn; the librarian yells a lot but seldom carries through; chewing gum is permitted in Mr. X's class but not in Mrs. G's, etc.

Involving Students in Making the Rules

It is human nature, even for adults, to feel that rules made by someone else are arbitrary. One of the major reasons why length of hair of students was such an issue was the difficulty in explaining how it might affect student behavior. There probably are some relationships (just as the clothes one wears reflect and affect one's personality), but the difficulty comes in explaining why. In general, the more opportunities the student has for input in making rules, the better.   In a classroom this can often be done with the whole group; in making school-wide rules, some form of representation is generally needed.   Clearly, some rules which affect the safety of students and personnel need to be enforced routinely but, at the same time, many rules enforced in the name of "safety" are not related to safety at all.   One reason for student involvement is to keep the staff "honest"; it is easy for rules, like laws, to remain on the books long after they have ceased to serve any useful purpose (Swift and Spivak, 1975).

Providing Consistency in Enforcing Rules

One skill that must be acquired in the American culture is to learn when to obey the rules and when it is not necessary.   Educators profess to be consistent, but in reality there are many little subtleties which affect whether or not a rule in schools will be ignored or enforced.   It is often extremely difficult for some young people to interpret the subtle clues which determine how they will act.   It must be very confusing, for example, for a young child to determine the difference between "tattling" and "responsible reporting" of things that other children are doing (Randolph and Catterall, 1964).   The bell system, especially in a modern school, can be extremely confusing.   Five or six rings and nothing seems to happen; then suddenly at the sound of another bell everyone gets up and starts to move.   The process of learning to ignore some of the extraneous sounds or "static" is true for bells; it is equally true for rules.   Many foreign exchange students, just starting in an American high school, are intimidated by teachers who start the year by "laying down the rules."   Not knowing whether or not to take the teacher seriously, the students frequently become alarmed that they are going to have to work extremely hard and that they are likely to "get thrown out" if they break a single rule.   True, their understanding of the rules is complicated by the fact that they still do not have sufficient English to understand all of the nuances of the language.   Their problem, however, is not very different from the students who have used English all their lives but still do not really have the *conceptual* development to make the fine distinctions required. As in many things, once one has grasped a concept, it is difficult to understand why other people do not understand it. Similarly, when teachers understand the rules, it is hard for them to comprehend why students do not; it is easy to assume that the student is purposefully disobeying. The amount of structure needed by different students varies; it is necessary to watch their behavior and to be doubly certain that they really do understand all of the facets of the situation before one starts to reprimand.

The advice about rules is "be consistent." Like many rules, this is not always possible when all of the fine shades of differences are taken into consideration; few rules in life are really adhered to consistently. "Be as consistent as you possibly can" is a more acceptable rule, and a meaningful next step is "help students as much as possible to understand why a rule must be enforced," especially when there has been a major infringement. To repeat, when a student is frequently markedly out of line, increase the amount of structure around him/her (Swift and Spivak, 1975) .

Providing Additional Structure

Most educators now agree that students need some structure in order to learn. They have difficulty in agreeing how much structure is needed, but in general, the concept of ultrapermissiveness once advocated by some is no longer accepted. The question becomes one of how much structure to give students. Most schools have too much structure, too many rules, for the average student. As previously indicated, the more opportunity the students have to decide what their goals are, the better. At the same time, some students cannot function without quite a number of rules. One strategy is to use individual "contracts" which provide certain students the structure they need within the total climate of limited structure.

In general, more capable students should be given the elements of a problem and should be encouraged to build their own structure. Some students have a great deal of difficulty "shifting gears" when they move from one activity to another. This can be helped by giving them advanced information of what is going to be expected of them. It is good strategy to work out with them a carefully designed schedule and then stick to it as much as possible (Hewett, Stillwell, Artuso, and Taylor, 1972).

A large segment of students are likely to get into trouble when they do not have enough to do or when what they are doing is boring or repetitious. A frequent problem is seen when the more academically capable students finish an assignment long before the less capable. It is best to indicate the amount of freedom students have in choosing things to do when assignments have been completed. Many students who are able to complete an exercise very rapidly are not learning much from it, anyway. It is often best to give these students a completely different assignment, not just more of the same, as is often the case. Otherwise, the very bright students soon learn that the price they pay for doing well is more and more drudgery.

Providing Less Structure

Although some students need more structure, the tendency of most people working with large groups is to provide too much structure. After making careful classroom observations, Leonard (1968) has estimated that as much as 80 percent of the time students spend in school is time spent *getting ready* to learn. Some of this is necessary, e.g. getting the appropriate materials, but much of it involves a process of waiting for all students to become quiet or perform some other required task. The more these necessary but time-consuming "housekeeping" tasks can become routine, the more time and energy can be spent on new learning.

In the lower grades many "wiggly little boys" consume an unreasonable amount of time that is counterproductive for both those boys and the other members of the class. Stand-up desks should be devised for them in which they can do their work standing at a desk in the back of the room. Most people can sit still just so long before they have to get up and work off some energy.

The introduction of carpets in some classrooms makes the idea of working on the floor much more possible. The use of "stand-up desks" and working on carpeted floors heightens the informal nature of learning and reduces the amount of time spent providing structure for the entire class.

Classes at most levels spend more time sitting "quietly" listening to the teacher than is conducive to the best learning. This is not to say that there is not a need for well-organized presentations on the part of teachers. It means that another powerful strategy for helping students is to shorten lectures and introduce different kinds of activities to vary the pace. Unfortunately some of the activities that have been traditionally used to reduce tension, e.g. cleaning the erasers by pounding them on a wastebasket, have been taken away from us as "more efficient" methods, e.g. cleaning erasers by use of a modified vacuum cleaner, have been employed. For younger students, a strategy such as having a child "run to the fence and tap it and run back again" does not fill an authentic need, such as getting erasers clean, but they do help some children work off counterproductive energy (Barsch, 1965; Swift and Spivak, 1975, p. 161).

In addition to the "more activity" kinds of strategies, another technique for providing less structure in the classroom is to allow students to earn "free time." In most schools there is almost no time to "goof off"; learning task follows learning task; the reward for finishing one is the necessity of starting another one. It is little wonder that some students fail to get motivated by this routine. A plan to alter this procedure gives students the opportunity to earn the right to do "anything they please" or nothing at all. If one is working with only one child, the "anything you please" must not conflict with other students who are still working. A still more powerful strategy (usually at the elementary school, but sometimes at the secondary level) is to agree on a certain amount of work which must be accomplished by the whole class before a certain amount of free time is given to them. In the past, teachers made use of reading an exciting book to the class as a reward to students for finishing their work. The goal of all of these strategies that reduce the amount of structure is to provide a change of pace that will make formal learning more efficient and will make possible, and capitalize on, the social learning that takes place in the intervals (Kyzar, 1972; Madden, 1973; Rathbone, 1971).

In the secondary school there are very few students (no matter how "turned on" they are to school) who would not desire to have some time away from school. In a situation which, by its very nature, is quite routine, anything that a student can do constructively to earn some free time becomes a tremendously reinforcing process and spurs greater learning. The ultimate goal, however, is that the free time should be filled with another kind of learning such as the student's favorite subject or instructional activity; in this instance, one kind of learning is reinforcing other learning.

When discussing less structure, educators must recognize their need to continue to help students to have more to say about where they are going with their lives, more opportunity to decide what they want to learn, and more power to structure their activities. One could look at the average curriculum (which in Latin means "race track") and get the feeling that all students are aimed at the same goal; a course has been devised which leads to that goal (and nowhere else) ; and the role of the school is to drag the students through that course toward that goal. In all fairness, it should be said that some of this "dragging" of students through the curriculum is forced upon educators, since they must educate students in groups. The major strategy and major challenge before educators is to identify, perfect, and use a variety of strategies for involving students in the process of helping each other; to individualize their goals, and to actively work to see that all of their peers can achieve the goals they have set for themselves. Educators must arrange the total educational environment in such a way that most students learn the greatest number of skills relevant to their unique expression of life. If all educators work together it would seem that this is a reasonably achievable goal.

REFERENCES

Abeson, A., Bolick, N., & Hess, J. *A primer on due process: Education decisions for handicapped children.* Reston, Va.: The Council for Exceptional Children, 1975.

Alpern, G. D., & Boll, T. J. *Development profile manual.* Indianapolis: Psychological Development Publications, 1972.

American children out of school. *APA Monitor*, February, 1975, 7, 1.

Arena, J. I. (Ed.). *Teaching through sensory-motor experiences.* Belmont, Ca.: Fearon Publishers, 1969.

Barclay, J. R. *Measuring the social climate of the classroom.* Monograph #40, Educational Technology, 1971.

Barsch, R. H. *A movigenic curriculum.* Madison: Wisconsin State Department of Public Instruction, 1965.

Bereiter, C. *Must we educate?* Englewood Cliffs: Prentice-Hall, 1974.

Birch, J. W. *Mainstreaming: Educable mentally retarded children in regular classes.* Reston, Va.: Council for Exceptional Children, 1974.

Bulletin of the National Association of Secondary School Principals; *Computer in Education.* Washington, D. C., 1970, *54, 343.*

Calovini, G. (Ed.). *Papers on the early identification of exceptional children.* Springfield: State of Illinois, Department of Exceptional Children, 1971.

Calvin, A. D. (Ed.). *Programmed instruction: Bold new adventure.* Bloomington: Indiana University, 1969.

Chamberlin, G. L., & Catterall, C. D. Acceleration for the overage potential dropout? *Phi Delta Kappan,* 1963, *45,* 98-100.

Children's Defense Fund of the Washington Research Project. *Children out of school in America.* Washington, D. C.: Author, 1974.

Chilman, C. The effectiveness of parent intervention programs. In B. Caldwell & H. Ricciuti (Eds.). *Review of child development research,* Vol. 3. Chicago: University of Chicago Press, 1972.

Circus. Princeton: Educational Testing Service, 1972.

Cohodes, A. Voucher system gets chance to show how it would work. *Nation's Schools,* 1970, *86, 20.*

Coordinating Council for Handicapped Children. *How to organize an effective parent group and move bureaucracies: For parents of handicapped children and their helpers.* Chicago: Author, 1974.

Croft, D. J., & Hess, R. D. *An activities handbook for teachers of young children* (2nd ed.). Boston: Houghton Mifflin, 1975.

Davis, H. *Organizing a learning center.* Cleveland: Educational Research Council of America, 1968.

Department of Elementary School Principals, National Education Association. *The non-graded school.* Washington, D. C.: Author, 1968.

Frankenburg, W. K., Dodds, J. B., & Fandel, A. W. *Denver developmental screening test, 1968.* Denver: Lacoca Project and Publishing Foundation, 1970.

Frostig, M., Maslow, P., Lefever, D. W., & Whittlesey, J. R. B. *The Marianne Frostig developmental test of visual perception.* Palo Alto: Consulting Psychologists, 1964.

Gearheart, B. R. *Learning disabilities: Educational strategies.* St. Louis: C. V. Mosby, 1973.

Gibbon, S. Y., & Palmer, E. L. Prereading on Sesame Street. In D.D. Hammill, & N. R. Bartel. *Teaching children with learning and behavior dis-*

orders. Boston: Allyn & Bacon, 1975.

Gibson, R. *Career development in the elementary school.* Columbus: Merrill, 1972.

Ginsberg, E. *Career guidance, who needs it? Who provides it? Who can improve it?* New York: McGraw-Hill, 1971.

Goodlad, J. I. Research and theory regarding promotion and nonpromotion. *Elementary School Journal,* 1952, *53,* 150-155.

Goodlad, J. I. Some effects of promotion and non-promotion upon the social and personal adjustment of children. *Journal of Experimental Education,* 1954, *22,* 301-308.

Goodman, L., & Hammill, D. The effectiveness of the Kephart-Getman activities in developing perceptual-motor and cognitive skills. *Focus on Exceptional Children,* 1973, *4,* 1-9,

Gordon, A. K. *Games for growth: Educational games in the classroom.* Chicago: Science Associates, 1972.

Goss v. Lopez, 95 S.Ct. 729 (1975).

Grzynkowicz, W. M. *Meeting the needs of learning disabled children in the regular class.* Springfield: Charles C Thomas, 1975.

Haden, H. I. Von, & King, J. M. *Innovations in education: Their pros and cons.* Worthington, Oh.: Charles A. Jones, 1971.

Hammill, D. D., & Bartel, N. R. *Teaching children with learning and behavior problems.* Boston: Allyn & Bacon, 1975.

Hammill, D. D., Goodman, L., & Wiederhold, J. L. Visual-motor processes: What success have we had in training them? *The Reading Teacher,* 1974, *27,* 469-478.

Haring, N. G., & Phillips, E. L. *Analysis and modification of classroom behavior.* Englewood Cliffs: Prentice-Hall, 1972.

Hart, V. *Beginning with the handicapped.* Springfield: Charles C Thomas, 1974.

Hartman, H. *Let's play and learn: Early education/parent education.* New York: Behavioral Publications, 1976.

Harris, M. M. Learning by tutoring others. *Today's Education,* 1971, *60,* 48-49.

Hess, R. D., & Croft, D. J. *Teacher of young children* (2nd ed.) Boston: Houghton Mifflin, 1975.

Hewett, F., Stillwell, R., Artuso, A., & Taylor, F. An educational solution: The engineered classroom. *Strategies for teaching exceptional children.* Denver: Love Publishing Co., 1972.

Heyman, M. Learning from the British Infant Schools. *Elementary School Journal,* 1972, *72,* 335-342.

Hillson, M., & Bongo, J. *Continuous progress education: A practical approach.* Chicago: Science Research Associates, 1971.

Hobbs, N. *The futures of children.* San Francisco: Jossey-Bass, 1974a.

Hobbs, N. (Ed.). *Issues in the classification of children.* San Francisco: Jossey-Bass, 1974b.

Hobson v. Hanson, 269 F. 410 (1967).

Hoffman, B. *Tyranny of testing.* New York: P. F. Collier, 1962.

Hoffman, D., Jordan, J., & McCormick, F. *Parent participation in preschool day care* (Monograph #5). Atlanta: South Eastern Educational Laboratory, 1971.

Holmes, J. A., & Finley, C. J. Under and over age placement in school achievement. *Journal of Educational Psychology,* 1957, *48,* 447-456.

Humphrey, J. H. *Education of children through motor activity.* Springfield: Charles C Thomas, 1975.

Informal schools in Britain today. New York: Citation Press, 1971-1972 (series of 23 paperbacks).

Iowa Department of Public Instruction. *Student suspension and expulsion procedures: A model policy and rules.* Des Moines: Author, 1975.

Jones, R. L. (Ed.). *Problems and issues in the education of exceptional children.* Boston: Houghton Mifflin, 1971.

Keiser, J. C., & Wampler, E. C. *Career education curriculum guide.* Indianapolis: Indiana State Department of Public Instruction, 1974.

Keogh, B. K., & Becker, L. D. Early detection of learning problems: Questions, cautions, and guidelines. *Exceptional Children,* 1973, *39,* 5-11.

Kephart, N. C., & Radler, D. H. *Success through play.* New York: Harper & Row, 1960.

Klinge, P. (Ed.). *American education in the electric age: New Perspectives on media and learning.* Englewood Cliffs: Educational Technology Publications, 1974.

Knitzer, J. Parental involvement: The elixer of change. In D. N. McFadden (Ed.). *Early childhood development programs and services: Planning for action.* Columbus: Battelle Memorial Institute, 1972.

Kowitz, J. G. T., & Armstrong, C. M. The effect of promotion policy on academic achievement. *Elementary School Journal,* 1961, *61,* 431-443.

Kyzar, B. Research on the effects of open space. *CEPF Journal,* 1972, 13-14.

Larsen, S., & Hammill, D. D. The relationship of selected visual perceptual skills to academic abilities. *Journal of Education,* 1975, 157.

LaVor, M., & Krevit, D. The handicapped children's early education assistance act: Public Law 90-538. *Exceptional Children,* 1969, *35,* 379-383.

Leonard, G. B. *Education and ecstacy.* New York: Delacorte Press, 1968.

Levine, E. S. *Lisa and her soundless world.* New York: Behavioral Publications, 1974.

Lindsley, O. R. *Pinpoint, record, and consequate.* Kansas City: Behavior Research, 1967.

Lowder, R. G. *Perceptual ability and school achievement.* Unpublished doctoral dissertation, Purdue University, 1956.

Madden, P. C. Skinner and the open classroom. *The School Psychology Di-*

gest, 1973, *2*, 4-43.

Mann, P. H. (Ed.). *Mainstream special education: Issues and perspective in urban centers.* Reston: Council for Exceptional Children, 1974.

Mardell, C., & Goldenberg, D. *Learning disabilities/early childhood research project: Developmental indicators for the assessment of learning.* Springfield: Office of the Superintendent of Public Instruction, 1972.

Markoff, A. M. *Teaching low achieving children reading, spelling, and handwriting: Developing perceptual skills with the graphic symbols of language.* Springfield: Charles C Thomas, 1976.

Mastors, C. *School volunteers: Who needs them?* Bloomington: Phi Delta Kappa Educational Foundation, 1975.

McBeath, P. M. *The effectiveness of three reading preparedness programs for perceptually handicapped kindergarteners.* Unpublished doctoral dissertation, Stanford University, 1966.

McFadden, D. N. (Ed.). *Early childhood development programs and services: Planning for action.* Columbus: Battelle Memorial Institute, 1972.

McNeil, D. *The relationship between psychological and behavioral characteristics of primary teachers and the concept of classroom psychological climate.* Unpublished doctoral dissertation, University of Michigan, 1972.

McNeil, J. D. Programmed instruction versus usual classroom procedures in teaching boys to read. *American Educational Research Journal*, 1964, *1*, 113-119.

Miller, W. H. *Teaching reading in the secondary school.* Springfield: Charles C Thomas, 1974.

Mills v. Board of Education of the District of Columbia, 348 F. Supp. (D. D. C., 1972).

Monson, C. H. Jr. (Ed.). *Education for what?: Readings in the ends and means of education.* Boston: Houghton Mifflin, 1970.

Mott, M. *Teaching the pre-academic child: Activities for children displaying difficulties in processing information.* Springfield: Charles C Thomas, 1974.

Neff, H., & Pilch, J. *Teaching handicapped children easily: A manual for the average teacher without specialized training.* Springfield: Charles C Thomas, 1975.

Newcomer, P., & Hammill, D. D. Visual perception of motor impaired children. *Exceptional Children*, 1973, *39*, 335-337.

Noue, G. R. La. *Educational vouchers: Concepts and controversies.* New York: Teachers College Press, 1972.

Nurturing intelligence. *Time*, January 3, 1972, 56-57.

Oakland, T., & Williams, F. *Auditory perception.* Seattle: Special Child Publications, 1971.

Ogle, G., & Menuey, J. *Good time box set.* San Diego: Pennant Educational Materials (n. d.).

Olson, W. C. Concept of organismic age. *Journal of Educational Research*, 1947, *35*, 525-527.

Open Education: Can British school reforms work here? *Nation's Schools,* 1971, *87,* 47-51.

Otto, H. J. *Nongradedness: An elementary school evaluation.* Austin: University of Texas at Austin, 1969.

Pennsylvania Association for Retarded Children v. Commonwealth of Pennsylvania, 343 F. Supp. 279 (E. D. Pa., 1971).

Postman, N., & Weingartner, C. *Teaching as a subversive activity.* New York: Dell Publishing Co., 1969.

Preston, R. C. Reading achievement of German and American Children. *School and Society,* 1962, *90,* 350-354.

Pucinski, R. D., & Hirsch, S. P. (Eds.). *The courage to change: New directions for career education.* Englewood Cliffs: Prentice-Hall, 1971.

Purdom, D. M. *Exploring the ungraded school.* Dayton: Institute for Development of Educational Activities, 1970.

Quick, A. D., Little, T. L., & Campbell, A. A. *Lesson plans: Guides to teaching preacademic skills.* Belmont: Fearon Publishers, 1973a.

Quick, A. D., Little, T. L., & Campbell, A. A. *The training of exceptional foster children and their foster parents: Enhancing developmental progress and parent effectiveness.* Belmont: Fearon Publishers, 1973b.

Randolph, N., & Catterall, C. D. *Self enhancing education: Processes that enhance.* Cupertino, Ca.: Cupertino School District, 1964 (out of print).

Rathbone, C. H. (Ed.). *Open education: The informal classroom.* New York: Citation Press, 1971.

Reardon, R. C., & Burck, H. D. *Facilitating career development.* Springfield: Charles C Thomas, 1975.

Reger, R., Schroeder, W., & Uschold, K. *Special education: Children with learning problems.* New York: Oxford University Press, 1968.

Reisman, F., Kohler, M., & Gartner, A. *Children teach children: Learning by teaching.* New York: Harper & Row, 1971.

Rendfrey, K. *Individually guided motivation: Setting individual goals for learning.* ERIC, ED057412 (microfiche), 1971.

Rhodes, J. A. *Vocational education and guidance: A system for the seventies.* Columbus: Charles E. Merrill, 1971.

Sabatino, D. A. An evaluation of resource rooms for children with learning disabilities. *Journal of Learing Disabilities,* 1971, *43,* 84-93.

Silberman, C. *Crises in the classroom.* New York: Random House, 1970.

Smuck v. Hobson, FO8 F.2d 175, (1969).

Spodek, B. Alternative to traditional education. In J. E. DeCarlo & C. A. Madon (Eds.). *Innovations in education for the seventies: Selected readings.* New York: Behavioral Publications, 1973.

Stock, J. R., Wnek, L. L., Newborg, J. A., Schenck, E. A., Gabel, J. R., Spurgeon, M. S., & Ray, H. W. *Evaluation of handicapped children's early education programs* (HCEEP). Columbus: Battelle, 1976.

Swift, M. S., & Spivak, G. *Alternative teaching strategies: Helping behavior-*

ally troubled children achieve: A guide for teachers and psychologists. Champaign: Research Press, 1975.

Syphers, D. F. *Gifted and talented children: Practical programming for teachers and principals.* Arlington: The Council for Exceptional Children, 1972.

Talmage, H. (Ed.). *Systems of individualized education.* Berkeley: McCutchan Publishing Corporation, 1975.

Telford, C. W., & Sawrey, J. M. *The exceptional individual* (2nd ed.). Englewood Cliffs: Prentice-Hall, 1972.

Thiagarajan, S. *The programming process: A practical guide.* Worthington, Oh.: Charles A. Jones, 1971.

Trump, J. L., & Baynham, D. *Focus on change.* Chicago: Rand McNally, 1962.

Wadsworth, H. O. A motivational approach toward the remediation of learning disabled boys. *Exceptional Children,* 1971, *38,* 33-42.

Wampler, E. *The counselor and career education.* Indianapolis: Indiana Department of Public Instruction, 1973.

Weber, E. *Early childhood education: Perspective on change.* Worthington, Oh.: Charles A. Jones, 1970.

Weber, L. *The English infant school and informal education.* Englewood Cliffs: Prentice-Hall, 1971.

Wedell, K. *Learning and perceptuo-motor disabilities in children.* Sussex, England: Wiley, 1973.

Wyatt, N. M. The reading achievement of first grade boys versus first grade girls. *The Reading Teacher,* 1966, *19,* 661-665.

Chapter 5

CORRECTIVE/REMEDIAL
INTERVENTIONS

ALTHOUGH IT IS ASSUMED that a carefully planned and executed developmental program will help most students to acquire most of their needed academic/intellectual skills (Chapter 4), it is also logical to assume that virtually all students, at one point or another and in one or more academic areas, will require and profit from some sort of a Corrective/Remedial Intervention (the subject of this chapter). All students have unique learning styles and unique learning needs; the goal, therefore, is to avoid forcing them into the same mold. The classroom teacher, in conjunction with the Learning Facilitation Team, will identify any academic-intellectual needs in a student or a small group of students which have not been met by the regular program. This chapter brings together and briefly describes those *interventions* which are designed to help remediate or to correct academic learning problems. Although the authors assume that most, if not all, behavior (including emotional behavior) is learned, for purposes of emphasis and clarification this chapter will emphasize what would ordinarily be considered learning problems. Social-emotional and behavioral problems will be discussed in Chapter 7.

The Corrective/Remedial Interventions listed here have the following primary purpose:

To implement a full range of corrective/remedial services designed to help students to acquire needed academic/intellectual skills by encouraging each person who comes in contact with the school to make his/her own unique contribution to this process. This can be done both by offering his/her own services and by contributing to a social climate in which it is considered appropriate and desirable to receive and to give these services when needed.

In many instances the *remedial techniques* are only an extension of the ones being used in the regular development program. In this sense intervention is designed to remove, whenever possible, the cause for the deficiency. *Corrective* is used to mean adding or subtracting an additional service to make the student's performance more adequate. The *intervention* process, which will be described in more detail later, is used to actively introduce a service into the lives of students in order to help them function more adequately in the total school situation. For example, one cannot "correct" a condition such as congenital deafness, but one can provide corrective/remedial interventions which will help the afflicted student to achieve more fully. The full title, "Corrective /Remedial Interventions," implies a full range of services which exist in the school in addition to the regular curriculum designed to help all students achieve to their highest potential. In brief, the interventions are all of the specialized things that can be done *for* the student (see Table 5-I).

Two of the interventions, *tutoring* and *adding stimulation,*

TABLE 5-I

INTERVENTIONS THAT CAN BE DONE FOR THE STUDENT

	Developmental/ Preventative	*Corrective/ Remedial*
Academic/ Intellectual Skills		*Corrective/Remedial Interventions* Things that can be done *for* the student
Life Skills		

involve providing additional stimuli for the student. In *reducing stimulation*, the intervention calls for the withdrawal of something from a student's life. Once a child does something, i.e. responds, two other interventions are available, *reinforcement* and *punishment*. In general, the positive approach has been found more applicable in the school setting and represents a powerful potential for helping students. Once again there is a great overlap between the categories which have, in some cases, been separated for the sake of emphasis.

TABLE 5-II

ORGANIZATION OF STRATEGIES FOR
CORRECTIVE/REMEDIAL INTERVENTIONS

Tutoring	*Reinforcement*
A. Other Students	A. Tangible Rewards
B. Professional Staff	B. Tokens
C. Other Adults in the School	C. Money
D. Parents and People from the Community	D. Peer Recognition
	E. Free Time
Adding Stimulation	F. Attention
	G. Contingency Contracting
A. Sensory Stimulation	H. Praise
B. Experiential Stimulation	
C. Language Development and Speech Correction	
D. Conceptual Development	
E. Academic/Intellectual Help	
F. Competition	
G. Physical/Medical Stimulation	*Punishment*
	A. Failure to Deliver a Reward
Reducing Stimulation	B. Withdrawing of Something Pleasant
A. Time Out	C. Introduction of Unpleasant Stimuli
B. Carrels or Offices	D. Negative Reinforcement
C. Limited Day	
D. Systematic Exemption	
E. Moratorium	
F. Limiting Excessive Services	
G. Relaxation Techniques	
H. Medical Destimulation	

Any attempt to isolate an activity as corrective or remedial as opposed to being developmental or preventive is artificial. It is difficult to think of any intervention on behalf of students that could not, at the same time, be considered preventive in one situation and corrective in another. Everyone involved in education is encouraged to think of all *strategies/interventions* for helping students as a long series of activities (a program) which can be skillfully used to assist students to develop to their fullest. Seldom will any one strategy or intervention work in isolation for even one student in one subject area, let alone for a total class. The good that any one activity can do is counterbalanced by its limitations. Educators' inability to choose any one intervention with precision forces them to listen to and observe carefully the students in order to be sure that what the authors have suggested is doing what it was proposed to do. For almost every force there is a counterforce; for every strategy there is probably a counterstrategy.

In trying to use specific interventions with students it has been helpful to keep in mind the simple *life-force* illustrated by taking a shower. If the water is too hot, one can correct this either by reducing the hot water or by increasing the cold water. One often forgets that every time one moves a muscle (for example in bending the arm to get the biceps to bulge) one must at the same time relax counterbalancing muscles on the other side of the arm. People who want to help students must learn to use strategies and interventions in stereo and to check constantly and to observe the behavior of the student to evaluate whether what has been prescribed is getting the desired results. The complexity of this process and the limited state of the art makes writing a "cook book," i.e. "for this kind of a student you must use this strategy," virtually impossible.

Although describing some activities as *developmental* and some as *corrective* seems artificial, keeping in mind that there should be two separate but complementary forces for helping students can be very helpful. These basic strategies constantly overlap and both have their place. Educators should constantly try to sharpen the strategies which help to improve the broad curricular program of the school. Early programs designed to improve mental health in the schools stressed the fact that those interested in the field of mental health should not only find *corrective/therapeutic* ways of helping those who need it (see Chapter 7), but they should also attempt to make the path of normalcy so wide and so easy to follow that almost everyone would be able to progress along it. Society has labeled many actions as "odd," "eccentric," "abnormal," "crazy," etc., and even put individuals into institutions when their behavior really did not harm anyone. "Talking out loud to yourself" is one example; consequently, one is impressed with the amount of normal behavior one sees in a mental institution and the amount of abnormal behavior one sees in ordinary life *(Mental Health is 1,2,3,* 1951).

The effective curriculum should also be broad and deep and flexible and effective enough to make it possible for every student to profit from it. To achieve this goal, curriculum development cannot be left to curriculum specialists or even, for that matter, to professional educators but rather it will be necessary to achieve total staff, student, and community involvement (Monson, 1970).

Concurrently with curriculum modification/development, it will be necessary to develop a full complement of Corrective/ Remedial Interventions which effectively interplay with the developmental strategies as another way of helping students. Although it has not been faced squarely, it is becoming increasingly obvious that the goal of educating *all* American students is not being reached. There are many who either cannot get admitted to schools or who do not try. There is an increasing number who enter, but eventually drop out or are pushed out for a variety of reasons. There is probably an even larger group who come to school and "go through the motions" but who are never quite "with it" and never quite "get it all together." Whether or not any of these young people are truly educated, in the best sense of the word, is questionable. The pressure is on education to be accountable, to improve its offerings, to continue to push toward the ultimate goal of educating *all* American youth.

Educators no longer have the excuse that they cannot provide full-service education because the schools are growing so rapidly. National statistics indicate that the total public school population in the United States is declining, especially in the elementary school. Many students that have been placed in special classes will have to be brought back into the mainstream. Students who have been put out of school in other community resources will have to be brought back into the regular educational program. The same forces that are working on the school are working on other institutions. Numerous students who have been sent out of the community to various residential treatment centers will be transferred back to the community and will need an educational program. It is becoming increasingly difficult to suspend or expel students. All of these events point to the need for an improved "mainstream" curriculum and a carefully constructed and operated corrective/remedial program. Once again, it cannot be left to the specialists; to reach the goal of a full-range, corrective/remedial program that is carefully integrated with the mainstream operation, it will be necessary to involve the total educational staff, student body, and community.

A word about the interaction between the regular curriculum program and the corrective/remedial services seems necessary. Unquestionably, the more of a student's need that can be met in the mainstream, the better. The more flexibly corrective/remedial services have been interwoven with the main program, the less noticeable it will be when a student has to make use of these services and the less the child will have to feel different, discouraged, unworthy, "out of it," etc. A tremendous amount of effort is currently being spent by all specialized personnel, undoing the feeling of defeat and the resistance to helpful attempts. This is bad enough at the elementary level; it is disastrous at the secondary level. There have been instances where the raw scores of a class of twelve high school students actually dropped after a year of intensive remedial instruction under the guidance of a well-trained teacher. Even though some of the special class placements are able to overcome this feeling of being "slow" or "different" while the student is in the class, it often shows up in the after-school activities. It is certainly an issue when the student returns to the regular classroom or when he/she leaves school to look for a job. Obviously, some children are so seriously retarded or handicapped that there is no alternative to full-time special class placement. If these programs can be conducted close to where there are regular students, it is better for the feelings of self-worth for the handicapped, and the regular students can, at the same time, get a more realistic total view of life (Reynolds and Davis, 1971).

Another problem with much special or remedial grouping is that it takes away much of the curative, remedial value of the interaction between normally developing students. As one psychologist, Harold F. Burks, would often say, "If you want to train a wild elephant you don't put it with a group of other wild elephants; you put it between other elephants going about their regular work." There is nothing less conducive to helping a hyperactive student settle down and work at his/her own level of ability than to put him/her in a class full of other hyperactive children. In many areas of corrective/remedial work better use is being made of mixing students, where some are able to "model" the appropriate behavior, and where the natural student-helping-student interactions can take place.

Since it has already been recognized that there will be some who need to be removed from the mainstream, i.e. the severely retarded, the question, as always, becomes one of, "Where do you draw the line?" Whom do you remove and whom do you retain? How flexible is the coming and the going? At one point in time some states made it illegal for a student who had been placed in a special class for the educable retarded to spend any time in a regular class, and vice versa (no regular student could get any help in the special class). Even in areas such as physical education and music, where some of the special students could function with the normal students, they were not allowed to do so; similarly, when a student in the regular program who was doing satisfactorily in all areas except reading, for example, needed some extra help, he/she could not receive it in the special class. Some of these rules were dictated by the tremendous problems associated with funding these early special programs, but some also originated from the process of labeling and by other similar errors (Warfield, 1974).

This brings up the question of "labeling." It is perfectly obvious that all students do not learn or develop at the same rate in any area. As children enter school, it is estimated that there is at least a five-year spread in their ability to achieve. When school begins, by definition, there is a full year in age difference possible even if no child has been held out of school or no one has been granted the right to "early admission," and traditionally there has usually been at least one of these "exceptions" in almost every class. The fact that some children are a full year younger than others is quite significant since it represents one fifth of the total life span of that child at a time when his/her development is taking place very rapidly. Typically, between one half and two thirds of young children fall within an average group (although there is wide variation in the ability of these "average" children to perform tasks assigned to them). Approximately 20 percent of a given class will be able to perform, on the average, a year above the "average" group, with one or two performing as much as two years above and with wide variations in specific subject areas. It has been facetiously said that some infants learn to read by studying the label on the baby bottle. At the other extreme, another 20 percent are a full year below and still others are two years below the average. Some may be very low in prereading activities but do much better in beginning number/counting concepts.

The five-year spread in the ability to achieve continues and even increases throughout the full school experience for a given class despite a curriculum that "holds back" the more able students and the remedial help that is provided the less able students. The situation at the beginning of school is complicated by a major sex difference. Boys have more variability at all ages and, on the average, mature more slowly than girls. Younger boys are frequently "high risk" students as they enter school. They vary more throughout the total school experience, have more speech problems and more reading problems, are placed in all kinds of special classes more often, and are even identified more often as "gifted." Boys have about an 85 percent greater chance of being placed in a learning disability class (this has been observed in state and in national samples). In one informal study, a district found that those boys who were among the youngest 25 percent of their class when they entered school were 90 percent more likely to be identified as "learning disabled" later in their school experience than were those boys in the oldest 25 percent of the class. Although this was not a carefully controlled study it is doubtful if it is an isolated case. Boys seem to have both social and biological problems (mainly the latter) which cause them to have difficulty in school. More boys, for example, are stillborn or die in the first year of life. If boys enter school at a very young age and continue to have difficulty throughout their early school years, one would have to suspect that the "pecking order" of the school had helped to maintain their differences. This suggests the strategy of trying to identify high risk boys early and to get extra help for them (see Chapter 4).

In every classroom there are "accelerated" and "slow" students. The problem is what to call the "slow" ones. One would think that it would be relatively easy to call the accelerated students "gifted," but giftedness varies greatly from individual to individual and the label, therefore, often ignores more information than it defines. There is also the problem of the gifted label starting the process of separating certain children from their peers.

The major problem, however, comes when one starts to use labels for children at the other end of the achievement continuum. The term "retarded" also ignores more information than it defines, but it has the additional problem of possibly setting into motion a series of negative feelings about the self; no one enjoys being at the "bottom of the heap" (*A very special child,* 1972). The problem cannot be overcome by simply avoiding the use of the term in front of the child (few educators are so insensitive as to call a young child "retarded"). There is evidence that this negative labeling also sets up certain expectations in the mind of the teacher. The label "retarded" not only has the connotation of being slow in school, of being "out of it," but it also implies that the student will be that way the rest of his/her life. It would seem that the teacher's thinking about a retarded boy might be: "He is slow so I can't push him. I won't ask him to do as much as the rest of the class. I will give him less work to do. Since he is slow, I won't ask him to run the errand that takes more skill. I will accept whatever he does and praise him for it." Over a period of time, it is little wonder that this will indeed continue to reduce what the child can produce, which in turn will confirm what the teacher, in all good faith, thought in the first place. This cycle is what has come to be known as the "self-fulfilling prophecy." It must be repeated that teachers are not usually "irrational" or "mean" or "prejudiced" or "unprofessional"; they are simply carrying out, in most cases, what they have been taught and what in many instances is supported by what they have observed (Rosenthal and Jacobsen, 1968).

Why is it necessary to use labels? Unfortunately, in the efforts to obtain funding to help students with special needs, educators have been forced to play the labeling game. Educators cannot just go to the state legislature and say, "There are students who need special help." The legislators, being prudent people, want the students to be identified, counted, and the help they need defined—in short, to label the students. The difficulty, therefore, appears when one has to decide which students to label "retarded," to identify the numbers of children who are so severe that they must have extra help, to establish the classes, and to provide the services that are needed. Labeling leads to ignoring a lot of differences within the individual child resulting in the conclusion that, all things being considered, this child is more retarded than not. Then there is the additional problem of deciding what cutoff point to use. In one sense of the word, everyone below average is "slow" or "retarded." If the slowest one is labeled "slow" and removed there are still two or three that are "borderline." In the extreme case, the entire bottom half of the class could be labeled "slow," resulting in a new average considerably higher than the old one with a new group of students who are now below average or "borderline," and so the process could continue. Over the years, admission procedures for special classes for the "educable mentally retarded" have used cut off scores varying as much as 15 IQ points (based on an instrument where the scores could vary by chance as much as 6 more points) (Hobbs, 1974a,b).

Within the last year or two different states (in response to all of the pressures currently on special education) have started to use "cut off points" 15 IQ points apart. So in one state, in order to label a child "educably retarded" the child (together with other data, of course) has to have an IQ below 70, which would make this label apply to only one child out of 100. In another state any child with an IQ below "one standard deviation" (which is usually about an IQ of 85) can be labeled "educably retarded." In a typical school this would make the label applicable to about fifteen children out of 100. It is not uncommon to find whole schools in the lower socioeconomic (often inner-city) areas, where the average IQ in the school is around 85, which would include 50 percent of the children as "educable retarded." It is not the authors' purpose to belittle these honest efforts to help students. The complexity of these problems does not permit easy solutions. Educating all students is a tremendously complex, challenging job; finding ways to help those who are "not making it" is even more so. Much of the labeling of the past has been created to provide the money to help students who needed specialized services.

To counteract the problems introduced by negative labeling of students, a great deal of pressure has been brought against special placement, initiated by parents of minority children but rapidly spreading to representatives of other groups. The objections were numerous, such as the following: The special classes, they argued, are taking away their children's right to a normal education; being in these classes affects their children's ability to get a job following graduation, etc. Since an unusually high percentage of students placed in classes for the "educable retarded" were from minority groups, it was claimed that the school personnel were prejudiced and were using these classes to "hold the minority groups down." The tests that were used to place the children in these special classes were felt to be invalid, especially for the children who were bilingual or who used a nonstandard English dialect. The parents also felt that they had not been properly informed of the changes and were not made aware of all of the social ramifications of such special class placements. If the parents had disagreed with the placement, they felt that there was nothing they could do about it. Once the student was in the program, there was no way out.

First the courts and then professionals began increasingly to question whether the intervention of special placement of students might not be introducing as many problems as it solved. Perhaps the decision to take these students out of the mainstream had been based too much on just looking at the difficulty these students were having keeping up with the regular classroom work. Maybe not enough thought had been given to the long-range social effects of such placements. Certainly there had been no intention of taking away the student's rights; it had been seen as a way of trying to help, and so there had been little emphasis on parental/student rights. Studies on the achievement changes of students in special classes showed few increases; in fact, in some cases they were worse than the same kinds of students who were left in the regular class. Certainly more is known about how to help these youngsters than once was the case. Much of what had gone on in Special Education could be considered "Experimental Education" and could now be transferred back to the regular class. Educational supplies and technologies for all kinds of special problems are in much greater supply, and distribution systems are being expanded which could come much closer toward bringing these supplies to the student who needed them in the regular classroom. The sophistication and the technology shown by the regular classroom teacher have improved significantly over the years. Staff development techniques are improving. Regular classroom teachers are becoming more open to keeping these students in their rooms, provided they are given the appropriate training and auxiliary services (Catterall, 1972; Deno, 1970).

The best solution to the labeling-to-get-funds problem would seem to be as follows. It is obvious that there is a large group of students who respond well to the regular curriculum. Efforts continue to be made to increase the flexibility of the regular offerings of the school to make sure that a larger percentage will succeed. But there will still be a certain percentage whose needs are so great that they will need the special help that requires extra money. Accurate information regarding how many blind, deaf, and learning-disabled children there are is now available. Formulas can be developed which will indicate how much money will be given to help the mainstream (and of course there has never been enough money allocated for this purpose; this again points out that what will be paid out is more of a function of the state of the economy than it is the number of children in need). The needs of all exceptional children have not been met as witnessed by the fact that large groups are bringing "Right to Education" action against the schools to get their children into a special program. (The plan currently in existence, which is closest to this model, is the Texas Comprehensive Special Education Program, 1970.)

Schools would be provided special money for a certain percentage (say 10 percent) of their total population, providing they could prove that the money was actually being spent for the needed services for these students with exceptional needs. There would be little emphasis on the older concepts of diagnosis, labeling, and counting of these children and of trying to force them into categories into which they really did not fit. The highly trained personnel who had been working on identifying and treating special students could then work with the teacher in the regular classroom, providing for student needs in a relatively normal setting. There would still be a need for special placements for the seriously handicapped, but these would be integrated as much as possible, and students would move back into the mainstream more flexibly. Children who had been in institutions would often need to be placed in these special classes as a "half way point," helping them become reintegrated into the public school. None of this would save money, but it would direct the services where they would do the most good.

As far as the labels are concerned, it is not likely that they can be completely abandoned. As soon as individuals try to communicate with each other about the needs of a group of children they are, in a sense, forced to label. Indeed our very thought process requires that students and their needs be grouped into some unit for purposes of communication in order that a plan to meet their needs can be implemented. The negative labels which do so much harm, especially those which erroneously imply some sort of a life-long condition that is irreversible, can be minimized. Not enough is known in many cases about whether or not these conditions can change. Teachers and students should use only labels which imply the *next instructional step* or service that a student needs. From the standpoint of the educator the major reason for a label is to provide a basis for bringing together a group of students with relatively similar educational needs so that appropriate supplies and educational technology are available. The state of the art indicates that students can be helped to make significant gains, and educators should be making that a high priority.

A label that has become more popular lately is that of "learning disability." Although there is not always agreement on the definition or the way one should treat it, as used in this book it will refer to students who have a learning difficulty (moderate to severe) in one or more of the academic areas (with reading being perhaps the biggest problem) which *cannot* be accounted for by reason of retardation, cultural deprivation, or any of the traditional categories of handicapping conditions (deaf, blind, etc.). Early efforts to identify a cause for the learning problem attempted to locate neurological deficits in these children (Los Angeles County Superintendent of Schools, 1963).

Although there was some support for the neurological deficits theory, it certainly was not true for all students with learning difficulties and did not seem to lead to useful strategies for helping those students with essentially educational problems (Catterall, 1967). Once again it would seem to be more helpful to spend the time identifying programs for helping these students in the classroom rather than spending so much time doing a "high powered" medical-psychological work-up. There are, however, an increasing number of resources available to those who are concerned about this kind of child (Glaser, 1974; Lerner, 1971; Smith, 1969; Waugh and Bush, 1971; Wisland, 1974).

A great deal of use has been made of behavior modification techniques with the learning disabled, first in special classes (Hewett, Stillwell, Artuso, and Taylor, 1972; Valett, 1967), but increasingly in the mainstream of education (Haring and Phillips,

1972; Kozloff, 1974; Stephens, 1970). A summary of some of the techniques associated with this movement will be discussed later in this chapter.

Other approaches have tried to identify a broader range of educational techniques which seem to be helpful in the regular classroom (Blackwell and Joynt, 1972; Grzynkowicz, 1975; Hammill and Bartel, 1971; Kozloff, 1974). Still others have specialized in an instructional or media approach, i.e. what special kinds of material are most helpful for these children (Hammill and Bartel, 1975; Schloss, 1975; Special Education Instructional Materials Center, 1972). Since there are so many children who could be labeled as learning disabled, the strategies which have been found helpful in working with them and with other related kinds of problems are discussed throughout this chapter. Good educational procedures for the learning disabled would almost always be good educational procedures for all children.

It is apparent that in order to accomplish the tasks described in this chapter, education must begin to take the information that is available from the corrective/remedial services and use it in improving the normal developmental curriculum. Educators must examine the reasons why some students are not learning, and find ways insofar as possible to place strategies within the regular curriculum which will help others coming after them. Educators must look at all children who have to leave the mainstream to see what services could have been provided them in a more nearly normal setting. Every instructional technique which has been proven to be effective with the exceptional child must be analyzed and adapted insofar as possible, for use with other students. Every drop-out and every push-out must be studied to see what additional strategies are needed to hold on to these wasted human resources. This is not to imply that all of these problems are necessarily created by the school, but just as students should learn to make a "creative use" of their errors, so too should educators look to their "rejects" in order to improve.

This chapter describes a series of interventions. As used in this book, an *intervention* is an action or service that is introduced into a student's life-space which is designed to fill a specific, identified need. Interventions are different from the strategies described in the preceding chapter since they deal with needs that are typically more severe, are more corrective/remedial in nature than the regular curriculum can usually handle, and are more likely to involve the cooperative planning and action of a specialist as well as the regular classroom teacher. The intervention, whenever possible, will be carried out in the normal classroom setting, but there will also be provisions for working with students in other settings.

Interventions can and should be identified and carried out by a variety of people working together as a *Learning Facilitation Team*. The team of teachers that will ordinarily be working on the strategies in Chapter 4 will normally be joined by one or more specialist/interventionists and often will include the local school administrator. Teachers should insist that they have the support of well-trained specialist/interventionists who are available to them when they are needed. Just as the family doctor needs the support of other professionals, so too, teachers cannot and should not try to function alone. Many of the traditional specialists will be involved in this process: corrective reading teachers, nurses, speech teachers, counselors, social workers, psychologists, etc. Other specialists will probably emerge as new ways are identified for providing students with more help in the regular classroom. Professional assistants, paraprofessionals, and aides will be trained for specific interventionist roles. Parents will be brought in on the intervention planning stage more often and will also assume responsibilities for carrying out the plans. Specialists outside the school will continue to be called on to provide their special services. The learning facilitation team will ordinarily involve and be under the direction of a school psychologist, school counselor, or special education teacher.

Once a well-trained learning facilitation team has been assembled, true professional problem solving will take place. Each interventionist will provide information and assume responsibilities to fill a specific need on the basis of his/her ability to help rather than on the basis of role definitions. Most specialists and teachers become "role bound" and have only a relatively limited repertoire of intervention skills, i.e. teachers teach, counselors counsel, and psychologists test. One of the primary goals of the learning facilitation team is to help each person make his/her best contribution because we desperately need the best everyone has to offer to solve some of our major problems and to learn a variety of new intervention strategies. Whenever possible, the students who are the concern of the Learning Facilitation Team will also be involved in the process up to the level of their ability. (For an approach that relates the current "due process" concerns to the multidisciplinary approach, see Tracy, Gibbons, Kladder, and Daggy, 1975.)

It is essential that the interventionist bring the special services needed to the student's regular classroom (Ebersole, Kephart, and Ebersole, 1968; Grzynkowicz, 1975; Kephart, 1971). Each interventionist must learn how to relate his/her special skills to the mainstream of education. Nurses have to become more involved in health education in the classroom. It is suggested that counselors become more involved in the total curricular development in the area of humanistic education (see Chapter 6). Librarians ought to become more involved in the total curricular offerings, rather than just as an isolated service. Speech correctionists must become more involved in assisting the teacher with developmental speech. Reading specialists should get involved with integrating their services into the regular classroom. Teachers who have special skills in working with the mentally retarded should bring in necessary services to the child in the mainstream. The learning disability teachers must modify their special techniques devised for working one-on-one toward an instructional program for the regular class. Psychologists will have to become more skillful in using carry-through interventions in the classroom. The great majority of these specialists, however, are willing and able to make these changes. They have been allowed to get bogged down with other activities which, although important, too often have been less effective because they were being carried out in isolation. The "growing edge" of helping most students and the challenge of this total approach exists in the curricular modifications in the regular classroom (Catterall, 1972).

TUTORING

By this time the reader should be aware of some of the excitement in education and the increased pace in bringing people together to help other people. There is increasing evidence that it is helpful to both persons involved. With the reduction in the number of new teachers entering the teaching ranks, with the tight school budgets seen almost everywhere, and with the continuing pressures on educators to work with an ever-increasing number of individual needs, probably the brightest hope with the widest possible application is the systematic use of paraprofessional people in the process of helping other people. The traditional concept of a tutor as a fully-trained person who serves as a "private teacher" has been around for a long time and does not excite great hopes of solving the major problems of education. The word conjures up the vision of an elderly lady, seeing five or six students, working in isolation on afternoons and Saturday mornings, in her home, etc. What these people have done is valuable, but it is hard to believe that this is a new, dynamic intervention that would even begin to solve some of the major problems which face education.

For a long time it was felt that the only people who could help other people were those who were highly trained. Once again, we do not want to go overboard and move the point of saying that training is not important. We are beginning, however, to see the value of involving a large number of untrained people helping others. Most jobs, especially teaching, entail a large number of details which, in the press of time, do not always get completed. It is extremely difficult to meet the needs of even the small group of students who are having problems. The need for knowledge of results discussed in the preceding section of this chapter is one example. Teaching machines showed promise of taking over some of these details. Some educators, however, feel that these machines are "inhuman." This, together with their expense and the problems of trying to keep their programs flexible, have kept teaching machines from becoming widely used. The increased use of tutors, especially with those students who are not progressing satisfactorily, holds great promise.

There is increasing evidence that the teaching act can, and

probably should, be broken down into smaller units. This indicates that some of the details in teaching not only can be handled, but sometimes can be handled better by tutors. One source of this type of information is an emphasis on differentiated staffing. Here the responsibilities for working on large learning units have to be broken down into specific assignments for people with different levels of teaching skills. Not only is there a need for "super" teachers in these programs, but it becomes obvious that all kinds of teaching aides can also be of major help in the teaching/learning act. Needs are identified for a small group or even for a one-to-one activity which can be handled by a teacher aide. Many of these same activities can also be handled by tutors (Olivero and Buffie, 1970).

Programmed instruction efforts have also indicated that a great many things can be taught more easily if they are broken down into their component parts and carefully sequenced (Thiagarajan, 1971). Educators began to accept the fact that if this material could be effectively "fed" to students through a machine, the same material could be introduced in other ways. Many teachers are using a variety of tutors to provide immediate feedback to students while they are being given instructional material which has been prepared in this same way. In addition to having certain instructional advantages, there are marked personal advantages in using a system of tutoring. Although the need for highly trained, professional skills in helping people has been stressed, it suddenly became evident that there was a great deal of strength in facilitating the learning process by bringing together two "regular" people. The emphasis is on the "magic" of one person having and being willing to take the time to help a certain student. Although unquestionably less efficient than a machine, a tutor adds a personal quality and provides the social praise or reinforcement which is so badly needed to help the person being tutored to be able to transfer into the classroom what he/she has been learning.

While it is not newsworthy that tutors can help, it was exciting that there were so many potential tutors (literally almost everyone, including other students) who could provide that help. It was *newsworthy*, however, when it became more and more evident that the process was helping both the tutor and the one being tutored (Gartner, 1971; Reissman, Kohler, and Gartner, 1971). There had previously been agreement, albeit somewhat luke-warm, that the child needing help could profit from this kind of arrangement. However, some people felt that it was not fair to take time away from another student's learning to serve as the helper. Evidence seems to be coming from all sides that if tutors are not too far advanced beyond the level where they are tutoring, the process helps both students, not only academically but prob-ably socially (although this is more difficult to measure and prove) (Stainback and Stainback, 1972). In terms of academic gains, as discussed under "cycle teaching," there are advantages to both. In fact, it became apparent that some of the best tutors were students who had previously had a great deal of difficulty themselves. The student who previously had a reading problem, for instance, did a better job of helping another student with a reading problem, and at the same time probably made more academic gain in the process than an average or above-average child would have (Harris, 1971).

In order for the tutoring process to be most effective, the tutor has to know whether or not the other student is making a correct response (Danish and Hauer, 1973). Although they are an impor-tant source, students are not the only source of tutors. The ways tutors can be used to help are almost as numerous as the problems of the students with whom they have been asked to work. In fact, it is hard to think of any academic problem that could not be al-leviated in some way by the tutoring approach. It has already been pointed out that tutors can help students learn both simple and increasingly complex tasks, depending upon the age and ma-turity level of the tutor. Tutors can utilize a "communications model"; one group of parents was given instructions to sit down with students on a one-to-one basis and simply engage in mean-ingful conversation with them. How many children, especially from underprivileged homes, ever have a chance to hold such a conversation with an adult in our culture? These students, mostly early elementary-aged boys who had been selected because of "com-munication problems," included some who were excessively shy, some who came from bilingual backgrounds, a boy whose conversation seemed to "drift off" the subject easily, some with rather typical developmental speech problems, and so forth. The results were amazing. Another group of adult tutors took some young students, mostly boys, with coordination problems and helped them through a series of musical and sports activities designed to make them feel more adequate physically, again with good results. Other adult tutors, with parental permission, have taken students out to grocery and department stores and on other kinds of field trips especially tailored to their individual needs. With appropriate training programs, and as long as the student and his/her parents give their permission, there is almost no limit to the educational activities in which tutors could become engaged (Hardy and Cull, 1973).

Some, who would otherwise be agreeable to this plan, would say, "But our school doesn't have that many places for tutors to work with students." In general the more these activities can take place in the regular classroom, the better. It would be unfortunate to disrupt the rest of the class, but the main advantage of using the regular classroom is that it does not isolate the student's special help from his/her regular work. There is usually an empty classroom or a multipurpose room that stands empty 70 percent of the time; simple "stations" around the outside will serve the purpose. Similarly, school halls can be converted to tutoring halls, sometimes in such a way that the student's teacher can also visually supervise. If the school has a library or a media center, much of the tutoring can take place there. In good weather, these activities can also go on outside. In the secondary schools there are usually a number of small rooms which can be used to carry on these activities. As previously indicated, every department should make available a space for these one-to-one and small-group activities near the resource materials needed for the subject being tutored. Some suggestions for sources of tutors will be listed in the following sections.

Other Students

A variety of examples of using other students have already been given. When one looks objectively at traditional American education, it becomes obvious that it has "walled off" students from each other (Montessori, 1963). The implication seemed to be that all ideas had to come from the teacher, and that the student would collect those ideas and integrate them and report them back to the teacher on demand. If, in the process, one student helped another, not only had the one student "cheated," but the one who gave him/her the help was also at fault. Whereas there may be some justification for this in a testing situation, it seems to have permeated our education in many learning situations when the social interaction between two students would be extremely helpful. As previously indicated, techniques need to be found for having all students shift back and forth between the role of the one who is tutoring and the one who is being tutored. This, of course, is only possible if one moves beyond the confines of a single class and starts to think of the total educational program across a school, district, or region (Gartner), 1971. In summary, some of the ways that other students have been used as tutors include the following:

CLASSMATES. When using other students in the classroom one would, as much as possible, want to provide the student being helped with a student that can model effective learning behavior (Christine, 1971; Moskowitz, 1972).

OLDER STUDENTS. These can be chosen either from older classes in the same school or from the school serving the next older group. These other students may or may not have previously had difficulty with the subject in which they are tutoring. The students can go through a formal training program in the process of becoming tutors (probably the best) or they can rely on the teacher of the child who needs tutoring to provide the training. Audiovisual training kits are available for training tutors (see Higgins, 1975). The tutoring can be done for school credit or as a volunteer activity (Goodman, 1971).

COLLEGE STUDENTS. Students from nearby colleges or universities can be asked to volunteer; many of them are seeking some avenue of service and are glad to give their time. It is especially valuable to work through a specific group or organization on campus in order to provide continuity. This can be a very useful experience for college students who are considering going into a profession where they will have to work closely with other people.

Many colleges and universities lack these kinds of experiences for their own students; thought should be given to finding the most convenient way to bring the two students together and to reinforce the older students for contributing their time.

STUDENTS IN TEACHER TRAINING. An especially valuable group to work with are those who are thinking of becoming teachers. With the surplus personnel, teacher training programs are beginning to think of a variety of professional/observation/exploration approaches whereby potential teachers get out into the elementary and secondary schools to observe a school from the vantage point of a potential professional (as opposed to the viewpoint of the student going through the process). As part of this procedure, the students in training begin to take part in tutoring one or more students. Many find this process naturally very stimulating, others feel the need for a lot more training before they can feel comfortable in the process (which should give direction to their studies). Some decide that it is "not for me." The one who makes the decision to change has saved several years of time which would have originally been spent in preeducation courses. It seems infinitely better to find this out when one is still in the first or second year of college rather than waiting until the fourth or fifth year when one traditionally starts to practice teach.

Professional Staff

Although other staff members are usually busy during the entire school day and are not available, there are occasions when they have time for tutoring, e.g. before or after school or during the "prep" period (Beach, 1973). A variation would be when a teacher has a student who needs help and he/she brings in another older student, who also needs help, to serve as the tutor for the younger student. The teacher provides guidance for both at the same time. Principals can often be pressed into service (if we could release them from some of the important but noneducational "administrativia," they would probably be glad to help a lot more). Schools are increasingly hiring tutors, but in many instances they are restricted to working with learning disabilities or with other students in special education programs (Olivero and Buffie, 1970).

Somewhere between another professional on the staff and a parent can be found the enormous number of people in every community who have been trained as teachers but who have quit (usually to have a family) and yet they still have a great many technical skills and a lot of personal maturity. Many are more than willing to become involved. Some want to "keep their hand in," thinking that they may wish to go back to teaching. Others want more of a sense of personal contribution than they are able to get from their regular housework. It staggers the imagination to think of how many of these highly trained people are around. One tremendously successful program included a carefully planned ten-day training program for these people and found that they could be trained to become excellent tutors even for students with relatively complex learning disability problems (Browning, 1974).

Other Adults in the School

Many school secretaries have gravitated toward the school because they like education. Many would like to become teachers but do not have the necessary formal education. Like principals, they are usually burdened with other details, but in some instances the "pay-off" for this person-to-person kind of help makes the rest of the work go faster (helping young people can be a tremendously rewarding task). Custodians, who are usually thought of as helping students in more physical types of activities, can also serve as tutors. Some schools have hired women bus drivers and have trained them as tutors for the period of time between their bus runs. Sometimes these people know a great deal about children's "real" environment (their home, neighborhood, etc.) and can relate what the children are learning in school to their real lives.

Parents and People from the Community

There are still reservations on the part of many administrators and school staffs about having parents from the immediate community serve as tutors. Where they have been used, they have been a tremendous amount of help; they create few complications when they are used in a "productive" sort of way. It was feared that they would spread "gossip" around the community. With a little training, however, they have been found to be just as reliable as any of the paid staff. If parents are not involved at a variety of levels, then educators have cut themselves off from one of the potentially most powerful resources at their disposal. There are parents who do not have much formal education, but they do have some of the natural instincts of a great teacher and frequently are willing to take the direction offered by the classroom teacher. (The process of having the parents reinforce, through the activities they have at their disposal in the home, the good behavior in the school that has been reported to them by the staff has been described by Cohen, Keyworth, Kleiner, and Libert, 1971.)

One model used the parents of children with learning disabilities (who were trained through their parent's group) to help the students with learning problems from other families (Sluyter and Hawkins, 1972). Educators still have a suspicion that whenever they find a child with a problem, they believe it must have been caused by a "disturbed parent." Of course some parents are disturbed; having some of these severely handicapped children would "disturb" any home. Parents should be given some training so they know how to assist their own child (which was positively forbidden for many years and is still quite rare) (Champagne and Goldman, 1972; Patterson and Gullion, 1971). There is good evidence that parents of retarded infants coming from limited educational, environmental, and ability backgrounds can, with training, actually raise the IQ of their children (Nurturing Intelligence, 1972).

Retired people can be another source of tutors; the retired engineer, for example, might take the time to find the practical examples to help a high school boy make progress with his "troublesome" math. How many older people are there in every community with little to do who could be put to work in this creative process? A "bank" of "fathers," "mothers," "big brothers," and "big sisters" who can help out with a variety of problems needs to be developed. In short, educators need to remember that they are part of a larger community and that parents and other members of the community want to and are able to make significant contributions to the education of their children and other children in the community. People who have "invested" themselves in the schools usually make the best public relations teams for telling others in the community the kinds of good things that the schools are doing (Carter and Dapper, 1972).

The question of whether or not to pay tutors has been avoided up to this point. To some extent, however, the answer depends upon how much money is available. Paid people (other things being equal) are more consistent, but this, to a large extent, depends upon how their involvement is structured, i.e. how the original task is set up. The "rules" should be, "If you want to help us with this crucially important task you will need to be consistent and come in when you say you are going to be here." Most people will respond to that kind of approach and those who have tried it have found that it works. Of course there may be other community problems that are crying for solution, such as providing money for low-income parents or students needing help to get through college (Hardy and Cull, 1973). Under these circumstances, by all means, pay. If adult volunteers are used, their task will have to be defined in specific terms: "Let's try two mornings a week for five weeks, and then we will take a look and see how we want to proceed." The interminable "come in and help" will usually not do the job. Once they are on the job, they will need encouragement and support in their learning and commitment just like everybody else; this, in a sense, is their "paycheck" (Rauch, 1972).

As a rule of thumb, if a teacher or specialist is trying to help a student on a specific task, he/she should identify components which can be done by a tutor. Then the teacher or specialist should spend 20 percent of the time he/she would have taken to do the job alone to find a tutor, and 30 percent of the time training and supervising the tutor, and use the remaining 50 percent on other students.

ADDING STIMULATION

The interventions described in this section all have in common the fact that they add something to the life of the student of a corrective/remedial nature in response to an academic/intellectual need identified by the classroom teacher and prescribed by a Learning Facilitation Team. Technically, tutoring could also be considered one part of an overall plan of *adding stimulation,* but it is so large and so potentially powerful that it has been treated separately in the preceding section.

Sensory Stimulation

Stimulation can be provided in any of the major sensory areas: the sense of touch (haptic stimulation), the sense of smell (olfactory stimulation), the sense of hearing (auditory stimulation), and the sense of sight (visual/perceptual stimulation). For normally developing children, educators stress auditory and visual/ perceptual experiences because these are both"distance receptors" and are not as restrictive as the other two. This is true because one does not have to come into direct physical contact with the object to see it or hear it as one does with the sense of touch.

Both touch and smell, which are in many ways more primitive, are rarely as fully developed as the other senses. For handicapped children such as the deaf or blind, these added senses take on greater importance because they are often a major avenue to learning. Fortunately, few children are totally blind or totally deaf. One aspect of sensory stimulation, however, involves amplifying and teaching the handicapped child to learn to more efficiently use the remaining sensory inputs, i.e. optical corrections and hearing aids. In general, the earlier that the correction is given the better.

Audiometric devices are available which can be used routinely to test hearing at birth. Not only are hearing aids being put on children very early, but if there is any residual hearing, binaural devices will pick up the sound and send it to both ears. This helps the child to use the remaining hearing to begin to localize the direction from which the sounds come. Dramatic increases in the magnification of sound and in the miniaturization of hearing aids have made it possible for many hard-of-hearing children to lead much more normal lives.

The impairment of hearing is a *major* handicapping condition unless powerful interventions are provided which help the child to minimize the handicap. One primary reason that hearing loss is so critical is that it dramatically reduces the ability of deaf persons to use language. This, in turn, dramatically reduces their ability to think and to conceptualize, thus cutting into their ability to communicate with others. The adult deaf in our country tend to band together into "deaf communities" which, needless to say, provide much-needed social contacts for these people. Unfortunately, they also tend to contribute to the learning problems of the often normal-hearing children of deaf parents. More precise interventions providing a total spectrum of services are needed earlier to help the deaf and hard-of-hearing to become more fully integrated into society. As in other cases, parents are being used more systematically to help their deaf children. (For a general discussion of the issues of educating the deaf and hard-of-hearing, see Jones, 1971, Part IV; and Telford and Sawrey, 1972, Chapter 12.) Most states fund programs for the deaf starting at age three. This, of course, is much too late to start providing needed services. Educational programs must either be continued downward or other community/health agencies must be developed to work with these children, literally from birth.

Early special programs for the partially sighted were unfortunately called "sight saving" classes. One cannot "save" sight just as one cannot save any function which requires muscles to perform the activity; if you do not use a muscle, it atrophies and becomes even more useless. The eyes are controlled by some of the most complex muscles in the body, normally as an integrated function with both eyes working together. This movement is critically important to how much sensory input the child is able to receive and send to the occipital portion of the brain. To show how important vision is to total learning, almost half of the total brain is devoted to the occipital areas which collect and store visual images. Normally developing children, in a manner of speaking, also begin to "tack on" a great many nonvisual clues to the visual image. For example, when they look at a piece of metal, most of them think it "looks" cold.

Dramatic advances have been made and are being made in

magnifying the remaining vision; in some instances visually handicapped children are fitted with almost telescopic devices which
magnify the usable vision hundreds of times. Unfortunately, they
have the disadvantage of any telescope and restrict the field of
vision considerably.

Although virtually every state has a state school for the blind,
many people responsible for educating the blind have long advocated a program based on the following: There should be early
identification and medical/optical interventions where indicated.
Parents will often work with the child from birth, but formal preschool training will often begin about three-and-a-half years of age.
When it is the normal time to start kindergarten, the partially
sighted and most of the blind will go into regular classes in schools
which are able to support them with a resource program. This
will provide both the specialized equipment, the educational
materials, and the technical-instructional help the child needs.
The partially sighted may only require a little additional help to
make the early transitions into reading and other aspects of the
normal academic program. The child who is blind (or a child
who is losing his/her vision) is taught Brailling skills. The resource teacher helps the child understand the assignments, rewrites
the regular teacher-made tests into Braille, and transcribes (types)
the child's responses which, in turn, are corrected by the regular
classroom teacher. Gradually, often starting about the third
grade, blind children are also taught to type on a standard typewriter. Once they have acquired that skill they can often be
moved into the neighborhood school where material is increasingly introduced to them through tapes and records and the students complete the assignments on the typewriter. This phase requires a great deal of supervision and assistance by an itinerant
teacher who also provides the specialized educational materials
needed by the blind child.

Countless hours of volunteer labor have to be spent in transcribing new books into large print and Braille (with the explosion
of educational materials in the regular classroom, this is a never-
ending task), in transcribing books onto tapes and records, and in
many other ways. The technical capacity exists (although it has

still not been put to use except in a very limited, experimental way) of having someone read into one computer where the voice signal is translated into typed form. This, in turn, is fed into another computer where it is transcribed into Braille. Incidentally, computer printouts can be modified relatively simply to come out as "bumps" similar to Braille rather than as printed symbols. This computer capability dramatically opens up the world of computer sciences as a career for the blind. With highly skilled educational interventionists, with countless hours of time given by dedicated volunteers, and with this type of increasing technology, the blind are being able to lead increasingly normal lives both in school and in everyday life. (For a general discussion of the problems of educating the visually handicapped child see Jones, 1971, Part III, and Telford and Sawrey, 1972, Chapter 3.)

The concept of sensory stimulation is not restricted, however, to the severely handicapped. Experiences which help the developing young child to become aware of and to integrate the sensory experiences are a standard part of the preschool program (see Chapter 4). Although most children coming to school are able to see and hear, there has been a great deal of interest lately in finding ways to help some of those children having difficulty to learn to improve their visual skills (Mott, 1974). It is one thing, for example, to be able to hear and another thing to be able to make the fine auditory discriminations between the sounds in the words that the child will have to differentiate (Oakland and Williams, 1971). Similarly, most children can see but may not be able to make the necessary visual distinctions required in beginning reading. There have been a number of tests designed to measure visual perceptual skills, such as the Frostig (Frostig and Horne, 1964; Frostig, Maslow, Lefever, and Whittlesey, 1964). Other strategies have been devised which have based whole educational programs on this type of sensory stimulation and training (Markoff, 1976).

Since the main way we have of knowing whether or not children have "perceived," (added together the incoming sensory stimulations into some sort of a new meaningful "whole") is through their ability to *do* something; since movement patterns are so basic to all aspects of learning, other strategies have attempted to help children develop integrated movement patterns as a means of assisting them to make more progress in academic areas (Bower, 1976; Wedell, 1973). These programs are to be distinguished from muscle building and physical-skill building exercises (although they are related) which would be considered as a part of a physical education program. This work is based on the following premise: Perceptual-motor functions develop through certain identifiable stages of maturation. Many children who have difficulty with early, formal learning also show some degree of perceptual-motor dysfunction. Both maturation and the ability to integrate separate sensory experiences depend upon appropriate sensory stimulation and the child's ability to respond appropriately (Arena, 1969). The main unifying force behind the concept of sensory stimulation is the idea of providing experiences which are carefully devised and systematically introduced into the child's developing organism in such a way that it promotes or facilitates maturation and readiness for later educational learning. Its primary tools for doing this include helping the child isolate the information coming in from the various senses, making appropriate discriminations between increasingly finer differences, and then integrating the total information into new meaningful wholes upon which later learning can be based (Getman, 1962; Humphrey, 1975).

Like every other strategy, it can be both misused and overused. Although most of this training will not hurt any child, its use as a preliminary program for formal learning should be considered a corrective/remedial strategy for only a few children (Frostig, 1970; Goodman and Hammill, 1973; Hammill, Goodman and Wiederhold, 1974; Heckelman, 1969). In order to teach children to learn to read and write there is no substitute for carefully devised and introduced reading and writing programs. Some children need extra help to learn to integrate perceptual-motor functions, preliminary to, but not as a substitute for, formal training (Frank and Frank, 1950). Used in this way, these procedures will prove to be yet another effective strategy for helping some children achieve better.

Experiential Stimulation

To some extent, the concept of producing total experiences to increase learning is an extension of the sensory stimulation experiences described above. Here the emphasis is on building larger units of life experience which enable students to bring to the learning task the experiential background needed to get meaning out of what they are learning. The typical child comes to school with a large enough vocabulary so that in the first phases of *learning to read* he/she does not run into very many words that he/she has trouble understanding. Much beginning reading material, however, is somewhat sterile, in that it portrays idealized situations which do not jibe with a child's real experience.

Starting in the third grade, the emphasis typically shifts to one which requires the student to be able to take beginning reading skills and *read to learn*. At this point it becomes increasingly important whether or not a student has had the experiential background to get the meaning out of the reading. An extreme example would be a boy who lived in the tropics and had never seen snow, trying to comprehend a story about an Eskimo boy whose life depends upon making distinctions between different kinds of snow. (The Eskimo language is reported to have thirteen different words for snow.)

Numbers and mathematics may rely upon life experiences more from the very first. The concept of a "number," that numbers have an order, and that a number can be transferred from object to object, e.g. from the third block to the third child, etc., is all quite abstract. Although children can probably learn to do early rote counting without much conceptual background, so-called "modern math" requires them to make some fairly high-level computations, even in the first grade, which are related to the experiences they have had in their lives and bring the knowledge they have into the classroom. An example is the "zero" concept on a number line. This requires the child to conceptualize just as much "distance" between the zero point and the first item as there is between the first item and the second. Not as many children had difficulty with beginning mathematics when it was taught in a rote fashion, as it once was. Once modern math was introduced it became more difficult, especially for the child without the necessary background experiences.

The intervention of using sensory experiences was used extensively in the early stages of the educational "War on Poverty." Unfortunately it was used without carefully thinking through how a specific experience would really help a child to learn, and the results were not very encouraging. In some instances, whole classes of lower socioeconomic minority children were taken on field trips to the opera as a part of a "cultural enrichment" program. It would be more beneficial to have field trips near the child's home so that everyday experiences could be integrated with and related to the learning tasks at school. (American education has much to learn from the way the Japanese systematically use field trips in their public schools.) When planning prescribed experiential field trips for specific students, school personnel will often have to make use of parents or volunteers. Hard-core poverty (whether one's skin is black or white) can dramatically "cut into" a child's experiential background for learning. Providing the necessary background for the Appalachian child is also difficult to do. The use of an experiential stimulation approach can help some of these students, but it is not a complete answer (Cull and Hardy, 1975; Figurel, 1970; Weikart, 1967).

In many areas, the economically impoverished group takes on the additional dimension of being members of a different racial/ethnic group. Examples include the following: the Mexican Americans and American Indians of the Southwest; the blacks in many of our large cities; the Puerto Rican and Cuban families in New York and Florida, and the children of French Canadian descent in the Northeast. In these instances, we not only frequently have economic factors cutting into the learning process; we often have also a second language or nonstandard English. Major differences in value standards are sometimes associated with different cultural heritages. Many such children have been "walled off." One intervention is to introduce these children to "another way of life" which, although not necessarily better, might help them to be better able to compete in the mainstream of life, should they care to do so. (Also see the earlier discussion of language development for these children.)

Another group which is somewhat of a mixture of the two mentioned above, but with other specialized problems, is the group of migrants that still represent a sizable minority in our country. In addition to the poverty associated with this way of life and the social/ethnic/language differences of some of them, the rootless, disorganized quality of their lives gives them still other educational problems. There are the additional difficulties associated with the constant changing of schools and the frequent absences created by this life-style. A student appears at a school and by the time the staff can determine the student's educational level he/she is suddenly gone. One school, in order to help solve this problem, set aside a special teacher who administered "rapid surveys" in the basic learning areas. Thirty minutes after first entering a school, the migrant student was walking down the hall with a slip of paper indicating the room to go where he/she could most profitably "plug in" to the curriculum during his/her brief stay in that school. This is a service that would be helpful for most new students. The educational survey was also designed to be taken with the child whenever the family moved again.

On a much larger scale, the problem has been attacked by the capabilities of a computer. In one of the major efforts to cut across state lines to help migrant children (and needless to say the solution has to involve more than one state), an overwhelming majority of the states have jointly started to keep information on children of migrant workers on a centrally located computer. A fifth grade teacher in Arizona, for example, who has a migrant child put into his/her class, could contact a computer in that area which would hook into the central computer, and the information on that child would be sent over telephone lines to operate a local terminal, so the cumulative record report could be available to the teacher the following morning. Obviously, a computer is not going to solve all of the complex human and educational problems associated with this type of child. This example does show promise of how educators are beginning to solve more systematically some of their common problems.

Other countries have similar problems; we could learn much from the efforts of Israel to educate the tremendously large number of Jews, who, after "roaming through the deserts" for generations are now in their public schools (Feuerstein and Krasilowsky, 1972).

Language Development and Speech Correction

For a long time schools have used interventionists called *speech teachers* who have unfortunately worked altogether too often in isolation on the very important problems of helping children improve their speech and articulation problems. They have traditionally worked with youngsters (alone or in small groups) from the late primary or elementary grades. As in other forms of corrective/remedial activities, not very much has been done at the high school level and that which has been done has not been very successful. Like many other special education areas, this important work has not been actively integrated with the program of the regular classroom. Children with speech problems were relatively easy to identify and the speech teachers developed and utilized a high degree of skill in correcting the identified problems. There was little time and/or encouragement for these teachers to get back into the regular classroom to work on developmental speech difficulties.

Another outgrowth of the relatively new emphasis on preschool screening and programming for the handicapped has been a major emphasis on an earlier corrective/remedial approach with children before they formally enter school (Karnes, 1968). Speech sounds, like most other developmental tasks, normally appear in a systematic sequence which makes detection possible at an early age. The developmental emphasis is also being seen more in the primary grades (Simonds, 1975). In many states, the speech teachers are being asked to take part of their time away from the speech correction work and go into the regular class and work with the teacher on developmental speech. As in many areas, if systematic instruction is provided, fewer children are likely to need major corrective work. Once a problem has been identified, the earlier the corrective work can begin before it impedes the academic work the better, and the less likely the child is to have emotional problems as a result of the speech defect. There will probably continue to be some who will need the individualized correctional work, but the total educational program will improve because of the better utilization of all of the skills of these corrective speech personnel (Blumberg, 1975; Nist, 1974; Swift, 1970).

Another kind of language stimulation program is rapidly developing for students coming from bilingual families. One major emphasis has been under the heading of "Teaching English as a Second Language." There appears to have been a great deal of confusion about the "problem" of being bilingual. It has come to the point where many people feel that if the second language is French or German, it is a "plus" factor; if, however, the second language is Spanish, it has come to be considered a negative influence on learning. The problem seems to be that many of the children who come from bilingual homes are also economically deprived. Their life-style has not permitted them (or required them) to speak concisely or to think clearly in either language, even though language is so basic to our total thought process. A young student who is functioning well in one language can shift to another quite easily. The average child's vocabulary is "exploding" at about the time he/she enters school. To have exposure to two different languages will normally make their vocabulary grow that much faster. Such auto-instructional techniques as "language masters" can help students to develop quite rapidly the basic vocabulary of another language if their experiential/cognitive level is satisfactory. The effective use of "English as a second language" has the potential of providing cognitive exercises built around language development activities. It can, at the same time, help these young people to come out of the experience feeling proud of their heritage and thus become a powerful intervention for helping them learn better (Blank, 1970; Ogeltree and Garcia, 1975; Thonis, 1967).

Still another use of language-centered activities is to help students express their feelings better in their relationships with other adults and children. Activities of this nature will be discussed in the next two chapters.

Conceptual Development

Closely related to language development (because of the major overlap between language and conceptual thinking) are a group of procedures designed to facilitate growth in a student's ability to form meaningful, accurate concepts (Blank, 1970; Kohlberg, 1972). One of the reasons why culturally deprived children have so much difficulty in moving on to the appropriate conceptual development is that their language often does not support the proper use of abstract thinking.   Language/conceptual development programs should help these children see the world around them as having logical, conceptual relationships.   They need to receive more help in organizing new information into some sort of a relationship with the things they already know than do children coming from home environments where this is already more heavily stressed (Getman, 1962).   The program should assist children to acquire a group of cognitive skills which would help them to develop new strategies for thinking and for processing information, i.e. ability to delay gratification, appropriate use of "self-talk," planning ahead to future events, etc.   Too often education stresses the learning of new facts or information which the child is supposed to repeat or to recall when asked.   There is not sufficient stress placed on helping the child to see how this information is related to other things he already knows and how to apply it to present and future problem solving.   If possible, the program should permit every child to respond every time rather than the traditional method of the teacher asking a question and only one child responding.   Continued success should be experienced as children get constant practice in increasing their language/conceptual development (Bereiter and Englemann, 1966; Blank, 1970; Englemann, 1969; Engelmann and Bruner, 1969; Engelmann and Osborn, 1970; Johnson, 1970).

Remedial work with the child who is having difficulty in school points to the way that education can be improved for all.   Although conceptual development seems more difficult for the culturally deprived than for many others, large numbers of children have difficulty with this and need some special assistance.   Language acquisition, especially as it moves on to the higher levels, tends to be limited by the child's level of conceptual development. This is one reason why language has to be taught in relationship to all of the child's experience and should be infused throughout his/her whole school experience.   There is a definite relationship between the way children use language and the way they think, even though in some ways they are separate processes. The complex problems of helping children experience the joys of communicating their feelings, their thoughts, and their impressions are just now beginning to be understood (Schiefelbusch and Lloyd, 1974). The work of Piaget is rapidly being brought into classroom training programs with good results (Piaget, 1952).

Other efforts have used the term "critical thinking" to organize activities and interventions helpful to specific students. Procedures are followed which help a student "order" the factors in his/ her life (either directly or through simulated activities) in more precise ways so as to be better able to make decisions. In some cases, workbook activities have been devised using an approach similar to that frequently used in a mystery story. Certain facets are introduced within the framework of a "true-to-life" story; certain actions are taken, and then the student has to perform the critical thinking to come up with the best solution. There is some evidence that there is a tendency for people to form concepts even when they do not have all of the needed information (or have not used it properly). Some of the students who were originally labeled as "brain damaged" (a term no longer used) appear to display this characteristic. They would abstract a concept or similarity which was not accurate because they had not correctly perceived the total situation. An analogy would be to assume that when one gets intoxicated after drinking "Scotch on the rocks," "Bourbon over ice," or "crème de menthe over shaved ice" that it was the ice that was making one drunk because it was the common denominator. As previously mentioned, one of the main goals of education is to help students take the isolated bits of information given to them (many of which would be useless to try to memorize) and make new, meaningful units or concepts out of them. Teaching some students to use a critical approach to test the accuracy of their thinking can be very valuable (Schiefelbusch and Lloyd, 1974). (For a discussion of how the modern media are affecting language, learning, and conceptual development, see Tyler and Williams, 1973.)

Academic Intellectual Help

Obviously all students need some sort of academic intellectual help both of a developmental and a corrective/remedial nature (and probably all students will need some extra help in some subject during their schooling). In another sense of the word all of the strategies previously listed in this section are, broadly speaking, "academic." Where it is most important to consider this as a separate strategy, however, is when one is working with both extremes of ability, the retarded and the gifted, and when one is introducing an essentially academically oriented program in some subject such as reading or math.

The most obvious group of retarded are the Mongoloid or Down's syndrome children, but there are several other conditions that also cause severe retardation. Research has identified a physical cause for some kinds of retardation which, in certain instances, has produced ways of preventing or controlling the severe retardation from having its crippling effects. However, there is no known cure for most types. Although there are some individual variations in ability, it has been traditionally assumed that very few severely retarded would ever be able to read more than a few words or do anything more than the most limited kind of rote counting. Once again, some of the newer educational techniques are producing better results and so judgment must be withheld regarding possibilities for change by the severely mentally retarded. Certainly the great majority will probably never be able to become integrated into the normal classroom (Telford and Sawrey, 1972). There is a great deal of pressure from parents of these children who have not been receiving service to demand for their students a right to an education. Similarly, some of the types of youngsters who had previously been in residential schools or institutions are being transferred back to the community. Some of the more able ones are being moved out of the severely retarded classes into classes for the educable retarded. Even though most of the severely retarded will never be able to function in a regular class, the trend is to arrange the classes for them in conjunction with schools for normal children (Abeson, Bolick, and Hess, 1975). Many of the Down's syndrome children used to die at a relatively early age, few getting past their teen years. With modern drugs, however, they are now living to an older age.

The public school classes for the retarded have traditionally been for the educable mentally retarded (EMR). Most of these children are able to perform academic tasks, although not up to their age level. This is the label that has been under such criticism lately. The question is not whether they are really having difficulty in the regular class; the question is, what can be done about it? An unusually large percentage of the lower socioeconomic and minority groups have ended up in an EMR class. With the more capable, the trend is to put them back into the regular classroom or not remove them in the first place. The challenge is to find ways of getting the needed service to them much earlier and to provide a more comprehensive program of intervention to make it possible for them to remain in the mainstream. Some programs include sending specialists into the homes of EMR children while they are still infants and providing a training program for their parents (who also often have limited educational backgrounds). Results indicate that this can help these children develop faster (Nurturing Intelligence, 1972). Preschool programs are also helping to provide a better transition into the regular school program. Many states are helping to provide special teachers who bring special services to the child in the regular class.

Some of the interventions described under "Sensory Stimulation," "Experiential Stimulation," "Language Development and Speech Correction," and Conceptual Development" are proving helpful. The academic work given to the mentally retarded has traditionally been relatively concrete; as more is learned about educating students to think more abstractly, this may no longer be satisfactory. When classes for the EMR first began, there was a great deal of emphasis on crafts. Unless the craft projects lead back to a more formal academic learning, modern classes now do not use this sort of activity much more often than would classes for the nonretarded of the same age. As previously indicated, the challenge is to find ways of leaving the borderline students in the mainstream and provide the services they need there. There will, however, continue to be a need for special classes for a much smaller number of children (Birch, 1974; Dempsey, 1974; Grzyn-kowicz, 1975; Neff and Pilch, 1975).

There has traditionally been another special group called the "remedial reading group." These children are supposed to be of normal intelligence but have difficulty with traditional academic work, especially reading. Remedial reading groups are not usually funded through Special Education money in the various states. Some of the Title I funds (Federal money provided to help children from underprivileged homes) are being used for remedial reading. Although there is some variation between the programs sponsored from state to state and district to district, nationwide there is an attempt to help certain children who have reading problems with *all* of their academic problems, especially reading.

Another large intervention program is for so-called learning disability (LD) students (sometimes called programs for the learning and behavior disordered, LBD). Although there are some variations, the general category is one in which the students have normal ability (or at least do not qualify for classes for the educable retarded) but they are having difficulty with their academic work. Many also have some behavioral problems, quite often associated with hyperactivity. Many others of them will have some perceptual problems which will prevent them from integrating the visual stimuli which they receive into a meaningful whole.

There is an exploding technology of ways of helping the "learning disability" type of child to learn. Many states have both full-time classes and a tutoring type of program; the early emphasis was on the special classes, but the trend is to leave these students in their normal setting and bring a special teacher to them. Under the tutoring model, they are usually seen from three to five hours a week, either alone or in very small groups. The objective is to enable them to function more capably in their regular classroom. Some states have a limit on how long a student can remain in an LD (or LBD) program. The intention of this ruling was to get help to them as soon as possible, but also to try to get them to the point where they no longer need special help (Blackwell and Joynt, 1972; Glaser, 1974; Hammill and Bartel,

1975; Kirk and McCarthy, 1975; Kozloff, 1974).

A group of students who needed "remedial reading" had been identified in many school settings throughout the country (Ekwali, 1970). The overlap between this group and those that are now called "learning disabled" is great. Some districts, with the perennial shortage of money, would not take students for remedial reading unless they had normal or better ability. The logic that those who were borderline in ability did not need or deserve as much help as those who were of average or above average ability is hard to justify. One of the problems with remedial reading, for example, is getting material that has a low enough reading level but has a sufficiently high interest level that it appeals to this type of child. There was a period of rapid development of specialized instructional materials for this purpose (i.e. Colemena, Berres, Hewett and Briscoe, n.d.; Darby, 1966) but this material does not seem to be used as much as it once was. Other curriculum specialists (Engelmann and Osborn, 1970; Gattegno, 1962) have tried to approach the complicated reading task with unique instructional programs.

Still another group that would come under this intervention category would be the gifted (Burt, 1975; Concannon, 1957; Syphers, 1972). The problems and promises of working with this group were discussed under the placement/grouping section in the last chapter. Conceivably, however, all students at one time or another would come to a subject or level in which they would need some extra academic/intellectual help. Many of the skills which have been developed in working with the exceptional child can now be used to help the normal student over a period of difficulty.

Competition

Because of its potentially harmful affects, there is a great deal of argument about whether or not school personnel should introduce and encourage competition. There is little question that it is used extensively in our culture: in business, in sports, and in almost every other sphere of life. The strength of the intervention makes it potentially very valuable if used properly. The main consideration seems to be in finding ways to get two students or teams that are going to compete to be as equal as possible before they start. Certainly one way that this can be done is to have a student compete against his/her own past performance. He/she can try to work faster, work more problems, or try to improve the quality of his/her work.

Although it may not be technically called competition, it is generally helpful to students (and especially those with specific needs) to find some way for them to be aware that they are making good progress. Good teaching breaks learning into such fine steps that it is sometimes difficult for children to see their progress. There are many other ways of helping to show this progress: saving a set of papers from the first of the year and handing them back to be compared with end-of-year work; or, in the elementary years, the teacher can compare work students are doing currently with the work being done by the next lower class. Older students can be encouraged to keep a "personal advancement" chart; this works best in subjects where advancement can be easily changed into numbers such as the "words per minute" measure used in typing classes. Some healthy use of competition against past performance produces an increased rate of learning.

When teachers are planning competition between groups, they should equalize the groups on some sort of a pretest measurement. Names of students could be rank ordered on the basis of their scores and every third or fourth one (depending on how many groups are needed) put into separate groups. Letting students choose team members can also help in this regard. Another way to even out the groups is to give one individual or group a "handicap" based upon past performance. Group A has received an average score of 7 over the last three tests; Group B has averaged 10. Competition starts with the understanding that the handicap score of 3 will be added to the final score obtained by Group A. There are a variety of somewhat more complicated ways of equating the scores that would challenge older students, e.g. transformation into standard scores, in their attempt to set up a good handicap system.

Some students who have constantly "lost" in the process of

competing in academic/intellectual areas may become "all tied up in knots" when competition is introduced. Although some anxiety and tension are helpful to most learning, when tension gets beyond a certain level it does more harm than good. The corrective/remedial situation should probably minimize competition, but once the student comes to that point where he/she will have to work with the regular group (without extra help), some controlled reintroduction of the use of competition is probably a good idea.

Some of the gaming/simulation activities which will be discussed in Chapter 6 use games where the outcomes are "rigged" so that either a preselected group always wins, as in the game of "Star Power," or, for younger children, "Powderhorn" (see Shirts, n.d.). In other games, those who compete always lose and those who cooperate always win (as in "Win As Much As You Can," see Pfeiffer and Jones, Vol. 2, 1974, pp. 66-70). Whether the results are "rigged" or not, competition will occasionally bring out some openly hostile feelings. The teacher who uses competition will have to be ready for this and have a plan for dealing with it. Rather than avoiding situations which produce this hostility, it is usually preferable to bring the feelings out into the open and work them through.

When one talks about competition, the question is raised, "What are we competing for?, i.e. "What is the prize?" When students are competing against themselves, of course, no prize is necessary. There tends to be enough excitement in the process of competition in general that it also reduces the need for a prize. This is especially true if the interest in the subject is fairly high to begin with and the competition is not too one-sided. For other situations, some sort of "prize" is indicated. For corrective/remedial groups the prize may have to start off being quite tangible (see the subsequent section on reinforcement), but it should be related to social praise as much as possible. The winners get a certain amount of "free time" while the losers have to perform some undesirable (but socially useful) task, etc. For older students, competition which can be directed to "real life" events and rewards is very good: the cosmetology students who are competing in class to see who will pass the state boards with the highest score, the students competing for better scores on the written exam for a driver's license, and the like. In short, although there are risks involved in using competition, the process can be very motivating if it is controlled so that it is not damaging to the less competitive child.

Physical/Medical Stimulation

The clearest use of medical stimulation within the context of this section would be to prescribe a stimulant for certain types of depression. Although used quite extensively with adults, this is not done very often with students. At one time there was a great deal of interest in prescribing thyroid medication for hypoactive children, with only minimal results, and this type of intervention is now seldom used. Endocrinology, the field of medicine that deals with this kind of medical problem, does not seem to be actively working on learning-related problems at this time. The closely related intervention of making certain that children have an appropriate nutritional background for appropriate learning is still useful, but even here it is hard to identify interventions that directly affect the learning process.

So-called "psychic energizers" were designed to help students focus their attention better. If medication could help in this regard, i.e. help students focus their attention for longer periods of time, it would probably be a helpful strategy; but the results to date are not impressive. Others are experimenting with megavitamin therapy in which massive doses of vitamins (in some cases many times the minimum daily requirements) are being tried. There has probably not been enough research either to encourage or to discourage this type of intervention. Further research progress in this area should be undertaken.

Whereas medical stimulation of depressed children in the traditional sense is not followed extensively, it is interesting to note that many hyperactive children have what is called a "paradoxical reaction" to many medications. This means that what would normally serve as a stimulant will actually serve to calm these children. This is offered as evidence of a basic chemical imbalance in the student. In that regard, probably one of the most frequently used drugs for students with learning problems is Dexidrene®. This is normally considered to be a stimulant, but it seems to have a calming effect on some students and it also appears to help them concentrate more and thus to learn better (Gittelman-Klein, 1976).

There are, of course, whole families of drugs being tried with children with learning problems; the field is very complex. Obviously educators should never try to prescribe medication for a child. Concern over the amount of medication given to children is mounting. Some litigation has been introduced which would seriously limit the amount of drugs that could be used. For some time it appeared that even though some had negative side effects, they might lead to a major breakthrough, but interest in them seems to be diminishing. However, there is a new, related interest in giving hyperactive children caffein, either in a pill or in coffee. Instead of having the stimulating effect it has on most people, there is some evidence that this has an overall calming effect. Caffein merits consideration, since there would be very few side effects and it probably would be accepted by more people who fear the "controlling" aspect of more severe drugs.

There is also a whole series of medical interventions which have as their goal encouraging or maintaining the physical health of the child. Although these are beyond the scope of this book, it should be understood that for learning to take place it has to make some imprint or some change in the physical body (in many ways when something new is learned what actually occurs physically is unknown). Educators should be constantly alert to medical/physical conditions in the classroom which impede normal physiological growth but also (and in the context of this book, more importantly) pay attention to those factors which can be related to the child's approach to learning (Haslam and Valletutti, 1975; Kalafatich, 1975; Peterson and Cleveland, 1975).

Obviously students need to eat, but it is too often taken for granted that children are getting enough food to actively support good learning. What makes this strategy more complicated is the fact that there are undoubtedly nutritional deficiencies in the same school where large amounts of food are wasted (Screening Children for Nutritional Status, 1971). As would be expected, the problem is complicated by factors of poverty and ethnic identity (Bullough and Bullough, 1975).

The importance of physical growth and maturation as a "backdrop" for learning has been discussed elsewhere (in the section on preschool development and earlier in this section under Sensory Experience). In addition to nutrition, children need a well-developed curriculum in physical education which enhances intellectual development (Means and Appelquist, 1974). Too often physical education in the elementary school takes the form of allowing the children to "go play." In the intermediate and high schools frequently only the most physically gifted students get to play (thirty students, one ball, one player, and everyone waits). Elementary schools need a great deal more sophistication in building movement into their curriculum (Barsch, 1965; Frostig, 1970). Attention span is closely related to the physiological functioning of the young child. For children in the middle school and later, there needs to be thought given to corrective and remedial programs in the area of physical education both for their potential contribution to the physical functioning of the child and because of its close relationship to the student's feelings of self-worth.

REDUCING STIMULATION

In addition to the interventions attempting to stimulate a response by *adding* something to the life of a student, other interventions involve *reducing* the amount of stimulation in a student's life. In general, these interventions involving reducing stimulation are used with students who are overstimulated or with the student who is unable to "sort out" all of the incoming stimuli that surrounds him/her. Normal development helps most children learn to "attend" to some signals and to ignore others. One factor which some hyperactive students display quite often is the difficulty of focusing their attention on the most important "signals" or details. In almost every situation, and especially in a classroom full of students, there are a lot of extraneous noises which most students learn to shut out. A good example of such a situation is when a student learns to study in spite of a noisy radio blaring in the background. There is even some evidence to indicate that when one has become used to a specific noise while concentrating, then one will need that noise to help focus attention.

A person can pay attention to any number of factors as long as all of them have become routine except one. One of the authors learned this lesson as a high school student when he atended an assembly which featured a "mental genius," who illustrated this fact by doing the following three or four things at one time: quoting from Shakespeare, juggling balls, and computing the square roots of numbers called to him from the audience. He clearly demonstrated how he had made some of these factors routine so that he could do them "in his sleep," without thinking. This left him free to really focus his attention on just one task. Some students are so disorganized that they can never make anything truly routine, so almost any stimulus produces an "overload" to the point that their ability to "attend" is seriously reduced.

Another illustration is the common task of driving a car. The law in most countries requires one to drive on the right side of the road. When this becomes automatic, the driver can drive down the road and carry on a conversation while at the same time thinking about other things. While driving, the driver does not have to make a decision every time a car is approached, "Am I going to pass on the right or on the left?" (Although this must be decided when one drives in England or Japan.) If drivers had to keep making these decisions it would take all of their energy and concentration and any conversation would be very distracting.

Obviously, one of the great distractions to many students comes from the complex, social stimuli in the average classroom. For most students these reinforce good learning; for others, they only serve to confuse the student and cut down learning efficiency. Some students respond to the difficulty of sorting out the stimuli by getting nervous and hyperactive; others become explosive and violent. In either case, the intervention should involve some technique of cutting down on the amount of stimulation that is affecting the student.

The following should be considered: No one focuses his/her attention completely on any subject for a long period of time. This is especially true for things that are either boring or very difficult to understand. The reader is encouraged to stop for a moment and think of the lapses (sometimes called "birdwalks") in attention he/she has had in just the last few minutes. Most individuals learn to "cut in" and to "cut out" with sufficient ease and efficiency that they know what they are reading or what the other person is saying, and so learning takes place. Each of us learns to identify very subtle clues, such as pauses in speech, raised eyebrows, or underlined words which signal the listener/reader to refocus on these subtle cues. It is effective for the person trying to help such students to introduce other, more forceful, cues, e.g. a sound signal or touching the person's arm, which will help the distracted student switch back to the important instructions or ideas that are about to be introduced. Again, good teachers have learned to do this instinctively; others will have to concentrate on it as an effective intervention skill.

Time Out

There has been a great deal of talk in recent years about an intervention called "time out." In the elementary classroom it might involve a special area or "box" or may be simply another seat; for older students it might be another room or area in the building. When students become disruptive, they are sent to the "time out" place for either a predetermined length of time or until they can control themselves again. There are some parallels in "time out" to holding of young students who are having temper tantrums until they can regain control of themselves. Although some may see this as a punishment (and there is something in the competitiveness of the American society that tends to make many of us see it that way), the model is essentially one of reducing the amount of stimuli and helping students calm down before they come back to resume work. The interventionists should be clear in their thinking; if they really are using the action as punishment (which, as will be described later, is a much-used intervention), then they should make this clear to the student. Some schools serving older students will often try to locate a specific place or room for this purpose.

Many teachers, sensing that a particular student is "about to blow" will use a variation of the intervention technique and will send him/her off on some sort of an errand, both to "change the pace" and to reduce the amount of frustration and overstimulation the student is facing in the classroom. Although trying to do this for all students would be prohibitively time-consuming, the teacher soon learns that such corrective/remedial interventions are only needed for a very small percentage of students. However, some teachers may be more sensitive than others to the kind of fidgeting in a student that signals the introduction of a stimulus reduction intervention (Swift and Spivak, 1975).

Carrels or Offices

Another way of cutting down on the visual stimuli that are impinging on a student at any one time is the use of a small office or carrel. The original research on classes for the so-called "brain damaged" students, stressed the need for a very low-stimulus environment, including the use of cubicles and of opaque windows that let in the light but could not be seen through. Although this is not practical in the regular class and has not been found necessary in most special learning disability classes, the concept of observing students to determine if they are being overstimulated by the class is important. With younger children, it is often possible to introduce such a place for one or two students who are having this kind of difficulty. (A common place in a primary classroom is behind the piano.) When there are classroom discussions going on, however, these students need to be brought out to interact with the other students. They are usually able to adjust to the total-class stimulation for increasing periods of time.

Limited Day

This intervention will work with students of all ages. As in the "time out" technique, both the school staff and the parents have to clarify whether they are trying to help the students by reducing the amount of stimulation on them or whether they are trying to punish them. If the concept is one of cutting down the distraction, the child should be allowed to do what he/she wants when out of school. Parents frequently want to punish or restrict the privileges of the child. The approach should be, "We are here in this school to help you. We are sorry that you cannot take advantage of this help. We are sending you home to help you. We want to make it possible for you to come back and enjoy all the desirable things that are going on in the school. We want you here whenever you can take advantage of them." It is, of course, necessary to work out such an arrangement with, and get permission from, the parents since they will have to be available for supervision. If that is not possible, a "time out room" variation has been found to be satisfactory when it is supervised.

Many children who can handle the classroom are overstimulated by the free play of recess and the playground activities during the lunch period. Identifying substitute activities such as working in the office or with the custodian tends to reduce possible sources of conflict.

As in any technique which takes the student away from the learning environment, use of the limited day is not a good long-range solution. The goal is to go back as soon as possible to where students can spend the whole day in school. A variety of other interventions which will be described next may be needed to help make this possible.

Systematic Exemption

This intervention, also called the "contract method," is an extension of "time out," limited day, etc. It requires that the student be old enough to understand, at least in general terms, what it means to "sign a contract." It seems to work best when there is a question about whether or not the student is really trying hard enough to control his/her own behavior. In essence a contract is signed by the child, the teacher, the principle, or the parents indicating that the adults in the student's life will stop "yelling, nagging, punishing," i.e. will reduce these negative stimuli, if the child agrees to become responsible for his/her behavior. Specific rules are laid down in the contract of what the student will be expected to obey; what signal will be given by the teacher to indicate that it is time for him/her to leave; how he/she will get home; and how long he/she will stay. Needless to say, since this takes a long time to set up, the situation has to be monitored by the interventionist or it can "blow up." It is difficult to use for this and other reasons, but it does take the responsibility from the teacher and put it with the student. A useful analogy for this is that "The responsibility for behaving is like a suitcase: There is only room for one hand on the suitcase handle; when teachers or parents pick it up, it is their responsibility to make the students behave; when they put it down and the students pick it up, they become responsible for their own behavior."

Moratorium

There is a related series of techniques in which either the students or the adults in their lives are encouraged and agree to stop a particular behavior of theirs for a period of time because of a variety of reasons. The behavior can be almost anything that has been contributing to the problem, e.g. "nagging" on the part of the parent, "assigning homework" by the teacher, or "bugging the teacher" on the part of the student. The reasons for using this technique can be varied. An "experimental moratorium" suggests that certain things should be tried out, e.g. see what the student will do when not being either encouraged or "nagged." A diagnostic moratorium indicates "the stopping of doing something to see what will happen," e.g. the teacher agrees to allow the student to stand up while working. A "medical moratorium" is an agreement (after consultation with the child's doctor) to take him/her off medication to see how he/she will get along in school without it.

Some other variations of this intervention are the following: The teacher agrees to stop giving the student tests for a certain period of time. Demands for achievement in some areas are lifted or reduced, so that the student can concentrate and gain success in another specific area of learning. In a more drastic form, the teacher and/or parents may agree to make no attempt to educate the student unless he/she requests help. The teacher stops asking the student to do homework. Even though the student has not completed any assigned work at home for a long time, it is surprisingly difficult for some teachers to accept the fact that they are not going to harm the student by not assigning any.

These moratorium techniques tend to have the common goal of helping the student begin to learn again through the removing of some stimulus which has become counterproductive. In some instances students have so strongly defended their points of view or their actions in response to conditions or requirements placed on them by others, that by removing these requirements the students are able to function again. In other cases parents may be "trying too hard" to help. Sometimes the interventionist is only buying time and will have to find other ways of helping the student get started during the moratorium. In still other instances, the moratorium is created to help a student get through a particularly difficult period of time. Some would hypothesize that during the interim the natural, positive, growth-producing forces within the student tend to start working again and help the student to cope better with the demands on him/her when the moratorium is lifted. Others would stress that the help comes from the positive reinforcement that the student gets for positive actions during the moratorium. Whatever the reason, if the results are good, there is often no need for either party to return to the original behavior.

Limiting Excessive Services

In educators' eagerness to help students they occasionally find that students are getting too many different services at the same time, e.g. remedial reading, counseling, group activities, and the like. In some homes the parents want so much to have the student improve and "make something of himself/herself" that they have lined up a whole array of academic and social experiences which are overwhelming to the student. Some parents who are strongly identified with a different nationality or ethnic group, in their legitimate desire to help their child take advantage of both cultures, send their children to the regular school during the day and to an ethnic school in the afternoon or evening. Sometimes the same thing happens in families with strong religious convictions where the student receives extensive after-school religious instruction. Of course, some students thrive under this extra stimulation. However, if the interventionist determines that the student is overloaded, he/she must convince the parent and the student that it would be best to focus on just one set of learnings at a time.

Relaxation Techniques

A series of procedures for helping students "cut out" or reduce the distractability of the world are coming both from interventionists who are developing desensitization procedures (Clarizio and McCoy, 1970; Hammill and Bartel, 1975) and from the heightened interest of young people in this country in various aspects of yoga and meditation. These have not been used extensively in schools to date but there is enough support coming from the research in two areas to suggest that these are possible corrective/remedial interventions of the future. One area comes from the teaching of controlled breathing (to clear the body of excessive carbon dioxide which collects when one does not breathe deeply enough). The other area, which is in some ways even more complicated, is called biofeedback where some of the basic body functions, including even the basic rhythm of the brain, are capable of being controlled (Paskewitz, 1975). Although biofeedback is being used a great deal in private practice, it will still be a while before it is available to school personnel and even then its use will probably be limited. All of these techniques have the potential of helping students to relax, for example, before taking a major examination.

Medical Destimulation

There has been increased use over the past twenty years of various forms of medication to control the behavior of hyperactive students. Usage of these drugs, popularly called tranquilizers, is quite complex. While many doctors will not prescribe them, others tend to give them to every student no matter what the initial reason for referral. Some of the drugs have strong side effects such as drowsiness. Choosing the correct drug involves a high degree of "trial and error" as the doctor varies types and dosages. Getting consistent results from the medication is another problem because parents sometimes forget to give it to the student, or the student may resist taking it. If the doctor prescribes the medication to be taken at school, there is a problem as to who should actually give it to the child. Usually school nurses, if they are available, can do this with a doctor's order. There is, as previously indicated, a growing public opinion against these drugs, for obvious reasons.

With all of these problems, however, there are many who have been able to remain in school with the help of these different kinds of medications, when otherwise they would have been put out of school. When it gets to this kind of value judgment, drugs look more attractive. Fortunately, in-school techniques are being discovered which are proving just as powerful in aiding learning and with fewer side effects. The so-called "paradoxical reaction" has previously been mentioned; some children have to be given what would ordinarily be considered a stimulant to get "calmed down," and vice versa. These paradoxical interventions should not be ruled out as useful techniques (Gittelman-Klein, 1976; Kameya, 1972).

REINFORCEMENT

Although teachers have always used praise, a powerful reinforcer, its systematic application to the problems of education has been made since approximately 1968. At that time some of the principles of behavior modification or social learning theory began to be applied to a variety of learning and behavior problems both in schools and in a wide variety of other settings in the culture. It has proven to be a tremendously potent type of intervention. Like many other corrective/remedial procedures, some of the behavior modification techniques have application to the regular developmental curriculum for all students. It is, however, in the area of working with students who have had the most severe learning and behavior problems that behavior modification has had the most dramatic results. This is partially because the techniques are probably most effective when applied to building basic skills, such as paying attention or staying in one's seat. Behavior modification is also best in teaching relatively small units of learning, e.g. beginning reading or number facts. It has not been as powerful in the teaching of larger units of thought or in developing some of the humanistic skills described in following chapters. In short, while it has not been as helpful with the average or above-average student, behavior modification has been used to develop a very complete series of ways to work with students of all ages who are having difficulty. The literature is so complete in this area that it would be impossible to list all of it. (See Brown, 1972, for an extensive bibliography of resource material in behavior modification. Other references include: Ackerman, 1972; Blackham and Silberman, 1975; Blackwood, 1971; Brown and Avery, 1974; Buckley and Walker, 1973; Daniels, 1974; Deibert and Harmon, 1973; Hall, 1974; Haring and Phillips, 1972; Harris, 1972; Lovitt, 1973; Macht, 1975; Morreau and Daley, 1972; and Sulzer and Mayer, 1972.)

Any small, discrete, well-defined act or behavior, called the "target behavior," has three components. Certain acts, behaviors, or cues have preceded the target behavior. Out of all the myriad sounds, syllables, or cues available to a person at any one point in time, there are certain ones which have "triggered" or elicited the target behavior. Teachers either have or can gain control over many of the academic factors which precede the specific target behavior in question. Some of the factors, such as stimulation by other students, are much harder to define and control. Teachers can, however, "arrange the conditions of learning" in such a way as to increase desirable behaviors and decrease undesirable, unproductive ones.

This suggests that there are two major types of target behaviors which are as follows: those that contribute to the learning of the student (these should be increased) and those that get in the way of their learning (these should be decreased). Many complex behaviors can be separated into separate or discrete parts, which in turn, can be arranged in such a way as to progress toward the larger, more complex behavior. The more the total behavioral goal and the separate parts are based upon an appropriate understanding of the developmental aspects of growth and learning, and the more they can be related to the personal goals and understanding level of the student who is involved, the less pressure has to be exerted and the faster the learning can take place. It is artificial either to separate social learning from academic learning, or learning problems from behavior problems; they are all parts of the same process.

As soon as the target behavior occurs, it should be reinforced either positively, if an increase in the behavior is desired (described here under the heading "Reinforcement") or negatively, if the behavior should be "decelerated" or decreased (described in the next section under the heading "Punishment"). When the factors which trigger the target behavior cannot be identified or controlled, the interventionist waits until the behavior (or a close proximity of it) occurs, and then reinforces it in an appropriate manner. When the separate steps which lead toward the more complex act or behavior are difficult to arrange, a system of "successive approximations" is used in which any behavior which represents the closest approximation of the desired behavior is reinforced (Sarason, Glaser and Fargo, 1971). These techniques are being used to train some laboratory animals to do increasingly complex acts. Whenever possible it is desirable to reinforce a response that is incompatible with what one is trying to eliminate (Krumboltz and Krumboltz, 1972).

Behavior modification techniques are relatively simple but unquestionably powerful. Few would argue with the right and the responsibility of the school to "arrange the conditions" to increase effective learning. The problem comes in deciding how much "right" or "say" the students have in determining what the most appropriate goals are for them. How much "right" do students have to resist the interventionist from trying to "control" them? There is enough power in the technique and enough question about this right to control that the use of behavior modification programs has been prohibited in some areas. There is sufficient question that it is probably inadvisable to undertake a stringent behavior modification program with either a total group or an individual unless one has gained the "informed consent" of the student and/or his/her parents. There is unquestionably a middle ground between the behavior modification techniques and the goals of humanistic education that will be described in the following chapters. Educators will have to keep working to make certain that they can find and make use of that middle ground in the specific areas of learning where they want to use these techniques (Trotters and Warren, 1974; Wexler, 1973).

Tangible Rewards

When research with reinforcement techniques was first begun, there was a great emphasis on specific, tangible rewards such as candy or prizes. In fact it becomes known as the "M and M™ Technique" in certain parts of the country. As someone said, "The student is learning very rapidly but he/she won't have any teeth left because of all of the candy." Educators soon learned that other kinds of reinforcement produced just as desirable results. Obviously, whatever is chosen to reinforce desirable behavior has to be considered desirable by the student. A tangible reward may still have to be used with young children or with the very severe cases until other reinforcers can be substituted which have the same effect. It may be necessary to establish a "good behavior clock" (Swift and Spivak, 1975, pp. 125-126) so each minute a child is working, he/she gets some reward (also see Kubany, Weiss, and Sloggett, 1971). There is a long list of tangible rewards that includes the following: candy, raisins, breakfast cereal (especially the sweetened variety), plus a variety of toys and trinkets. It is important that the student be given warm, honest verbal praise at the same time that the tangible reward is given. Ultimately students will no longer need the tangible reward and will be able to function with normal amounts of praise (Carter, 1972).

Tokens

This intervention includes any system where marks or tokens are given which can be traded in for something the student wants.

These include the following: marks on a score card, poker chips, trading stamps, stars, and similar items. Almost anything that can be allocated to the student to indicate specific progress toward a predetermined goal can be used. What the tokens can be traded for varies with the age of the child and the amount of money available. One person, working with high school dropouts, took them on "shopping tours" in the department stores of the city (which unfortunately turned into "shoplifting" tours on occasion) to identify what it was that the student wanted (Schwitzgebel, 1967). In general, it is probably best to have a small variety of things for which the tokens can be traded. The rewards can require different numbers of tokens, and students can choose their own goals toward which to work.

One system for involving the parents in this process, which would help to make the procedure economically more practical, involves a "checking account." Students earn points or "money" by working in the school situation. The teacher then fills in a "check" indicating that the student has earned a certain amount for each day. When the fund gets large enough, the parents buy whatever they and the child have agreed upon as a reward (Stainback, Payne, Stainback, and Payne, 1973; Walker and Buckley, 1974) .

Money

An extension of the above two reinforcers is the use of money. This differs from "paying students for learning" in that, instead of paying by the hour, the student earns money for specific steps of progress. As one would expect, the amount of money needed to be reinforcing varies with the age of the student. In some studies, severely disadvantaged high school and college youths have been motivated to go all the way through college on this system. It is essential that the student be involved in setting up such long-range goals. There is nothing quite so validating in the American culture as being paid; of course the money can, in some instances, also supply older students with some of the necessities of life (Payne, 1976) .

Peer Recognition

In this category would be classified a whole group of ways of helping the student to earn special privileges. The focus is on the effect that these privileges have in the eyes of other students. This type of peer relationship is especially important with older students. Examples are special responsibilities or duties, opportunity to do a special project away from school, and anything that is considered desirable by both the student and the peer group. An interesting variation for younger children is the earning of "points" for their progress, which in turn leads toward a class party. This procedure gets many students involved in encouraging their peers to succeed; a student's productive behavior becomes the "trigger" for total group approval. Another variation is to reinforce the helping behaviors of the remainder of the class for helping a particular student. There seems to be an almost limitless variety of ways to use this kind of procedure (Solomon and Wahler, 1973; Swift and Spivak, 1975).

Free Time

Some teachers are afraid that they do not have enough reinforcers at their disposal to utilize this approach. Free time is an illustration of how educators "aimlessly" give away reinforcers in schools. If the free time involves the opportunity to leave school, use of this approach would be quite applicable to older students. Younger children, however, could spend their free time in approved ways within the school. A score card or tab sheet could be used to tally the earned points, which could be paid off at some predetermined time or whenever the student wanted it. There is something magical about having an amount of saved up time. In some cases, students have become so "hooked" on having free time that they never actually use it; they just keep "storing it up."

Attention

Students win the attention of the teacher, other students, another interventionist, their parents, or any other adult that is significant in their lives. One of the most powerful events for some physically active young boys, for instance, is to earn the privilege of having a "wrestling match" with their father. The basic, gut-level affection seems to come through better in this instance than it does through words. One of the great strengths of the whole rein-forcement approach is to help teachers and parents realize that in many instances they are putting all of their attention on the nega-tive or "bad" behavior of the child and in most instances a shift of emphasis to where they are paying attention primarily to what the student is doing "right" produces good results. When tied in with a problem that the student has previously helped to identify and when the attention comes after an honest effort on the part of the child, it is even more reinforcing. To put it another way, we all like to be praised (at least it is preferable to being "bawled out"), but it is much more meaningful and helpful to come at a time when we feel that we have made a good effort and have produced good results (Broden, Bruce, Mitchell, Carter, and Hall, 1971; Swift and Spivak, 1975).

Contingency Contracting

One special variation on these reinforcement strategies which bears specific mention is a technique known as "contingency man-agement." In its simplest form, this is the process of allowing children to do something that they want to do following some-thing that the teacher wants them to do (Homme, 1973). An ex-ample might be: After the student completes the homework, he/ she can watch television. In school, it might be that after com-pleting math, they can do independent activities. Again hopefully what the teacher asks them to do is something they are able to do and that is in their best interests, not simply something the teacher is trying to force upon them. What students are allowed to do depends upon their age, the subject area, the conditions prevailing in the educational situation, and the amount of time and money available. Any reinforcer discussed in other parts of this section can be used. There is a great deal of evidence that this approach works for lower-achieving students (Barnett, 1973); there is still some question about whether or not it will work with all students or with more normally developing groups (Nelson and Jones, 1970).

As a rule of thumb, however, it is well for the teacher to think through those things which the children want to do and those which they should do but for which they lack any real motivation. Then the instructional strategy is to allow the students to do the things they want to do once they have completed some of the less motivating tasks. Although teachers have been doing this for a long time, current research has indicated when and how it can be most effectively used (Homme and Tosti, 1971).

Praise

As indicated throughout, when more "artificial" reinforcers are used, they should be accompanied with strong, warm, verbal praise. Gradually the tangible reward is only given intermittently, having the effect of reinforcing good behavior over longer periods of time. The ultimate goal is to help students respond to and keep motivated by the normal reinforcing activities of the school, i.e. praise and attention. Someone may say that grades are the primary way of reinforcing students. This is probably true for some average students and many above-average ones, but the students needing corrective remedial help are usually not "turned on" by them. Once they can get started again and begin to feel some personal satisfaction from their progress, reasonable amounts of praise from their peers and teachers will go a long way toward keeping them motivated (Buys, 1972; Carter, 1972; Friedman, 1973).

PUNISHMENT

Punishment has been used a great deal in the schools (and indeed in the whole of society); some people have felt that punishment is the only intervention that is used. As a means of changing or improving behavior, the punishment that the schools "hand out" tends to be ineffective. Research with animals supports evidence that although the behavior one is trying to get rid of seems to go away at first, it tends to come back again. The unusually high percentage of prisoners who have to return to prison indicates that this may also be true in higher animals. Another reason that undesirable behavior returns is that it is ex-

tremely difficult in a complex school to administer the punishment consistently enough, immediately after the behavior, and
with sufficient intensity to make it an effective procedure. A third
reason why it has not been very effective is that punishment is
often accompanied with feelings of hostility on the part of the student toward the person administering the punishment. In the
typical principal or assistant principal/student relationship, there
is little opportunity to constructively work through a hostility
associated with being "paddled" to get back to more positive feelings as there would be in the parent/child relationship. The risk
that is taken is that, for older male youths particularly (which is
where most of the punishment takes place), educators may alienate
the youth from the school as well as from the total society (Clark,
1974; Farson, 1974).

Added to the above reasons contributing to the ineffectiveness
of punishment are the growing movements from both the courts
and the teaching profession itself, to do away with corporal punishment. Much of the punishment that is carried out is done under
provisions of standing *in loco parentis* (in place of parents). This
is the same "authority" that has been used to put students into special classes without parental permission and to expel students from
school. In all instances these so-called "rights of the school," are
being eroded. One United States District Court (in Virginia) has
ruled that paddling in school violates a child's civil rights (Landmark decision: Judge recognizes children's rights, 1974); others
are sure to follow. In the meantime the report of the National
Education Association (1972) Task Force on Corporal Punishment represents a strong position against the use of corporal punishment in the schools. Several large districts (Boston, New
York, St. Paul, and Washington, D.C.) do not indicate any adverse
effects from outlawing corporal punishment. Three states—
Massachusetts, Maryland, and New Jersey—have also stopped using
it. To help other districts come to this same conclusion, studies
are needed concerning what happens when this type of punishment is abolished (Violence against Children, 1973).

Many school counselors and school psychologists, who have
been convinced that most punishment in schools is at best inef-

fective and often completely wrong, have stood up against it. Because of this they are often seen as too permissive or "spineless" in an environment that uses punishment excessively. It has been described in this system of interventions because it is used so extensively by schools. If it is to continue to be used, punishment will be most effective in the following situations: when it comes as a *natural consequence* of the student's behavior; it is administered as *humanely and objectively* as possible; it comes as *close as possible* to the act for which the student is being punished; and is reserved for students who are *testing the limits,* but have a great deal of personal strength.

Another intervention related to punishment which has not been used very much but which might have usefulness with younger students, is called the *exhaustion* method. Exhaustion has probably been used most effectively with eliminating behaviors that have previously been forbidden. The method involves using behavior that has been pleasurable to the student and require the student to repeat it so many times that it becomes unpleasant. The classical example (which would preferably take place out of school) is to force the child who has been caught playing with matches to light and extinguish a large box of them one by one. Some young children, who have used spitting as a way of "getting back" at other children, have been helped to stop with the exhaustion method.

A related strategy is called *extinction* (Hammill and Bartel, 1975); it has been used to reduce excessive talking, tantrum behavior, and academic errors. The approach is to withdraw all reinforcers, such as in the case of ignoring the temper tantrums of young children. One of the powerful aspects of behavior modification is the positive attention paid to certain behavior in specific ways often makes it unnecessary to attend to or punish unacceptable behaviors.

Punishment and reward are closely interrelated in the sense that they both manipulate the application of pleasant and unpleasant consequences. They can be "added," promised but "never delivered," or "taken away." Table 5-III, listing these variables, is given below. In the previous section the term *rein-*

forcement has been used to mean the giving of a pleasant response, or positive reinforcement. It also shows the true meaning of negative reinforcement as the taking away of an unpleasant stimulus.

TABLE 5-III

POSITIVE VERSUS NEGATIVE REINFORCEMENT

	Something Pleasant	*Something Unpleasant*
Add to	Positive Reinforcement (Reward)	Pain (Punishment)
Failure to Deliver	Disappointment (Punishment)	Relief (Reward)
Take Away	Deprivation (Punishment)	Negative Reinforcement (Reward)

Failure to Deliver a Reward

It is important to remember that one does not have to actually add or take away something in order to produce punishment. The failure to deliver a positive reinforcement that has been promised can cause punishment in the form of disappointment and will therefore tend to reduce the accompanying behavior in the future. This is probably another reason why underprivileged people are so often difficult to motivate; they have been promised so many things (either explicitly or implicitly) that they have never received, that it is difficult for them to try to work toward another goal.

Withdrawal of Something Pleasant

The obvious application of this is the taking away of grades, prizes, honors, and similar incentives. Fines of money could be considered a subclassification. Another major category would be the attempt to reduce social support for the actions of a student. One major problem with the discipline often used in the school is that, although, it is unpleasant at the moment, the "culprit" often gets a lot of silent approval (and sometimes not so silent) from his/her friends. For some, the peer approval is needed so much or is such a powerful reinforcer that he/she is willing to risk the punishment in order to get the approval.

One powerful intervention for helping out in such a situation is to get the peers to withdraw their social support and even their attention. Some of the techniques described in the next chapters will be helpful in this regard. In our "other-directed" culture, one needs to find more techniques which will reduce the amount of support for negative behavior, especially with older students. Isolating or restricting students can also be used. For younger students, a special section of the room can be used. For older students, a special room, the principal's office, or detention might be used. One problem with all these strategies is that it is difficult to know whether or not the student is obtaining social support for the misbehavior. If the intervention actually takes away the social support, it would fit under this category. Inasmuch as what the teacher requires the student to do is seen as an unpleasant activity, it would be classified as negative reinforcement. Another major problem with using this type of "discipline" is that it frequently is difficult to tell whether the total effect is considered "good" or "bad" by the student.

Introducing Something Unpleasant

The growing problems concerning corporal punishment in the schools have already been discussed. Less physical punishments can, of course, also be used; e.g. sarcasm, ridicule, "bawling the student out," or asking parents to come in. Whenever educators have to punish students, it should be made clear to the students that they continue to validate or approve of them as a person, but what they disapprove of is their behavior. Unfortunately, this is a difficult distinction to make, both for the person handing out the punishment and for the one receiving it. Again, some of the techniques described later will suggest other approaches to be used when students do "get out of line."

Suspensions and expulsions represent other techniques for punishing students. Whether suspensions and expulsions should be classified under the "Withdrawal of Something Pleasant" or under the "Introduction of Something Unpleasant" depends upon the way the student views school. Most students, even those that get into the most trouble, generally enjoy the social climate of school, although they will often not admit it. If there is *nothing* in the school, that the student likes (assignments, boring work, artificial rules), and if there is *something* on the outside that they do like (friends, TV, the chance to loaf), then being expelled can reinforce whatever behavior started the process. Of course many administrators are thinking of the large remaining group of students and may have to make the practical decision that they had better "get rid" of the *one* to save the *many*. Even though this decision is done to help the majority, it has to be taken against an individual, and his/her best interests must be weighed (Corporal punishment is an issue, 1974).

Court actions are, once again, attacking school practices which "take away the students' rights to schooling" without adequate attention to "due process" procedures *(Goss v. Lopez, 1975)*. There is little question that even the first suspension reduces the chance that the student will finish high school. Furthermore, this process of putting the student out of school takes away from the school an opportunity to positively reinforce desirable behavior. The recent Supreme Court action noted above clearly indicates that the student cannot be put out of school for just any reason without a proper hearing.

Although a lot of use of corporal punishment in schools has been made, educators have not experimented very much with introducing other unpleasant stimuli to students. Some parents have made use of a mild electric shock for children who wet their beds, with fair results. It might also be possible to introduce unpleasant sounds to students when they make a wrong response, if it could be done without disturbing the other students (with earphones, for instance). Squirting water in the face has been used in some experimental classrooms, but such strategies are seldom used.

Negative Reinforcement

Since administering an unpleasant stimulus is difficult in the first place, negative reinforcement (which technically refers to the taking away of an unpleasant or noxious stimulus) is not very practical in the school situation. In experimental schools working with severely disturbed children, where mild electric shocks are used to help children stop doing such things as biting themselves, the withholding of the electric shock in precise ways would be an example of the use of this intervention (Lovaas and Simmons, 1969). An analogy in a regular school might be when an interventionist convinces other students to stop their teasing or "picking on" another student in question when he/she makes an undesirable response (assuming that the student saw the teasing as obnoxious and did not enjoy the attention he or she was getting from the other students).

In summary, although punishment has produced a great many problems as a corrective/remedial intervention (Maurer, 1974), it continues to be used extensively (Hall, Axelrod, Foundopoulos, Shellman, Campbell, and Cranston, 1972). Working with highly disruptive students in the school setting is a major problem for which there is no simple answer (Madsen and Madsen, 1970). It appears as though educators have clung to punishment techniques even though their usefulness is seriously challenged. In lieu of traditional punishment techniques, educators must all work together to find a variety of other strategies and interventions for helping students. In addition to the techniques that have already been discussed, some of the humanizing techniques that follow point encouragingly to possible solutions.

REFERENCES

Abeson, A., Bolick, N., & Hess, J. *A primer on due process: Education decisions for handicapped children.* Reston: The Council for Exceptional Children, 1975.

Ackerman, J. M. *Operant conditioning techniques for the classroom teacher.* Glenview, Il.: Scott Foresman, 1972.

Arena, J. I. (Ed). *Teaching through sensory-motor experiences.* Belmont: Fearon Publishers, 1969.

A very special child: Conference on placement of children in special education programs for the mentally retarded. Washington, D. C.: President's

Commission on Mental Retardation, 1972.

Barnett, J. B. *Effects of self-management instruction and contingency management to increase completion of work.* Unpublished doctoral dissertation, The Ohio State University, 1973.

Barsch, R. H. *A movigenic curriculum.* Madison: Wisconsin State Department of Public Instruction, 1965.

Beach, R. G. *Help in school: Establishment of a paraprofessional program.* Philadelphia: Dorrance, 1973.

Bereiter, C. *Must we educate?* Englewood Cliffs: Prentice-Hall, 1974.

Bereiter, C., & Englemann, S. *Teaching disadvantaged children in the preschool.* Englewood Cliffs: Prentice-Hall, 1966.

Birch, J. W. *Mainstreaming: Educable mentally retarded children in regular classes.* Reston: Council for Exceptional Children, 1974.

Blackham, G. J., & Silberman, A. *Modification of child and adolescent behavior* (2nd ed.). Belmont: Wadsworth, 1975.

Blackwood, R. O. *Operant control of behavior: Elimination of misbehavior; motivation of children.* Akron: Exordium Press, 1971.

Blackwell, R. B., & Joynt, R. R. *Learning disabilities handbook for teachers.* Springfield: Charles C Thomas, 1972.

Blank, M. Implicit assumptions underlying preschool intervention programs. *Journal of Social Issues,* 1970, *26,* 15-33.

Blumberg, H. M. *A program of sequential language development: A theoretical and practical guide for remediation of langauge, reading, and learning disorders.* Springfield: Charles C Thomas, 1975.

Bower, E. M. *Learning to play: Playing to learn.* New York: Behavioral Publications, 1976.

Broden, M., Bruce, C., Mitchell, M. A., Carter, V., & Hall, R. Effects of teacher attention on attending behavior of two boys in an adjacent desk. *Journal of Applied Behavior Analysis,* 1971, *4,* 191-199.

Brown, A. R., & Avery, C. (Eds.). *Modifying children's behavior: A book of readings.* Springfield: Charles C Thomas, 1974.

Brown, D. G. *Behavior modification in child, school, and family mental health: An annotated bibliography.* Champaign: Research Press, 1972.

Browning, A. W. *Optimizing individual instruction.* Centerville, Oh.: Centerville City Schools, 1974.

Buckley, N. K., & Walker, H. M. *Modifying classroom behavior* (6th ed.). Champaign: Research Press, 1973.

Bullough, B., & Bullough, V. L. *Poverty, ethnic identity, and health care.* West Nyack, N. Y.: Prentice-Hall, 1975.

Burt, C. *The gifted child.* London: Hodden & Stoughton, 1975.

Buys, C. J. Effects of teacher reinforcement on elementary pupil's behavior and attitudes. *Psychology in the Schools,* 1972, *9,* 278-288.

Carter, B., & Dapper, G. *School volunteers: What they do. How they do it.* New York: Citation Press, 1972.

Carter, R. *Help! These kids are driving me crazy.* Champaign: Research Press, 1972.

Catterall, C. D. *Interprofessional communication in identifying the educationally handicapped child.* San Jose, Ca.: Curriculum Associates, 1967.

Catterall, C. D. (Guest Ed.). Special education in transition: Implications for school psychology. *Journal of School Psychology*, 1972, *10*, 91-98.

Champagne, D. W., & Goldman, R. M. *Teaching parents teaching.* New York: Appleton-Century-Crofts, 1972.

Christine, R. O. Pupil-pupil teaching and learning team. *Education*, 1971, *91*, 258-260.

Clark, K. B. *Pathos of power.* New York: Harper & Row, 1974.

Clarizio, H. F., & McCoy, G. M. *Behavior disorders in school aged children.* Scranton: Chandler, 1970.

Cohen, S. I., Keyworth, J.M., Kleiner, R. I., & Libert, J. M. *The support of school behaviors by home-based reinforcement via parent-child contingency contracts.* Greenbelt, Md.: Behavior Science Consultants, 1971.

Colemena, J. H., Berres, F., Hewett, F. M., & Briscoe, W. S. *The deep sea adventure series.* Palo Alto: Field Educational Publications (n.d.).

Concannon, S. M. J. *Relationship of actual achievement to potential achievement in reading and study skills of gifted and average pupils.* Unpublished doctoral dissertation, Boston College, 1957.

Corporal punishment is an issue. *The American School Board Journal*, 1974.

Cull, J. G., & Hardy, R. H. (Eds.). *Problems of disadvantaged and deprived youth.* Springfield: Charles C Thomas, 1975.

Daniels, L. K. *The management of childhood behavior problems in school and at home.* Springfield: Charles C Thomas, 1974.

Danish, S. J., & Hauer, A. L. *Helping skills: A basic training program.* New York: Behavioral Publications, 1973.

Darby, G. *The time machine series.* Palo Alto, Ca.: Field Educational Publications, 1966.

Dempsey, J. J. (Ed.). *Community services for retarded children.* Baltimore: University Park Press, 1974.

Deno, E. Special Education as developmental capital. *Exceptional Children*, 1970, *37*, 236.

Deibert, A. N., & Harmon, A. J. *New tools for changing behavior* (6th ed.). Champaign: Research Press, 1973.

Ebersole, M., Kephart, N. C., & Ebersole, J. B. *Steps to achievement for the slow learner.* Columbus: Charles E. Merrill, 1968.

Ekwali, E. E. *Locating and correcting reading difficulties.* Columbus: Charles E. Merrill, 1970.

Engelmann, S. *Preventing failure in the primary grades.* Chicago: Science Research Associates, 1969.

Engelmann, S., & Bruner, E. C. *Distar: An instructional system.* Chicago: Science Research Associates, 1969.

Engelmann, S. & Osborn, J. *Distar: An instructional system.* Chicago: Science Research Associates, 1970.

Farson, R. *Birthrights.* New York: MacMillan, 1974.

Feuerstein, R., & Krasilowsky, D. Interventional strategies for the significant modification of cognitive functioning in the disadvantaged adolescent. *Journal of the American Academy of Child Psychiatry,* 1972, *11,* 572-582.

Figurel, J. A. (Ed.). *Reading goals for the disadvantaged.* Newark, De.: International Reading Association, 1970.

Frank, M., & Frank, L. D. *How to help your child in school.* New York: Viking Press, 1950.

Freidman, P. Relationship of teacher reinforcement to spontaneous student verbalization within the classroom. *Journal of Educational Psychology,* 1973, *65,* 59-64.

Frostig, M. *Movement education: Theory and practice.* Chicago: Follett, 1970.

Frostig, M., & Horne, D. *The Frostig program for the development of visual perception.* Chicago: Follett, 1964.

Frostig, M., Maslow, P., Lefever, D. W., & Whittlesey, J. R. B. *The Marianne Frostig test of visual perception.* Palo Alto: Consulting Psychologists, 1964.

Gartner, A. *Children teach children; Learning by teaching.* New York: Harper & Row, 1971.

Gattegno, C. *Words in color.* Chicago: Learning Materials, 1962.

Getman, G. N. *How to develop your child's intelligence.* Leverne, Mn.: Author, 1962.

Gittelman-Klein, R. *2603 recent advances in child psychopharmacology.* New York: Behavioral Publications, 1976.

Glaser, K. *Learning difficulties: Causes and psychological implications: A guide for professionals.* Springfield: Charles C Thomas, 1974.

Goodman, L., Tutoring for credit. *American Education,* 1971, 7, 26-26.

Goodman, L., & Hammill, D.D. The effectiveness of the Kephart-Getman activities in developing perceptual-motor and cognitive skills. *Focus on Exceptional Children,* 1973, *4,* 1-9.

Goss v. Lopez, 95 S. Ct. 729, (1975).

Grzynkowicz, W. M. *Meeting the needs of learning disabled children in the regular class.* Springfield: Charles C Thomas, 1975.

Hall, R. V. *Managing behavior. Part 1, behavior modification: The measurement of behavior.* Lawrence, Ks.: H & H Enterprises, 1974.

Hall, R. V., Axelrod, S., Foundopoulos, M., Shellman, J., Campbell, R. A., and Cranston, S. S. The effective use of punishment to modify behavior in the classroom. In K. D. O'Leary, & S. G. O'Leary, (Eds.). *Classroom management: The successful use of behavior modification.* New York: Pergamon Press, 1972.

Hammill, D. D., & Bartel, N. R. *Educational perspectives in learning dis-*

abilities. New York: Wiley, 1971.

Hammill, D. D., & Bartel, N. R. *Teaching children with learning and behavior problems.* Boston: Allyn & Bacon, 1975.

Hammill, D. D., Goodman, L., & Wiederhold, J. L. Visual-motor processes: What success have we had in training them? *The Reading Teacher,* 1974, *27,* 469-478.

Hardy, R. E., & Cull, J. G. (Eds.). *Applied volunteerism in community development.* Springfield: Charles C Thomas, 1973.

Haring, N. G., & Phillips, E. L. *Analysis and modification of classroom behavior.* Englewood Cliffs: Prentice-Hall, 1972.

Harris, M. B. (Ed.). *Classroom use of behavior modification.* Columbus: Charles E. Merrill, 1972.

Harris, M. M. Learning by tutoring others. *Today's Education,* 1971, *60,* 48-49.

Haslam, R. H. A., & Valletutti, P. J. *Medical problems in the classroom: The teacher's role in diagnosis and management.* Baltimore: University Park Press, 1975.

Heckelman, R. G. Sensory-motor sequencing experiences in learning. In J. I. Arena, (Ed.). *Teaching through sensory-motor experiences.* Belmont: Fearon, 1969.

Hewett, F., Stillwell, R., Artuso, A., & Taylor, F. An educational solution: The engineered classroom. *Strategies for teaching exceptional children.* Denver: Love Publishing Co., 1972.

Higgins, A. *Peer tutoring process: An audio-visual training kit.* Kettering, Oh.: Behavioral Products, 1975.

Hobbs, N. *The futures of children.* San Francisco: Jossey-Bass, 1974a.

Hobbs, N. (Ed.). *Issues in the classification of children.* San Francisco: Jossey-Bass, 1974b.

Homme, L. *How to use contingency contracting in the classroom.* Champaign: Research Press, 1973.

Homme, L., & Tosti, D. T. *Behavior technology: Motivation and contingency management, unit four, self management.* San Rafael, Ca.: Individual Learning Systems, 1971.

Humphrey, J. H. *Teaching elementary science through motor learning.* Springfield: Charles C Thomas, 1975.

Johnson, K. R. *Teaching the culturally disadvantaged: A rational approach.* Chicago: Science Research Associates, 1970.

Jones, R. L. (Ed.). *Problems and issues in the education of exceptional children.* Boston: Houghton Mifflin, 1971.

Kalafatich, A. J. *Approaches to the care of adolescents.* West Nyack, N. Y.: Appleton-Century-Crofts, 1975.

Kameya, L. I. *Biophysical interventions in emotional disturbance.* Ann Arbor: University of Michigan, 1972.

Karnes, M. B. *Helping young children develop language skills: A book of activities.* Arlington: The Council for Exceptional Children, 1968.

Kephart, N. C. *The slow learner in the classroom* (2nd ed.). Columbus: Charles E. Merrill, 1971.

Kirk, S. A. & McCarthy, J. (Eds.). *Learning disabilities.* Boston: Houghton Mifflin, 1975.

Kohlberg, L. Early education: A cognitive-developmental view. In C. S. Lavatelli, & F. Standler (Eds.). *Child behavior and development* (3rd ed.). New York: Harcourt, Brace, Jovanovich, 1972.

Kozloff, M. A. *Educating children with learning and behavior problems.* New York: Wiley-Interscience, 1974.

Krumboltz, J. D., & Krumboltz, H. B. *Changing children's behaviors.* Englewood Cliffs: Prentice-Hall, 1972.

Kubany, E. S., Weiss, L. E., & Sloggett, B. B. The good behavior clock: A reinforcement time out procedure for reducing disruptive behavior. *Journal of Behavior Therapy and Experimental Psychiatry,* 1971, *2,* 119-124.

Landmark decision: Judge recognizes children's rights. *The Last Resort,* 1974, *2, 3.*

Lerner, J. W. *Children with learning disabilities.* Boston: Houghton Mifflin. 1971.

Los Angeles County Superintendent of Schools. *An explanatory study of children with neurological handicaps in school districts of Los Angeles County.* Los Angeles: County Superintendent of Schools, 1963.

Lovaas, O. I., & Simmons, J. Q. Manipulation of self-destruction in three retarded children. *Journal of Applied Behavior Analysis,* 1969, *2,* 143-157.

Lovitt, T. C. Self management projects with children with behavioral difficulties. *Journal of Learning Disabilities,* 1973, *6,* 138-150.

Macht, J. *Teaching our children.* New York: Wiley, 1975.

Madsen, C. H., Jr., & Madsen, C. K. *Teaching/discipline: Behavioral principles toward a positive approach.* Boston: Allyn & Bacon, 1970.

Markoff, A. M. *Teaching low achieving children reading, spelling, and handwriting: Developing perceptual skills with the graphic symbols of language.* Springfield: Charles C Thomas, 1976.

Maurer, A. Corporal punishment. *American Psychologist,* 1974, *29,* 614-626.

Means, L. A., & Appelquist, H. A. (Eds.). *Dynamic movement experiences for elementary school children: Combining the traditional approach with movement education to produce a physical education that enhances and compliments intellectual growth.* Springfield: Charles C Thomas, 1974.

Mental Health is 1, 2, 3. Washington, D. C.: National Association for Mental Health, 1951.

Monson, C. H., Jr. (Ed.). *Education for what? Readings in the ends and means of education.* Boston: Houghton-Mifflin, 1970.

Montessori, M. *The absorbent mind.* Adyar, India: The Theosophical Publishing House, 1963 (originally published 1949).

Morreau, L. E., & Daley, M. F. *Behavioral management in the classroom.* New

York: Appleton-Century-Crofts, 1972.

Moskowitz, H. Boredom? No more! Seventh graders try teaching. *Science and Children,* 1972, *10,* 14-15.

Mott, M. *Teaching the preacademic child: Activities for children displaying difficulties of processing information.* Springfield: Charles C Thomas, 1974.

National Education Association. *Task force report on corporal punishment.* Washington, D. C.: Author, 1972.

Neff, H., & Pilch, J. *Teaching handicapped children easily: A manual for the average classroom teacher without specialized training.* Springfield: Charles C Thomas, 1975.

Nelson, D. E., & Jones, G. B. *Effect of contingency management and quasi-individualized instruction on academic performance and attitudes.* Palo Alto: American Institutes for Research, 1970.

Nist, J. *Handicapped English: The language of the socially disadvantaged.* Springfield: Charles C Thomas, 1974.

Nurturing Intelligence. *Time,* January 3, 1972, 56-57.

Oakland, T., & Williams, F. *Auditory perception.* Seattle: Special Child Publications, 1971.

Ogeltree, E. J., & Garcia, D. *Education of the Spanish-speaking urban child.* Springfield: Charles C Thomas, 1975.

Olivero, J. L., & Buffie, E. G. (Eds.). *Educational manpower: From aides to differentiated staff patterns.* Bloomington: Indiana University Press, 1970.

Paskewitz, D. A. Biofeedback instrumentation: Soldering closed the loop. *American Psychologist* (Special issue), 1975, *30,* 371-378.

Patterson, G. R., & Gullion, M. E. *Living with children: New methods for parents.* Champaign: Research Press, 1971.

Payne, J. S. *Living in the classroom: The currency-based token economy.* New York: Behavioral Publications, 1976.

Peterson, R. M., & Cleveland, J. O. *Medical problems in the classroom: An educator's guide.* Springfield: Charles C Thomas, 1975.

Pfeiffer, J. W., & Jones, J. E. (Eds.). *A handbook of structured experiences for human relations training,* Vol. 2 (Rev.), Iowa City: University Associates Press, 1974.

Piaget, J. *The origins of intelligence in children.* New York: International University Press, 1952.

Rauch, S. J. (Ed.). *Handbook for the volunteer tutor.* Newark: International Reading Association, 1972.

Reissman, F., Kohler, M., & Gartner, A. *Children teach children: Learning by teaching.* New York: Harper & Row, 1971.

Reitman, A., Follman, J., & Ladd, E. T. Corporal punishment in the public schools. *American Civil Liberties Union Report.* Washington, D. C.: ACLU, 1972.

Reynolds, M.C., & Davis, M. D. *Exceptional children in regular classrooms.* Minneapolis: University of Minnesota Press, 1971.

Rosenthal, R., & Jacobsen, L. *Pygmalian in the classroom.* New York: Holt, Rhinehart, & Winston, 1968.

Sarason, I. G., Glaser, E. M., & Fargo, G. A. *Reinforcing productive classroom behavior.* New York: Behavioral Productions, 1971.

Schiefelbusch, R. L., & Lloyd, L. L. (Eds.). *Language perspectives: Acquisition, retardation, and intervention.* Baltimore: University Park Press, 1974.

Schloss, P. J. *Learning Aids: Teacher-made instructional devices.* Springfield: Charles C Thomas, 1975.

Schwitzgebel, R. Short-term operant conditioning of adolescent offenders on socially relevant variables. *Journal of Abnormal Psychology,* 1967, *72,* 134-142.

Screening children for nutritional status. Rockville, Md.: Department of Health, Education and Welfare, 1971.

Shirts, R. G. *Powderhorn.* La Jolla, Ca.: Simile II (n.d.).

Shirts, R. G. *Starpower.* La Jolla, Ca.: Simile II (n.d.).

Simonds, L. *Language skills for the young child: A teacher's guide of language skills for the preschool and primary grades.* San Francisco: R & E Research Associates, 1975.

Sluyter, D. J., & Hawkins, R. P. Delayed reinforcement of classroom behavior by parents. *Journal of Learning Disabilities,* 1972, *5,* 20-28.

Smith, R. M. (Ed.). *Teacher diagnosis of educational difficulties.* Columbus, Oh.: Charles E. Merrill, 1969.

Solomon, R. W., & Wahler, R. G. Peer reinforcement control of classroom problem behavior. *Journal of Applied Behavior Analysis,* 1973, *6,* 49-56.

Special Education Instructional Materials Center. *Instructional materials and resource material available to teachers of exceptional children and youth.* Austin: Author, University of Texas, 1972.

Stainback, W. C., Payne, J. S., Stainback, S. B., & Payne, R. A. *Establishing a token economy in the classroom.* Columbus: Charles E. Merrill, 1973.

Stainback, W. C., & Stainback, S. B. Effects of student tutoring on arithmetic achievement and personal social adjustment of low achieving tutees and high achieving tutors. *Education and Training of the Mentally Retarded,* 1972, 7, 169-172.

Stephens, T. M. *Directive teaching of children with learning and behavioral handicaps.* Columbus: Charles E. Merrill, 1970.

Sulzer, B., & Mayer, G. R. *Behavior modification procedures for school personnel.* Hinsdale, Il.: Dryden Press, 1972.

Swift, M. S. Training poverty mothers in communication skills. *The Reading Teacher,* 1970, *23,* 360-367.

Swift, M. S., & Spivak, G. *Alternative teaching strategies: Helping behaviorally troubled children achieve: A guide for teachers and psychologists.* Champaign: Research Press, 1975.

Syphers, D. F. *Gifted and talented children: Practical programming for teachers and principals.* Arlington: The Council for Exceptional Children, 1972.

Telford, C. W., & Sawrey, J. M. *The exceptional individual* (2nd ed.). Englewood Cliffs: Prentice-Hall, 1972.

Texas Comprehensive Special Education Program. Austin: Texas Education Agency, 1970.

Thiagarajan, S. *The programming process: A practical guide.* Worthington, Oh.: Charles A. Jones, 1971.

Thonis, E. *Bilingual education for Mexican-American children.* Sacramento: California State Department of Education, 1967.

Tracy, M. I., Gibbons, S., Kladder, F. W., & Daggy, N. *Case conference: A simulation and source book.* Ann Arbor: University of Michigan Press, 1975.

Trotters, S., & Warren, J. Behavior modification under fire. *APA Monitor,* 1974, *5*, 1, 4.

Tyler, K., & Williams, C. M. *Educational communication in a revolutionary age.* Worthington, Oh.: Charles A. Jones, 1973.

Valett, R. E. *The remediation of learning disabilities: A handbook of psychoeducational resource programs.* Belmont: Fearon, 1967.

Violence against children. *Journal of Child Clinical Psychology* (Special issue), 1973, *2*, 1-49.

Walker, H. M., & Buckley, N. K. *Token reinforcement techniques.* Eugene, Or.: E-B Press, 1974.

Warfield, G. J. (Ed.). *Mainstream currents: Reprints from Exceptional Children, 1968-1974.* Reston: Council for Exceptional Children, 1974.

Waugh, K. W., & Busch, W. J. *Diagnosing learning disorders.* Columbus, Oh.: Charles E. Merrill, 1971.

Wedell, K. *Learning and perceptuo-motor disabilities in children.* Sussex, England: Wiley, 1973.

Weikart, D. P. Preschool programs: Preliminary findings. *Journal of Special Education,* 1967, *1*, 163-181.

Wexler, D. B. Token and taboo: Behavior modification, token economies, and the law. *Behaviorism,* 1973, *1*, 1-14.

Wisland, M. V. *Psychoeducational diagnosis of exceptional children.* Springfield: Charles C Thomas, 1974.

Chapter 6

STRATEGIES FOR DEVELOPING
HUMANISTIC/LIFE SKILLS

INTRODUCTION

T HE STRATEGIES listed in this chapter describe some of the developmental programs which have focused on helping the normally developing student to acquire needed humanistic or life skills. The goal of all these strategies is to do the following:

To help each student to develop an understanding and appreciation of him/herself;

To become increasingly better able to communicate effectively with and relate to others; and

To make age-appropriate decisions that will lead toward becoming a mature member of society.

This chapter describes the need for, the rationale behind, and a way to conceptualize and to organize the process of developing life skills. It suggests the need for a curriculum with six strands, each of which is developed in a nine-step process that should be interwoven through the academic/intellectual curriculum.

Just as a great deal of effective learning of academic/intellectual skills takes place as a result of helping students to solve everyday problems, so too does good humanistic education grow out of helping students to realistically solve their personal and interpersonal problems. While this is true, approaches in this section are *not* basically oriented to the "problem student." The emphasis is on facilitating emotional growth in the essentially normally developing student. Helping students to develop humanistic/life skills is not necessarily best accomplished by introducing a separate course called "Personal Growth" or "Humanism." It is becoming more and more apparent that it will be necessary for schools vigorously to assume the responsibility of systematically and sequentially helping students to develop personally and socially just as much as (and perhaps more so than) they have developed programs to help further academic/intellectual skills. Schools have only just begun to accomplish this task. Educators need to free the creativity of all classroom teachers and to work with them to create new approaches and good instructional materials to help students to develop life skills.

Education has always had its critics; there is nothing new about having a group of people who want to change almost all aspects of education. There does, however, seem to be an increasing crescendo of criticisms directed toward regimentation and lack of development of human potential in the schools. It would be difficult to trace carefully the history of this movement, but certainly Neill's (1960) book on the changes needed in elementary education, as demonstrated in the Summerhill program in England, would be an early major influence. Although this was relatively easy to dismiss as an "experimental" school program, Holt's (1964) book also had a major impact because it described in great detail how the American school was designed to help children fail rather than succeed in the real goals of becoming independent, mature thinkers. Holt feels that the present educational system seems to encourage students to drop out, either mentally or physically, or to identify with trivial goals. To the list of critical books must be added Leonard's *Education and Ecstacy* (1968), reported to be based on literally thousands of hours of observations in American classrooms with their extreme demand for conformity, almost always at the price of individuality and creativity. (See also Flescher, 1973, and Le Shan, 1971.) Silberman (1970) endorsed the informal education approach of the British schools and advocates a return to the techniques developed by Montessori (1964).

Later, the trend seemed to move towards more of a critique of the secondary schools, starting perhaps with Postman and Weingartner's *Teaching as a Subversive Activity* (1969). Their work initially involved an attempt to "turn on" some students from lower socioeconomic homes; they found that many of these students and "tuned out" the school because it had little or no relevance for their lives. In order to meet the "district standards," while at the same time meeting the needs of their students, Postman and Weingartner urge teachers to try to make their materials more relevant in order to increase learning not only for the culturally deprived but for all students. As before, many of the advances which have been brought about in attempting to improve education for the disadvantaged or exceptional child have major implications for helping all children.

An even stronger criticism of schooling comes from Illich (1971) who suggests that the only solution to all of these problems is to "de-school" society. He suggests that the way schools are organized takes from individuals the feeling of personal competence as they learn to depend on the institutional school to organize their lives and to make their decisions. His critique, that schools dehumanize students, has been given indirect support by a great deal of talk about the need for alternative schools. Once again, this started with alienated youth, but the concept is expanding to the point where it could serve the needs of a great many kinds of students. More recently, Bereiter (1974) asks the question through his book, *Must We Educate?* He suggests that if the government made basic educational training freely available and issued certificates of competence in specific skills at various levels of attainment, it would no longer be necessary to have compulsory education. Realistic job requirements would require certain skills which would provide the motivation for students to seek training. Haney and Zimbardo (1975) suggest the similarity between the high school and a prison. Others (Farson, 1974; Foster, 1974; Zuckerman, 1974) have urged change using a more legal approach, suggesting that students should have a "bill of rights." Whereas many of the problems described by these critics could be greatly alleviated by a well-developed plan of humanistic education, it would be untrue to indicate that all critics are requesting more humanism in the schools. While some are advocating *Beyond the Three R's: Training Teachers for Affective Education* (1974), others are requesting an even greater emphasis on the "basics" (Melton, 1975).

While it is true that some have advocated an overhaul of all major aspects of the schools, many others are stressing the fact that what American education needs is a strong program of humanistic education (Aspy, 1972; Association for Supervision and Curriculum Development, 1970; Brown, 1971; Chase, 1975; Forsyth and Gammel, 1974; Hamblin, Buckholt, Ferritor, Blackwell, and Kozloff, 1971; Hitt, 1973; Manning, 1971; Thomas, 1971). An interesting trend is also observed as the proponents of behavior modification have attempted to temper the efficiencies of that approach with more humanistic goals (Bateman, 1973; Bradfield, 1970; Skinner, 1971). Even such a strong critic as Bereiter (1974) has suggested the possibility that, so long as the behavioral techniques are used only with the student's consent, they may be able to help do away with "coercion and indoctrination" and will hasten to make the whole process of education more optional and therefore more meaningful.

Some programs would attempt to humanize education through closer cooperation and work with the parents. One reason why some aspects of life-skills education have not been used more consistently evolves around the problem of whether or not humanistic programs, i.e. values clarification techniques or family-life education programs, should be taught in the school or left to the home. Obviously the values taught by parents vary considerably, and any value taught in the school will differ from the values of some parents. Educators can circumvent some of this by opening up discussions where each child can look at his/her own values as opposed to trying to help him/her accept some predetermined value. This, of course, is easier said than done since a great deal of teaching of values comes through nonverbal communication. Some would see the school in a role of using some of the new behavioral techniques to help parents learn how to work with their children more effectively (Becker, 1971; Patterson and Gullion, 1971).

Others would encourage an approach combining some of the humanistic techniques with some of the behavioral ones (Fine, 1974; Moore, 1972; Willis, Crowder, and Willis, 1975). Still others would train the parents in an almost purely humanistic approach, i.e. helping them understand and work with the feelings and perceptions of the child (Fass, 1968). The Fass model is essentially one of helping parents work with their children in such a way as to help them develop appropriate life skills. Others have stressed the interplay between the family and problems in the school (Friedman, 1973; Pavenstedt and Bernard, 1971). Although not a new idea, some feel that one of the main strategies in helping students in this area comes through effective parent-teacher contacts where the true integration of the cognitive and the affective education of the child can take place.

Still another series of strategies would focus on the classroom in the elementary school. There is good evidence that most children with emotional problems can be identified early in the school experience, both by teacher referral and testing (Bower, 1974; Marmorale and Brown, 1974; Silver and Hagen, 1972) and through sociometric types of peer ratings (Barclay and Barclay, 1972). This suggests that a good strategy would be to introduce programs which improve the classroom climate in the elementary school (Phillips and Covault, 1973). It also suggests the related approach to using the group process in the classroom (as opposed to the one-to-one approach) to bring about a better humanistic education program (Caldwell, n.d.; Sheppard, Shank, and Wilson, 1973). Some programs deal with an approach that combines humanistic programs with the regular course work (Dreikurs, Grunwald, and Pepper, 1971; Hunter, 1972; Strang, 1969) or through a generalized process of "encouragement" designed to get and to keep the student motivated (Dinkmeyer and Dreikurs, 1963). Most of the strategies listed in this chapter are designed to be integrated into a regular curriculum. While attempting to do this, the following factors (suggested by Swift and Spivak, 1975, pp. 198-207) should be considered: (1) teachers should set up a one-to-one contact with the children to discover their interests and to establish mutually satisfactory individual signals; (2) teachers should be constantly aware that they are serving as a model (either for good or bad) to the student; (3) a positive classroom emotional tone should be established which accepts children as individuals even though some of their behaviors might be in question; (4) students should always know what is expected of them, both where they are trying to go and how they are going to get there; (5) teachers should foster self-control and independent problem solving; students "should be encouraged to act purposefully on the basis of their own best judgment and to risk success and failure because they are confident" (p. 208) ; (6) teachers should also help the students see that what they do actually makes a difference by means of linking their efforts to their work, by recording their successes, and by emphasizing the students' use of their own initiative (p. 185) .

There are those who believe that the main emphasis for improving humanistic education should be made in the junior high school (Overly, Kinghorn, and Preston, 1973; Sweat, Fink, and Reedy, 1974) and the high school (Cole, 1972; Hamilton and Saylor, 1969). Another approach is directed to the discipline (broadly defined) of the secondary teacher, suggesting different approaches for working on teacher-caused problems, student-caused problems, administrator-caused problems, and parent-caused problems (Jessup and Kiley, 1971). Jessup and Kiley (1971, pp. 148-152) point out that (1) Many inconsequential incidents which have become full-blown crises could have been controlled. (2) Adolescents expect and will accept behavioral limits in an atmosphere conducive to self-growth and learning. (3) Since all behavioral problems are caused, the teacher must become a diagnostician. (4) Effective teachers will have fewer problems, academic and behavioral, in their classrooms because of their professional competence and personal qualities. (5) Teachers do not operate in a vacuum or restrict their activities to the classroom; total involvement is essential to successful discipline (see also Le Grand, 1969). Others feel that the teachers' role in counseling should be improved (Ligon and McDaniel, 1970). Gazda and Folds (1968) stress that the total secondary school staff should participate in a continuous developmental approach to group guidance. They suggest a training program involving a "critical incidents" approach to help students with (1) orientation problems, (2) personal development, and (3) educational and vocational planning. Using a micro-teaching approach, Gregory (1972) sought to help the secondary teacher improve the process of teaching.

Still another approach focuses in on more effective use of the

"group process" in the secondary classroom.   Schmuck and
Schmuck (1971) suggest that all peer groups go through four
stages: (1) inclusion and membership, (2) shared decision making and friendships, (3) the pursuit of learning goals, and (4)
the maintenance of a supportive group once it has been established. They point out that the peer climate also has four dimensions: (1) influence over each other, (2) attraction for each
other, (3) norms (shared expectations), and (4) communication
patterns. As previously mentioned, another aspect of this movement has been to suggest the need for a wide range of alternative
schools at both the elementary and secondary level (Spodek, 1973).

As usual, life-skill education places great demands upon the
classroom teacher who should have the right (and the responsibility) to be able to reach out and to seek help from others in the
school. Since a large number of the techniques described in this
section are essentially experimental in nature, the teacher will
have to become part of a Learning Facilitation Team where a group
effort will be made to find solutions for the complex problems of
how to implement an effective humanistic education program.
The two professionals in the school with the most training in the
behavioral sciences are the school counselors and the school
psychologists. In general, the elementary field has more service
from the school psychologist and the secondary field has more
service from the school counselor. Although both of these groups
have tended to get involved in other activities, it is essential that
they be encouraged to turn their attention back to helping students learn. Both have definite contributions to make (Cottingham, 1970; Kaczkowski and Patterson, 1975) to a Learning Facilitation Team at both the elementary and secondary levels. Both must
learn to work cooperatively with teachers and to lead staff development programs on improving the process of education.
Valett (1972b) and Perry (1974) have suggested, for example,
that the school psychologist should serve as a human development
specialist. Lightfall (1973) suggests the need for a social psychologist in the schools who could help teachers and administrators
see how the group-process is affecting student learning. He suggests a strategy of having a "problem accountant" on the staff

who can monitor the problem-solving process of a faculty and school and determine where problem solutions tend to get "bogged down." The problems of implementing a good humanistic program are monumental; all educators are going to have to work together and each make his/her own personal and professional contribution if the goal is to be achieved (Beatty, 1969).

Toward this end, the programs in this chapter have been designed or modified essentially to be used with total classes under the direction of the regular classroom teacher. This is not to say, however, that the help of a specialist or specific instructional material would not be useful. Teachers are urged to teach to a "two-level" curriculum (Weinstein and Fantini, 1970): one which deals with the intellectual facts and the other with the level of how these facts affect the "humanistic" qualities of the student's life. It is in the latter area that educators are probably having the most trouble keeping the curriculum relevant; in most instances, what is taught is not presented in such a way as to encourage the students to relate the learning to the development of their own life skills. The total educational process (but especially tests) overemphasizes a "right answer" culture. Instead of forcing students (and teachers, for that matter) to "check their emotions at the door of the school," the students need to be helped to see that the only time a fact has personal significance is when it has been "sifted" through their own view of life. The curricular approach to developing life skills should come from the following three major sources: (1) teachers should use the unplanned learnings in the student's life, both at home and at school (the experiential learnings); (2) teachers should emphasize the humanistic values inherent within the regular subject matter that they are expected to teach; and (3) teachers should use special, planned, classroom, and total-school experiences based on experiences that the student is likely to meet in real life.

Such a program of humanistic education has, of course, to be developmentally based so that the valuing standard and the judgments that students are asked to make are appropriate to their level of development. As part of this developmental program, there will also be a process for identifying those who are not making the appropriate progress and who therefore need to be considered for corrective/therapeutic services. Before any student is "pulled out" of the main Life-Skill Developmental Program, every effort should be made to provide the needed help in the normal setting. The problems of resisting help once an individual feels he/she is different, e.g. the "identified patient," represents a monumental problem for the total corrective mental health field to solve. Although the activities described later in this chapter can, in some instances, be carried out with a small group or only one student, in general they have been developed to utilize total class and social interaction to gain their greatest power. They are all of the strategies that can be accomplished *with* the students.

TABLE 6-I

STRATEGIES THAT CAN BE DONE WITH THE STUDENT

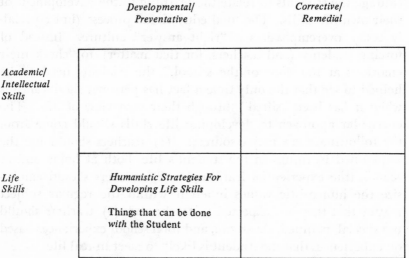

	Developmental/ Preventative	Corrective/ Remedial
Academic/ Intellectual Skills		
Life Skills	*Humanistic Strategies For Developing Life Skills* Things that can be done *with* the Student	

For a group with the greatest amount of expertise in helping students acquire skills in large groups, educators have been slow to systematically develop those classroom activities which promote humanistic/life skills. There has, however, been an increased

TABLE 6-II

THE SIX HUMANISTIC LIFE-SKILL STRANDS

Strand I: Understanding/Valuing Self and Others

I. Understanding Self and Others
   A. A Book About Me
   B. Developing Understanding of Self and Others
   C. Dimensions of Personality
   D. Developmental Guidance Series
   E. Toward Affective Development
   F. Explorations in Personal Adjustment
   G. High School Psychology Courses

II. Improving Self-Concept
   A. Self-Enhancing Education
   B. Developing Self-Concept
   C. Myself Checklist
   D. Focus on Self-Development
   E. Strength Bombardment Activities
   F. Bowman Early Education Series
   G. Getting to Know Me Filmstrips

III. Relating Effectively With Others
   A. Human Relations in the Classroom
   B. Comic Book Approach to Mental Health
   C. Reading Ladders for Human Development
   D. Human Behavior & Mental Health
   E. The Magic Circle
   F. Black-White Encounters
   G. Call them Heroes
   H. Using Audio-visual Materials
   I. Understanding/Accepting the Handicapped
   J. Games, Simulations, Human Relation Activities
   K. Becoming: A Course in Human Relations
   L. Small Group Dynamics
   M. Human Relations Development Program

Strand II: Clarifying One's Values

A. Values Clarification
B. Experimental Value Sharing Projects
C. The Human Value Series
D. Teaching Values Through Curriculum

Strand III: Improving Communication Skills

A. Inside Out Series
B. Using Gaming/Simulations
C. Class Meetings
D. Student Effectiveness Training
E. Helping Students use "Self Talk"
F. Learning Group Discussion Skills
G. Project RAPP
H. Other Communication Techniques

Strand IV: Solving Life's Problems

A. Inquiry Training: Asking Questions
B. Teaching Steps in Problem Solving
C. Games and Simulations
D. Project LIFE
E. Getting it All Together
F. Discovery Through Guidance Series
G. Life Space Interviewing

Strand V: Adopting More Satisfying Roles

A. Modeling
B. Role Playing
C. I'm OK, You're OK
D. Valett Human Development Program

Strand VI: Making Creative Decisions

A. Appropriate Sex-role Identification
   1. Sociology I
   2. A Time of Your Life
   3. Contemporary Family-life Education
   4. Other Approaches to Family-life Education
   5. Influence of Liberation Movements
B. Making Use of Academic Learning
C. Deciding How to Use Drugs
   1. A World to Grow In
   2. Project TRIAD
   3. National Clearinghouse for Drug Abuse Information
D. Making Comprehensive Career Decisions
   1. "Deciding"; "Decisions & Outcomes"
   2. The Santa Clara Guidance Program
   3. Life/Career Development System
   4. Life Careers Game
   5. Work Experience/Exploration
E. Promoting Creative Thinking
   1. Thinking Creatively
   2. Responsible Citizenship
   3. Zest for Life

amount of interest in this kind of activity over the past few years. The primary (and almost single) interest in curriculum development for years was in the traditional academic areas. This is not to conclude that some teachers did not teach values, interpersonal relationships, decision making, etc. It meant that, by and large, they had to teach life skills informally and essentially without the help of well-developed organizing techniques and materials. Although the situation is changing, it will still be a long time before there is really a systematic development of life skills in the average school.

In addition to the heavy emphasis on academic skills, another reason that development was so slow in this area was the concern on the part of many that emotions and feelings were not something that should be "tampered" with unless one was a trained therapist. Even if one were well trained, techniques for working with groups had not been well developed. Educators had somehow accepted the idea that the teaching/learning of academic facts or skills was different from the teaching/learning of humanistic skills. As time progressed and new programs began to be developed, it became more and more obvious that learning is learning—that learning about the concept of "democracy" or learning how to communicate with others are interrelated and both are governed essentially by the same "laws" of learning. It is obvious from this example that it is also becoming increasingly evident that life skills must be taught in relationship to developing concepts in the traditional academic areas. If it is to be "lived," it must be taught in groups where the special interactions between group members help the student to understand the real meaning of democracy in the first place, and where democratic interrelationships between the students reinforce and maintain those understandings once they begin to emerge (Kounin and Abradovic, 1969; Wood, 1975).

For purposes of clarification and emphasis, the process of developing life skills has been organized along six "strands." The life-skills curriculum develops each of these six strands for all students through a continuous cycle process which goes through three phases and nine steps.

THE THREE-PHASE, NINE-STEP, DEVELOPMENTAL LIFE-SKILLS CYCLE

Phase I: Perceiving—Collecting Information

THE PROCESS OF INTRODUCING A LIFE-SKILLS CURRICULUM

1. Developing Awareness—Consciousness Raising Activities to identify and become aware of the importance of specific life skills.
2. Observing Skill—The Use and Effects of the Skill in Others.
   I see the effect of this humanistic process in the lives of others.
3. Experiencing the Life Skill
   I assess the effects of this life skill on my own life through the significant others or models in my life.

Phase II: Processing—Personalizing Information

THE INTERNAL PROCESS OF THE STUDENT

4. Self-Awareness
   How do these experiences affect the real me? Do I want to adopt, change, or reject them?
5. Integration
   Who am I? How do I see/value myself?
6. Planning/Commitment
   Because I have developed a new life skill, I will plan to act accordingly.

Phase III: Implementing/Behaving—Actions Taken in the Outer World

BEHAVIORAL CHECKS TO BE USED BY THE STUDENT AND/OR SCHOOL TO EVALUATE PROGRESS OF THE SKILL ACQUISITION

7. Acting Consistently
   I act "transparently real" on the basis of my processing and planning.
8. Facilitating Growth in Others
   I accept others, and without dominating them, will help them to grow.
9. Evaluating the Results of this Behavior

On the basis of the feedback, I will either continue with the plan or use the information to start the life-skills processing cycle over again.

It is assumed that this life-skill developmental cycle will take place across each of the six major, overlapping strands which form the substance of a humanistic education program. The strands are:

1. Understanding/Valuing Self and Others,
2. Clarifying One's Values,
3. Improving Communication Skills,
4. Solving Life's Problems,
5. Adopting More Satisfying Roles, and
6. Making Creative Decisions.

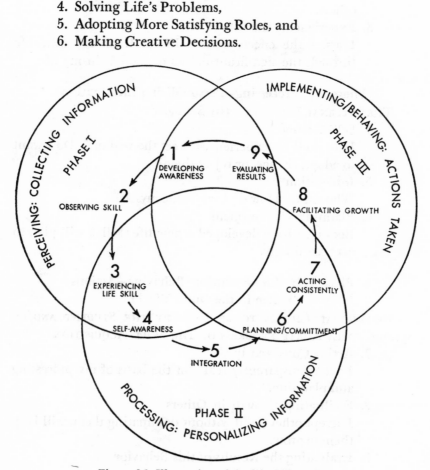

Figure 6-1. Illustration of the life-skills cycle.

THE SIX STRANDS AS THEY REFLECT THE NINE-STEP LIFE-SKILLS DEVELOPMENTAL CYCLE

Strand I—Understanding/Valuing Self and Others

PERCEIVING

1. I will identify specific life skills in the behavior of others.
2. I will observe/analyze the effect of this life skill in others.
3. I will assess how the use of the life skill by the significant others in my life affects my life.

PROCESSING

4. I will develop an awareness of self: Who am I?
5. I will develop a self-concept: How do I see myself?
6. I will plan to act on the basis of my self-concept: Because I know who I am, I will act accordingly.

IMPLEMENTING/BEHAVING

7. I will act consistently toward others, because I know who I am.
8. I understand my own and others' behavior: I will be sensitive to their needs and will attempt to facilitate growth.
9. I will proceed on the basis of the feedback I get.

Strand II—Clarifying One's Values

PERCEIVING

1. I will become aware of different values and how they affect behavior.
2. I will carefully observe the values of others as reflected in their behaviors.
3. I will actively experience how the values of the important people in my life affect me.

PROCESSING

4. I will become aware of both the conflicting and congruent values in my life.
5. I will learn and use the values clarification process so my values can be consistent in my own life.
6. I will make decisions based on my values.

IMPLEMENTING/BEHAVING

7. I will act consistently on the basis of my values.
8. I will make associations with others and will relate to them so as to facilitate their attempt to clarify their own values.
9. I will evaluate my progress (especially where I encounter value conflicts) and will continue to use my new values clarifying skills.

Strand III—Improving Communication Skills

PERCEIVING

1. I become aware that communication is a complicated process and that it is a skill that has to be learned in order to be effective.
2. I observe the effects of effective and ineffective verbal and nonverbal communication in others.
3. I develop the skill of active listening when communicating with others.

PROCESSING

4. I am aware that I use "self-talk" to cue myself.
5. Although much of this self-talk is helpful, I will identify and deal with any that tends to be self-defeating.
6. I will develop a plan which involves active listening, appropriate self-talk, and effective communication with others.

IMPLEMENTING/BEHAVING

7. I will attempt to communicate consistently and clearly with everyone I contact.
8. I will communicate in such a way as to facilitate open, effective communication with me on the part of others.
9. On the basis of the feedback that I get, I will check my progress and will plan and implement new strategies as necessary.

Strand IV—Solving Life's Problems

PERCEIVING

1. I will become aware of the steps in the problem-solving process.

2. I will observe the effects of unresolved problems and of the problem-solving process in others.
3. I will assess how the effects of the life skill of solving problems in others has affected me.

PROCESSING

4. I will become aware of the unresolved problems in my own life.
5. I will become aware of the ways in which these problems have kept me from becoming what I want to become.
6. I will establish a plan which will enable me to solve more effectively the problems which face me.

IMPLEMENTING/BEHAVING

7. To the best of my ability I will implement my personal problem-solving plan.
8. I will relate to others in such a way as to facilitate their process of problem solving, especially as it relates to me.
9. I will be continually alert to the need for using the problem-solving skill on unresolved problems and on new problems as they arise.

Strand V—Adopting More Satisfying Roles

PERCEIVING

1. I will identify the roles played by others.
2. I will carefully observe how these roles affect the lives of others.
3. I will assess how the roles played by others and their role-expectations for me affect my life.

PROCESSING

4. I will become aware of the effects of the roles I have played and identify new ones that I want to be able to play.
5. I will attempt to identify the real "me" behind the roles that I play.
6. I will plan to abandon self-defeating, useless roles and to develop those roles which promise to be self-productive.

IMPLEMENTING/BEHAVING

7. I will take the knowledge about behavior and values and attempt to act as consistently as possible within the roles that I play.
8. I will relate to others in such a way as to help them to develop a repertoire of self-satisfying roles.
9. I will decide, on the basis of feedback I get from others, whether or not my behaviors have been productive and self-fulfilling, and plan accordingly.

Strand VI—Making Creative Decisions

PERCEIVING

1. I will become aware of the life skill of making creative decisions in the lives of others.
2. I will attempt to find models who utilize creative decision making in their lives.
3. I will assess how the use or misuse of creative decision making in others has affected me.

PROCESSING

4. I will ascertain the effects of creative decision making (or lack of same) in myself.
5. I will attempt to make creative decisions and to become fully functioning in the light of my newly developed life skills.
6. I will develop a plan which will be most likely to lead to a full and creative future.

IMPLEMENTING/BEHAVING

7. I will act consistently, responsively, and productively with others.
8. I will do what I can to sponsor creative decision making in others.
9. I will be constantly on the alert to the need for starting the creative decision-making life-skill cycle again in order to develop new skills and plans.

Though there is a great deal of overlap and interrelatedness between the various strands (as there is in real life), there is even more overlap in the humanistic programs which have already been developed, i.e. almost all existing programs attempt to develop more than one strand. Even though this is true, existing humanistic education programs and emphases will be described next in this chapter under one of the six strands. Since much of the material that follows in this chapter is experimental and hard to obtain, exact addresses have been provided for the instructional material wherever possible (when a standard book reference will not suffice). Although some of the earlier material is out of print, it has been listed, when possible, for its historical and trend-setting value.

STRAND I—UNDERSTANDING/VALUING
SELF AND OTHERS

Some would say that understanding yourself and the behavior of others would be the central task of all humanistic education (Reichert, n.d.). Certainly no one would argue that this is not an important task, even though most educational programs have not put a great deal of effort into helping students develop these necessary understandings. It would be considered by many to be the basic building block upon which to base all of the other life skills. As always, the concepts that the students can understand will vary with their age and the quality and quantity of their experiences (Promoting Mental Health in the Classroom, 1973).

Understanding Self and Others

A Book About Me. Jay (1952) produced this simple children's workbook for use with the young child; since it requires no reading, it can be used even at the kindergarten level. By identifying with specific pictures (provided for this purpose) the child gives the teacher and other students clues about his/her home life or information about interests and attitudes. It probably represents one of the earliest attempts to put out instructional material of this nature (available from Science Research Associates, 259 E. Erie St., Chicago, Ill. 60611).

Developing Understanding of Self and Others. Dinkmeyer (1970) developed the DUSO Series in the form of kits which were field tested from 1969-72 (available from American Guidance

Service, Circle Pines, Minnesota 55014) .

DUSO Kit D-1—Kindergarten and Lower Primary. This kit uses stories, puppets, records, activity cards, etc., to help the student achieve the three following basic goals: to learn more words to express their feelings; to learn that feelings, goals, values, and behavior are dynamically related; and to learn to talk more freely about them.

DUSO Kit D-2—Upper Primary and Grade Four. This kit also uses a wide variety of materials to help the developing child in five basic areas: to develop an understanding and positive valuing of one's unique self; to understand interpersonal relationships; to understand the purposive nature of human behavior; to understand the dynamic relationships among ideas, feelings, beliefs, and behavior in order to express one's feelings accurately; and to understand competence and the components of accomplishment.

DIMENSIONS OF PERSONALITY. The DOP program started with a series of workbook texts by Limbacher (n.d.) in the fourth to sixth grades. They were designed to promote meaningful discussions of students' needs and emotions, and to provide classroom activities that facilitate student interaction. This series has now been extended to the following nine levels (available: the Pflaum-Standard Publishing Co., 8121 Hamilton Ave., Cincinnati, Ohio 45231) .

> Level K-1: *Let's Begin* (available in either a filmstrip or teacher "lap-card" format)
> Level One: *Now I'm Ready* (student worktexts and seven activity sheets)
> Level Two: *I Can Do It* (student worktexts and seven activity sheets)
> Level Three: *What About Me?* (student worktexts and seven activity sheets)
> Level Four: *Here I Am* (student texts and spirit masters)
> Level Five: *I'm Not Alone* (student texts and spirit masters)
> Level Six: *Becoming Myself* (student texts and spirit masters)

Junior High Level: *Search for Meaning* (seventy spirit masters covering thirty-six lessons)

Senior High Level: *Search for Values* (seventy spirit masters covering forty-four lessons)

NATIONAL FORUM FOUNDATION DEVELOPMENTAL GUIDANCE SERIES. Probably one of the earliest attempts to develop a total curriculum designed to help normally developing students to understand their personal-social problems and their interpersonal relationships was made by Shull who served as the Director and Managing Editor for the National Forum Foundation (n.d.) in Chicago, Illinois. Starting in the early 1950s, a series of guidance textbooks was designed first for high school students, then for junior high. The original material was designed for "group guidance activities" with teenage students. The extension of the series down to grades 4, 5, and 6 (which is currently available from the American Guidance Service, Circle Pines, Minnesota 55014) uses stories and materials designed to facilitate the students' understanding of social and emotional development by encouraging classroom discussions and thought which can help them clarify their values. The material is organized to stimulate the developing self-concept of the child in the following six areas: feelings or emotions, peer relationships, academic achievement, family relationships, appropriate use of drugs, and career choices. In addition to the texts, a series of charts are available to stimulate classroom discussion.

Grade 4: *Everywhere We Go* (textbooks and discussion charts)

Grade 5: *The People Around Us* (textbooks and discussion charts)

Grade 6: *Seeing Ourselves* (textbooks and discussion charts)

TOWARD AFFECTIVE DEVELOPMENT. An activity-centered program designed to stimulate psychological and affective development in students in grades 3 through 6 has been developed by DuPont, Gardner, and Brody (n.d.). TAD is organized and presented in five sections, divided into twenty-one units, making up a total of 191 lessons (each of which takes about twenty to twenty-five minutes). It is planned in such a way as to facilitate integration with the typical classroom schedule (available: American Guidance Service, Circle Pines, Minnesota 55014).

Section I: *Reaching In and Reaching* Out—5 units (51 lessons)

    Unit 1: Developing Group Participation Skills

    Unit 2: For Rainy Days and Fridays

    Unit 3: Brainstorming, Discussing, and Evaluating Ideas

    Unit 4: Developing Awareness Through Sensory Experience

    Unit 5: Encouraging Openness and Creativity

Section II: *Your Feelings and Mine*—6 units (45 lessons)

    Unit 6: Recognizing, Labeling, and Understanding Feelings

    Unit 7: Posturing

    Unit 8: Gesturing

    Unit 9: Facial Expressions

    Unit 10: Verbalizing Feelings

    Unit 11: Role-Playing

Section III: *Working Together*—5 units (37 lessons)

    Unit 12: Cooperating and Sharing

    Unit 13: The Individual and the Group

    Unit 14: Leading, Following, and Instructing Others

    Unit 15: Actions and Feelings that Weaken Social Collaboration

    Unit 16: Actions and Feelings that Strengthen Social Collaboration

Section IV: *Me: Today and Tomorrow*—2 units at each of two levels (39 lessons)

    Unit 17: Individual Differences—Level I

    Unit 18: Careers Open to Me—Level I

    Unit 19: Individual Differences—Level II

    Unit 20: Careers Open to Me—Level II

Section V: *Feeling, Thinking, Doing*—1 unit (19 lessons)

    Unit 21: Choosing Behavior

EXPLORATIONS IN PERSONAL ADJUSTMENT: A GUIDE TO SELF-

UNDERSTANDING. Another early attempt to provide a workbook aimed at the secondary student was published in 1949 by George Lehrner. The second edition (Lehrner, 1957) was, in many ways, a forerunner of many of the high school psychology courses which will be discussed next. It attempted to help the students to do the following: get acquainted with themselves; adjust to personal needs and goals; handle frustrations and conflicts; make an appropriate adjustment to their family and school; make good social adjustments; learn to communicate effectively; assume appropriate dating and courtship behaviors; make vocational and avocational adjustments; and understand "maladjustment." The final chapter was entitled "Personal Adjustment 'And the Pursuit of Happiness'" (available from Prentice-Hall, Englewood Cliffs, N.J.).

HIGH SCHOOL PSYCHOLOGY COURSES. There is a growing interest all over the country in developing high school courses variously called Psychology, Sociology, Human Relations, Behavioral Science, or Mental Hygiene (Fisher, 1974); and even an occasional experimental program is being tried in the elementary schools (Epstein, 1975). In some instances the primary organizational thrust is in the areas of drug education and sex education. The increasing requests on the parts of older students for more information about how to understand human behavior is often referred to as further evidence that students are moving toward a more humanistic position. This shift is seen in universities where students are switching from the physical sciences to majors in sociology, psychology, and other behavioral sciences. Although many of them will never actually work in these fields of behavioral science, most of them are probably interested in knowing what "makes people tick." Unfortunately, some schools turn the course into a "watered down" beginning psychology course, dealing with learning rates, and the like. A creatively taught psychology course can do much to make an entire high school aware of and understand a wide range of human behaviors. One creative teacher, for example, trained all of the students in the psychology class to collect data on a problem facing the school at a given point in time, i.e., whether the grades of those who used the senior lounge had dropped; they had not.   The American Psychological Association has established a committee on Precollege Psychology and a newsletter called *Periodically* under the sponsorship of the APA Clearinghouse on Precollege Psychology and Behavioral Science.   APA has also published a book entitled *The Psychology Teacher's Resource Book: First Course* (2nd ed., 1973) .   (All of these are available from: American Psychological Association, 1200 17th St., N.W., Washington, D.C. 20036). There are a great many different psychology text books available and being used, and some appearing now are specifically for the high school student (Whittaker, 1975) .   Such courses, if creatively and sensitively taught, can do a great deal to help students better understand themselves and others (Kasschau and Wertheimer, 1974) .

Improving Self-concept

The main idea behind the strategies in this section is to help students discover that the way they feel about themselves and how well they accept themselves, i.e. their self-concept, is of major importance in determining how they function both in school and in life in general (Brookover, Erickson, and Joiner, 1967; Hawley and Hawley, 1972) .   Although this idea has been around for a long time, the self-concept has always been hard to define in specific behavioral terms and even harder to measure (Webster and Sobieszek, 1974) .   One definition of the "self" (which, in a sense, dramatizes its resistance to change) is that it is that *part* of the individual which remains *unchanged* as the person moves from one experience to another (Coopersmith, 1967) .   Criticisms that the self-concept was really too difficult to define or to research won out for awhile, to the end that progress in this area was slowed.   However, efforts to devise programs which help students to develop a good self-concept are beginning to come forth.   The "self" would now be generally defined as follows: a composite of an individual's thoughts and feelings, strivings and hopes, fears and fantasies, his/her view of what he/she is, what he/she has been, what he/she might become, and his/her attitude toward his/her own worth.

SELF ENHANCING EDUCATION. SEE was a program developed primarily for use with primary and upper elementary children in the Cupertino (California) School District, starting about 1956. Randolph and Catterall (1964) put together an instructional guide *Self Enhancing Education: Processes that Enhance* (now out of print) which helped the teacher organize the year's instructional program around five "facilitating questions":

1. Who are we?   (What are our names, who are we as persons, what roles do we have?)
2. Where are we in time and space?   (Where are we in space, in history, in the growth of ideas, in terms of the stages of personal growth?)
3. Why are we here?   (Why are we in school, what is expected of us—by ourselves, our parents, our teachers, our culture?)
4. What are our operational problems?   (What will keep us from meeting our goals?)
5. How can we solve the operational problems?   (How can we arrange our room and our schedule so that we can get the things done that need to be done; how can we develop the necessary social skills; how can we establish and reach our goals; how can we manage ourselves?)

The process also stressed a total problem-solving concept and helped the students to see the value of working together to meet their common goals. A later publication by Randolph and Howe, *Self Enhancing Education* (1966), was published by Educational Development Corporation of Palo Alto, California. It can be seen that this approach, with slight modifications, could be used at all levels of the curriculum. At the high school level, for example, a potentially valuable approach would be to ensure that all students had something "going for them" in which they could become deeply involved somewhere in the high school program. This could be in sports, in some particular academic subject, in extracurricular activities, or in more informal personal relationships.

DEVELOPING THE SELF-CONCEPT. Another project, similar to SEE, was developed by Anderson and Coburn (1972) for the

Ocean View School District: *A Major Goal of Any School District Should be to Help Develop in Children a Healthy Self-concept* (Ventura County Superintendent of Schools, Ventura, Calif. 93001). This project identifies six major objectives, available materials and resources, together with ways for determining which students need help and suggestions for ways to help them achieve the following objectives:

> The child indicates awareness,
> The child indicates self-reliance,
> The child indicates an acceptance of self,
> The child indicates a feeling of well-being,
> The child indicates a feeling of being confident, and
> The child indicates a feeling of being accepted.

MYSELF CHECKLIST. Valett (1973a) devised a diagnostic checklist to be used by elementary and junior high school age pupils to aid both the teacher and the student in determining the pupil's progress in developing adequate self-concepts. It can also be used in planning cooperatively between the teacher and the student for an affective education or self-development program (available: Fearon Publishers, 6 Davis Dr., Belmont, Calif. 94002).

FOCUS ON SELF-DEVELOPMENT. This series has been designed to help students develop a better understanding and acceptance of self (available: Science Research Associates, 259 E. Erie St., Chicago, Ill. 60611). It is separated into two stages:

STAGE ONE—AWARENESS

> Unit A. Physical Attributes of Self
> Unit B. The Intellectual Self
> Unit C. The Emotional Self
> Unit D. The Social Self
> Unit E. Awareness of the Environment Through Hearing
> Unit F. Awareness of the Environment Through Seeing
> Unit G. Awareness of the Environment Through Smelling and Tasting
> Unit H. Awareness of the Environment Through Touch
> Unit I. Groups and Interaction of Group Members
> Unit J. Interaction of Family Members
> Unit K. Qualities of Older Children

Unit L. Unique Qualities of Another Person

Unit M. The Problem-solving Process

Unit N. Needs and Interests of Other People in Relation to Those of Self

Unit O. Possible Consequences of Decisions

Unit P. Factors that Influence Behavior and Attitudes of Other People

Unit Q. Factors that Influence One's Own Behavior and Attitudes

Unit R. Causes of Behavior

STAGE TWO—RESPONDING

Unit A. Self-concept

Unit B. Interests

Unit C. Abilities and Limitations

Unit D. Goals

Unit E. Concerns

Unit F. Responsibility

Unit G. Physical Environment

Unit H. Cultural Differences

Unit I. Social Influences

Unit J. Communication

Unit K. Honesty

Unit L. Companionship

Unit M. Acceptance and Rejection

Unit N. Respect

Unit O. Trust

Unit P. Loyalty

Unit Q. Competition and Cooperation

STRENGTH BOMBARDMENT HUMAN RELATIONS ACTIVITIES. There are a growing number of games or activities designed to help people relate to each other in a more positive way. Those called "team-building activities" have attempted to bring people together in many different settings. They have been used with classes of students, groups of teachers, and groups in the community, usually with good success. A class or large group is divided into subgroups with five or six people in each. One person serves as a timekeeper and each participant spends, for example, three minutes describing the major events of his/her life. After this is completed, participants provide each other (in the same order they followed at first) with feedback of what they remembered or what impressed them about each person's life history. After this is done, each person takes a large (approximately 18" by 22") horizontal sheet of paper and writes "Strengths People See In _____ (their name)" at the top left, and "Sees In Self" on the right. One person puts his/her paper on the wall with the other members of the group sitting around. Each member of the group who desires, uses a marking pen and writes (without speaking) a strength or asset he/she sees in the other person, on his/her paper. When they have completed this, each group member who so desires can say why he/she identified that strength. The person addressed can then "validate" whether or not he/she sees that strength in himself/herself (under "Sees In Self"). Whereas the great majority see this activity as a strongly positive experience, some may view it as not very meaningful because of the artificiality of the process and because negative points of view are not expressed. In general, however, this technique, with minor variations, has proven to be very positive in helping people to begin to identify and to reinforce strengths in each other.

As in most gaming activities, after the group has gone through this type of exercise, it is appropriate for the teacher to focus the discussion (sometimes called "de-briefing") around three points:

What happened? What did you observe? (It is best not to play "psychologist" and tell them what you think they experienced; let them describe it for themselves.)

Why is it important? (Let the group discuss, evaluate, and synthesize the experience.)

Now what? How does this relate to the "real" world? (What are some other things we can and should do?

BOWMAN EARLY EDUCATION SERIES. This series, designed by Jaynes and Woodbridge (n.d.), is designed to help young children develop a positive self-identity, an awareness of themselves as persons, and an ability to relate to others. It contains picture stories, story books, and recordings (available: Bowman Publishing Co., 622 Rodier Dr., Glendale, Calif. 91201).

GETTING TO KNOW ME FILMSTRIPS. This series includes four brightly animated color/sound filmstrips designed for grades K through 3. They were developed by Virginia Powers and are intended to encourage self-understanding and self-acceptance (available: QTED Productions, 2921 W. Alameda Ave., Burbank, Calif. 91505).

Relating Effectively with Others

As an outgrowth of better understanding of self and others and a better acceptance and valuing of self, the implementing/ behaving aspect of this strand is designed to help improve relationships with others, another major emphasis in humanistic education. Whereas there have been numerous attempts to develop this life skill, it should also be noted that there is some controversy about the value of this approach (Morris, Cinnamon, and Kanitz, 1975).

HUMAN RELATIONS IN THE CLASSROOM. One of the earliest organized attempts to put together any curricular material in any of the humanistic skill areas came in this category. In 1947, Bullis and O'Malley authored *Human Relations in the Classroom: Course I* (Course I, 5th ed., 1951, out of print) and later Bullis authored Course II (Course II, 2nd ed., 1950, out of print). These books set forth a series of units designed originally for use once a week with sixth–, seventh–, and eighth-grade students in the state of Delaware. The model was clearly an attempt to help these students to understand and to express their emotions, to begin to see how emotions affect their lives, and to prevent emotions from developing into major problems. The format was as follows: the teacher told a story from a book; the students were then asked to analyze the emotions involved, the conflicts and personalities of the people involved; and then they were encouraged to relate these feelings and conflicts to their own lives. These early attempts to help young students become more emotionally mature were well received, but this material is not currently being extensively used.

COMIC BOOK APPROACH TO MENTAL HEALTH. Soon after the introduction of the Bullis material, Joe Musial of the New York

Department of Mental Hygiene (1950) worked with Chic Young, cartoonist/developer of the "Blondie" series, to publish, under the sponsorship of the National Association for Mental Health, an issue of a comic designed to teach human relation concepts to students and adults. One issue, for example, contained the following four sections: scapegoating, everyone's need for love, the need for everyone to accept and follow through on their own responsibilities, and the value of working as part of a family unit and also on one's own. Although very popular, the series did not last very long.

READING LADDERS FOR HUMAN DEVELOPMENT. Another approach has been to utilize existing books, both fiction and non-fiction, to teach human relationship skills. The model is illustrated in the American Council on Education's *Reading Ladders for Human Relations* (1949). It classified and annotated a list of books for children in the following areas: family relationships, rural-urban ways of living, and living in ethnic and social groups. The work of Taba is closely associated with this movement (Taba, 1955; Taba and Elkins, 1950; Taba, Robinson, Brady, and Vickery, 1951). Although most of the stories classified in these earlier attempts now tend to be somewhat dated, the concept of using regular children's literature to promote better interpersonal understanding is still a very good one. Almost every juvenile story has some plot; classifying those plots in terms of human relationships and assigning them to students either as individuals or in small groups still has great potential. Children, for example, who are scheduled to go into the hospital for a tonsilectomy would be better prepared if they read a story about another child having the same operation. This process is effective all through the school years, and it has been used successfully by teachers in advanced courses in English literature—relating themes in either the current literature or the classics to the personal/developmental problems of the students.

A TEACHING PROGRAM IN HUMAN BEHAVIOR AND MENTAL HEALTH. Another person who has been working for a long time to improve the mental health of children is Ojemann (n.d.). In his capacity as the Director of the Education Research Council of

America, he has promoted the development of grade-level hand-
books for upper elementary aged students (available: Order
Department, Education Research Council for Greater Cleveland,
Rockefeller Building, Cleveland, Oh. 44113).

THE MAGIC CIRCLE. The work of Besell, *Methods of Human
Development* (1974), in teaching human relations material
should be noted. He, in conjunction with Palomares, developed
a training program which was designed to help preschool through
grade 3 children to understand themselves better and to become
"constructively" involved in their own personal effectiveness,
self-confidence, and an understanding of the causes and effects in
interpersonal relationships. They structured their material so
that it could be used for about twenty minutes a day in what they
called the "Magic Circle." The teacher, who serves as leader/
facilitator, begins by explaining the topic for discussion and, if
necessary, demonstrates what is expected of the children. Topics
include such things as "Something I do very well is. . . ." In preschool and kindergarten, children participate in "mastery sessions." These lessons are designed, through the use of positive
feedback, to build self-esteem. Goals at the preschool level are to
encourage the child to talk, listen, and succeed. In the kindergarten they add the dimension of helping him/her to understand
the negative and positive aspects of individual differences and
tolerance. In Grade 1, the objective is to help the child accept
ambivalent feelings and behavior, to see the differences between
reality and fantasy, and to begin to have leadership experiences.
In Grade 2, child leaders are guided by the teacher to help develop concepts of "awareness," "coping," and social interaction.
"Challenge," "commitment," and "confrontation" of peers are
used in a systematic program of character development. In Grade
3 there is an emphasis on "awareness," "responsibility," and
"keeping commitments." One aspect of building good social relationships stressed in the magic circle is to encourage children to
recognize and appreciate differences between the sexes. (Available: Institute for Personal Effectiveness in Children, Box 20233,
San Diego, Calif. 92190).

BLACK-WHITE ENCOUNTERS. Although not a developmental

curriculum, another human relation type of activity which has been used quite extensively in recent years is to devise a series of experiences which would help members of minority/majority groups to get along with each other more effectively. Some of the teaching of black history and Mexican-American history has been designed to help members of these groups know more about and be proud of their own heritage and thus be better able to relate to the dominant society. Some attempts to bring together the various ethnic and racial groups have assumed a very aggressive, confrontational approach which would not be categorized in this section. Whereas some individuals obviously do have hostile feelings toward each other, trying to bring the two groups together on the basis of "telling it like it is" does not seem appropriate to the regular school curriculum. Unless one has considerable time to work through the negative feelings and help to rebuild positive ones, more often than not these techniques serve to reinforce the negative. There is emerging, however, a series of experiences and/or exercises which stress the fact that people are all alike at the core and that they share common feelings such as warmth and love. Individuals can relate to each other in their expressions of these warm feelings, in their hopes for the future, and so on. The need of some of the "militant" minority members to stress the negative sides of the intergroup relations seems to be diminishing. There are still major social problems in the racial area, but within the confines of the developmental school curriculum, the establishment of human relations skills between minority members will probably go further if some meaningful, positive experiences can be shared with each other.

CALL THEM HEROES. Another approach to human relations, especially as it relates to multiethnic groups, is typified by this series of four books. They were developed by the staff of the Board of Education of the city of New York, under the direction of Loretan and Umans (1965) (available: Silver Burdett, Morristown, N.J.). They are designed to demonstrate the bravery and the contributions to the United States by many people representing minority groups and to help student members of the minority groups develop appropriate models so that they too, can make a significant contribution. Each of the four books contains twelve stories of people who "refused to accept life as they found it and who are willing to work for a better life." They can also be used with nonminority students to help them appreciate the contributions of these people from different ethnic groups.

USING AUDIOVISUAL MATERIALS TO TEACH HUMAN RELATIONS SKILLS. The Society for Visual Education (1345 Diversey Parkway, Chicago, Ill. 60614) has produced a large number of "Guidance" filmstrips for use with junior and senior high students. Their Guidance/Counseling filmstrips, with records and cassettes (most of which are in color) are listed under the following headings:

Popularity Problems
Life Issues
Dating Problems
Family Problems
Critical Areas of Health
Health and Social Problems
Social Problems
Why Wait Till Marriage?
About Sex and Growing Up
Being Responsible About Sex and Love
Love and the Facts of Life
Drugs in Today's World
Drugs in Our Society
The Problem of Drug Abuse

Ripples is a series of thiry-six, fifteen-minute films on videocassettes, designed for instructional TV. It is also available for preschool and primary-aged children. It includes many of the six strands mentioned previously.

Self-incorporated is yet another series of television shows (also in films and videocassettes) designed to explore day-to-day problems common to eleven- to thirteen-year-olds. They attempt to help the young adolescent cope with the problems that arise as a result of physical, emotional, and social changes that he/she is experiencing. The fifteen-minute lessons include:

By Whose Rules (systems and self)

Changes (physiological changes)
The Clique (cliques)
Different Folks (sex-role identification)
Double Trouble (family adversity)
Down and Back (failure and disappointment)
Family Matters (what is a family?)
Getting Closer (boy-girl relationships)
My Friend (ethnic/racial differences)
No Trespassing (privacy)
Pressure Makes Perfect (pressures to achieve)
Trying Times (making decisions)
Two Sons (sibling rivalry)
What's Wrong With Jonathon? (everyday pressures)
Who Wins? (morality)

(For further information about these and other AV materials, write to: Agency for Instructional Television, *1976 Television: A Catalogue of instructional television courses and related materials*, Box A, Bloomington, Ind., 47401.)

The general approach in using audiovisual materials is to show either a film strip or a 16-mm sound movie to present material or start a discussion designed to help students understand interpersonal and intergroup relations. Working with much younger students, one of the authors first attempted to use this kind of material in 1954 when he used one of the (even then) classical Silly Symphony Cartoons called "Elmer the Elephant" in kindergarten and first grade classes. As is true with most cartoons, it was filled with a great deal of aggression. When one thinks about all of the "humor" that "bombards" young children within our culture today, especially in the cartoons now shown primarily on TV, one becomes even more impressed with the need for schools to develop systematic programs working on human relations at a more mature level. At any rate, in "Elmer the Elephant," the children would laugh at all of the aggression, but at one point in the brief cartoon it became evident that the other animals (the children) had gone too far and were "scapegoating" Elmer, who was "different" because he had such a long nose. If a child was still laughing at this time, he or she had missed the point of the cartoon. Even these very young children were able to relate (through discussions) the incident in the film to human relations problems in their classroom.

Hello People. This is a multimedia, multiethnic program, designed for six- to nine-year-olds (available: Argus Communications, 3505 N. Ashland Ave., Chicago, Ill. 60657). Developed by O'Connell and Cosmos (n.d.), it focuses on the growth of the child's self-concept and attempts to help the child relate to others in a "people-oriented" way. The alert teacher will continue to be on the lookout for material of this nature which will help students begin to look at the way they relate to others. (A valuable resource book for media which teach in the affective domain has been published by the National Special Media Institutes, 1970.)

UNDERSTANDING/ACCEPTING THE HANDICAPPED. Another group that needs special understanding is the physically and mentally handicapped (Dibner and Dibner, 1973). With more of these students remaining in or being returned to the regular classroom there will be more of an opportunity to help the nonhandicapped get to know and to understand those with special problems. Since those who are handicapped will have to take their place in the regular society some day, the sooner the nonhandicapped learn to accept them, the better. One program, Facilitative Environments Encouraging Development (information: Project FEED, 10th and By-Pass 46, Bloomington, Ind. 47401), under the direction of Smith (1975), uses the model of taking junior high students and helping them to become teacher assistants in hospitals and preschool centers for the handicapped. These experiences provide the basis for questions and discussions at a later time. The model attempts to help these junior high school students learn first hand about child development and handicapping conditions. Once again, through the focus on abnormal development, the students can learn more about the normally developing child. In other situations, the literature approach has been used to help students understand the handicapped. They are assigned books such as Levine's *Lisa and Her Soundless World* (1974), the story of a deaf child, or Gold's book *Please Don't Say Hello* (1975), describing the frightening world of autism. Society needs to constantly guard against the tendencies which segregate the handicapped, thereby robbing most people of the opportunity to know them and help them, and robbing them of their right to make their own contribution to the larger group.

GAMES, SIMULATIONS, AND HUMAN RELATIONS ACTIVITIES. A growing number of techniques, which can broadly be called human relations activities, use interaction in a group setting to facilitate the development of human relations skills. The primary reference for these kinds of activities is a series of four books edited by Pfeiffer and Jones (1973, 1974a,b,c) called *Handbooks of Structured Experiences for Human Relations Training* (available: University Associates, 7596 Eads Ave., La Jolla, Calif. 92037). Although many of these activities were directly designed for use with adults, creative teachers will not have much difficulty in selecting and modifying the ones that will work in their classroom. Many of them are relatively simple techniques that provide the student with the structure of responding to another and getting a response back which will be meaningful to both. These should not be used too frequently and students should not feel compelled to respond at any particular time or occasion. Educators must not take away a student's right to be different in their eagerness to help them learn to relate better with other students. Teachers are not trying to run a therapy group; they are simply trying to structure the classroom experience in such a way as to facilitate maximum personal growth.

Most of the *games* have a win-lose component to them which can heighten motivation on the part of the students but can also obscure what the teacher wants to emphasize. It is possible to find games which do not stress competition so heavily (Washburn and Washburn, 1973). Another group of activities involves *role-playing* (to be discussed later). A number of *simulation activities* often grow out of social study units and have the potential of developing human relations understandings and skills. One such game, "Sunshine," simulates a small community with an all-white high school on one side of the tracks and an all-black high school on the other. Students are randomly assigned to the role of a black or a white in the simulation (stressing that no one had anything to say about their race before they were born). The "action" of the simulation evolves around the need to divide the town so that both high schools are integrated. Players earn "Imp" (for "importance") points for certain kinds of delaying or pressuring activities depending upon which side they are on. The debriefing discussion stresses the feelings of different players as they act out their roles. This kind of activity, especially when related to units of work in social studies or history, shows promise for helping students understand some of the problems in intergroup relations in the real world. Simulation activities usually try to (1) recreate some aspect of reality, (2) have some sort of a win-lose, competitive component, and (3) have some aspect of role-playing involved. In the simulation, students learn to pay attention to a variety of important stimuli, to use specific rules to make decisions (even though they may complain about the artificiality of the rules), and to begin to see the consequences of some of the decisions they have made, all in a controlled role-playing situation. A complete list of twenty-six simulation activities which relate to social studies units and most of which also teach development of life skills are available from Interact, Learning Through Involvement, P. O. Box 262, Lakeside, Calif. 92040. Other directories have been developed by Belch (1973), and Zuckerman and Horn (1973).

BECOMING: A COURSE IN HUMAN RELATIONS. This new program, developed by Cromwell, Ohs, Roark, and Stanford (1975a, b), has as its primary objective to help students to develop affective and constructive interpersonal relationship skills (available: J. P. Lippincott Co., Philadelphia, Pa.). It comes in the form of a leader's manual, a personal log for each student, a series of cassette recordings, photocards, and manipulative devices. The material (called "investigations") is divided into four parts: perspectives, consensus, helping, and becoming. The leader is encouraged to identify and to utilize a series of techniques to facilitate group interaction. Three broad stages of group development are identified: *aggregate* (or class) which is characterized by lack of cohesiveness; *team* (with a beginning sense of group identity and direction); and *group,* where there is sufficient identity and cohesiveness to encourage warmth and self-disclosure. Each activity is divided into the following three phases: the opening, an activity, and the integration. The activities are designed to give each participant: (1) an experience in a specific situation or task designed to elicit various reactions; (2) an opportunity to generalize their reactions as well as those of the group into a more generalized statement of principle about human behavior; (3) an opportunity to see how their own experiences relate to the newly formulated principles. The material is probably best suited for junior high or older students.

TEACHING HUMAN RELATIONS THROUGH SMALL GROUP DYNAMICS. Small group interaction can be used for many purposes, i.e. communication skills, leadership development, decision making, or motivation. In some instances, however, the spontaneous group interaction with a minimum of structured stimulus material has been used to help the participants improve their interpersonal relations (Flynn and La Faso, 1972; Hechlik and Lee, 1968). In some situations, teachers are encouraged to use the peer relationships in the regular classroom to help the students to become aware of others and of their own behavior. The work of Rardin and Moan (1971) would indicate that a child's cognitive development is affected by the quality of his/her peer relationships (judged by popularity rankings) but that the components of peer interaction have to be taught. Schmuck and Schmuck (1973) would also encourage the use of the normal group interaction to identify and to teach human relationship components. Others would suggest that it is between the teacher and the learners that the most valuable interactive process takes place in education (Gorman, 1974; Luft, 1970). Still others, however, urge that small groups be especially set up for the purpose of helping students learn about behavior and human interaction. Some of the techniques used in encounter groups have been used for this purpose. Most classroom teachers feel more comfortable, however, if they have some material or structure with which to facilitate this kind of learning.

HUMAN RELATIONS DEVELOPMENT PROGRAM. Although it is primarily designed as a manual to teach educators rather than a direct program to be used with students, the work of Gazda, Asbury, Balzer, Childers, Desselle, and Walters (1973) and Gazda, Walters, and Childers (1976) provides a comprehensive, systematic training program for improving human relationship skills. Drawing heavily upon the Carkhuff Model (1969), this work helps the educator to apply the helping relationship skills to the educational setting. It is aimed primarily at elementary and secondary teachers but has direct applications for other educators. It describes and trains in the use of the core dimensions of a helping relationship: the ability to employ empathy, respect, warmth, concreteness, genuineness, self-disclosure, confrontation, and immediacy. It also provides educators with separate scales for measuring their own ability to use these core dimensions. As such it tends to emphasize the listening and responding (facilitative) dimensions as opposed to the problem-solving/action dimensions of the model. This is probably the most complete program for helping educators develop these facilitative skills (available: Allyn and Bacon, 470 Atlantic Ave., Boston, Ma. 02110).

This model is currently being field tested with junior and senior high school students under the title *Realtalk: Exercises in Friendship and Helping Skills* (by Gazda, Walters, and Childers, 1976. It should be available for distribution some time in 1979).

STRAND II—CLARIFYING ONE'S VALUES

A major emphasis in the area of teaching life skills in recent years has come under the heading of *Values Clarification*. It has helped, among other things, to remind educators that they are modeling and teaching all humanistic skills in everything they do, but especially their values, whether for better or for worse. Educators really do not have a choice as to whether or not to teach values (Simpson, 1973). They only have a choice as to whether or not to teach them indirectly and inefficiently from their own actions, or more directly (and hopefully more efficiently) in a way which gives students the chance to abstract principles that transcend their teachers' own patterns of behavior and adjustment. This concept is well dramatized by the title of a book by Cullum (1971): *The Geranium on the Windowsill Just Died*

But Teacher You Went Right On. It follows from this line of logic that we cannot just "do nothing" in the area of values clarification; but what are we to do? Some say that teachers should directly transmit their own values, but this has the pitfall that their values may not be applicable to the students. Others say that teachers should not talk about their values, but should model them effectively. This, too, is hard to do because of conflicting values. Other possibilities include rewarding "good" values seen in students and explaining the value system of the culture. Still others feel that it is the job of the school to transmit the predominant values of the culture to the students. But once again, the culture has conflicting values and the future may require a change in value structure. Another option is to expose students to the best values of the culture and hope that they will find and adopt them for themselves. Probably the best approach, according to Harmin and Simon (1971), is to teach students a "value skills approach," i.e. to teach them to go through the process of clarifying the values that they hold and act upon. Even this approach, however, does not answer the question of what the teacher should or could do with the student who holds values which appear to be counterproductive (Baier and Rescher, 1969; Berkowitz, 1964; Raths, Harmin, and Simon, 1966; Rokeach, 1973).

SIMON'S APPROACH TO VALUES CLARIFICATION. Although in many ways much of this work is directed more towards teacher training programs than it is towards curricular programming strategies, there is little question but that Simon's work has been very influential in both pre- and in-service training for teachers and in actually modifying classroom techniques. By way of definition, Simon demands that anything called a "value" should pass all seven parts of a stringent test:

> It must be prized and cherished.
> It must be part of a pattern of behavior; it is repeated.
> It must be chosen from alternatives.
> It must be freely chosen.
> It must be chosen after due reflection.
> It must be publicly affirmed.
> It must be acted upon.

With such a strict definition, not very many things would pass the test which could be called "values." Simon calls other things "value indicators" or "beliefs," "attitudes," or "interests" (Simon, 1969). Simon and his co-workers have suggested a wide range of values clarification activities (Simon and Clark, 1975; Simon, Howe, and Kirschenbaum, 1972; Harmin, Kirschenbaum and Simon, 1973). The following strategies are some of those which have been used to help students to choose those values which they are willing to proclaim and which form the basis for them to make choices and decisions in their own lives.

Among others, Simon suggests the following strategies for values clarification. Ask students to reflect on their work in a nonjudgmental way on weekly reaction sheets. Each student should turn in a card (preferably at the first of each week) indicating something that is valued. Simon suggests that teachers should use an autobiographical questionnaire which helps to clarify the question: Who Am I? He also suggests a time diary indicating how one uses time, which is not read by the teacher but is for the students to use in clarifying their own values. The use of confronting questions is also advocated as another valuable technique. The teacher should also use a values-sheet at least once a week in which a provocative question or statement is posted; the students are encouraged to react in writing and in group discussion. Still another suggestion is to create what Simon calls a "value confronting experience" in which the students have to come directly into contact with an experience that will make them face their true values. Certainly there is much in this work that can and should be adapted to specific classroom techniques for students of all ages (Simon, 1969).

Yet another technique is to build a "reaction chart" on the floor by using masking tape and five different colors of construction paper. The papers should be marked "Strongly Agree" at one end and "Strongly Disagree" at the other. Stories are read discussing different value positions taken as people react to the pressures of life. Students measure their agreement with the character in the story by standing on the paper in the place they feel best expresses their feelings. As more information is given or conditions change, the student moves to different positions on the "reaction chart." This usually leads to heated and (hopefully) thoughtful discussions.

Another popular values clarification technique starts with giving each student a facsimile of a coat of arms, drawn on a full-size sheet of paper. In the six sections of the coat of arms, the students are asked to answer a question with a picture, design, or symbol. The only area where they can use words is area 6.

1. What do you regard as your greatest personal achievement to date?
2. What do you regard as your family's greatest achievement?
3. What is the one thing that other people can do to make you happy?
4. What is something you are striving to become? Or to be?
5. What would you do if you had only one year to live and were guaranteed success in whatever you attempted?
6. What three things would you most like to be said of you if you died today?

If they wish, students may share the meaning of their symbols in small groups.

EXPERIMENTAL VALUE SHARING PROJECTS. From 1959 to 1964, the Chicago Public Schools were engaged in a formal project designed to maximize the effective use of human values in the classroom. They attempted to extend the democratic ideal of human worth and dignity through the widest possible sharing of values. They built the program on the assumption that many mental and social problems were caused by low status and felt that the most important instructional activity was to create school practices which would help their students understand and enhance their values (Rucker, Arnspiger, and Brodbeck, 1969).

THE HUMAN VALUE SERIES. This series, consisting of a Teacher's Edition and Student Texts, was published from 1967-69 under the leadership of Arnspiger, Rucker, and Brill (available: Steck-Vaughn Publishing Co., Austin, Tx.). It was used experimentally in its early stages by a great many school districts, including the Santee (California) District and the Fannindel School District in Texas. This series has organized a large variety of values clarification instructional techniques around the following factors which are considered to be "indices" of the valuing process in an educational setting:

1. Affection—teachers and students promote congenial human relations.
2. Respect—the work and privacy of each member of the class is held in respect.
3. Skill—students are encouraged to develop and to utilize a full range of academic and interpersonal relationship skills.
4. Enlightenment—every effort is made to bring out the true facts on the part of the students and the teachers, both in subject areas and in interpersonal relationships.
5. Power—the widest possible base of students and teachers is used in making decisions.
6. Wealth (goods and services)—learning and producing handicraft materials is seen as wealth; students are encouraged to serve others and plan for their vocational future.
7. Well-being—the mental and physical well-being of all participants is safeguarded.
8. Rectitude—students are encouraged to establish and live by their own set of moral standards and conduct (Rucker, Arnspiger, and Brodbeck, 1969).

TEACHING VALUES THROUGH THE REGULAR CURRICULUM. Although there has been a lot of interest in these special activities (Ogle and Menuey, n.d.) and in such techniques as using role-playing to teach values clarification (Hawley, 1973, 1974), clearly the main use of values clarification techniques has come as a result of teachers relating the value-skills process to the regular subject matter which they are teaching (Curwin and Curwin, 1974; Harmin, Kirschenbaum, and Simon, 1973). Values clarification has probably been used most consistently in connection with the social studies curriculum (Barr, 1971). Other major uses have been in the teaching of composition writing in the English curriculum (Simon, Hawley, and Britton, 1973). Another area where it would appear that the valuing technology would be useful is in the area of moral development. Mattox and Koryda

(1974), for example, have related these techniques to the Kohlberg theories of moral development through the use of peer group discussion of a variety of dilemmas. Certainly what has been traditionally called moral development is closely related to the things now considered under the heading of values clarification. (For suggestions in the use of films, see Schrank, 1972.)

STRAND III—IMPROVING COMMUNICATION SKILLS

Another thrust that some life-skills programs have taken is to develop methods and materials to facilitate the awareness and expression of feelings and to improve interpersonal communication skills. The ability of children to be aware of and express their feelings is to some extent based on their ability to use the values clarification skills and somewhat on their ability to use the full-range communication process. Helpful questions in this regard are: Do the students know themselves, their needs, their feelings? Can they identify feelings within themselves such as fear and anxiety? Can they discover the source of their feelings and rehearse mentally how they might be able to deal with them? Do they accept their feelings as a legitimate part of themselves or do they tend to deny them? Do they understand the values and attitudes they hold and how they affect their behavior? Can they recognize the inconsistencies they see between their personal values or between their values and their behaviors? (See *Beyond the 3 R's: Training Teachers for Affective Education,* 1974; Le Shan, 1972; Robert, 1973.)

In the areas more typically associated with the topic of improving communication skills, the following questions will also help to set the stage for productive thinking: Does the student hear what other people say? Are they sensitive to both the verbal and nonverbal aspects of communication? Can they express a full range of feelings and know when and how it is appropriate to do so? Can they deal with problems in conflict-resolving ways rather than in a resolution-defeating manner? These skills require the student to draw actively upon a variety of internal processes. Teachers can help in the following ways: (1) by being aware of themselves, (2) by being aware of their roles as models of good or bad communication for the students, and (3) by establishing a facilitative process to encourage good communication (*Beyond the 3 R's: Training Teachers for Affective Education,* 1974). Communication cuts across almost all of the interpersonal skills; this makes it in some ways more difficult, but in other ways more important, for the school to structure a developmental program in this area.

The human transaction is a very complicated process. It typically includes something taken in from the "outside-our-skin" stimuli (light waves, sounds, tactile impressions, odors, tastes, etc.), something transformed (light and sound waves transformed into electrical "codes" for transmission to the brain and muscles); something retained (memory patterns stored in the nervous system as electrochemical codes); something created (codes changed into muscular reactions) ; something transmitted (muscular movements move objects so that they emit or reflect unique patterns of pulsed sound waves which are received by others as speech or events seen or heard) (Fabun, 1970, p. 108). The transaction process is further complicated in the classroom. Teachers often "verbally crowd" students; they ask a question but do not give the student a chance to answer before they ask another question. Teachers are afraid of (embarrassed over) silence. There are often similar complications between the dialogue of parents and their children. There are several programs that have been designed to develop this valuable life skill.

INSIDE OUT SERIES, a series of thirty, fifteen-minute films, was produced by National Instructional Television (n.d.) in the early 1970s (available: Agency for Instructional Television, Box A, Bloomington, Ind. 47401) through a consortium of thirty-three educational and broadcasting agencies and with the aid of a grant from the Exxon Corporation. This series has been used extensively both over educational television and in the form of 16-mm film. It was designed by health educators and learning specialists to help eight– to ten-year-olds understand and cope with their emotions. Everyday experiences which are common to this age group are used to open up discussions of social, emotional, and physical problems. The purpose is to extend traditional health education materials to help young people achieve and maintain their sense of well-being. The titles indicate feelings which the film/video cassette is designed to help the student become aware of and express, i.e. to get them *out*:

Because it's Fun (enjoy playing for the fun of it)

Breakup (emotions involved in separation or divorce, real or imagined)

Brothers and Sisters (recognize and cope with sibling rivalry)

Bully (cope with harrassment and understand the feelings of violence and terror that bullying situations produce)

But . . . Names Will Never Hurt? (recognize and deal with incidents of prejudice and discrimination)

But They Might Laugh (cope with fears of humiliation and failure)

Buy and Buy (make wise decisions in the face of conflicting emotions and group pressure)

Can Do/Can't Do (recognize the stages of growth and deal with the feelings these changes bring about in themselves)

Can I Help? (recognize how and when others can be helped and what the personal consequences may be)

Donna (Learning to be Yourself) (accept the things that make them different)

Getting Even (be aware of what it means to be accepted or rejected by a group)

Home Sweet Home (cope with feelings of mistreatment)

How Do You Show? (understand the many ways people express what they are thinking and feeling)

I Dare You (consider choices that involve risk, safety, and group pressure)

I Want To (deal with differences of opinion between themselves and adults on personal freedom and responsibility)

In My Memory (deal with feelings about the death of a person or pet)

Jeff's Company (recognize the need for a person to be alone as well as with others)

Just Joking (recognizes difference between "good clean fun" and ridicule)

Just One Place (develop personal convictions about the responsibility to maintain an environment of humane quality)

Living With Love (realize the benefits that love produces, recognize how love can be expressed, and cope with the lack of love in one's life)

Lost is a Feeling (recognize how persons feel lost and threatened in new situations)

Love, Susan (deal with the misunderstanding and conflict that arise even within a loving family)

Must I/May I (cope with the feelings caused by the tension between freedom and responsibility)

A Sense of Joy (aware of the joy to be found in familiar things and in the surprises of everyday life)

Someone Special (recognize that "crushes" are a normal part of growth and psychological development)

Strong Feelings (understand the physical effects of strong emotions)

Travelin' Shoes (aware of the emotions that moving arouses)

When I Help (aware of the consequences of helping either too little or too much)

Yes, I Can (recognize the benefits and limits of independent action)

You Belong (recognize the interdependence of all things; help increase a sense of responsibility to the environment)

Other resources designed to help students accept and express their feelings include Berger (1971), Lyon (1971), and the Association for Childhood Education International (n.d.). An approach by Maultsby (1974, 1975) called "Rational Self Counseling" is designed to help older students and adults to learn to understand and to control their emotions; it is a promising approach. His approach has been used with student-led discussion groups in several colleges and universities and seems adaptable to normally developing high school students.

USING GAMING/SIMULATION TO TEACH COMMUNICATION SKILLS. Some of the many new gaming techniques are being used to demonstrate the need for good communication (Adams, 1973).

In one called "one way communication" (Pfeiffer and Jones, 1974a), one member of the group volunteers to give instructions to other members of the group in order to help them draw a series of interrelated geometric forms, which can only be seen by the volunteer.   To further complicate the procedure, the volunteer stands with his/her back to the audience.   Members of the group cannot ask questions of the leader, even if they are not sure of the instructions.   The group is then shown the original forms and they discuss the difficulties in the communication process under this "one way" circumstance.   Real-life situations where the communication lines are equally "one way" are identified, i.e. "memos from the boss," announcements from the office, etc.   The "two-way communication" procedure is then introduced with another similar set of forms but where students can ask questions when they are not sure of the instructions.   The results of the class are compared with the standards, and the application of communication techniques to real-life situations is drawn.   (Other similar exercises are described in the four volumes by Pfeiffer and Jones, 1973, 1974a,b,c.)

There is much discussion about *nonverbal communication* these days.   Unquestionably there are many facets to all communication that come through other-than-verbal channels.   Students should focus on some of these.   Unfortunately, the interpretation of some nonverbal communication encourages the "junior psychiatrist" syndrome, e.g. "sitting like that means you hate your. . .," or "holding your mouth like that means. . .," etc.   There is very little evidence to support the hypothesis that any single move "means" something special to everyone who makes it.   It is possible to structure the class discussion on the basis that a given movement or stance is "likely to be interpreted" in a specific way by other members of the group, and it is also possible to help each student think about what "message" he/she is sending through his/her body (East, 1970; Morris and Cinnamon, 1975; Pfeiffer and Jones, 1974a,b,c).

CLASS MEETINGS.   Since Glasser's Reality Therapy approach (which appeared first in his book *Reality Therapy*, 1965) is essentially a one-to-one relationship, it will be discussed in the Corrective/Therapeutic Intervention section. However, his approach to working with the total group (especially in the elementary school but probably also for older students) is essentially a communications process called the "Class Meeting." He suggests that a relatively open style of communication be adopted by the teacher which encourages students to discuss the problems that they have encountered both in school and in life, and to work cooperatively towards solutions. Glasser's later books, including *Schools Without Failure* (1969), relate his theories more completely to the total educational system.

Some have complained that Glasser places too much emphasis on a simple solution, such as a class meeting, to solve complex educational problems. His technique involves working with and communicating with students that goes beyond but has its focus in the class meeting; this technique should be an effective one for life-skill development in the classroom. He recommends that this procedure be woven into the regular teaching process and that it take place at least once a day in the elementary school and three times a week in the high school.

STUDENT EFFECTIVENESS TRAINING. Gordon (1970) has taken some of the work of Carl Rogers, especially his Nondirective Counseling techniques, and has added creative thinking of his own, to train people to communicate better. Gordon's original emphasis was primarily on Parent Effectiveness Training. The aspect of this work that has been most used with students is to teach them what Gordon calls "active listening." When most people listen, they usually do not actually pay attention to the real feeling level that is being expressed, but only listen and respond at the surface or intellectual level. Through following a series of training exercises, each student learns to listen more carefully and communicate to the sender a clear statement reflecting the sender's real feelings. As teachers and students reach this level, the solution to mutual problems can take place much more easily.

HELPING STUDENTS BECOME AWARE OF AND USE *Self-talk.* Communication is more than sending and receiving a message. There is an internal response that mediates both immediate and

long-range communication called *self-talk.* It would appear
that much self-defeating behavior is caused by negative self-talk
and that much impulsive behavior can be helped markedly by
teaching impulse-prone children to learn to talk to themselves
(Swift and Spivak, 1975, pp. 72-73). It would appear, also, that
the "internalization" of verbal commands is a critical step in the
children's development of their ability to control their own behavior (Meichenbaum and Goodman, 1971). The procedure of
helping such children to slow down and to verbally rehearse what
they are going to do seems to be another way of helping them
improve their performance. Even the process of helping some
children rehearse the question they have been asked (to keep
them from forgetting it) is helpful. Assisting students to use self-
talk to enable them both to communicate more effectively and to
achieve their goals can be a valuable way of providing them with
a new life skill.

LEARNING GROUP DISCUSSION SKILLS. Just as human relations
and values clarification can be taught through group dynamics, so
too can the teaching of communication skills. Indeed, this is an
essential skill because in most schools most of the learning is done
in groups of twenty-five or more students. Group interaction is
an effective way to teach both verbal skills (Morris and Cinnamon, 1974) and nonverbal communication (East, 1970). A booklet by Stanford and Stanford (1969) on *Learning Discussion
Skills Through Games* describes a sequence of ten skill-building
games and activities designed to help the student develop proper
discussion techniques. The book also describes another group of
fifteen remedial activities to use when a group becomes aggressive
or inhibited, strays off the subject, argues about definitions, or
encounters other difficulties. These techniques would be helpful
in improving classroom discussions on many topics, but especially
those situations where student interaction is essential to getting
the point across. The book by Fabun (1970) also lists some very
effective ways to improve communication.

PROJECT RAPP. A project that is not well known but which
develops and utilizes a communications model for total school-
community problem solving at the high school level is "Reducing

Alienation and Activism by Participation" (n.d., available: Project RAPP, Centerville School District, 122 N. Main St., Centerville, Oh. 45459) . Although the title of the project suggests heavy corrective/therapeutic measures, in reality the project was entered into to improve total communication and participatory management in the district and was essentially preventive in nature rather than corrective. One component of the program was to help the school administration to obtain a greater "grass roots" involvement in the decision-making process from teachers, students, and parents. First of all, a series of workshops involving community members and the decision-makers in the school district was arranged. Gradually students in groups of about fifteen to twenty at a time were involved from the junior and senior high schools. One goal of the sessions was to obtain more interaction which included a greater awareness of the individuality of the self and others. Each person was helped to express his/her own values and to accept the values of others.

OTHER TECHNIQUES TO IMPROVE COMMUNICATION. There are an increasing number of ways that can help students to improve communication skills, which are not part of a complete program. In one high school, about 85 percent of the teachers volunteered, when asked, to lead relatively "open ended" *teacher-led student discussion groups* in which the group members could bring up any topic that they wished. All students in the school were asked if they wanted to take part, and about 70 percent participated. Students were assigned to groups as randomly as possible, both according to grade level, age, sex, and ability level, but some grouping was dictated by the teacher's free time and the availability of students for meeting before or after school. As one would expect, some groups did not work on deep concerns; they were content over several meetings to learn to enjoy cross-level, informal discussions together. Other groups "waded in" on some of the major problems facing the school and community and nation, and worked together with some very desirable results. We need to help students to become effective listener/communicators.

One total class technique which has been used, at least temporarily, to get a discussion group down to about fifteen is the "double horseshoe" method. It works especially well if there are two opposing points of view when the discussion begins. Under the direction of the leader (who sits at one end of the horseshoe), the group forming the inner ring of the horseshoe may start the discussion and continue for about ten minutes, while the outer ring observes the interaction of the first group in the center. Each member of the outer group can be assigned a counterpart on the inner horseshoe. The discussion stops and the second group shares ideas on the interaction they have observed. Then the groups change places and the discussion is carried on for ten more minutes while the group that had been participating observes. Eventually, all people are involved in one large group, discussing the topic from their different points of view.

An even more frequently used variation, called the *fishbowl* technique, places the large group in a circle with a small group of from three to five people in the inner circle with one empty chair. The group in the center starts the topic and anyone on the outside group may take the empty chair while making his/her contribution. The "core" group can remain in the center the entire time, partially change one at a time, or change completely in order to get more total involvement. This method is especially useful when there are students who might be reluctant to state a position where they felt they "had to" discuss a topic before they were ready for it.

The Agency for Instructional Television (1976) has produced a series called *Discussing Controversial Issues,* consisting of four twenty-minute lessons for high school students and their teachers. Teachers are helped to become effective discussion moderators who can facilitate an exchange of views without imposing their own value judgments. Students are helped to become active discussion participants, to develop insights into their own opinions, to understand the opinions expressed by others, and to form a rational basis for choosing between alternatives. (Available: Agency for Instructional Television, Box A, Bloomington, Ind. 47401.)

STRAND IV—SOLVING LIFE'S PROBLEMS

Many people who are knowledgeable in the learning process would disagree that problem solving is an independent life skill which can be taught separately; they believe that behavior change or problem solving is equated with total learning (Skinner, 1970). The problem-solving process is essentially the same regardless of whether it is the student who wants to solve his/her individual problems, the teacher who wants to solve classroom problems, or the administrator who wants to solve school-wide problems. For the purposes of this book, however, teachers should make certain that they are making good use of their own problem-solving skills in teaching their classes before they start to introduce these skills as life-skills subject matter. Teachers will find *Problem Solving to Increase Classroom Learning* by Schmuck, Chester, and Lippitt (1966) a valuable resource. Lippitt, Fox, Schmuck, and Van Egmond (1966) support the efforts of schools and teachers to understand and to improve the mental health and learning climate of the classroom because their ten years of research support the hypothesis that the mentally healthy student learns more efficiently (see also Spivak and Shure, 1973). There is also evidence that the ability to manage one's own behavior is a behavior that has to be learned and reinforced. Barnett's (1973) study indicated that nonproductive students in an elementary school learned better when they were encouraged to manage their own behavior through the use of behavioral modification techniques. The emphasis in Strand IV is on finding tension-reducing solutions for everyday problems and crises that everyone faces, rather than leaving these problems essentially unresolved (Fish, 1970; Mohr, n.d.).

INQUIRY TRAINING/ASKING QUESTIONS. A number of years ago much emphasis was placed on the approach to learning which required that teachers start the learning process with appropriate questions. Although this terminology is not used as much any more, the problem-solving process often starts by asking appropriate questions, especially those which are open-ended. An example of a closed question would be, "Who discovered America?" Presumably there is a right answer: Columbus (although the recent controversies over whether or not other explorers came earlier than Columbus makes one wonder at how many truly "open-ended" questions have been treated as "closed," i.e. there may have been artificially forced "right answers"). An example of an open-ended question would be, "Why do we learn to read?" Although, to a large extent, society has established the rule that all children who can must learn to read, asking such open-ended questions and helping the students feel that their suggestions and criticisms are legitimate is a helpful strategy. In this way, students can feel that the teacher understands their negative feelings. Sanders (1966) authored a book complete with the kinds of questions that could be asked in the classroom. Others have built a whole theory of critical thinking and learning from the way questions are asked (Raths, Wasserman, Jonas, and Rothstein, 1967). The kinds of questions teachers should ask of students are included in a chapter entitled "138 Questions" in Postman and Weingartner's book *The Soft Revolution* (1971). By asking and appropriately utilizing students' responses to well-phrased questions, teachers can set the stage for a complete program of life-skill education and can begin students on a lifetime process of problem solving. For students to become effective inquirers there must be three conditions present: (1) There must be a sense of freedom which makes it possible for students to make choices (teachers should help students find ways to approach and solve problems rather than emphasize the "right answer"); (2) Learners must also be in a responsive environment which gives them the data and the right to pursue them as they see fit (teachers must encourage students to theorize, because without theories around which to organize facts that they collect, the data-gathering process does not make sense); (3) The students will occasionally need focus, i.e. someone to remind them of the discrepancies in their theories. (if carried out properly, the students will learn to process ideas for themselves, but at first the teacher must provide the appropriate focus for them).

TEACHING THE STEPS OF THE PROBLEM-SOLVING PROCESS. Many people have identified and encouraged the teaching of the steps of the problem-solving process (Carkhuff, 1973; Randolph and

Catterall, 1964). Although they all differ slightly, the important thing to remember is that there are identifiable stages or steps that cut across essentially all problem solving and that this process can be taught. Carkuff's stages are as follows:

Stage One—*Developing the problem*. This flows out of the questions referred to above which, if properly asked, help the student to explore and to understand the problem. (Questions, however, are rarely the best method to use in developing the specific problem when it is of a personal nature.)

Stage Two—*Breaking down the problem*. This involves accurately interpreting the problem, which in turn leads to properly defining the goal that one wishes to attain.

Stage Three—*Considering courses of action*. This stage includes considering all of the alternatives which might possibly lead to the goal.

Stage Four—*Choosing courses of action and implementing them*. This involves choosing the course of action which is most likely to lead to the goal and acting upon that decision.

The problem-solving steps of Randolph and Catterall (1964) might be more appropriate to the teaching of younger students; they are as follows:

Step One—*Present the problem*. Either the teacher or one of the students clearly presents the problem as they see it.

Step Two—*Listen*. The teacher should take time to listen to each student's view of the problem.

Step Three—*Clarify*. Once the significant data are gathered from each person, the teacher clarifies the problem as he/she sees it.

Step Four—*Ask for feedback*. When the problem has been clarified, ask the students for feedback. Do they feel that you have stated the problem well?

Step Five—*Invite solutions*. If the problem has been properly clarified, students will usually be able to come up with a supply of possible solutions. Then the group decides on a solution and acts on that decision.

The classroom teachers should feel free to develop or modify the system with which they feel comfortable and which will meet the needs of the students they serve.

GAMES AND SIMULATIONS. Although there is a lot to be said for using the real-life problems which arise in the school and in the student's life to teach problem-solving skills, another approach which is rapidly growing in popularity is to use either a simulation or a game to start this process. There are a wide number of these different activities; the best references are Zuckerman and Horn's (1973), which lists 600 simulations in twenty different subject areas, and Belch's (1973), which lists 900 decision-making or problem-solving exercises in three major areas, spread over seven grade levels. Other valuable references on this topic include: Bower (1976); Carlson (1969); Heyman (1975); Inbar and Stoll (1972); Shears and Bower (1974); and Teaching Research Division, Oregon State System of Higher Education (1967).

A game is essentially a simplified slice of reality. Its structure reflects a real-world process that the designer wishes to teach or to investigate. The game serves as a vehicle for testing that process or for learning more about its workings. In playing games, students tend to develop feelings of effectiveness and control because the actions they take in the game usually produce results. Teachers can help students study either attitudes or problems by having them actually play out their implications and subsequent effects in the classroom. Nobody suggests that games should be used to teach all subject matter, but if they are as effective in teaching processes as has been suggested, they should prove to be a valuable tool in the teaching of life skills (Gordon, 1972).

Simulations, on the other hand, place the learners in a role-playing position where they assume a decision-making role and where, although they can (to some extent) play the role the way they want, they must follow certain procedures and rules to achieve specific objectives. Simulations often force individuals to participate in decision making, under conditions that tend to be highly motivating. The degree of involvement is usually more a function of the psychological reality than it is how well the simulation reproduces real life. For both games and simulations, it is essential to identify the goal to be achieved before they are used.

After the game or simulation, the participants must be "debriefed." This should start with the "What?" concept, a chance to look again at the way the game was played, i.e. what happened, what were the communication patterns, what critical decisions were made, what was the turning point? One can also identify intergroup roles, i.e. what decisions were made, who influenced whom, who emerged as the leaders? Under the heading of "Now what?", the teacher can explore other ways of playing the game; for example, "What rules might be changed?" Then the group progresses to the "So what?" stage, or interpretive part, i.e. "What does it all mean?" Depending upon the objective, the students can challenge the games' norms and can look critically at "justice" and the use of power in the game. Students should be encouraged to compare the elements of the game or simulation with the real world. Most games tend to have a competitive element in them; for a resource on common games that can be changed to meet classroom needs which at the same time deemphasize the "win-lose" component, see Washburn and Washburn (1973).

Many games and simulations have been used to help students learn more about problem solving. *Lost on the Moon* is one of the best known which has been used for this purpose; it was devised by Hall (available from American Behavioral Science Laboratories, Houston, Tx.), and has been included in many National Training Lab Programs. Each participant (from Grades 7 through 12) is given a list of fifteen items which they have to rank in order of their usefulness as if they were really "lost on the moon." The individuals then join small groups and rank the items again. Both scores for each individual and for the total group are compared with the official NASA rank order. A discussion is directed as follows: toward the factors influencing group and individual decisions, and to the conditions under which it would be best to use a group decision, and the like. Some other points that can be considered include the roles taken by different members of the group, how to identify the members with the most information, different styles of group decision making, and the value of collaboration. This game usually involves a very "heated" discussion, even if several members have previously gone through the exercise.

Another group decision-making/planning activity starts by dividing a class of students (it could be anywhere from upper-elementary age upward) into four groups. Each group is assigned a piece of paper attached to the floor at the four corners of a square, approximately twelve feet apart. They are given a supply of common drinking straws, some thread, four paper cups, and two balloons. Without talking, the groups work for twenty minutes trying to build a tower which will reach across to the towers built by the other groups, without letting it touch the floor anywhere except on the four pieces of paper. If, after twenty minutes, the groups have not completed the task, they are given ten more minutes with talking allowed. The debriefing brings out the leadership roles, group decision making, and the importance of verbal communication in both our thinking and in communicating our ideas.

An activity which facilitates the problem-solving process is called *Problems and Hints.* A large group (this can be larger than one class but should not be less than twenty people) is divided into small groups of five or six seated around tables. They are given (or may select) a single, relatively complex, real-life problem which has meaning to the entire group, e.g. how to get more students involved in the decision-making process in the school. Each group is given papers labeled "problems" on which they write all of the major roadblocks that they are likely to encounter before they can reach their goal. These are put into an envelope and passed to the next group; however, before that group can open the envelope, they must "brainstorm" and write down helpful "hints" which they think will help to overcome the problems. After they have completed this task, they open up the "problems" and begin to match their hints with the problems, and they also invent new solutions for situations that they have not considered. Discussion brings out the larger issues surrounding the problem and the best possible hints for the solution. Then a plan of action is devised.

PROJECT LIFE. A small but unique unpublished project that

had a somewhat different "flavor" to it was called *Learning Is For Everyone* (Project LIFE). In this project, college-student volunteers were trained to work with groups of fourth, fifth, and sixth graders in schools with a high percentage of underprivileged children, many of whom were Mexican Americans. Each college student worked with a group of ten to twelve youngsters. The group was told that they had a certain amount of money to use (approximately $60) in any way that they wanted to spend it. They "brainstormed" all kinds of ideas; the steps of solving a problem were given to them and they were helped to use this process to decide what was possible, what they actually would do, and how to plan and to execute their decision. While they were on the trip (or whatever they did), they were given inexpensive cameras with which to take pictures. The slides were then used to help them tell the story of their adventure to the rest of the students at the school, and to reinforce the problem-solving steps they had taken in order to get where they went.

GETTING IT ALL TOGETHER: A GUIDE FOR PERSONALITY DEVELOPMENT AND PROBLEM SOLVING. Valett (1974b) has authored a forty-eight-page workbook presenting a series of affective-emotive lessons for use by adolescents in an attempt to help them develop skills in their personal and social problem-solving (available: Academic Therapy Publications, 1539 Fourth St., San Rafael, Calif. 94901). Valett (1972a) has also devised a similar instrument for younger students called *My Goal Record*. This is a four-page self-evaluation form for involving pupils in the consideration of their own behavior and in planning ways to progress toward a goal. The students are encouraged to identify: a goal, why it is so important to them, and the specific steps to be taken to achieve that goal. There is also a place to specify where they will need help and to plot their progress toward the goal.

DISCOVERY THROUGH GUIDANCE SERIES. This series of four student activity workbooks and teacher's guides was developed for upper elementary-aged pupils, grades 4 through 6, by Bruck (1968a,b, 1969) and by Bruck and Vogelsong (1969) based on a problem-solving approach (available: Bruce Publishing Co., 850 Third Ave., New York, N.Y. 10002). Although *Discovery*

Through Guidance is not closely graded, the four workbooks are as follows:

    Build (Bruck and Vogelsong, 1969)
        Unit I—Building Happiness and Success in School
        Unit II—Building a "Me" I Can Always Respect
        Unit III—Building My Life With Others
        Unit IV—Building Into a Future
    Search (Bruck, 1969)
        Unit I—Searchlight on School
        Unit II—Searchlight on Self
        Unit III—Searchlight on Others
        Unit IV—Searchlight on the Future
    Quest (Bruck, 1968)
        Unit I—Educational Quest
        Unit II—Social Quest
        Unit III—Personal Quest
        Unit IV—Vocational Quest
    Focus (Bruck, 1968)
        Unit I—Educational Focus
        Unit II—Social Focus
        Unit III—Personal Focus
        Unit IV—Vocational Focus

This series represents an example of an attempt to use the group process to teach elementary students to examine the school of which they are a part, themselves as they are influenced by the school, their relationships with others, and how it all affects their personal and vocational future. The Teacher's Guides have good lists of audio visual and printed material for facilitating the problem-solving approach for personal guidance.

LIFE SPACE INTERVIEWING. Hammill and Bartel (1975, pp. 139-143) describe a technique aimed at dealing with the everyday problems that occur in the classroom which they call "Life Space Interviewing." Although it was originally designed for use with crisis situations, it is also encouraged for use with more typical interaction problems in the classroom. Life Space Interviewing involves a rational and semidirectional approach to structuring the situation so that students can work out solutions to their own problems. The teacher listens and facilitates in the problem-solving process worked out by the students; the following method is nonjudgmental and encourages the provision of immediate, concrete consequences for the students, without the typical pleading that often accompanies this process:

Step I—The teacher attempts to get the point of view of both sides (at this point, the facts are not as important as getting at each child's perception or understanding of the incident) ;

Step II—The teacher attempts to find out, through objective questioning, the extensiveness of the argument and how well the two sides understand the situation;

Step III—The two sides are asked to explain what they *can* (not should) do about it, thereby involving the value standards of the two sides. If the solution is acceptable to both sides and to the teacher, the matter is closed with a minimum of verbalization by the teacher.

Step IV——If the problem is not resolved, the teacher must take a more direct stand and point out (as objectively and simply as possible) the consequences of the behavior if it occurs again.

Step V—The teacher attempts to find some approach which will be suitable to both sides.

Step VI—The last step involves the teacher in developing and discussing with the two sides a follow-through plan in the event that the same problem should arise again in the future. Of course the consequences are clearly and succinctly stated by the teacher.

Throughout the process the teacher attempts to minimize "why" questions, since children seldom have the insight or verbal ability to explain their actions. Life Space Interviewing is seen as an efficient "first aid' 'technique which is designed to prevent the problem from spreading. It does present the problem of taking time from the entire class but, if used properly, the whole class can use the process to develop a new life skill.

STRAND V—ADOPTING MORE SATISFYING ROLES

The modern study of groups continues to support the assumption that most people play a series of "roles" as they move from one type of situation to another. In the American culture, probably more than any other, the people around us tend to influence what kind of role we will play at any one time. In this sense of the word, "role" refers to the behavior that is typically expected of persons either when they are alone or, more especially, in a group. One of the developmental life skills that students need to learn is how to identify an appropriate model from whom they can adopt a satisfying role (Sarason and Ganzer, 1971; Sarason and Sarason, 1974; Stumphauzer, 1972; Sulzer and Mayer, 1972). Modeling is a term that has been popularized by the behavior modification movement, but it has found acceptance in many other approaches to working with students. Assertiveness training is a closely related technique (McFall and Lillesand, 1971). Another life skill, therefore, is to learn how to play a series of flexible roles which can enable the student to function in a variety of groups and situations (Powell, 1969). Some older students have trouble because they can only play one role, e.g. the "tough guy" or the "shy girl." Even when they do not feel tough or shy, they have to go on playing the same role. Helping students enact the "role" of other people can assist them increasingly to adopt more satisfying roles for themselves (Blatner, 1973; National Education Association, *Unfinished Stories for Use in the Classroom,* 1968). Many of the techniques which are described later under the heading of *Role-playing* are useful in teaching this life skill. Although Transactional Analysis cuts across communications and other life-skill processes, it will also be discussed in this section as it relates to helping the student to identify and to learn more satisfying roles.

MODELING. The terms "modeling" and "observational learning" are often used interchangeably. They refer to behavior that is learned or modified as a result of observing the behavior of others. The person or group whose behavior is observed and imitated is referred to as the "model." Sarason and Sarason (1974) list the following six basic assumptions related to the effectiveness of modeling:

1. Seeing someone else do something increases the likelihood that the observer will also do it. This is exemplified by the way some people imitate clothing fashions or behavior they see in television stars.

2. If the model is rewarded or reinforced for a certain behavior, the observers are even more likely to imitate that behavior. There is a great deal of evidence to support the fact that rewarding the good behavior of one student will make it more likely that that behavior will be adopted by others, especially if the one being observed is regarded as a desirable model (Woody, 1969).

3. If the behavior of the model is punished, the observers are less likely to imitate the behavior. Similarly, if the observers do not know what happens to the model, i.e. whether they will be rewarded or punished or why, the effect of the reinforcement is reduced. It is important in using modeling behavior that the observers clearly relate the reward or punishment directly to the specific behavior under question.

4. When modeling is effective, behavior is observed and then copied by the onlookers. Students who need to become more aggressive are more likely to adopt that behavior if they see assertive behavior effectively modeled and reinforced in another student or adult. This can be carried out through a fairly direct process of role-playing or a more indirect process of behavioral rehearsal.

5. As one would expect, the observers will imitate the model more readily if they are credible, if they admire them, or, if for some other reason they want to imitate them. Many attempts to help underprivileged youngsters emulate upper-middle class, achieving models have failed because the observers did not admire or want to imitate that kind of model. Certainly teachers are potential models for their students if a good relationship has previously been established. The model, however, does not have to be "all perfect"; in fact, for many students perfection would detract

from the ability to serve as a model. Students usually serve as models (either for better or for worse) for other students.

6. It is obviously necessary for the observers to have the necessary academic skill background or level of physical development if they are to be able to imitate specific academic or physical skills that they see modeled by other students.

Although the process of modeling goes on continuously in the educational endeavor and throughout life in general, when it is to be selected as a strategy for helping students adopt more satisfying roles, several points must be considered. Modeling will be most helpful when: (1) there is a clear picture that what students are doing is maladaptive and (2) that one can be reasonably certain that substitute behaviors would improve the student's adjustment. The behavior that one is trying to modify has to be carefully identified as well as the substitute behavior that one is going to introduce. To ensure that the students to be helped will pay attention to the behavior being modeled, the demonstrated behavior must be clearly observable and it must be seen as a desirable behavior by the student observers. (The process of role acquisition may be enhanced by introducing some of the role-playing or role-rehearsal techniques described in the next section.) Whether or not these techniques are used, the modeling has to be arranged so as to increase the likelihood that the observers will have the opportunity to use the new life skill in their lives. When they perform the new behavior, they will also need to be rewarded or reinforced (either by the teacher, or preferably, by their peers or other natural life forces). The more related the new behavior is to the students' repertoire of behaviors, the more they would naturally adopt the new behavior (Sarason and Sarason, 1974).

ROLE-PLAYING. Theoretical discussions of role-playing have been going on for a long time, but it has not actually been used a great deal. Shaftel has long advocated its use in the school setting (Shaftel and Shaftel, 1967). It would appear that its original conceptualization was "ahead of its time." It will probably be used and accepted more now that we are becoming concerned about life-skill education. Role-playing can be distinguished from dramatization insofar as the roles are ones that would normally have been observed by the students in their real lives (Blatner, 1973; Greenberg, 1975). In structuring role-playing, the following steps are suggested by Shaftel and Shaftel (1967):

1. *Setting the correct climate.* Stress the fact that there is not any "right" answer and that we are exploring what *will* happen, not what *should* happen. Role-playing usually starts with a story that stops in the middle followed by the actors playing out the roles; another approach is for the teacher to simply "set the scene" before the enactment.

2. *Selection of the role-players.* During the warm-up, ask for reactions and choose students who seem to be identifying with the problems and roles. For the first try, it may be well to choose students whose solutions are either unusual or likely to be seen as less satisfactory; other solutions can be used later.

3. *Preparing the students who will observe.* Students who are not in the enactment should be asked to do something fairly specific, e.g. to identify with a particular role, pay attention to the feelings of certain students in the enactment.

4. *Enacting the role-play.* Help from the leader may come from such questions as, "Where will this take place?", or "What are the various people doing?" Once the players have demonstrated their idea of what will happen, the teacher can stop the enactment to save more time for the discussion.

5. *Discussing and evaluating.* The teacher should not be judgmental. Questions should be open-ended, i.e. "What is happening?" "How does _____ feel?" "Are there other ways this situation could end?" The teacher should ask some questions which help the students to apply the enactment to their own lives.

6. *The reenactment.* This may represent other students' ideas about how the roles should be played. The teacher may also ask a player to "switch roles."

7. *Sharing experiences and generalizing to real life.* When the students are ready to generalize, the teacher should

facilitate the generalization with a question such as, "Where are we now?"

Thus it can be seen that role-playing becomes problem-solving in action, in a setting with one's peers, often the most powerful teachers.

I'M OK, YOU'RE OK. A widely used teaching/learning approach to working with young people these days is one adapted from the book by Harris, *I'm OK, You're OK* (1967). This is a modification of the work of Berne, whose book *Games People Play* (1964) (see also Berne, 1972) established a different therapeutic approach called Transactional Analysis. *I'm OK, You're OK* identified three elements or roles in each person's makeup: The Parent (who provides the "do's" and "don'ts"), the Adult (whose role of making reality decisions needs to be strengthened), and the Child (who represents spontaneous emotion). Although Transactional Analysis has many facets, the part that is easiest to teach to students is that there are four ways in which one can approach life:

1. I'm Not OK, You're OK (the dependency of the immature),
2. I'm Not OK, You're Not OK (the "give up" or despair position),
3. I'm OK, You're Not OK (the criminal position), and
4. I'm OK, You're OK (the response of the mature adult at peace with himself/herself).

Adaptations have been also made for the use of these approaches with young children by Ernst (1972), Freed (1971, 1973), and Hesterly (1974).

VALETT HUMAN DEVELOPMENT PROGRAM. Although this particular program directs itself to the development of a much fuller range of life skills than just adopting more satisfying roles, this is one of the major emphases of the program. Based on Valett's (1974a) book, *Affective-Humanistic Education,* which describes his total approach to affective-humanistic education, the Human Development Program is aimed at upper elementary grades (available: Lear Siegler, Fearon Publishers, 6 Davis Dr., Belmont, Calif. 94002). The full-range program is based on five points:

1. *Understanding Basic Human Needs.* A six-point hierarchy of the following basic needs of children: physical security, love, creative expression, cognitive mastery, social competency, and self-worth.
2. *Expressing Human Feelings.* In such basic areas as love, fear, or hate, and secondary areas such as politics or religion.
3. *Self-Awareness and Control.* Uses the "Myself Checklist" (1973a).
4. *Becoming Aware of Human Values.* Principles of value clarification in personal values, social values, and cultural values.
5. *Developing Social and Personal Maturity.* Improving skills in predicting personal consequences, adapting to change, and assuming social responsibility.

Although field-tested on a large number of children, it is too early to tell how effective programs such as this will be.

For teachers, Valett (1974a) suggests a five-point program of what he calls "Pupil Behavior Through Effective Teaching—Model LEARN."

*L*ove and Concern: Do you love and are you concerned about your students?

*E*valuate and Assess: Do you evaluate and assess their progress carefully?

*A*ssign and Record: Do you assign tasks and homework systematically and record individual pupil progress?

*R*einforce and Reward: Do you reinforce desirable behavior?

*N*egotiate and Contract: Do you involve students in critiquing and setting up the class rules?

A word of warning is in order in helping students adopt more satisfying roles. It would be very easy to fall into the trap that students should adopt teacher roles or that teachers can identify roles for them that are more "mature," more "satisfactory," more "productive," and so forth. For this to be a truly humanizing, life-skill developing process, however, teachers must allow students (and themselves) to try a range of roles which will not always appear to be "more mature" or "better." Teachers can help to facilitate students to evaluate the effectiveness of the roles that they have adopted (a major life skill) but they should be very hesitant to try to force students into any predetermined role that they feel would be best.

STRAND VI—MAKING CREATIVE DECISIONS

This strand is closely related to other strands in the life-skill education process (especially the problem-solving strand which helps students face and solve the problems they meet in their day-to-day lives). This strand focuses on helping students: (1) to take what they know about themselves and the world, and (2) to make some decisions about what their goals are and how they want to live their lives. As in all of the other life skills, decisions in this area do not come all at once. A systematically developed, comprehensive program of humanistic education will start by helping very young children to make increasingly important decisions about their lives as they have the information and the maturity to do so. The material in this section will be organized around five major decision-making areas which are as follows: (1) Making an Appropriate Sex-role Identification; (2) Making Appropriate Use of Academic Learning; (3) Using Drugs and Alcohol Appropriately; (4) Making Comprehensive Life Career Decisions; and (5) Promoting Creative Thinking.

MAKING AN APPROPRIATE SEX-ROLE IDENTIFICATION. An area of life skills or humanistic education which has been debated for a long time is variously referred to as "sex education," "family life education," "family living," and the like. In general, these titles refer to attempts that have been made to find ways to help students make decisions about their sexual identities and their sex roles as they affect relationships with other people, and how students relate to family living both now and in the future. This life-skill area has been very difficult to put into operation in the past, primarily because of various pressures from parent groups. Introducing such a program is becoming even more complex, and perhaps more important, because there is more debate about human sexuality and different life-styles than the ones that have been traditionally dictated to us by our basic sex-role identification.

1. *Sociology I.* An early attempt to formalize education in the area of family-life education was developed by the Hayward Unified School District from 1947 to 1967. In 1967, it published *Teacher's Guide for Sociology I (Family Living Instruction): Grade 12* (available: Rapid Printers and Lithographers, Inc., 733 A St., Hayward, Calif. 94541). It was designed as an optional course for high school seniors and contained the following units:

I. Introduction (two to three days): History, Philosophy, and Purpose of Course

II. Human Behavior (five weeks): Heredity and Environment (one-half week), Physical Growth and Development (one and one-half weeks), Personality and Emotional Development (three weeks)

III. Looking Towards Marriage (three weeks): Dating, Courtship, Engagement

IV. Marriage (four weeks): The Family as an Institution, Legal Aspects, Customs, Areas of Adjustment

V. Parenthood (three weeks): Approaching Parenthood, Human Reproduction, Prenatal Care, Infant Care, Child Development and Training, Explaining Sex to Children

VI. Home and Society (two weeks): Changing Nature of the Family, Crises in Marriage, Satisfactions and Problems of Grandparents, Social Problems that Affect the Home, Sources of Community Help, Contributions of the Family to Society Evaluation— (two days)

2. *A Time of Your Life.* The fifteen twenty-minute lessons of this series are designed to help intermediate students consider interpersonal relationships, self-understanding, and family structure. This series stresses individual worth and the need for controlled self-expression; sex education is included as a natural part of the study of family life. (Two thirty-minute teacher programs are included.) The lessons are:

Where Are You? (mutual respect and similarities and differences)

Who Runs Your Life? (self-control and freedom)

Decisions, Decisions, Decisions (self-control and freedom)

How Does a Family Get Along? (conflict, rules, and compromise in the family)

Different Kinds of Families (variations in family compositions)

How Do We Get Through to Each Other? (communications)

What Makes a Friend? (the elements of friendship)

Marriage (the commitment of husband and wife)

Being a Boy—Being a Girl (masculinity/femininity as a part of personality)

Time of Your Future (sociological and technological changes)

The Male (body functions and changes related to puberty)

The Female (follows pattern set in the male)

Questions, Please (questions and answers of three previous shows)

Growing Up (sex can and should be controlled)

(Available: Agency for Instructional Television, Box A, Bloomington, Ind. 74401).

3. *"Contemporary Family Life" course.* Another approach to family life education (Allen and Johnson, 1973) was originally developed for a nine-week unit for high school seniors. Units include:

a. Becoming a Well-adjusted Individual (students take personality tests to help them understand themselves)

b. Preparation for Marriage (students learn to relate to others and deal with the problems of dating, engagement, sex, unwed mothers, etc.)

c. Marriage (students are assigned marriage partners, go through mock ceremony, plan for children, etc.)

d. Family Finance (students learn about how to plan for their spending, about credit and insurance)

e. Home Ownership (students discuss renting vs. buying, how to get loans, etc.)

f. Dissolution of Marriage (students discuss divorce and death).

This approach has been very popular with students and has a breath of reality in it which takes it beyond the usual class discussion or lecture technique.

4. *Other approaches to Family Life Education.* There have obviously been a number of other approaches to sex and family life education, many of which were introduced much earlier in the student's life. As has already been indicated, many of the early decisions regarding appropriate sex-role identifications start in infancy when the culture begins to teach sex-linked roles to the young child. Where such material should be introduced in the curriculum is difficult to say. Most attempts to introduce this type of material tend to use an informal approach, using already available materials for subunits within the larger teaching program. SIECUS, the Sex Information and Education Council of the United States (n.d.) has produced a series of fourteen Study Guides intended for all persons who are concerned with education for sexuality and with increasing their own understanding in this area. Although not specifically designed for classroom use, they have frequently been adapted for that purpose. The study guides are as follows: (1) Sex Education, (2) Homosexuality, (3) Masturbation, (4) Characteristics of Male and Female Sexual Responses, (5) Premarital Sexual Standards, (6) Sexual Relations During Pregnancy and Postdelivery Period, (7) (not available), (8) Sexuality and the Life Cycle, (9) Sex, Science, and Values, (10) the Sex Educator and Moral Values, (11) Sexual Encounters Between Adults and Children, (12) Sexual Life in Later Years, (13) Concerns of Parents About Sex Education, and (14) Teenage Pregnancy. (Available: Behavioral Publications, 72 Fifth Ave., New York, N.Y. 10011.)

Another book by Valett, called *Sex and TLC* (1973b), was written with adolescent classes on marriage and family living as part of its intended audience. It stresses the importance of tender, loving care as the essence of love and helps the reader to appreciate how a great deal of self-realization can be obtained through such a positive relationship. There is also increasing interest in the counseling and education of the handicapped in the area of sex education (Fischer, Krajicek, and Borthick, 1974).

5. *The influence of liberation movements on sex-role identification.* Both the Women's Liberation and the Gay Activist

movements are having an effect on how sex-role identification topics should be treated in the school. They are making it possible to help students look more critically at the sex-roles assigned to them by society and to decide more clearly how these pressures affect their own lives. The pressures of the society to exact conforming behavior in the area of sex-role identification can be more easily understood, and alternative life-styles in marriage and human relations can be considered. Many of the instructional materials which are already being used in the schools can be examined for their assumptions about sex roles and life-styles. Some attempts have been made to help elementary school girls become more aware of the expanding role of women in our society (Gerson, 1973; Harrison, 1973).

As in many other life-skills areas, the amount of published material which is available for the school to use directly with the students is quite limited. On the one hand, it reflects the lack of interest historically paid by school personnel in these areas. In the case of sex-role identification, in some instances it also reflects an organized pressure on the part of certain people in the culture to keep the school from developing adequate humanistic education programs for all students. There does, however, appear to be growing support (both legislative and social) for those educators who are trying to start programs in this important life-skill area.

MAKING APPROPRIATE USE OF ACADEMIC LEARNING. By law, students attend school, and almost by definition it is the responsibility of the school to help them become educated (however "educated" is defined). It is important to help students understand the facts and information that are presented to them by the school; to make decisions about how to use this information; to organize themselves so they can get the greatest profit from these experiences; to decide what course to take, and how long they want to continue in school. In the area of humanistic education, it has already been pointed out that students' achievement may be aided when they view their teachers as friendly persons who wish to encourage communication rather than as powerful, authoritative figures (Gaudry and Spielberger, 1971). The teacher interested in this approach will find helpful a booklet by Mager, (1968) *Developing Attitude Toward Learning*. The booklet is not about what to teach, but about a way of helping students get the best use out of what they have been taught and how to influence them to learn more while they are in (and after they have left) school. Mager discusses the conditions that influence this attitude in students under three questions: Where am I going? How shall I get there? How will I know when I have arrived? This approach is similar to the one listed under the heading of "Five Facilitating Questions" in the earlier section of "Self-identity" described under the Self-enhancing Education Program (see also Alschuler, 1971). Closely related to Mager's approach is the one which encourages students to make comprehensive career decisions discussed later in this section. Students who have made realistic plans about the kind of career they want to pursue are more ready to relate what they are being taught today to the long-range goals they have set for themselves.

Bread and Butterflies is a series of fifteen, fifteen-minute (with several lessons aimed at the teacher) audiovisual programs for intermediate level students. It is designed to give students a clearer understanding of successful work behavior and the connection between school and the real world. It also encourages each child to develop his/her own special capabilities and goals (available: the Agency for Instructional Television, Box A, Bloomington, Ind. 47401). The fifteen programs include:

> Treasure Hunt (self-independence and the economic system)
> Work Means (why people work)
> Me, Myself, and Maybe (self-clarification)
> Decisions, Decisions (decision-making)
> Schools and Jobs (relationship: school, work, and society)
> Taking Care of Business (the responsible self)
> I Agree—You're Wrong (interpersonal skills)
> Success Story (what is success?)
> The Way We Live (life-styles)
> Planning Ahead: The Racer (shaping one's destiny)
> Things, Ideas, People (people at work)

People Need People (interdependency of workers)
Our Own Two Hands (human dignity)
Power Play (power and influence)
Choosing Changes (freedom to hope, to choose, and to change) .

Another approach that has been used to give greater meaning to academic learning is helping students learn to take tests more effectively (Millman and Pauk, 1969) and learn to study. In general, these approaches are more effective when they come after students are able to relate learning to their own life goals. It is not always possible, however, to wait until students have established such objectives before they are helped to make the most of their schooling. It would appear that much could be done to help students step back from the process of education and learn how to "play the game" of going to school. This could be done through role-playing or simulation and it might help the student to look objectively at the processes and procedures which they will have to go through in order to receive a good education.

There are a great many books on helping students improve their study skills (Zifferblatt, 1970). Once again, to show the interrelatedness of life skills, teachers should be aware of the fact that students who have a good self-concept are more likely to achieve than those who do not (Brookover, Erickson, and Joiner, 1967).

Still another approach might be to make students aware of their rights in regard to the educational process. When they know their rights they might not feel so "put down" by the school (Sandman, 1971).

DECIDING HOW TO USE DRUGS APPROPRIATELY. There has been a great deal of interest in how to introduce "drug education" programs into the school. This was brought on by the high incidence of students who were experimenting with and actively using a wide variety of drugs (Scott, 1972). The impetus to help students make appropriate decisions in this area overcame some of the fear and resistance by school personnel regarding these complex life-skill areas and resulted in a great movement toward a broad series of humanistic education programs (Coronado Plan

Teacher's Guide, n.d.). There has been a problem in finding an appropriate name for these programs. They traditionally place very little emphasis on drugs and their effects partially because this is not where the real problem is and partially because many students have already acquired quite a bit of knowledge about these drugs from their peers. In some instances earlier attempts at "drug education," became just that, i.e. the programs had the net effect of students trying out some of the drugs that they had heard about. The programs rapidly moved into a humanistic/ life-skill approach or decision-making program (Light, 1975).

There are so many substances that are technically "drugs" which we use almost constantly and so many ways to get "high" that it becomes necessary to start talking about "substance abuse prevention programs." One attempt to put together a total K-12 curricular approach uses many of the humanistic education foci which have been discussed in this section; it is described below.

1. *A World to Grow In: A K-12 Drug, Alcohol, Tobacco, and Human Behavior Approach.* This material was developed by a Title III Project of the Ohio Department of Education and was cooperatively prepared by the Educational Research Council of America and the school systems of Dayton and Lima, Ohio (available: the Ohio State Department of Education, 65 Front St., Columbus, Oh. 43215). It is based on the assumption that in order for students to avoid "substance abuse" behavior they must learn to understand the following: the nature of life tasks, the nature of frustrations, the differences between constructive and nonconstructive methods of resolving frustrations (including both remote and immediate consequences), and to use constructive and enjoyable methods for working out the daily tasks required in life.

In the primary grades students learn about the need for keeping their physical, social, and personal surroundings in balance. They also learn how to use curiosity about substances without taking undue chances. Both the teachers and their students are helped to understand the frustrations experienced by children at various ages and how they can be helped to deal with their difficulties.

In the elementary school and later, students learn about the long-term effects of various drugs and of the alternative ways of meeting personal needs for self-respect, personal worth, or being loved. Upon exploring alternative ways of meeting these needs, students are helped to identify what effects they want and what they want to do with their lives. They are, in short, helped to clarify the purposes they want their lives to serve and how most effectively to meet the daily demands of life in a way consistent with that life purpose. This behavioral approach assumes that "taking drugs" is understandable as a behavior (just as is any other behavior) and that students can be taught humanistic and decision-making skills related to whether or not they want to get involved.

2. *Project TRIAD.* Another approach to substance abuse education is typified by the Project TRIAD in the Genesee Intermediate School District (information: 2413 West Maple Ave., Flint, Mich. 48504). Its publication (Project Triad: Road Notes, 1974) presents a philosophy that the best drug education has its foundation in establishing a healthy emotional environment and the promotion of sound mental health and self-understanding. Instead of a fixed curriculum, David Hall, Project Director, brought together a group of people who emphasized a process of education with the following components:

Self-concept: A New View of the Identity Process
Communication Skills
Empathy Training
Introductory and Advanced Values Clarification
Influences
Decision Making and Risk Taking
Self-defeating Behavior
Alternatives to Drug Taking—"Alternative Highs"

TRIAD attempted to take the staffs of the schools and train them in a new way of understanding and working with students by using these skills.

3. *National Clearinghouse for Drug Abuse Information.* The National Clearinghouse (n.d.) has reprinted the Drug Abuse Curricula for all of the schools listed below. (Single copies are

available from the Clearinghouse: Education Services, 5454 Wisconsin Ave., Chevy Chase, Md. 20015. Multiple copies can be purchased from the U.S. Government Printing Office, Division of Public Documents, Washington, D. C. 20402). Price and order number are indicated in parentheses.

> Baltimore Co. Board of Education, Grades 6, 9, 12 (Prex 13.8:Ed 8 $1.00)
>
> Flagstaff Public School, Grades K through 12 (Prex 13.8: Ed 8/2 $ .65)
>
> Great Falls School District #1, Grade 6 (Prex 13.8:Ed 8/8 $1.25)
>
> New York State Education Dept., Grades 4, 5, 6 (Prex 13.8: Ed 8/3 $ .65)
>
> Rhode Island Dept. of Education, Grades K through 12 (Prex 13.8:Ed 8/5 $1.25)
>
> San Francisco Unified School Dist., Grades K to 12 (Prex 13.8:Ed 8/7 $1.75)
>
> South Bay Union School Dist., Grades K through 12 (Prex 13.8:Ed 8/4 $1.25)
>
> Tacoma Public Schools, Grades 6 through 12 (Prex 13.8: Ed 8/6 $ .65)
>
> Resource Book for Drug Abuse Education (Fs 2.22:D 84/12 $1.25)

MAKING COMPREHENSIVE CAREER DECISIONS. Needless to say, one decision that all students have to make sooner or later is what kind of a career they will enter. As previously mentioned, many students and educators have not wanted to face this decision either very early or very directly. Early attempts seemed to try to "force" the student to say that he/she wanted to be a lawyer or something else; this is no longer the emphasis. Much effort is being devoted to the development of programs from K through 12 in which students are systematically introduced to the world of work; helped to understand themselves and their needs in relation to a career choice; taught to assess a career choice in terms of its requirements and the ways it affects a life-style; encouraged to make several possible choices; given guidelines to determine which ones are likely to be best for them; helped to make and to follow a career development plan; and encouraged to remain flexible in case a change is indicated (Dunn and Payne, n.d.; Ginsberg, 1971; McCure, 1975; Wernick, 1973). It should be somewhat apparent that most of the humanistic approaches discussed in this part of the text could be readily included in such a comprehensive career development model (Holland, 1973; Reardon and Burck, 1975).

Two general approaches to career development show great promise and need further development. One helps students (at approximately the fifth, sixth, or seventh grade) to do a comprehensive "life-style assessment" of the vocation chosen by the breadwinner in their family, especially as it has affected their own life. It makes sense to help all students understand that vocational choice is more than just a way to earn money. The other approach involves the use of immediate follow-up data of what the graduates of a high school are doing one or two years after graduation. The students may be told, "Just two years ago, there were _____ students sitting in the desks you are sitting in now. Here is what they are doing two years later. What does this information suggest regarding your plans and what you will be doing two years from now?" (*You, the Decision Maker: Counselor's Manual*, 1967).

1. *"Deciding"* and *"Decisions and Outcomes."* Gelatt and other members of the Palo Alto (Calif.) Unified School District staff prepared two workbooks and leader's guides published by the College Entrance Examination Board. They both focus on the development of decision-making skills by helping students to determine and recognize their personal values, to collect and effectively use relevant information, and to convert this information into a sound course of action. They are both designed to be used separately as a course in decision making, or they can be used as a unit in other courses such as English, history, human relations, drug education, or health education. They both rely on peer interaction and group discussions and use values clarification to teach personalized decision making. The two workbooks are:

Deciding (for junior high students) : Values, Information, and Strategy (Gelatt, Varenhorst, and Carey, 1972a), and *Decisions and Outcomes* (for senior high and older). The Starting Point, The Deciding Self, Before Deciding, and Applying Skills (Gelatt, Verenhorst, Carey, and Miller, 1973a).

2. *The Santa Clara Educational-vocational Guidance Program.* (n.d.) This program (now out of print) was developed in conjunction with the Santa Clara (Calif.) Unified School District and the American Institute for Research, in Palo Alto. It was designed in the form of Individualized Teaching Learning Units (TLU's) for students from the seventh through twelfth grades. Each unit listed the objective that the students were expected to be able to achieve in using that unit, the materials and procedures which would be used to reach the objective, and the way they would be able to evaluate whether or not they had attained the objectives. In addition to helping students gain an orientation to the units, there were six major guidance skill areas divided into twenty units:

Understanding the Problem (two units)
Searching for and Using Information (nine units)
Getting Alternatives (two units)
Selecting Goals and Making Plans (three units)
Carrying out Plans (three units)
Finding Out if it Works (one unit).

3. *Life/Career Development System.* This program was developed by Waltz (n.d.). Nine modules are included for students in grades nine through twelve. Each unit takes from six to nine hours to complete. The units can be used by total classes or individually (available: Human Development Services, Inc., Ann Arbor, Mich.). The units are:

Exploring Self,
Determining Values,
Setting Goals,
Expanding Options,
Overcoming Barriers,
Using Information,

Working Effectively,
Thinking Futuristically, and
Selecting Mates.

4. *Life Careers Game.* Another approach involving career decisions which has been very useful is the Life Careers Game developed by Boocock and Varenhorst. Small groups of students read a case study about high school students in different kinds of situations. They then "play through" the life of the student, making decisions about how they spend their working hours and how they progress through school. The grades obtained in the courses "their" student is taking are determined by the throw of dice, which leads to interesting discussions about how grades are really determined. Chance cards bring in accidental factors which affect the individual's career decisions. The involvement in the process and the discussions which follow seem to be very helpful in assisting students to evaluate what they are doing with their own lives (Boocock, n.d.) .

5. *Work Experience/Exploration.* It is not desirable to try to bring all of the career decision making into the classroom. One of the most exciting strategies utilized outside the school involves the increased use of work experience and career exploration programs by the student. These programs give the student an opportunity to explore the world of work firsthand, and under supervision. Although in the past the work experience model has been used primarily for the student who either had a great deal of difficulty with school or who had to work for financial reasons, it would appear that there would be almost no student who would not profit from some sort of on-the-job experience. For those students who are capable and motivated enough to consider professional careers, it would seem likely that professional people in the community could be located who would be willing to take them in for brief periods of time to help them become oriented to that profession. Educators continue to try to "reinvent the wheel" and bring all of the world in canned, predigested form into the classroom. It would appear to be time to further humanistic, career-decision education by making it possible for large numbers of students to get out of the school and begin to relate what they

are taking there to some possible career explorations in the "real" world.

PROMOTING CREATIVE THINKING. Life is more than solving the "hum drum" problems that face us here and now. The end result should be more than an efficient person who relates well to all. Effective life-skill education should produce individuals who are in touch with their feelings (Jones, 1968); who reach out to make effective interpersonal relationships (Johnson, 1972); who can take sides on important public issues (Oliver and Shaver, 1966); who are in harmony with their environment (Terry, 1971); who can take the necessary risks in life to get the job done (Carney, 1971); who can face crises effectively (Mohr, n.d.); who are creative people (Torrance and Meyers, 1971); and who can realistically face the future even to their ultimate death (Zeligs, 1974). As idealistic as it sounds, individuals should also be able to do all of this with a sense of joy and a zest for life. Some beginnings in the area of teaching for creativity have been made, but most of the other areas remain only shadows in the current state-of-the-art in humanistic/life-skill education.

1. *Thinking Creatively.* Although this discussion of creativity comes at the last of this section, it also needs to be developed as a continuing strand throughout all levels of the curriculum. Whereas the behavior modification approaches appear to work well with certain children who have various learning and behavior problems, there are good reasons to assume that many students prefer to think and to learn in a more creative fashion where they attempt to "fill the gaps" in what they know in some original way. This process involves more than just step-by-step problem solving; it involves some productive attempt at putting together the things in the environment in a new way (new to the students, at any rate). Creative drama has been effectively used to promote this in many grade levels, but especially with young children to foster creativity (Feudo, 1975). The role-playing techniques described earlier can have a similar effect with older children. Once again, our schools too often teach for convergent (i.e. "right answer") thinking which does not help the divergent, innovative thinker (Frymier and Hawn, 1970; Kravetz, 1970).

Torrance (1971) lists the most fundamental things that a teacher can do to encourage creativity:

> Respond to the creative needs of the learner.
>
> Know the learner.
>
> Build creative skills in the learner.
>
> Heighten anticipation on the part of the learner (use a period of warm-up).
>
> Build creative reading skills.
>
> Encounter the unexpected and deepen the students' expectations (use the unexpected ending, etc.).
>
> Go beyond the textbooks, classrooms, and curricula (keep encouraging the students to find new ways to look at the material and world in which they live).

2. *Responsible Citizenship.* Another aspect of the creative decision-making curriculum should be designed to help the student relate to others and to the society in a productive, useful way. *Rights and Responsibilities* is a series of (what will eventually be) ten, twenty-minute lessons aimed at junior high and high school students. It is designed to help them examine the privileges of the individual in our society, to understand the interplay between privileges, obligations, and limitations inherent in citizenship. The series deals with rights and responsibilities in the school, at work, and in society as a whole. The six lessons already developed (available: Agency for Instructional Television, Box A, Bloomington, Ind. 47401) are:

> I Don't Care (the life story of Larry, a convict, from age 9 to 19)
>
> Dead Path (from the time of arrest to the sentence)
>
> Change (the time in prison, his rehabilitation, and desire to live responsibly)
>
> An Interview With Larry (four students interview him about his past, his feelings, etc.)
>
> Police Officer (two officers encounter juveniles breaking the law)
>
> An Open Mind (the thoughts of students about police and law are contrasted with those of police officers).

3. *Zest for Life.* Although there is much that can be done in

the improvement of a curriculum in the area of developing life-skills and there is much that can be done in teaching groups of students to make better decisions (Eisman, 1969), it is undoubtedly going to be very difficult to devise a curriculum which will help large groups of students to develop a creative look at life. It will probably have to rely much more on the creative ways in which teachers and students relate to each other and in the ways they handle the unexpected problems as they arise in and out of school (Harris, 1973). Although everyone can aspire to such high levels of teaching, it is more practical to hope that every student will come into contact with one or more creative teachers at one or more critical points in their lives so that they will come out of the formal aspect of their educational process with a confident look toward the future and a zest for life. Some of this quality of a creative quest for freedom seems to have caught the imagination of people in the book *Jonathon Livingston Seagull* (Bach, 1970) which can be used as part of a humanistic education program. The words to popular music may also be helpful (Walker, 1969). Similarly, many of the modern posters which students buy and display quite proudly have strong valuing statements and reflect different life-styles which could become the basis for still further life-skill programs (see Rinder's, 1970, *Love is an Attitude,* a book made up of small reproductions of a large number of these posters).

It is hoped that the suggestions which have been given in Chapter 6 will serve to draw out the creative thinking of teachers and other people interested in improving education. The techniques discussed are a long way from being a complete (K through 12) developmental program in life skills. Until such a program is developed and implemented there will be large groups of students who have unmet personal-social needs and it will continue to be necessary to "put out the fires" with some of the Corrective/ Therapeutic Interventions discussed in the next chapter.

REFERENCES

Adams, D. M. *Simulation games: An approach to learning.* Worthington, Oh.: Charles Jones, 1973.

Agency for Instructional Television. *1976 television: A catalog of related materials*. Bloomington: Author, 1976.

Allen, C., & Johnson, W. *Contemporary family life: A course guide*. Portland, Or.: Allen, Johnson, & Roberts (Parkrose High School, 11717 N. E. Shaver, 97220), 1973.

Alschuler, A. *Teaching achievement motivation*. Middleton, Co.: Education Ventures, 1971.

American Council on Education. *Reading ladders for human relations*. Washington, D. C.: Author, 1949.

American Psychological Association. *Psychology teacher's resource book: First Course* (2nd ed.). Washington, D. C.: Author, 1973.

Anderson, L., & Coburn, J. *A major goal of any school district should be to help develop in children a healthy self-concept*. Ventura, Ca.: Ventura County Superintendent of Schools, 1972.

Arnspiger, V. C., Rucker, W. R., & Brill, J. A. *The human value series*. Austin: Steck-Vaughn, 1967-69.

Aspy, D. *Toward technology for humanizing education*. Champaign: Research Press, 1972.

Association for Childhood Education International. *Feelings and learning*. Washington, D. C.: Author (n.d.).

Association for Supervision and Curriculum Development, NEA. *To nurture humaneness*. Washington, D. C.: ASCD, 1970.

Bach, R. *Jonathon livingston seagull*. New York: MacMillan, 1970.

Baier, K., & Rescher, N. *Values and the future*. New York: Free Press, 1969.

Barclay, J. R., & Barclay, L. K. *Appraising individual differences in the elementary classroom: A user's manual of the Barclay Classroom Climate Inventory*. Lexington, Ky.: Educational Skills Development, 1972.

Barnett, J. B. *Effects of self-management instruction and contingency management to increase completion of work*. Unpublished doctoral dissertation, Ohio State University, 1973.

Barr, R. D. (Ed.). *Values and youth: Teaching social studies in an age of crises*. Washington, D. C.: National Council for the Social Studies, 1971.

Bateman, B. Humanistic goals and behaviorist technology. *School Psychology Digest*, 1973, *2*, 3-9.

Beatty, W. H. (Ed.). *Improved educational assessment and an inventory of measures of affective behavior*. Washington, D. C.: Association for Supervision and Curriculum Development, 1969.

Becker, W. C. *Parents are teachers: A child management program*. Champaign: Research Press, 1971.

Belch, J. *Contemporary games*. Detroit: Gale Research, 1973.

Bereiter, C. *Must we educate?* Englewood Cliffs: Prentice-Hall, 1974.

Berger, T. *I have feelings*. New York: Behavioral Publications, 1971.

Berkowitz, L. *The development of motives and values in children*. New York: Basic, 1964.

Berne, E. *Games people play*. New York: Grove, 1964.

Berne, E. *What do you do after you say hello?* New York: Grove, 1972.

Bessell, H. *Methods of human development: Secondary level activity guides.* San Diego: Human Development Training Institute, 1974.

Beyond the three R's: Training teachers for affective education. Atlanta: Southern Regional Education Board, 1974.

Blatner, H. *Acting in: Practical application of psychodramatic methods.* New York: Springer, 1973.

Boocock, S. S. *Life career game.* New York: Western (n.d.).

Bower, E. M. *Early identification of emotionally handicapped children in school* (2nd ed.). Springfield: Charles C Thomas, 1974.

Bower, E. M. *Learning to play: Playing to learn.* New York: Behavioral Publications, 1976.

Bradfield, R. H. (Ed.). *Behavior modification: The human effort.* San Rafael: Dimensions, 1970.

Brookover, W. B., Erickson, E. L., & Joiner, L. M. *Self-concept of ability and school achievement, III: Relationship of self-concept to achievement in high school.* East Lansing: Human Learning Research Institute, Michigan State University, 1967.

Brown, G. *Human teaching for human learning: An introduction to confluent education.* New York: Viking, 1971.

Bruck, C. M. *Focus: Discovery through guidance.* New York: Bruce, 1968a.

Bruck, C. M. *Quest: Discovery through guidance.* New York: Bruce, 1968b.

Bruck, C. M. *Search: Discovery through guidance.* New York: Bruce, 1969.

Bruck, C. M., & Vogelsong, M. O. *Build: Discovery through guidance.* New York: Bruce, 1969.

Bullis, H. E. *Human relations in the classroom, Course II* (2nd ed.). Wilmington: Delaware Society for Mental Hygiene, 1950 (out of print).

Bullis, H. E., & O'Malley, E. E. *Human relations in the classroom, Course I* (5th ed.). Wilmington: Delaware Society for Mental Hygiene, 1951 (out of print).

Caldwell, E. *Group techniques for the classroom teacher.* Chicago: Science Research Associates (n.d.).

Carkhuff, R. R. *Helping and human relations: A primer for lay and professional helpers,* Vol. 1, *Selection and training.* New York: Holt, Rhinehart & Winston, 1969.

Carkhuff, R. R. *The art of problem solving.* Amherst, Ma.: Human Resource Development, 1973.

Carlson, E. *Learning through games.* Washington, D. C.: Public Affairs, 1969.

Carney, R. E. *Risk taking behavior: Concepts, methods, and applications to smoking and drug abuse.* Springfield: Charles C Thomas, 1971.

Chase, L. *The other side of the report card: A how-to-do-it-program for affective education.* Pacific Palisades, Ca.: Goodyear, 1975.

Cole, H. P. *Process education: The new direction for elementary-secondary schools.* Englewood Cliffs: Educational Technology, 1972.

Coopersmith, S. *Antecedents of self-esteem.* San Francisco: Freeman, 1967.

Coronado Plan Teacher's Guides. San Diego: Pennant Press (n.d.).

Cottingham, H. *Elementary school guidance: Conceptual beginnings and initial approaches* Washington, D. C.: American Personnel and Guidance Association, 1970.

Cromwell, C. R., Ohs, W., Roark, A. E., & Stanford, G. *Becoming: A course in human relations.* Philadelphia: Lippincott, 1975a.

Cromwell, C. R., Ohs, W., Roark, A. E., & Stanford, G. *Personal log for becoming: A course in human relations.* Philadelphia: Lippincott, 1975b.

Cullum, A. *The geranium on the windowsill just died but teacher you went right on.* New York: Quist, 1971.

Curwin, R. C., & Curwin, G. *Developing individual values in the classroom.* Palo Alto: Learning Handbooks, 1974.

Dibner, S. S., & Dibner, A.S. *Integration or segregation of the physically handicapped?* Springfield: Charles C Thomas, 1973.

Dinkmeyer, D. *DUSO: A program to develop understanding of self and others.* Circle Pines, Mn.: American Guidance, 1970.

Dinkmeyer, D. & Dreikurs, R. *Encouraging children to learn: The encouragement process.* Englewood Cliffs: Prentice-Hall, 1963.

Dreikurs, R., Grunwald, D. B., & Pepper, F. C. *Maintaining sanity in the classroom: Illustrated teaching techniques.* New York: Harper & Row, 1971.

Dunn, C. J., & Payne, B. F. *World of work: Occupational-vocational guidance in the elementary grades.* Dallas: Leslie, (n.d.).

Dupont, H., Gardner, O. S., & Brody, D. S. *Toward affective development: An activity-oriented program designed to stimulate psychological and affective development.* Circle Pines, Mn.: American Guidance, (n.d).

East, J. *Body language.* New York: East, 1970.

Eiseman, J. W. *The deciders.* Menlo Park, Ca.: Institute for Staff Development, 1969.

Elder, C. A. *Making value judgments: Decisions for today.* San Diego: Pennant Press, 1972.

Epstein, S. Teaching psychology to elementary school students: A new role for the school psychologist. *DUO, A Joint Publication of the California State Psychological Association and the California Association of School Psychologists and Psychometrists,* 1975, October, *1,* 13-14.

Ernst, K. *Games students play: And what to do about them.* Millbrae, Ca.: Celestial Arts, 1972.

Fabun, D. *Three roads to awareness: Motivation, creativity, communications.* Beverly Hills: Glencoe, 1970.

Farson, R. *Birthrights.* New York: MacMillan, 1974.

Fass, J. S. *A primer for parents.* New York: Trident, 1968.

Feudo, V. J. *Creative drama for young children.* New York: Behavioral Publications, 1975.

Fine, M. J. *A parent education short course.* Lawrence, Ks.: Author, 1974.

Fischer, H. L., Krajicek, M. J., & Borthick, W. A. *Sex education for the developmentally disabled: A guide for parents, teachers, and professionals.* Baltimore: University Park, 1974.

Fish, K. L. *Conflict and dissent in the high school.* New York: Bruce, 1970.

Fisher, H. *Developments in high school psychology.* New York: Behavioral Publications, 1974.

Flescher, I. *Children in the learning factory: The search for a humanizing teacher.* Philadelphia: Chilton, 1973.

Flynn, E., & La Faso, J. *Group discussion as learning process.* Paramus, N. J.: Paulist-Newman, 1972.

Focus on Self Development. Chicago: Science Research Associates (n.d.).

Forsyth, A. S. Jr., & Gammel, J. D. *Toward affective education: A guide to developing affective learning objectives.* Columbus, Oh.: Battelle Center for Improved Education, 1974.

Foster, H. H. *A "Bill of Rights" for children.* Springfield: Charles C Thomas, 1974.

Freed, A. M. *T.A. for kids and grown ups too.* Sacramento: Jalmar Press, 1971.

Freed, A. M. *T. A. for kids and tots and other prinzes.* Sacramento: Jalmar Press, 1973.

Friedman, R. (Ed.). *Family roots of school learning and behavior disorders.* Springfield: Charles C Thomas, 1973.

Frymier, J. R., & Hawn, H. C. *Curriculum improvement for better schools.* Worthington, Oh.: Charles C. Jones, 1970.

Gaudry, E., & Speilberger, C. D. *Anxiety and educational achievement.* New York: Wiley, 1971.

Gazda, G. M., Asbury, F. R., Balzar, F. J., Childers, W. C., Desselle, R. E., & Walters, R. P. *Human relations development: A manual for educators.* Boston: Allyn & Bacon, 1973.

Gazda, G. M., Asbury, F. M., Balzer, F. J., Childers, W. C., Desselle, R. E., & Walters, R. P. *Instructor's manual to accompany human relations development: A manual for educators.* Boston: Allyn & Bacon, 1973.

Gazda, G. M. & Folds, J. H. *Group guidance: A critical incidents approach.* Chicago: Parkinson Division, Follett Educational Corporation, 1968.

Gazda, G. M., Walters, R. P., & Childers, W. C. *Realtalk: Exercises in friendship and helping skills.* Authors, 1976.

Gelatt, H. B., Varenhorst, B., & Carey, R. *Deciding.* New York: College Entrance Examination Board, 1972a.

Gelatt, H. B., Varenhorst, B., & Carey, R. *Deciding: A leader's guide.* New York: College Entrance Examination Board, 1972b.

Gelatt, H. B., Varenhorst, B., Carey, R., & Miller, G. P. *Decisions and outcomes.* New York: College Entrance Examination Board, 1973a.

Gelatt, H. B., Varenhorst, B., Carey, R., & Miller, G. P. *Decisions and out-*

comes: A leader's guide. New York: College Entrance Examination Board, 1973b.

Gerson, B. The theory and practice of consciousness-raising groups with elementary school girls. *School Psychology Digest,* 1973, *2,* 38-44.

Ginsberg, E. *Career guidance, who needs it? Who provides it? Who can improve it?* New York: McGraw-Hill, 1971.

Glasser, W. *Reality therapy.* New York: Harper, 1965.

Glasser, W. *Schools without failure.* New York: Harper, 1969.

Gold, P. *Please don't say hello.* New York: Behavioral Publications, 1975.

Gordon, A. K. *Games for growth: Educational games in the classroom.* Chicago: Science Research Associates, 1972.

Gordon, T. R. *Parent effectiveness training: The tested new way to raise responsible children.* New York: Wyden, 1970.

Gorman, A. H. *Teachers and learners: The interaction process of education.* Boston: Allyn & Bacon, 1974.

Greenberg, I. A. (Ed.). *Psychodrama: Theory and therapy.* New York: Behavioral Publications, 1975.

Gregory, T. B. *Encounters with teaching: A micro-teaching manual.* Englewood Cliffs: Prentice-Hall, 1972.

Hall, J. *Lost on the Moon.* Houston, Tx.: National Training Laboratory Institute, 1970.

Hamblin, R. L., Buckholdt, D., Ferritor, D., Blackwell, L., & Kozloff, M. *The humanization processes: A social, behavioral analysis of children's problems.* New York: Wiley, 1971.

Hamilton, N., & Saylor, G. (Eds.). *Humanizing the secondary school.* Washington, D. C.: Association for Supervision and Curriculum Development, 1969.

Hammill, D. D. & Bartel, N. R. *Teaching children with learning and behavior problems.* Boston: Allyn & Bacon, 1975.

Haney, C., & Zimbardo, P. G. It's tough to tell a high school from a prison. *Psychology Today,* 1975, *26,* 29-30, 106.

Harmin, M., Kirschenbaum, H., & Simon, S. *Clarifying values through subject matter: Applications for the classroom.* Minneapolis: Winston, 1973.

Harmin, M., & Simon, S. B. Values. In D. W. Allen & E. Seifman, (Eds.). *The teacher's handbook.* Chicago: Scott Foresman, 1971, 690-698.

Harris, S. J. *Winners and losers.* Chicago: Argus Communications, 1973.

Harris, T. A. *I'm OK, you're OK: A practical guide to transactional analysis.* New York: Harper & Row, 1967.

Harrison, B. G. *Unlearning the lie: Sexism in school.* New York: Liveright, 1973.

Hawley, R. C. *Human values in the classroom: Teaching for personal and social growth.* Amherst, Ma.: Education Research Press, 1973.

Hawley, R. C. *Value exploration through role playing.* Amherst, Ma.: Education Research Press, 1974.

Hawley, R. C., & Hawley, I. L. *A handbook of personal growth activities for classroom use.* Amherst, Ma.: Educational Research Press, 1972.

Hechlik, J. E., & Lee, J. L. (Eds.). *CAPS current resources series: Small group work and group dynamics.* Ann Arbor: ERIC Counseling and Personnel Services Information Center, 1968.

Hesterly, S. O. *Parent package: To raise a winner (a T. A. program for parents of winners).* 8 Brookfield Cove, Little Rock, Ar.: Author, 1974.

Heyman, M. *Simulation games for the classroom.* Bloomington: Phi Delta Kappa, 1975.

Hitt, W. D. *Education as a human enterprise.* Worthington, Oh.: Charles A. Jones, 1973.

Holland, J. L. *Making vocational choices: A theory of careers.* Englewood Cliffs: Prentice-Hall, 1973.

Holt, J. *How children fail.* New York: Dell, 1964.

Hunter, E. *Encounter in the classroom: New ways of teaching.* New York: Holt, Rinehart & Winston, 1972.

Illich, I. *Deschooling society.* New York: Harper & Row, 1971.

Inbar, M., & Stoll, C. (Eds.). *Simulation and gaming in social science.* New York: Free Press, 1972.

Jay, E. S. *Book about me.* Chicago: Science Research Associates, 1952.

Jaynes, R., & Woodbridge, B. *Bowman early childhood series.* Glendale, Ca.: Bowman (n.d.).

Jessup, M. H., & Kiley, M. A. *Discipline: Positive attitudes for learning.* Englewood Cliffs: Prentice-Hall, 1971.

Johnson, D. W. *Reaching out: Interpersonal effectiveness and self-actualization.* Englewood Cliffs: Prentice-Hall, 1972.

Jones, R. *Fantasy and feeling in education.* New York: New York University Press, 1968.

Kaczkowski, J., & Patterson, C. H. *Counseling and psychology in elementary schools.* Springfield: Charles C Thomas, 1975.

Kasschau, R. A., & Wertheimer, M. *Teaching psychology in secondary schools.* Washington, D. C.: American Psychological Association, 1974.

Kounin, J. S., & Abradovic, S. Managing emotionally disturbed children in regular classrooms: A replication and extension. *Journal of Special Education,* 1969, *2*, 129-236.

Kravetz, N. The creative child in the un-creative school. *The Educational Forum,* 1970, *34*, 219-222.

Le Grand, L. E. (Ed.). *Discipline in secondary school teaching: A book of readings.* West Nyack, N. Y.: Parker, 1969.

Lehrner, G. F. *Explorations in personal adjustment: A guide for self-understanding* (2nd ed.). Englewood Cliffs: Prentice-Hall, 1957.

Leonard, G. B. *Education and ecstacy.* New York: Belacorte, 1968.

Le Shan, E. J. *The conspiracy against childhood.* New York: Athenium, 1971.

Le Shan, E. J. *What makes me feel this way?* New York: Macmillan, 1972.

Levine, E. S. *Lisa and her soundless world.* New York: Behavioral Publications, 1974.

Light, P. K. *Let the children speak: A psychological study of young teenagers and drugs.* Lexington, Ma.: Lexington Books, 1975.

Lightfall, F. F. Social psychologists in schools: Some concepts and interventions. *School Psychology Digest,* 1973, *2,* 10-15.

Ligon, M. G., & McDaniel, S. H. *The teacher's role in counseling.* Englewood Cliffs: Prentice-Hall. 1970.

Limbacher, W. J. *The dimensions of personality series.* Cincinnati, Oh.: Pflaum-Standard Publishing Co. (n.d.).

Lippitt, R., Fox, R., Schmuck, R., & Van Egmond, E. *Understanding classroom social relations and learning.* Chicago: Science Research Associates, 1966.

Loretan, J. O., & Umans, S. *Call them heroes,* Books 1-4. Morristown, N. J.: Silver Burdett, 1965.

Luft, J. *Group process: An introduction to group dynamics* (2nd ed.). Palo Alto: National Press, 1970.

Lyon, H. C. *Learning to feel — feeling to learn.* Columbus: Charles E. Merrill, 1971.

Mager, R. F. *Developing attitude toward learning.* Palo Alto: Fearon Publishers, 1968.

Manning, D. *Toward a humanistic curriculum.* New York: Harper & Row, 1971.

Marmorale, A. M., & Brown, F. *Mental health intervention in the primary grades.* New York: Behavioral Publications, 1974.

Mattox, B. A., & Koryda, M. M. *Getting it all together: Dilemmas for the classroom.* San Diego: Pennant Press, 1974.

Maultsby, M. C., Jr. *More personal happiness through rational self-counseling.* Lexington, Ky.: Author, 1974.

Maultsby, M. C., Jr. *Help yourself to happiness.* Lexington, Ky.: University of Kentucky Medical Center, 1975.

McCure, L. *Career education survival manual: A guidebook for career educators and their friends.* Salt Lake City: Olympus, 1975.

McFall, R. M., & Lillisand, D. B. Behavioral rehearsal with modeling and coaching in assertion training. *Journal of Abnormal Psychology,* 1971, *77,* 313-323.

Meichenbaum, D. H., & Goodman, J. Training impulsive children to talk to themselves: A means of developing self control. *Journal of Abnormal Psychology,* 1971, *77,* 115-126.

Melton, D. *Burn the schools — Save the children.* New York: Crowell, 1975.

Millman, J., & Pauk, W. *How to take tests.* New York: McGraw-Hill, 1969.

Mohr, G. *When children face crises.* Chicago: Science Research Associates (n.d.).

Montessori, M. *Spontaneous activity in education.* Cambridge, Ma.: Bentley, 1964.

Moore, D. J. *Preventing misbehavior in children.* Springfield: Charles C Thomas, 1972.

Morris, K. T., & Cinnamon, K. M. *A handbook of verbal group exercises.* Springfield: Charles C Thomas, 1974.

Morris, K. T., & Cinnamon, K. M. *A handbook of non-verbal group exercises.* Springfield: Charles C Thomas, 1975.

Morris, K. T., Cinnamon, K. M., & Kanitz, M. *Controversial issues in human relation training groups.* Springfield: Charles C Thomas, 1975.

National Clearinghouse for Drug Abuse Information. *Selected drug education curricula.* Washington, D. C.: U.S. Government Printing Office (n.d.).

National Educational Association. *Unfinished stories for use in the classroom.* Washington, D. C.: Author, 1968.

National Forum Foundation. *Everywhere we go* (4th grade). Circle Pines, Mn.: American Guidance (n.d.).

National Forum Foundation. *The people around us* (5th grade). Circle Pines, Mn.: American Guidance (n.d.).

National Forum Foundation. *Seeing ourselves* (6th grade). Circle Pines, Mn.: American Guidance (n.d.).

National Instructional Television Center. *Inside out: Films and videocassettes.* Bloomington: National Instructional Television Center (n.d.).

National Special Media Institutes. *The affective domain: A resource book for media specialists.* Washington, D. C.: Communication Service Corporation, 1970.

Neill, A. S. *Summerhill: A radical approach to child rearing.* New York: Hart, 1960.

New York Department of Mental Hygiene. *Blondie.* New York: National Association for Mental Health, 1950.

Nylen, D., Mitchell, J., & Stout, A. *Handbook of staff development and human relations training: Materials developed for use in Africa.* Washington, D. C.: National Training Laboratories Institute for Applied Behavioral Science, 1967.

O'Connell, J., & Cosmos, J. *Hello people.* Chicago: Argus Communications (n.d.).

Ogle, G., & Menuey, J. *Good time box set.* San Diego: Pennant (n.d.).

Ojemann, R. H. *A teaching program in human behavior and mental health.* Cleveland: Education Research Council of Greater Cleveland (n.d.).

Oliver, D. W., & Shaver, J. P. *Teaching public issues in the high school.* Boston: Houghton-Mifflin, 1966.

Overly, D. E., Kinghorn, J. R., & Preston, R. L. *The middle school: Humanizing education for youth.* Worthington, Oh.: Charles A. Jones, 1973.

Patterson, G. R., & Gullion, M. E. *Living with children: New methods for parents and teachers.* Champaign: Research Press, 1971.

Pavenstedt, E., & Bernard, V. W. (Eds.). *Crises of family disorganization: Programs to soften their impact on children.* New York: Behavioral, 1971.

Perry, N. E. *The school psychologist as a human development specialist.* Madison County, Oh.: Madison County Schools, 1974 (mimeo).

Pfeiffer, H. W., & Jones, J. E. (Eds.). *A handbook of structured experiences for human relations training,* Vol. 1 (Rev.). Iowa City: University Associates Press, 1974a.

Pfeiffer, H. W., & Jones, J. E. (Eds.). *A handbook of structured experiences for human relations training,* Vol. 2 (Rev.). Iowa City: University Associates Press, 1974b.

Pfeiffer, H. W., & Jones, J. E. (Eds.). *A handbook of structured experiences for human relations training,* Vol. 3 (Rev.). Iowa City: University Associates Press, 1974c.

Pfeiffer, H. W., & Jones, J. E. (Eds.). *A handbook of structured experiences for human relations training,* Vol. 4. Iowa City: University Associates Press, 1973.

Phillips, A. M., & Covault, T. J. *Improving classroom climate for children with special problems: An in-service education program.* Columbus: Central Ohio Education Research Council, 1973 (mimeo.).

Postman, N., & Weingartner, C. *Teaching as a subversive activity.* New York: Dell, 1969.

Postman, N., & Weingartner, C. *The soft revolution.* New York: Delacorte Press, 1971.

Powell, J. *Why am I afraid to tell you who I am?* Chicago: Argus Communications, 1969.

Powers, V. *Getting to know me.* Burbank, Ca.: QTED Productions (n.d.).

Project TRIAD: Road notes. Flint, Mi.: Genessee Intermediate School District, 1974 (mimeo.).

Promoting mental health in the classroom: A handbook for teachers. Rockville, Md.: National Institute for Mental Health, 1973.

Randolph, N., & Catterall, C. D. *Self enhancing education: Processes that enhance.* Cupertino, Ca.: Cupertino School District, 1964 (mimeo., out of print).

Randolph, N. & Howe, W. *Self enhancing education.* Palo Alto: Educational Development Corporation, 1966.

Rardin, D. R., & Moan, C. E. Peer interaction and cognitive development. *Child Development,* 1971, *42,* 1685-1699

Raths, L. E., Harmin, M., & Simon, S. *Values and teaching: Working with values in the classroom.* Columbus: Charles E. Merrill, 1966.

Raths, L. E., Wasserman, S., Jonas, A., & Rothstein, A. M. *Teaching for thinking: Theory and application.* Columbus: Charles A. Merrill, 1967.

Reardon, R. C., & Burck, H. D. (Eds.). *Facilitating career development.* Springfield: Charles C Thomas, 1975.

Reducing alienation and activism by participation: Project RAPP. Centerville, (Ohio) School District (n.d.).

Reichert, R. *Self-awareness through group dynamics.* Cincinnatti: Pflaum-Standard (n.d.).

Rinder, W. *Love is an attitude.* San Francisco: Celestial Arts Publishing, 1970.

Robert, M. *Loneliness in the schools: What to do about it.* Niles, Il.: Argus Communications, 1973.

Rokeach, M. *The nature of human values.* New York: Free Press, 1973.

Rucker, W. R., Arnspiger, V. C., & Brodbeck, A. J. *Human values in education.* Dubuque, Ia.: Kendall-Hunt Publishing Co., 1969.

Sanders, N. M. *Classroom questions: What kinds?* New York: Harper & Row, 1966.

Sandman, P. M. *Students and the law: A guide for high school and college students to help recognize their rights to free speech and due process.* New York: Collier Books, 1971.

Santa Clara Educational-Vocational Guidance Program. Santa Clara, Ca.: Santa Clara Unified School District (n.d., out of print).

Sarason, I. G., & Ganzer, V. J. *Modeling: An approach to the rehabilitation of juvenile offenders.* Final Report to Social and Rehabilitation Service of the Department of Health, Education, and Welfare (Grant # 15-P-55303), 1971.

Sarason, I. G., & Sarason, B. R. *Constructive classroom behavior: A teacher's guide to modeling and role-playing techniques.* New York: Behavioral Publications, 1974.

Schmuck, R., Chesler, M., & Lippitt, R. *Problem solving to improve classroom learning.* Chicago: Science Research Associates, 1966.

Schmuck, P., & Schmuck, R. Classroom peer relationships: What can the school psychologist do? *School Psychology Digest,* 1973, *2,* 4-12.

Schmuck, R. & Schmuck, P. *Group processes in the classroom.* Dubuque, Ia.: W. C. Brown, 1971.

Schrank, J. *Feelings: Exploring inner space.* Paramus, N. J.: Paulist-Newman, 1972.

Scott, E. M. *The adolescent gap: Research findings on drug using and non-drug using teens.* Springfield: Charles C Thomas, 1972.

Scott, J. *Teaching for a change.* New York: Bantam, 1972.

Sex information and Education Council of the U. S. *Study guides* (1-14). New York: Behavioral Publications (n.d.).

Shaftel, F. R., & Shaftel, G. *Role playing for social values: Decision making in the classroom.* Englewood Cliffs: Prentice-Hall, 1967.

Shears, L. M., & Bower, E. M. *Games in education and development.* Springfield: Charles C Thomas, 1974.

Sheppard, W. C., Shank, S. B., & Wilson, D. *Teaching social behavior to young children.* Champaign: Research Press, 1973.

Silberman, C. *Crises in the classroom.* New York: Random House, 1970.

Silver, A. A., & Hagen, R. A. Profile of a first grade: A basis for preventive psychiatry. *Journal of American Academy of Child Psychiatry,* 1972, *4,* 645-674.

Simon, S. B. Seven value-clarifying strategies for teachers. *Educational Opportunities Forum,* 1969, *1,* 75-84.

Simon, S. B., & Clark, J. *More values clarification: Strategies for the classroom.* San Diego: Pennant Press, 1975.

Simon, S. B., Hawley, R. C., & Britton, D. D. *Composition for personal growth: Values clarification through writing.* New York: Hart, 1973.

Simon, S., Howe, L. U., & Kirschenbaum, H. *Clarifying values: A handbook of practical strategies for teachers and students.* New York: Hart, 1972.

Simpson, B. K. *Becoming aware of values (2nd ed.).* San Diego: Pennant, 1973.

Skinner, B. F. *Beyond freedom and dignity.* New York: Alfred A. Knopf, 1971.

Skinner, B. F. On teaching thinking. In C. H. Monson, Jr. (Ed.). *Education for what: Readings in the ends and means of education.* Boston: Houghton-Mifflin, 1970.

Smith, G. R. *FEED (facilitative environments encouraging development): Brief description of program.* Bloomington, In.: Project FEED, 1975.

Spivak, G., & Shure, M. *Social adjustment of young children: A cognitive approach to solving real-life problems.* San Francisco: Jossey-Bass, 1973.

Spodek, B. Alternative to traditional education. In J. E. De Carlo & C. A. Madon, (Eds.). *Innovation in education for the seventies: Selected readings.* New York: Behavioral Publications, 1973.

Stanford, G., & Stanford, B. D. *Learning discussion skills through games.* New York: Citation, 1969.

Strang, R. *Guidance and the teaching of reading.* Newark, Del.: International Reading Association, 1969.

Stumphauzer, J. S. Increased delay of gratification in young prison inmates through imitation of high-delay peer models. *Journal of Personality and Social Psychology,* 1972, *21,* 10-17.

Sulzer, C. H., & Mayer, G. R. *Behavior modification procedures for school personnel.* Hinsdale, Il.: Dryden, 1972.

Sweat, C. H., Fink, A. K., & Reedy, L. *Humanizing instruction in the junior high school.* Danville, Il.: Interstate, 1974.

Swift, M. S., & Spivak, G. *Alternative teaching strategies: Helping behaviorally troubled children achieve: A guide for teachers and psychologists.* Champaign: Research Press, 1975.

Taba, H. *With perspective on human relations.* Washington, D. C.: American Council on Education, 1955.

Taba, H., & Elkins, D. *With focus on human relations.* Washington, D. C.: American Council on Education, 1950.

Taba, H., Robinson, J., Brady, E. H., & Vickery, W. *Diagnosing human relation needs.* Washington, D. C.: American Council on Education, 1951.

Teacher's Guide for Sociology 1 (Family living instruction), Grade 12. Hayward, Ca.: Hayward Unified School District, 1967

Teaching Research Division, Oregon State System of Higher Education. *In-*

structional uses of simulation. Eugene, Or.: Author, 1967.

Terry, M. *Teaching for survival.* New York: Ballantine, 1971.

Thomas, W. L. *Towards a concept for affective education.* Rosemont, Il.: Combined Motivation Education Systems, 1971.

Torrance, E. P. *Encouraging creativity in the classroom.* Dubuque, Ia.: W. C. Brown, 1971.

Torrance, E. P., & Meyers, R. E. *Creative learning and teaching.* New York: Dodd, Mead, 1971.

Valett, R. E. *My goal record.* Belmont: Fearon, 1972a.

Valett, R. E. School psychology and the design of humanistic education. *California School Psychology,* 1972b, *19,* 2.

Valett, R. E. *Myself checklist.* Belmont: Fearon, 1973a.

Valett, R. E. *Sex and TLC.* Belmont: Fearon, 1973b.

Valett, R. E. *Affective-humanistic education: Goals, programs, and learning activities.* Belmont: Fearon, 1974a.

Valett, R. E. *Getting it all together: A guide for personality development and problem solving.* San Rafael: Academic Therapy, 1974b.

Walker, J. L. (Ed.). *Favorite pop-rock lyrics.* New York: Scholastic, 1969.

Waltz, G. R. *Life/career development system.* Ann Arbor: Human Development Services (n.d.).

Washburn, J., & Washburn, W. *Re-created games for the classroom.* Healdsburg, Ca.: Teacher's Desk, 1973.

Webster, M. Jr., & Sobieszek, B. I. *Sources of self-evaluation.* New York: Wiley Interscience, 1974.

Weinstein, G., & Fantini, M. D. *Toward humanistic education: A curriculum of affect.* New York: Ford Foundation, 1970.

Wernick, W. *Teaching for career development in the elementary school: A life centered approach.* Worthington, Oh.: Charles A. Jones, 1973.

Whittaker, J. O. *Psychology and modern man.* New York: Behavioral Publications, 1975.

Willis, J. W., Crowder, J., & Willis, J. *Guiding the psychological and educational growth of children.* Springfield: Charles C Thomas, 1975.

Wood, M. M. *Developmental therapy: A textbook for teachers as therapists for emotionally disturbed young children.* Baltimore: University Park, 1975.

Woody, R. M. *Behavioral problem children in the schools: Recognition, diagnosis, and behavioral modification.* New York: Appleton-Century-Crofts, 1969.

World to grow in: A K-12 drug alcohol, tobacco, and human behavior approach. Columbus: Ohio Department of Education (n.d.).

You, the decision maker: Counselor's manual. Chicago: Follett Publishing Co., 1967.

Zeligs, R. *Children's experience with death.* Springfield: Charles C Thomas, 1974.

Zifferblatt, S. *Improving study and homework behaviors.* Champaign: Research Press, 1970.

Zuckerman, D., & Horn, R. *The guide to simulation games for education and training* (2nd ed.). Lexington, Ma.: Information Resources, 1973.

Zuckerman, H. *Adolescence is a required course.* Chicago: General Learning, 1974.

Chapter 7

CORRECTIVE/THERAPEUTIC
INTERVENTIONS

INTRODUCTION

THE INTERVENTIONS DESCRIBED in this chapter have in common the fact that, instead of being essentially developmental in nature, they are designed to help students with specialized or unique problems in the humanistic or life-skills area. As was pointed out in the beginning of Chapter 5, the curriculum designed to develop life skills will often grow out of normal problem-solving activities. Since this is true, there is no clear line between where a normal developmental, preventive strategy will become a Corrective/Therapeutic Intervention. However, for purposes of illustration and clarification, it is meaningful to think of all of these activities as part of a continuum or series which can and should be used quite flexibly. Just as the regular academic program should continue to try to meet as many needs as possible and should have a component which identifies particular students who need Corrective/Remedial Interventions, educators should continue to try to improve the development of humanistic/life skills in the regular curriculum while being alert to those who need extra help or assistance of this nature.

The Corrective/Therapeutic Interventions have the following common goal:

To implement a full range of corrective/therapeutic services designed to help students work on problems caused either by the deficits in the development of their humanistic/life skills or to work through some unique situational problem or concern. In order to do this, each person and agency that comes in contact with the school should be encouraged to assist in this process both by offering their own services and by contributing to a social climate in which it is considered appropriate and

283

desirable to receive these services when needed.

As stated before, the more normal the setting in which the *corrective* procedures take place, the better. Whereas it was once believed that help with all "personal" problems was best provided individually, this position is now questioned. Educators must learn to identify ways to use normal interaction and to capitalize on the helping quality of warm, positive relationships with others in order to implement these Corrective/Therapeutic Interventions. The concept that these procedures are *corrective* highlights the fact that the process starts with a problem or concern which has been identified either by the student or by school personnel.

The activities are *therapeutic* insofar as they build upon the normal health-producing forces found within the individual, the school, and the community. Traditional techniques of "therapy" involved long, intensive, one-to-one work with a highly trained therapist. The feedback from this type of service has been discouraging, as measured by observable behavior in the classroom. Although there will continue to be need for such specialized services, the trend is definitely toward bringing those specialists into the school and classroom in order to try to bring about the desired change there (see the last part of this chapter).

The activities are *interventions* in the sense that they actively introduce a service or process into the lives of students in order to help them solve a problem or attain a higher level of personal adjustment. Whereas school personnel have at their disposal a great many helpful interventions not ordinarily available to outside agencies, they do have the limitation of not being able to spend a great deal of time with any one student. They also frequently have the additional limitation of not having had adequate training in individual therapeutic techniques.

In this day of a renewal of interest in the student's rights, there is also a question about whether or not school personnel have the right to take students into intensive, individualized therapy relationships even with the student's and/or his or her parent's permission. While limitations of time and training and other factors preclude educators from employing psychotherapy techniques, they do have available to them a whole range of counseling strategies and Corrective/Therapeutic Interventions. Even though there are other community agencies that are prepared to provide a full range of specialized services for the student, school personnel should not "give up" on their responsibility to the individual student until they have done everything possible for him/her within the total spectrum of school services. When other agencies do become involved, however, effective liaison with the other community services is essential.

Because the distinction is somewhat artificial between learning academic/intellectual skills and learning humanistic/life skills, many of the Corrective/Remedial Interventions (discussed in Chapter 5) will also work as Corrective/Therapeutic Intervention. In attempting to select an intervention, it is still helpful to ask oneself whether or not the student has a deficit of skills which needs to be developed or whether he/she has the necessary skills but is either not able to use them or is unwilling to do so (see Chapter 8).

A great many so-called "emotionally disturbed" children in the early years of school have major academic skill deficits (Blain and McArthur, 1971; Hewett, 1975; Rhodes and Tracy, 1972). Some have felt that the emotional disturbance caused the poor achievement (Bower, 1974); others have pointed to evidence that inability to do the academic work creates an overlay of emotional problems. Unfortunately, the label "emotionally disturbed" has a tendency to set up barriers in the thinking of teachers and other educators which, in turn, sets up the hypothesis that because students are "disturbed" they cannot be helped in the regular classroom. Educators are beginning to find that, in most instances, this fortunately is not true.

When in doubt as to whether or not the emotional problem caused the learning deficit or the other way around, it is best for school personnel to use their greatest expertise, i.e. providing corrective remedial services rather than trying to move too rapidly into the Corrective/Therapeutic Interventions. This is not to say that one should ignore the social-emotional side of the student; one should approach all students with appropriate consideration for their human worth and dignity. As an extension of the rule that "the best strategy is to provide treatment in as normal a setting and manner as possible," the first intervention should be to investigate whether or not the young student has academic-skill deficits. For the older student, this may be less true; perhaps the first consideration should be given to the Corrective/Therapeutic Interventions.

Virtually all of the techniques under the heading "Behavior Modification" (described in Chapter 5) have some research to show that they are equally effective with both learning and behavior disorders (Clarizio and McCoy, 1970; Daniels, 1974; Gardner, 1975; Haring and Phillips, 1972; Kozloff, 1974; Nielson, 1974). As a generalization, behavior modification has been most helpful in working on specific, discrete segments of behavior with younger children who have not responded to the normal socialization process which keeps most persons motivated. To avoid duplication, and to highlight or emphasize another set of interventions available to school personnel, only those behavior modification techniques which have been specifically adapted to the counseling process will be reintroduced into this chapter.

Although separated in this book, it must be continually emphasized that there is no hard and fast line between Corrective/Remedial and the Corrective/Therapeutic Interventions. There is virtually no occasion when one should use one without considering the other. These considerations suggest a gradation of emphasis between the two major types of interventions depending upon the developmental level of the student. They should be thought of in stereo, each overlapping and complementing the other (see Figure 7-1).

One of the problems that has to be faced is finding the time to implement the counseling and other Corrective/Therapeutic Interventions. Just as tutoring has emerged as a valuable intervention in the Corrective/Remedial area, so too has peer counseling emerged as another means of providing the needed Corrective/Therapeutic Interventions. As with peer tutoring, peer counseling seems to help both the one providing the service and the one being helped (Mattson, 1970). For these and other reasons, there is a growing interest in how to use students in the counseling pro-

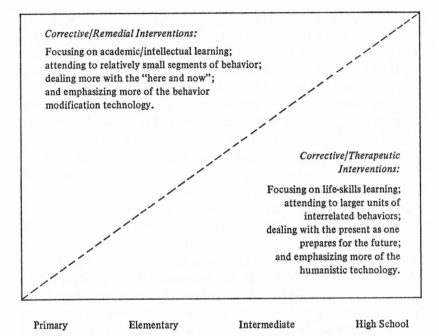

Corrective/Remedial Interventions:

Focusing on academic/intellectual learning;
attending to relatively small segments of behavior;
dealing more with the "here and now";
and emphasizing more of the behavior
modification technology.

*Corrective/Therapeutic
Interventions:*

Focusing on life-skills learning;
attending to larger units of
interrelated behaviors;
dealing with the present as one
prepares for the future;
and emphasizing more of the
humanistic technology.

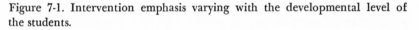

| Primary | Elementary | Intermediate | High School |

Figure 7-1. Intervention emphasis varying with the developmental level of the students.

cess. Since peers are typically of such importance in the decision-making processes of other teen-agers, it would seem that there is a tremendous potential in the further development of this area. It may also assist in relieving the human power shortage in providing help to students. Many of the same considerations and decisions discussed under "cross-age tutoring" will need to be made here. In general, slightly older students would probably be most effective as peer counselors, which is another reason for developing cooperative relationships with schools serving older students.

The peer counseling model may be limited to providing information or services, e.g. helping new students become oriented to a school, providing more information about the courses being offered, or giving information about club activities and colleges. In other settings, peer counseling could be directed toward a broader range of personal counseling techniques.

Students can be directly recruited to be peer counselors, or they can be given the opportunity to volunteer to be interviewed for the position (Landefeld, 1975). The peer counselor can either do it as a volunteer activity or can receive course credit. A training program will, in all likelihood, be needed depending on the goals of the program. General counseling would take considerable training; giving information regarding available courses would not take as much (Hamburg and Varenhorst, 1972). Educators should be able to use some of the training techniques being used with "counselors" at coffee houses, runaway homes, and drug centers. These other institutions may be serving a different clientele, however, and may lack some of the structure available in the school. Certainly one aspect of the training would be to teach the peer counselor something about understanding behavior (Banas and Wills, 1972) and the qualities of the helping relationship (Carkhuff, 1969; Gazda, Walters, and Childers, 1976). Another aspect would be to help them know when to involve an adult counselor, either indirectly by getting consultation services from them or directly by referring the case to them. The process of learning what kinds of problems they will face and what to do about them should be an extremely valuable experience for the majority of these peer counselors. A greater availability of counseling information and help to the student who has a problem should also make this a very valuable program.

Although there will be some discussion of general approaches to counseling, this chapter will not deal *specifically* with counseling theories or counseling techniques. Both of these topics relate to Corrective/Therapeutic Interventions, but they have been described well elsewhere (Barclay, 1971; Downing, 1975; Hackney and Nye, 1973; Meyer and Meyer, 1975). Furthermore, no major distinction will be made between those counseling techniques usually applied to groups and those typically used in a one-to-one situation, since most techniques can be used with either. The emphasis will be on the focus of the intervention rather than on the process or structure.

The preference is for educators to become more skillful in helping students develop appropriate life skills so that less emphasis will need to be placed on "putting out fires" of severe social problems or emotional disturbance. At the same time, since each learner is unique, it is doubtful if a normal developmental program (no matter how complete or how well executed) will take care of all of the social-emotional, life-skill problems of any given individual. There will always be some time when students will need some individualized help.

The remainder of this chapter will focus on all of those things which are under the control and responsibility of the school for those who are having difficulty in the personal, social/emotional life skill areas. The interventions are much broader, therefore, than those typically thought of as the "counseling" or "guidance" function of the school. Some of the interventions described will be more effective when carried out in groups (Hechlik and Lee, 1968; Luft, 1970; Rose, 1972). If used effectively, normal peer interaction can be very therapeutic. Some procedures, however, work best with a small number of people interacting. Other groups, such as Family Therapy, are made up of "natural groups." In some situations, the level of personal involvement and trust needed would be difficult to develop in large groups. In other instances, the problems being discussed are of such a personal nature that it would be unwise to discuss them before large numbers of students. In some cases, we will work with "self-formed groups" made up of several students wanting to work on the same problem. Putting together the right elements and interpersonal relationships to make an effective group takes a lot of time and preparation. If handled carefully, however, the time spent in forming such a group will pay dividends in increasing the speed with which it will proceed and how far it can go (Berkovitz, 1975, Gazda, 1971).

In summary, some of the interventions available to schools for helping students with life-skill problems are designed to help them primarily through providing appropriate *environmental supports*. Others, which tend to be more direct and intense, are used in *overcoming life-skill deficits*. As services are needed and/or provided by agencies outside the school, other interventions identify ways of establishing an *effective liaison with community agencies.* In short, the Corrective/Therapeutic interventions represent all of the things that can be done *in behalf of* the student (see Table 7-I).

TABLE 7-I

INTERVENTIONS IN BEHALF OF THE STUDENT

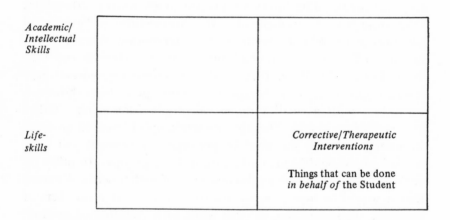

	Developmental/ Preventative	*Corrective/ Remedial*
Academic/ Intellectual Skills		
Life-skills		*Corrective/Therapeutic Interventions* Things that can be done *in behalf of* the Student

Although there is an almost limitless number of interventions that can be used with students who are having major difficulties, those that will be described in this chapter (see Table 7-II) should be sufficient to help the teacher and other educators be aware of the many resources available to them. Schools have at their disposal a tremendous spectrum of ways of working with and helping students. We should all be about the business of using them more effectively.

ENVIRONMENTAL SUPPORTS

Just as there are indirect ways of helping students with academic/intellectual problems, so too are there interventions providing help and support for students with humanistic/life-skill problems which do not work directly on the life-skills deficit.

TABLE 7-II

ORGANIZATION OF STRATEGIES FOR
CORRECTIVE/THERAPEUTIC INTERVENTIONS

Environmental Supports

Time to Reorganize
Change of Situation
Activities
More Structure
Punishment
Special Classes

Overcoming Life-skill Deficits

Difficulty Understanding/Accepting Self and Others
Problems Relating with Others
Value Conflicts
Communication Problems
Difficulty Making Decisions
Need for More Satisfying Roles
Sex/Role Problems
Concern Over Grades
Drug-related Problems
Difficulty Making Career Decisions
Difficulty in Planning for the Future

Effective Liaison With Community Agencies

Liaison with Health Agencies/Services
Liaison with Social Agencies
Liaison with Law Agencies
Liaison with Mental Health Agencies

TIME TO REORGANIZE. Not all acting-out behavior reflects deeply rooted personal problems. Indeed, it is well accepted that some of the most conforming and complacent students are sometimes (but certainly not always) the most disturbed ones. Under appropriate circumstances, acting-out behavior is very healthy. Therefore, if the student is temporarily out of line or out of control, the intervention might be to give him/her some time to "cool off" or to reorganize. Redl (1966) points out that even the youths who have been labeled as delinquent (and Redl indicates that he has never seen a "delinquent" who deserves that name) almost always have large reserves of healthy behavior. One way to help some students is to enable them to get through an emotional crisis with a minimum of friction and allow their natural tendencies toward stabilization to take over.

CHANGE OF SITUATION. When the environment of a student is contributing to his/her emotional outbreaks, especially if this problem has been recurring over a long time, another intervention that can be used is to try to bring about a change in the situation. This can involve the following: a change of seat, a change of groupings within a class, a change of class, a change of school, or even a transfer to another school district. This change will sometimes give the student the time to reorganize in a new setting which is less likely to trigger the undesirable behavior. At times, of course, the same behavior is seen in the new situation and other interventions have to be used. Certain theories emphasize that such a strategy is only treating the symptom, not the real problem, and that either the same problem or another would recur. Although there is some truth to this, it is equally true that the behavior that one exhibits is a combination of inner problems and stimuli in the environment which serve to trigger specific kinds of behavior. Working with the large numbers of students in schools, it is often difficult to know what is the specific cause of a behavior. Educators will often have to work with the surface symptoms of behavior. This makes it even more important to observe carefully the behavior of the student to see if the desired changes are being attained.

ACTIVITIES. The intervention of helping a student join a club or engage in activities can be utilized for a variety of reasons; e.g. to help a particular student find new friends, to improve social or physical skills, or as a change-of-pace activity in an otherwise purely academic day. At one time, there was extensive use of a related approach with upper elementary aged boys, i.e. "activity group therapy" (Slavson and Shiffer, 1975). Drawing from the ideas of play therapy then in vogue, the model was to take a small group of these boys, together with a therapist, into a room where they could be engaged in a variety of "building" activities. Fighting between the students was accepted; growth presumably came from releasing hostilities and tensions, from the positive relationships developed with other students, and from the insight gained in the brief discussions which followed. This approach was impractical in most school situations because of the requirement for having a room where the students could do "anything they want." It has been replaced by much more precise ways of helping students. It is still valid, however, to bring a group of students together to do something constructive which also helps the members of the group begin to relate to each other more effectively. Although such an approach is effective with students at all ages, it is perhaps most useful with younger students who have not developed good verbal skills.

MORE STRUCTURE. Many of the factors discussed in Chapter 5 also apply here. Within the context of this chapter, the concept would be that some students are having difficulty in a given social situation because they do not understand all of the social nuances and/or because they are confused either by the number of rules or their ambiguity. Some hyperactive students have sufficient difficulty in attending to details that they need more structure to help them to be able to survive. In the past, it was stressed that those students who were emotionally disturbed should be given more freedom to do what they want, but the trend in this field is to provide them with a set of rules that are simple, easy to understand, and followed as consistently as possible. This tends to reduce some of the restlessness that we have seen in this type of student.

PUNISHMENT. Once again, this was discussed at great length in

Chapter 5. Corporal punishment and a variety of other techniques for punishment are unfortunately still used a great deal on students judged to be acting-out or aggressive. There is sufficient overlap between the Corrective/Remedial and the Corrective/Therapeutic interventions to make it equally (if not more so) ineffective in this area (and for many of the same reasons as indicated in Chapter 5). This is not to say that some forms of "discipline" are not indicated. In order for the harsher forms of discipline to be effective, however, they have to be worked out in the context of a caring relationship. It is extremely difficult in most school situations, especially with older students, to express this caring relationship while at the same time handing out the harsher forms of discipline. Punishment as an intervention has been mentioned again as a reminder that: (1) punishment continues to be frequently used, (2) it has many limitations, and (3) it illustrates the fact that some interventions are often continued even though they do not bring about the desired results.

SPECIAL CLASSES. Special classes exist for the emotionally disturbed as well as for students with learning problems. Although the label is not used extensively, there is considerable evidence that a high percentage of acting-out students are screened into all kinds of special education classes no matter what they are labeled. Since there is so much variability in students, there are undoubtedly some that need to be placed into special classes and even into special institutions. Taking a student out of the mainstream should only be done after a wide range of other interventions have been tried. Otherwise, these classes become the "dumping grounds" for all kinds of students who are denied their rights to an education in a normal setting.

OVERCOMING LIFE-SKILL DEFICITS

DIFFICULTY IN UNDERSTANDING/ACCEPTING SELF AND OTHERS. Some students will need more direct interventions to solve the problems they face and to overcome their life-skill deficits. Problems can be associated with extremes in all of the life-skill areas described in Chapter 6; i.e. the development can come too early or too late, students may be too sensitive or insensitive to the needs of others. In other instances, life appears to present certain students with more problems or decisions than they can make at one time. In this section, interventions will be discussed which are primarily designed to help students with problems of self-understanding and acceptance and in their relations with others.

1. *Helping Students Gain Insight.* Earlier views of counseling which focused on the process of helping students to develop insight into their "unconscious motivations" are being used less and less in the schools. Counseling is now seen much more as a process of "clarifying" one's intellectual and emotional thoughts and feelings. This is accomplished through techniques such as reflecting back to the student, asking for clarification when the message is not coming through properly, helping the student see things the way others do, and similar procedures. One of the reasons that the goal of developing insight is not considered sufficient is that just understanding why a person does something does not necessarily lead to a plan to do something different. Typical methods of counseling in the modern school include helping students establish specific goals for themselves and assisting them in devising and implementing a plan which will help them reach their goals (Agoston, 1969; Walsh, 1976).

Early therapy group models brought together people with the same or similar problems to gain "insight," primarily through the skillful leadership of the therapist and, to a lesser extent, by discussing the problems with other members of the group. Fortunately, however, there are many new variations of group therapy which have been adapted for use in the schools. They include: involvement of students with various kinds of problems in a group, providing students who do not have identified problems to serve as models for the group, reduced emphasis on the role of the leader, more use of the concept of using a "facilitator" to introduce a structure which truly makes the group interaction a learning process, and more emphasis on short-term experiences to facilitate the normal growth process within the individual. With all of these changes, however, it must be said that there is often inadequate provision for working with small groups in modern schools (Gazda, 1975). Some of the counseling/therapy approaches which have been found to be most applicable to groups will be discussed on the following pages.

2. *Basic Encounter Groups.* There has been a major trend in recent years toward a series of groups variously called "Sensitivity, Leadership Training," or "Basic Encounter Groups" (Schein and Bennis, 1965). These have been used primarily for adults in an out-of-school setting. Several districts have attempted to use these techniques to improve communication lines within the administrative staff of a district and to improve leadership styles. It would appear that this approach has a great potential for helping people, such as teachers, who must constantly relate to other human beings. This should be one source of renewal for many educators who have to use themselves continually in intensive interpersonal relationships (Golembiewski and Blumberg, 1970; Rogers, 1970).

Although there has not been much use of this approach with students in schools, with some modifications and proper precautions, it would appear that there is much potential in this type of

THE JOHARI WINDOW

	Known to Self	Not Known to Self
Known To Others	I OPEN	II BLIND
Not Known To Others	III CONCEALED	IV UNCONSCIOUS

Figure 7-2. The Johari Window: I. The public self that is obvious to all and can be dealt with in almost any setting. II. The individual can be helped to see and understand more about this area through interaction within the encounter group. III. The individual only volunteers information from this area to the group when he/she is ready to do so. IV. Material from this area is not available and not applicable to this type of group process. (From Luft, J. GROUP PROCESSES: AN INTRODUCTION TO GROUP DYNAMICS (2nd Ed.) Palo Alto: National Press, 1970. Reproduced by permission.

focus for older students. One major problem is to find the time for this process for both the students and the interventionist. The "encounter" is usually relatively unstructured and uses the interactions between members to help each person learn more about him/herself (Lieberman, Yalom, and Miles, 1973). One tool which has been used extensively in this type of group and which helped to explain the process is called the Johari Window.

Since the role of the leader or facilitator has been minimized, there has been a lot of experimentation with so-called leaderless groups. Although this model would probably work with the professional staff (assuming there is enough sophistication to keep the process within the limits that such a group can handle), leaderless school-sponsored student groups are probably not indicated (Haas, 1975).

3. *Existential Counseling.* This approach, even more than other forms of counseling, stresses that there is within all individuals a force which helps them to move toward becoming more mature or "self-actualized." The techniques of the counseling relationship are minimized; the emphasis is on helping the students in their process of "becoming." Existential counseling stresses that the true standard for "valuing" must come from within, and it encourages the student to focus on his/her own experiences. The existential approach can be used in both individual and group counseling, but it has probably become best known as a group procedure (Hora, 1975; Pine, 1976).

One group approach, called the "Existential Group," which has been well received in the school setting, has been the model used by Bates and Johnson (1972). They make the distinction between groups designed to "make ill people better" (the remedial approach) and this process, which they call "the existential group," which is designed to facilitate "adequate personality functioning." They suggest two essentially equal co-counselors (preferably one of each sex) who work with groups of about ten students, usually late junior high age and older. The younger the students, the more the need for some kind of activity and some kind of directed teaching. Group members should be interviewed to make certain that they know what the process entails and that they wish to participate. Signed parental permission should be obtained (as it should in all groups of this nature). The group should have a variety of personality styles, i.e. not too many acting-out and not too many shy. The basic tone of the group should reflect the hypothesis that the group has come together in order to extend their basic "normality" into greater areas of "growth." The group is organized to meet for a specific number of sessions (usually from six to ten) during the regular school day. The co-counselors sit across from each other and establish the following rules:

a. The discussion should be about the "here and now." The only legitimate stimulus that group members can react to is what they see going on in the group; if members talk about something outside the group, the others cannot help them with that. This rule also keeps the discussion away from the privacy of the student's home, which should not be violated.

b. Positive feelings are emphasized. This stems from the concept that "positive tends to generate positive." In such groups there is usually no time to work through negative feelings. While positive expressions will best facilitate growth, some honest expression of anger or other emotions is accepted.

c. Co-leaders and members should stress statements of how they *feel* and should not ask questions of each other. Questions tend to "demand" answers or responses before members are ready to give them. This position is related to the existential philosophy which discourages the leader "playing the role" of knowing what is wrong with everyone and asking the "correct" question to help the other person understand what is wrong with them. The leaders use their interaction with each other as well as their interactions with the members to "model" good group behavior. They also use a variety of techniques (human relations type activities) to keep the group moving (Bates, 1975a). The use of the co-counselor model has many advantages: it provides the normal interaction of these two people to be used as a model of effective interaction; serving as a co-leader can help provide on-the-job experience in group counseling; and the second person provides an additional stabilizing force within the group.

Although somewhat distinct, it can be seen that there is much overlap between the basic-encounter and the existential groups. Some believe that the existential approach is not enough "problem oriented" or "goal oriented." It will probably continue to be modified and will receive more attention in the future because it fits in so well with the attitudes and values that many modern youth bring with them as they enter into the counseling situation to "try to get it all together." In some aspects, it has been the forerunner of the whole modern "humanistic" movement that has been so attractive to our modern young people.

4. *Meditational Techniques.* Although they have not been used a great deal yet in the schools, there is certainly an increase in student interest in a variety of meditation techniques which would broadly be grouped under the heading of techniques for improving self-understanding. There are many who feel that Western education and culture have left something out of our science, medicine, psychology, and our concept of how the individual develops; some of them have turned to Eastern religions and concepts of the human condition. Another approach comes from the increased interest in biofeedback mechanisms which help individuals come more into contact with themselves and their biological functioning (Wickramasekera, 1976). Both of these techniques have been explored only superficially in the school setting. They are not sufficiently refined to be listed as a well-established, school-based intervention. They are showing sufficient promise, however, that they should be kept in mind as additional ways of helping students.

5. *Attempted Suicide.* Students that have attempted to take their life, or who have threatened to do so, present a unique problem to the interventionist and/or the Learning Facilitation Team. Certainly there are many reasons why an individual threatens to take his/her life; there are also a large majority who never really intend to do so. As a generalization, they probably have a low opinion of their self-worth and/or are dramatically seeking help for their problems. Many of these students will need help from medical and mental health agencies outside the school, which will be discussed later in this chapter. Because of the po-

tential need for medical supervision, the role of the school is often one of working with the individual students and their parents to the point where they need to seek more professional help.

PROBLEMS IN RELATING TO OTHERS. These would include any major difficulty in relating to other people; this problem can be manifest in a variety of symptoms, i.e. lying, stealing, bossing, scapegoating, excessive arguments, etc. One cannot assume what the underlying problem is from the surface symptoms. The following interventions or approaches, although working on a broader range of life skills than just that of relating to others, have been found to be useful.

1. *Indirect, Nonverbal Techniques.* Not every student relates best at the verbal level; younger children especially will often respond best to some of the nonverbal interventions described below (Morris and Cinnamon, 1975; Widerman and Widerman, 1976). In most instances, the interventionist is trying to find more indirect ways of helping students change their personal/social behaviors which do not necessitate that they feel that they are "different" or "crazy" and therefore need help.

a. *Touch Therapy.* Although touching in and of itself would seldom be considered therapy, it is mentioned here to remind teachers and school people in general that one of the ways of helping express positive, warm feelings for students (especially, but not exclusively, with younger ones) is to provide warm physical contact. When working with those children who tend to be discouraged or confused by abstract words, good basic communication through the sense of touch can be very helpful. As in positive reinforcement, the pat on the shoulder or other approving gestures should be given each time the child does something right. Cruickshank found that this approach was very helpful in working with so-called "brain-damaged" children. The "wrestling match" with the father can be very therapeutic for the young boy. Whenever a student (especially a younger one) does not respond to the normal verbal/visual clues, educators should try to provide information to the child through the still more primitive senses of touch, taste, or smell.

b. *Play Therapy.* This method was originally used extensively in child guidance clinics for children with problems (Carek, 1972). It was based on the theory that many of the problems of young children were caused by "bottled up" emotions such as anger, fear, and hate. The play therapist would engage the children in "play" activities which would either allow them to get rid of the aggression or to express themselves in ways which might otherwise be forbidden. The calm acceptance on the part of the therapist would be reassuring to the child. This would help him/ her get rid of the feelings that were causing the problems, and they would presumably begin to act more normally outside of the therapy situation. The same approach was the basis for the Activity Group Therapy discussed earlier. Most of these theories are no longer held so firmly and so the technique is not used very much, especially in the school setting. It is included here to remind the teacher that some of the problems seen in students are created by the school's restrictive environment, and one means of helping them is to get rid of nervous tension by some sort of physical activity. The concept of allowing children to do otherwise forbidden acts in play therapy (which often produce some feelings of guilt) is no longer widely used.

There is rather general current agreement that there is much that is growth-facilitating (as opposed to therapeutic) in the normal play of the child. This, in a sense, is their "work," insofar as play permits the child to exercise and to try out new developmental skills which in turn enable them to take on ever more complex tasks. In this sense of the word, then, play is considered a major aspect of the development of normal children. This is an extension of the thinking used in Corrective/Remedial Interventions for young children with developmental lags (Chapter 5).

2. *Supportive Counseling.* Although supportive counseling was traditionally thought of as a major counseling approach, it is generally used as only one of several techniques in modern counseling. The counselor may provide some direct help in assisting students to identify and to plan for meeting personal goals or to analyze problems. The main concern is to provide the student with encouragement and approval. However, if overused, it can also make the student become too dependent upon the counselor.

It is included here to remind the reader that not all students who come with personal problems are on the "wrong track," and some times the only thing that they need is a "sounding board" and some support that says they seem to be moving in the right direction. Unless stated properly, however, the reassurance could sound like, "I have listened to what you have to say, and according to *my* value systems, what you are doing is okay." This overemphasizes the counselor's values as opposed to the student's.

3. *Confrontation.* Although really just one part of the counseling process rather than a total approach, many people agree that there are times when students need to be confronted with the possible consequences of their action. In another sense of the term, the older student will also frequently "confront" the counselor or teacher on his/her position, values, beliefs; this is something else the interventionist must learn to handle. There has long been a debate about how closely related counseling should be to the school's discipline process. Most counselors feel that they should be quite separate; this may be because these interventionists do not feel that the typical punishment program of the school is effective (see the discussion of punishment in Chapter 5). It is the absence of the warm, supportive, and positive feelings in the usual punishment procedures which often makes them so ineffective. The normal guidance of a parent has to weave the two together. Most people get "out of line" occasionally, and if everybody else acts as if "it didn't happen," then these persons are not faced with the natural consequences of what they have done.

Although the confrontation process in counseling should not be equated with punishment, it does point out the need for building a good relationship with students before one begins to confront them. The risk in both confrontation and punishment is that, if the students do not feel that it was done with their best interests in mind, they are much more likely to "rebel"; then the process will do more harm than good. It is essential for anyone using discipline and confrontation in the schools to look at his/her own motivation. There can be a destructive "need for power" which destroys rather than builds the student's attempt to move toward becoming a more mature person. If used wisely, on the other hand, both discipline and confrontation can be powerful techniques. Although it can be used in a group setting, confrontation is more frequently used in individual counseling techniques (Bates, 1975b).

4. *Reality Therapy.* The "reality therapy" of Glasser (1965) is based on the following assumptions and techniques:

a. *Needs.* Everyone has needs for love and for a feeling of self-worth. All of the "problems" with which educators are so concerned in school are symptoms of the fact that the students have needs which are not being met.

b. *Involvement.* In order for the teacher or counselor to help students who are having difficulty, they must be willing to reveal themselves *to* and involve themselves *with* the students. Students, in turn, must be willing to involve themselves with the teacher or counselor and with other significant people in their lives.

c. *Focus on Current Behavior.* Educators must work with the student in "the present." The typical cumulative record in school is a history of all of the failures of the past and should be ignored, since students cannot do anything about the past.

d. *Evaluating Behavior.* One should not talk as much about the feelings of the student (which are hard to "pin down") but should stress their behavior (which is easier to verify and which the student can change). It is difficult for a counselor to help students who are "feeling bad," but there are many things that can be done to redirect their specific behaviors. There is a good deal of confrontation of students in order to get them to see the consequences of what they are doing. This, however, only comes after the initial stage of "involvement."

e. *Planning Responsible Behavior.* The student must be helped to formulate realistic plans for change.

f. *Commitment.* The students are challenged to make a commitment to the plan of action which they have devised and which is based on their own value system.

g. *Accept No Excuse.* Glasser's earlier work stressed that, if the plan was indeed a good one and really reflected the student's value system, he/she should be expected to carry it out (with appropriate help) and it should not be put off or diverted for superficial reasons.

h. *No Punishment.* Punishment (as opposed to the natural consequences of irresponsible behavior) is one of the surest ways of breaking the involvement, to reduce the trust and confidence, and to eliminate the feeling of caring.

Many of the aspects of Reality Therapy were originally developed by Glasser for use with delinquents at the Ventura School for Girls in California; it has been used successfully in a wide spectrum of school settings, including the elementary school (Hawes, 1976). Although many think of it as an individual technique, it still continues to have great potential as a group approach (Kaltenbach and Gazda, 1975).

5. *Rational Counseling.* The original work of Ellis (Ellis 1971; Ellis and Harper, 1972) with the modifications of Maultsby (1975) called Rational Emotive Counseling is directed toward a wide spectrum of life-skill deficits. It attempts to help students to direct their behaviors of thinking (mental behavior), feeling (emotional behavior), and acting (physical behavior). It draws heavily from learning theory and stresses that you can "learn" to act rationally as well as you learn anything else, i.e. that your behaviors are not "driven" by emotions which are not learned. The student is taught that behavior is rational if it contains the following elements: is based on objective reality, protects one's life, helps one achieve one's goals, eliminates significant trouble with others. What is rational behavior for one student may not be rational for another. What is rational for one student at one time may not be rational for the same student at another time. In each situation, it is the student's responsibility to decide for him/herself what seems to be most rational for him/her (Goodman, 1975).

This approach is based upon six basic ideas:

    a. Useless happenings keep an individual from enjoying life more;

    b. Faulty thinking is a major cause of emotional problems (the brain controls one's emotional and physical behavior, but since all individuals direct their own brain, they can control their feelings and actions) ;

c. Self-supplied psychological needs are the best (people with normal intelligence can supply most of the psychological needs they must have for emotional security) ;

d. Each person is fallible and it is best to act like that (although people admit they are fallible, when they make errors, they often blame and punish themselves) ;

e. People have more emotional choices than they think (people act like "robots" because: (1) they were taught to act that way, (2) they do not have an effective way of stopping those reactions, and (3) they believe that they cannot stop) ;

f. A miserable past does not have to hold a person back (just because they have acted that way all of their lives does not mean they have to continue to act that way) .

Rational counseling de-emphasizes the role of the counselor and works on the assumption that all of these ideas can be systematically taught. In fact, much of how this can be done is in a book which describes a process of self-counseling (Maultsby, 1974). It is also adaptable as a group counseling process (Ellis, 1975).

6. *Human Relations Developmental Counseling.* Although Gazda's work was described (in Chapter 6) as a part of a developmental program, Understanding/Valuing Self and Others (Gazda, 1971), it has also been used as a basis for a corrective, group counseling approach. A group of workers under the direction of Gazda (Gazda, et al., 1973) have developed a program which can help students improve their relationships with others. This model has been found to be effective in working with teachers and other educational personnel as well as with students; it is assumed that the helping relationship is essentially the same no matter who is being helped. (The reader is encouraged to review the basic principles of this process described in Chapters 2 and 3 of this book.)

7. *Sensitization Techniques.* This series of interventions is designed to help students decrease or increase their sensitivity to specific stimuli, usually, but not always, in a social situation. The

general goal is to help increase the ability to tolerate difficult situations more easily.

a. *Immunization.* This approach has not been used very often. It attempts to help students learn to meet or "cope with" difficult situations. At one time, there was a belief that the best way to help young people become mentally healthy adults was to keep them from falling into pitfalls and hardships. This is no longer believed, but it is held that students, instead, must be helped to learn to handle the frustrations of life. For a child who is easily bothered by the "jibes" of other students about a "big nose," for instance, an immunization technique might be to "kid" him/her about that nose in a sheltered counseling situation. Unless it is carefully used, however, his/her anger at the criticism of the other students can become directed at the counselor. Similarly, there are some "crutches" that can be taught to students to help them turn "taunts" back onto the person who makes them, or to shift the emphasis into humor for all. Here, of course, the object is to at least "put up a front" that the student is not bothered and thus to turn the anger away from him/herself.

b. *Desensitization.* This is a technique which developed from the work of those applying behavior modification to the problems of the school. It does not attempt so much to reduce the stimuli that affect the student as it does to reduce his/her reaction to them. One difficult problem to work with is a child with "school phobia." The act of leaving home, saying good-bye, walking to and entering the school, and putting up with all of the noise is more than the child can handle. In many instances, it gets to the point where the anxiety is created not only by entering the school, but also by just thinking about it. Desensitization is the process of systematically introducing at first small, but increasingly larger, doses of the fear-producing stimulus in the presence of the interventionist with whom the child feels secure. In this instance, it may mean successively walking first a block away from the school, then past the school, then to the steps, then through the door for a moment, and then staying for increasingly longer periods of time until the child gets to the point where he/she can again function in the regular school program (Bugg, 1976).

8. *Arguments With Other People.* Although not specifically an approach, certainly a common problem that needs assistance in the school environment is to help students get through a situation where they are having an argument with someone else. The "someone else" could be a teacher, another student, parents, school administrators, the police, etc. The intervention is usually begun by allowing the student to "spill out" the frustration and anger. The next steps include helping them to be better able to understand their own feelings and then to explore various alternate paths of action.

VALUE CONFLICTS. In some ways, any disagreement could be labeled as a case of value conflict. As used here, it will be restricted to those situations where individuals or groups have pervasive, long-standing, major differences in the way they view or value the world.

1. *Black-White Encounters.* Although basic encounter groups have been briefly discussed as a life skill developmental program, there are obviously occasions when Corrective/Therapeutic Interventions are needed in this area. Some groups are assumed to have differences that are racial in nature, but the same techniques could be used with groups disagreeing on any major issue. The original concept included bringing people together with major differences to work out their disagreements—letting all of the hatred and negative feelings that individuals had for each other come out. Unfortunately, all too often this only served to reinforce the negative feelings, so it was often unsuccessful in its attempts to bring people closer together. The movement in this area is now toward finding the common denominator of thoughts and feelings as a means of bringing the two groups into agreement. Just as the Bates and Johnson (1972) approach to group counseling described earlier stressed only positive feelings, in the school setting it is much safer and seemingly as effective to stress the positive. This does not mean that there are not many negative, hostile feelings within individuals. Unfortunately, it takes a long time to work some of them through, time which groups in schools usually do not have. In many ways, the culture seems to support the expression of negative feelings almost more than it does posi-

tive ones. Whatever the reason, the violence often associated with hostile feelings is frequently very hard to contain within a small group in a school setting and becomes rapidly communicated throughout the school. This tends to confirm the negative feelings with little opportunity to move on to either a middle ground or toward more positive ones. At one level, it seems unrealistic to structure groups so that they only can bring up positive feelings, but experience has indicated that this is frequently the best procedure.

COMMUNICATION PROBLEMS. Since language plays a central role in so much of one's thinking, communication is a critical part of the corrective/therapeutic process (Bandler and Grinder, 1975). There are many reasons why students have difficulty in communicating: e.g. they may be hesitant to talk in front of others and need some sort of a "crutch" or technique which will help them get started; they may have been dominated by someone else and have not had the necessary opportunity to communicate; they may not have a sense of direction which is reflected in their inadequate communication; there may be a discrepancy beween what they are saying and what they are feeling; and there may be a discrepancy between what they are doing (their behavior) and what they are saying.

1. *Records-Production Techniques.* For some students, it is helpful if they are asked to prepare something before they come to work on it in the presence of the interventionist. These interventions have in common the fact that they produce or make something which will in turn help to create a more meaningful relationship with the counselor. In some instances, they are assigned either for the good that the students will get out of them or as something for which the counselor can later praise the student. Variations of this technique include the following:

a. *Art Work.* The students can be asked to produce a picture each time, either just before they come or during the counseling situation. There should be some significance in the fact that the art work is produced in sequence; it might depict different stages in the child's life, the way they feel just before coming to the session, or pictures of the important people of his/her life.

This process gives a visual clue upon which the counseling can focus and can be used to show students their progress.

b. *Construction.* The model for this type of activity at one time was to build model airplanes or cars either just before the counseling or as part of the process. Working with model dinosaurs is often a very interesting process for young boys.

c. *Games.* Some children enjoy the competition or intellectual challenge of games such as chess or checkers. If the goal is to increase verbal interaction, however, it may be best if the game has a high element of chance so either the student or counselor can win without too much time spent thinking about the game.

d. *Serial Testing.* A variation on the above techniques has the student take the same test over time (to show progress) or different parts of it each time they come in. This process is probably most effective if the results can be readily interpreted to the student.

e. *Counseling Homework.* A related, although somewhat different, approach is to have students accept some sort of an assignment which they are to do outside of the counseling situation, e.g. listening to a recording of the counseling session, or taking a small step which leads them in the direction of a goal they have set for themselves.

2. *Autobiographical Techniques.* These can be used to help shy students find it easier to talk in the counseling situation or to help other students who are too talkative use the techniques to focus their attention and organize their thoughts ahead of time. Others have found it easier to express hostility in the counseling situation if they have written about it ahead of time.

a. *Calendar-Diary.* The students are asked to keep a daily record of their activities together with their thoughts and feelings about them. If the students are able to express themselves better in art, they can also produce pictures or make a collage of their life using photographs, symbols, mementos, etc.

b. *Autobiography.* This technique was used more when counseling tried to go back into the student's past to find the "reasons" for his/her present actions. It is not used as much at this time, but it can still be a legitimate intervention. In both this and the calendar-diary technique, it may be easier for some to speak into a tape recorder rather than to write it down (although this takes longer for the student and the counselor to process when they are together).

　　c. *Bibliotherapy.* Several examples of this approach have been mentioned in connection with helping students overcome specific problems. The process is to select carefully and to prescribe reading books which reflect some concern or problem in a student's life. Even at the very early stages of reading, most of the children's books have some sort of a plot. Working with the school librarian, one could find out which books would be useful for this purpose. For example, a child might be able to learn something about how to cope with his/her parents' divorce by reading a book on the subject. The technique is applicable all the way through high school (and even college).

　　3. *Nondirective Counseling.* The original work of Rogers (1942) stressed that instead of counselors trying constantly to interpret behavior to the student, they should initiate a process that reflects back the student's feelings. Through this process, students are encouraged to organize their own resources and to find solutions to their own problems which are satisfactory to them. The rather simplistic technique of reflecting back to the student his/her feelings (by a process often humorously labeled the "you feel" techniques) is not used very much any more. One of the major goals of counseling in the schools is to assist the students in the process of solving their own problems. Even though Nondirective Counseling has probably had more influence on both general education and counseling than any other single theory, it is seldom used as rigidly as it was when it was first proposed.

　　The much used modification called "active listening" which has been discussed elsewhere and which has been developed by Gordon (1970) has its roots in this approach to counseling. Similarly, the concept that counseling should hold up a "mirror" in front of students so they can better understand themselves, i.e. Is this the way you wanted to communicate? is the product of Nondirective Counseling. The modern counselor typically enters much more personally into the process than was originally advocated by Rogers (who now has moved into more active approaches for helping people; Rogers, 1970). The nondirective approach de-emphasized the "gadgetry" of counseling and focused on the mature qualities desirable not only for the counselor but for everyone who desires to enter into a helping relationship. To reach that goal, everyone, according to Rogers, must continue to stretch and develop the tremendous potentiality toward the "direction of growth" that is within them. Although normally thought of as an individual technique, this approach has also been modified for use with groups (Meador, 1975). Nondirective Counseling has perhaps the strongest research evidence to support it of any of the Corrective/Therapeutic Interventions. It was in many ways the forerunner of the basic encounter group described earlier.

4. *Rap Sessions.* Although the theory behind the use of rap sessions has not been well defined, it is important to remember that they represent another potential intervention. The original rationale was greatly influenced by psychoanalytic thought which held that certain students have difficulty because of deep-seated hostilities and problems and that the major process of counseling is to help them release that anger and frustration, i.e. experience catharsis. Whereas there is still some truth in this, modern interventions would place more stress on helping the students move on to some sort of positive (at least in their eyes) action. There is still some value in "griping" and feeling that one is being heard if there is appropriate follow-through. Some schools are experimenting with self-selected groups (Berkovitz, 1975) and others are turning their detention periods into rap sessions where trained counselors try to assist the students to move on to positive plans of action. Too often, educators do not give the students a chance to tell "their side of the story" which can be the first step of a powerful helping, intervention.

5. *Student Effectiveness Training.* Although it was originally devised as a means of helping parents learn to communicate more effectively with their children and with each other, the concepts of Parent Effectiveness Training (Gordon, 1970) have also been used extensively with older students. This was discussed as part of the process of developing and improving communication skills

in Chapter 6, but the process can also be used with smaller groups (or even individuals) in a corrective/therapeutic way.

6. *Groups to Improve Communication Skills.* Rather than focusing on the underlying dynamics of communication, other groups may be formed to identify and to train students in the essentials of effective communication. A series of verbal group exercises may be used (Morris and Cinnamon, 1974) or the emphasis may be on using the normal social interaction of the group to identify and to work on problems that are identified as the interaction proceeds. Communication difficulties can be encountered first of all in the way the message is "sent." One may talk "over the head" of the listener (either in general or as it relates to a particular topic) ; mannerisms, tone of voice, or general appearance may distract from one's effectiveness; not timing the communication properly (talking too often, not enough, etc.) can be a problem; not really paying attention to the receiver; not really sending information that the listener needs or wants; all of these can produce ineffective communication.

Problems in "receiving" the message include not giving the sender adequate feedback at either the intellectual or feeling level when needed, inappropriate valuation of what is being said, being preoccupied with other thoughts, or rehearsing what you (the receiver) will say next. But communication is more than simply speaking to another person and receiving the spoken reply. It means sending effective, meaningful, consistent messages by tone of voice, by facial expression, by the use of silence, and by body movements. As the term "active listening" implies, listening is a very dynamic process of receiving and understanding messages at both the intellectual and feeling level.

Communication groups often use a technique to focus attention on some particular aspect of the communication process. Many of the techniques which were previously discussed in the section on the development of human communication skills can be used. Games such as the "one-way" and "two-way" communication (which have previously been described) as well as training techniques in "active listening," especially the component where the feelings behind the words are given as feedback to the sender,

have been used. Still another training method is to help participants learn to paraphrase what has previously been said to the satisfaction of the "sender."

7. *Discussion Groups.* Rather than working directly on effective communication, discussion groups can also be used to help
students. These can be either groups that are formed specifically
for this purpose or they may be discussion groups formed for other
purposes. Problems which may be encountered (together with
appropriate remedial devices) are described by Stanford and Stanford (1969) as follows:

a. Problems in obtaining feedback,
b. Groups polarized into warring factions,
c. Hostile, overly aggressive groups,
d. The silent group,
e. Groups that are not acquainted with each other,
f. Groups that ignore the contributions of others.
g. Dealing with problem members,
h. Groups that stray off the topic,
i. Inflexible groups that use fixed patterns of interaction,
j. The inhibited group,
k. Groups that only toss ideas around rather than building
   toward a product,
l. Groups that argue without agreeing on definitions,
m. Groups that use illogical reasoning,
n. Groups where everyone talks at once, and
o. Groups with a low level of trust.

8. *Nonverbal Exercises.* There is much interest in helping
students become aware of and learn to derive meaning from nonverbal cues, often referred to as "body language." Unfortunately
there is a great tendency for students and educators to move too
rapidly into simplistic explanations of certain body movements,
i.e. sitting with one's arms folded means one is "shutting out
people," and the like. In groups dealing with these issues, it is
much safer and more effective to put the emphasis on the group
interaction and the meaning that the student's peers are likely to
"read into" the observation of such behaviors. It is true that

educators have overemphasized verbal communication in the schools and in life in general to the exclusion of any appreciable emphasis on communication in other than verbal ways. Deep feelings are often better expressed nonverbally than they are with words. Students should at least be helped to understand and give appropriate, consistent verbal and nonverbal messages (Morris and Cinnamon, 1975; Widerman and Widerman, 1976). A word of warning is in order when small groups, organized by the public schools, work with nonverbal communication; these groups move rather naturally into exercises where students touch one another. A lot of bad public relations can result if the idea gets around that the school is encouraging a "touch-feely" group (the anxiety this creates shows how strong the basic feelings communicated through the sense of touch really are). In general, it is best to impose the rule of "don't touch" each other in expressing nonverbal communication. It may be that specific rules can be introduced which will keep this under control, e.g. different ways to express feelings through shaking hands, etc. but the potential good that can be done in this type of program can be undone by the possible public opinion that can be raised against it.

DIFFICULTY MAKING DECISIONS. Some students need help in making decisions. This may require a relatively simple procedure of providing them with the necessary information, to helping them think through and use the problem-solving skills, to becoming more assertive, or in setting up some sort of a center to help students through periods of crises in their lives.

1. *Direct Information Giving.* Although some may argue that this is not technically "counseling," there is little question that students have unique needs and questions which must be answered. The more this information can be prepared and provided to students in systematic ways (such as in printed form), the better. For every student who asks for a specific piece of information, there may well be four or five more who do not know how to ask, or for some other reason never try to find out. Both the professional and the peer counselor should be alert to the fact that although the student is, on the surface, asking for specific information, he/she may have used this as an "excuse" to make the con-

tact and may have something else on his/her "agenda." An "open-ended" approach will make the student feel more comfortable about bringing up the second topic.

2. *Decision Making.* Some students have most of the facts but are seeking some help in making one or more specific decisions. Many of the problem-solving techniques discussed in Chapter 6 can be used; this is a good time to introduce techniques to help the student analyze his/her values as they relate to the decision-making process. The counselor should reassure the students that they have the right to make their own decisions and, when appropriate, to provide the feedback that they are going in the "right" direction. This approach can be used with both individuals and groups (Eiseman, 1969).

3. *Assertion Training.* There is an increased interest in Assertion Training which derives from behavior modification technology. It helps students establish goals for themselves and then, through a system of modeling, coaching, and role-playing, they are helped to put their plan into action (McFall and Lillesand, 1971; Sarason and Sarason, 1974). In some aspects it stresses components of decision making; in other ways it would be valuable in helping students to adopt new roles.

4. *Crises Intervention.* There is also a growing interest in establishing crises intervention centers (sometimes called student service centers) for students who are "in over their heads." Although students have been facing crises for a long time, the major impetus for starting centers of this type came during the periods of heavy drug experimentation. In some communities they have been established outside of the school by other agencies. Since the school has a much wider range of interventions to help students than is typically available to outside agencies, it is generally preferable to organize and operate them within the school. At the same time, they should be separated from the regular school counseling program which, very often in the student's mind, is too closely related to the school administration (Project TRIAD, 1974). In addition to the problem of threatened suicide, drug problems, and some of the sex-related problems (which are all discussed elsewhere) some examples of the kinds of problems covered

by these Student Service Centers are as follows:

a. *New Member of the Family.* Although the problem of having a new child born into the family is typically associated with younger children than would ordinarily be using a service center, educators should remember that teen-agers are not the only ones who have crises. A bibliotherapeutic approach would be to ask a child to read a story about another child whose family is having a new baby (Arnstein, 1974). For older students the new member might be a new step parent who may be causing a temporary imbalance in the student.

b. *Facing Death.* At the other end of the life continuum is the crisis in which a student is shocked by the death of a close friend or relative. Neither young people nor adults, for that matter, have been very well prepared to face death; it, like sex, has in many ways been a taboo subject. Some progress is being made, however, both directly and through the use of bibliotherapy (Fassier, 1971). Needless to say, this topic should be included in a developmentally based life-skills curriculum. Even if it is, however, there will still be some students who need help as they face this problem (Zeligs, 1974).

c. *Runaways.* Students who are actually "on the run" are usually handled by juvenile agencies or by the growing series of "halfway" houses that are being established across the country for this purpose (Gang, n.d.). While in some ways this moves the interventions outside the school, there are, as in suicide, many students who threaten to run away but who never do. It usually is a signal that the student is "in over his/her head" in some basic dimension of his/her life.

d. *"Hot-Line" Counseling.* This procedure allows students to call to get information or advice on a variety of problems. Whereas they have been traditionally operated by nonschool agencies, they should be investigated as another appropriate school-related Corrective/Therapeutic Intervention. Many of the outside agencies are using volunteer "counselors" with apparently satisfactory results.

These topics bring up the issue of the school's responsibility to contact the student's parents. It is almost always preferable to bring the crisis intervention to the point where the student's parents are involved in finding solutions. The rights of the school personnel to work with students without notifying the parents are frequently defined by state statues and/or by school board policies. The educators who are working with youth at this level are strongly encouraged to learn the rules and regulations that govern their activities in this area. If the educator has no choice except to notify the parent, the student should know this from the beginning. Many young people who come to the schools for help do so because they are having difficulty with their parents. Many can be helped early in the counseling process to seek their parents' involvement. The problem comes when this does not take place. In some states the student's rights to confidentiality (these reside in the student, not in the school personnel) are provided when they are talking to a school psychologist (especially if they are both licensed and certificated by the state). In general, however, these rights are very limited with school personnel. In the final analysis, it may be necessary to let the student decide either to permit the interventionist to inform the parents or to seek help elsewhere.

NEED FOR MORE SATISFYING ROLES. The range of behaviors to be handled by this series of interventions is great. They can range all the way from the student who is vaguely discontent with his/her way of life to the one who faces a major problem in school or with life in general. The interventionist should remember that the new role has to be seen as potentially more satisfying to the student, not just to the interventionist.

1. *Role/Attitude Shift.* The importance of helping the student learn to identify and play a variety of roles has already been discussed under "Role-Playing." To take the part of someone else tends to change the view of the person playing that role and increases his/her empathy for the other person. At the same time it makes his/her own identity bigger and more complex. An attitude is more pervasive than a role and is more likely to affect the way students react in the various situations of their lives. Because attitudes tend to be vague and difficult to define (especially in oneself), it is often difficult for students to see the need for

changing them. In fact, many protect themselves from the fact that it is their attitude that is keeping them from getting along with others.

It may be necessary to "assign a role" on an experimental or "as if" basis, in order to make a change in attitude. "Let's see what would happen if you acted more friendly toward that other student." The student may need some "role rehearsal" in learning how to play roles that are completely out of his/her repertoire. Among others, the following possibilities of roles can be assigned in the school: room counselor, assistant librarian, "listener," "teacher watcher," game referee, or one who helps another student. It is possible that taking on these new roles will help the student break up old habit patterns and establish new, more effective ones. Such a role assignment will be more effective if the "new behavior" is recognized and reinforced by the other students and the teacher. The desired goal is to initiate a change in the student's total social system in such a way that the new behavior will be supported once it has taken place. If the student finds success in several of these new roles, it may be that he or she will begin to be seen by others as having a different attitude. Of course, not all students who are "out of line" are that way because they want to be; some have just never developed any other way to act.

2. *Role-Playing*. The use of modeling and role-playing was discussed in Chapter 6 under the heading "Adopting More Satisfying Roles." Assertion training, another related technique, was discussed earlier in this chapter. Traditional role rehearsal techniques tend to lend themselves more to group work than they do working with an individual. Although a suggestion might be made during an interview which would encourage the student to rehearse a specific role, for example, in his/her home, if the desired results are not obtained, it is difficult for the counselor to help the student understand what went wrong. There is a renewal of interest in psychodrama, which is an extension of these techniques into a more intensified, therapeutic format. This work is essentially carried on outside of the schools at the current time (Blatner, 1973; Greenberg, 1974).

3. *Transactional Analysis.* The elements of Berne's (1964) TA approach were discussed under the heading of *I'm OK, You're OK* (Harris, 1967) in Chapter 6. Its original conception was designed for use with short-term therapy groups outside the school. The rather intense level of training required to lead a real TA group is usually far above that available in the schools. The principles of this approach have been modified, however, for a variety of programs in and out of the school (Goulding, 1975). Some of the most important concepts of this approach are as follows:

a. There are three *major roles* in life. The *Parent* refers to any authority figure which has influenced the child; it includes appropriate parental attitudes but is also contaminated by dogmatic, critical, judgmental, and evaluative factors, i.e. telling someone he/she "should do something." The *Adult* represents the awareness, choice, options in behavior that are free from the autonomy of the Parent and the Child. The *Child* represents behavior that is a result of urges and reactions to the environment. The child is helpless and a victim of strong feelings.

b. From infancy on, people require *stroking,* both physically and verbally; it is vitally necessary for mental survival.

c. There are six ways to *structure time:* "Rituals" are a stereotyped series of transactions; they are noncommittal, but imperative. "Pastimes" are semiritualistic, predictable behaviors played at parties, group meetings, etc. "Activities" are those projects designed to deal with the material of the external reality, e.g. earning a living. "Withdrawal" is seen when the body is there but the mind is involved in fantasy. "Games" are stereotyped maneuvers to gain an ulterior motive with an ultimate pay-off. Although some games are good, many attempt to avoid reality, conceal ulterior motives, and avoid intimacy or closeness. "Intimacy" involves a complete commitment, a maximum fulfillment, and a total involvement-relationship. The first five ways to structure time essentially keep one from establishing intimacy.

4. *Family Therapy.* Whereas family therapy is typically conducted outside of the school, because of the dependent nature of most students upon a family unit, some of the techniques which have been developed in this process have direct application

in the school. The family is what some people call a "natural group" because it exists as a group outside of the therapy session. Too often in the past specialists have referred a student and/or his/her parents as individuals when the problem stems from the ineffective communication between family members. The practice of seeing all of the members of a family who are able to contribute to the sending/receiving communication is rapidly growing. Although this approach cannot be strictly classified in this section, it does tend to highlight the part played by different members of the family unit. In family therapy, for example, there is the "identified patient" within the family, the one that all have agreed is the "sick one." There must be a willingness on the part of all members of the family to participate. They should all agree on entering into the process for a given amount of time. Family therapy is based on some of the following concepts:

a. All individuals have the basic need for survival and desires or "wants" for intimacy, productivity, uniqueness, and a sense of order.

b. The self-concept of each member of the family is affected by the interactions of the family.

c. The way individuals "see" and "act upon" their world is affected by their feelings of self-worth.

d. The family is an assemblage of individuals, in which each member has his/her own needs, wants and self-concepts. It is a system which has devised some rules (some of which are productive and some of which are nonproductive) for getting "the job done."

e. At the basis of defining and carrying out the rules is the communication system within a family.

f. Families tend to "maintain the status quo" and to resist change.

Therapy is a process of looking at the family process, especially as seen in its communication (in the broadest sense) patterns. Choosing an intervention requires answers to the following questions: Is the family process promoting growth? What innovations are wanted? The goal is to improve the process through improved communication and through improved self-concepts. There are many student/parent interaction problems which are helped by this approach, but especially in situations where there is a "school phobia." The intervention in the school will often be to help students and parents understand this process enough so they will seek this kind of assistance in the community (Sugar, 1975; Wiseman, 1971).

SEX/ROLE PROBLEMS. There are a variety of problems which can be associated with deviations from the normal pattern of sexual development. All of these problems are complicated by a strong expectation for social conformity in this area of development. Some students are "precocious" in their early development of relationships with the opposite sex; others are worried about being slow in this area. There are students who are concerned about having contacted venereal disease; students who feel guilty about homosexual feelings or contacts; students who get married early and create a problem in school settings where most students are still single; and unwed girls who become pregnant. The interventions listed below can be handled in the regular counseling program, through a crisis intervention program, or through the regular health programs of the school.

1. *Supportive Counseling.* Most sex/role problems are complicated by the expectations that society establishes for its members; although sexual patterns are changing, students who get "too far out of line" frequently find that the reaction of others is "blown all out of proportion," at least in their minds. The students often need to be given some help in understanding why their behavior is creating so much concern on the part of others. They may need a better understanding of development; others may need information about health and counseling programs in the community or other forms of supportive counseling.

2. *Referral to Medical Agencies.* Although most interventions which require referral to agencies outside the school are discussed later in this chapter, they are of such importance to some of the problems in this area that they will also be mentioned here. Certainly suspected venereal disease and pregnancies require medical service and supervision beyond the health services normally available in

the schools. Getting a girl with a suspected pregnancy to the right medical facilities can still be quite a problem. Many schools have rules that will not allow pregnant girls to attend regular school programs; this complicates the problem. In many states these girls are considered "emancipated minors" and can be treated as adults, no matter what their chronological age. There is still the intervention of helping these girls find homes for unwed mothers although this is less common than it once was. In other cases they may be encouraged to stay close to their home and begin to make the necessary adjustments before the baby arrives. In all of these areas, a great deal of medical supervision is necessary.

3. *Making Plans.* In addition to supportive counseling and getting appropriate medical care, many students with sex/role problems also need help in planning for some changes in their lives. In some cases they may want to change something about themselves; in others, they may decide to approach the problem through different relationships with others. Many of these problems will often force a student to begin looking at his/her life after school much more realistically and he/she will want to start making plans in that direction. In almost all cases, the student has the problem of relating to the important people in his/her life who may begin to see the student in a different light as a result of these sex/role problems and/or adjustments.

CONCERN OVER GRADES. Some students will come in for help because they are concerned about the grades they are receiving; equally as often the concern comes from the students' parents or teachers. Occasionally gifted students will come in even though they are still getting average grades or better. In other instances the low grades are related to absenteeism or cheating.

1. The traditional approach to helping students with grade problems has been one of trying to help the student become more motivated, but this is often unsuccessful. Helping students evaluate their values and their short- and long-range goals is sometimes helpful.

2. Other students can be helped by getting them to appraise the ways they are using their time and by helping them with their study skills (Zifferblatt, 1970). Frequently the parents of the

students will need to be considered both because they are often "at the throat" of the student and because they will need to be involved in the process of remediation. Some of the new behavioral techniques have been found to be helpful in these situations.

3. With all students showing grade difficulty, but especially with the underachieving gifted, the interventionist should look into the possibility that the student has an inadequate self-concept or self-worth (Purkey, 1970). With the slower student, the low self-concept may be the end result of having met much failure. For the potentially more capable student, the low self-image may be one of the factors contributing to the cause of low grades. Of course being gifted in some areas does not mean that one is going to do well in all subjects, since there is a lot of variability within giftedness.

4. Some success has been experienced in using group approaches with the truant student (Berkovitz, 1972). Once again, however, it is generally best not to form groups where every student has the same behavior problem; such a situation often tends to reinforce the negative behavior rather than helping to diminish it. There are obviously a great many reasons why students are truant. We will continue to have trouble with this problem until we can make school more meaningful for older students so they can see some advantages in attending. Some states are allowing students to drop out of school before they have reached the required age or before they graduate if they can pass a high school equivalency test. Variations in establishing competency must be found, otherwise older students will continue to drop out of school before receiving the high school diploma.

DRUG-RELATED PROBLEMS. Various aspects of this problem have been already discussed in Chapter 6 and earlier in this chapter as a form of crisis intervention. If a student is in a drug overdose condition, immediate medical attention is essential.

1. *Drug Overdose.* If students are frightened by a bad reaction or a strong overdose, they may seek help from school personnel. In other instances, students are found in this condition at the school. Even if they have to be sent for immediate medical help and supervision, the students should be encouraged to return

at a later time to explore the total picture of their drug usage. The crisis can often make them appraise themselves more critically.

2. *Counseling Approaches.* In working with students in this area, the counselor typically spends very little time dealing with the physical effects of taking drugs; in general the students often know more about this than the school personnel. Although the adults in the student's life are usually very concerned, the counseling is complicated by the fact that there is so much peer-approval of taking drugs. Even the term "taking drugs" is confusing because virtually everyone is using something which would be classified as a "drug." The concept of "substance abuse" is preferable because it stresses the misuse of chemical agents, many of which have a socially accepted and recognized usefulness. Considerations about "risk taking" are also frequently discussed. Another way of assisting some of these students is to help them find legitimate ways of "alternate highs" which will help them get some legitimate "thrills" and which will be more likely to bring about long-range satisfactions (Project TRIAD: Road Notes, 1974). Once again, the willingness of the interventionist to listen and to be a good sounding board for these students has proven to be very helpful. To some extent the problems in this area are diminishing as the laws against marijuana are being relaxed.

DIFFICULTY MAKING CAREER DECISIONS. Out of the great majority of students who are having difficulty in making decisions about their occupational future, a few will come in to seek help in this area. Since this is such a major decision, however, most students seem to put off thinking about it as long as possible. The following strategies for helping to facilitate career development are suggested by Reardon and Burck (1975).

1. *Occupational Information.* An intervention that has been around for a long time (although it has not been very effective) has been to provide students with good information about different careers. Good information is hard to obtain, difficult to use, and becomes dated very quickly. There are some new advances in this field which show promise of improving this aspect of career counseling. The schools must decide that this is an important service and

allocate enough resources to get the job done. The interventionist should model good information-seeking behavior for the students who must be helped to find the personal meaning of the material once they have obtained it. They will often need help in identifying the next step which would help them move toward their identified goals. The objective of helping students make comprehensive career decisions is not to have them choose a specific vocation. In a much broader sense, interventionists are trying to get them to investigate the world of work and evaluate themselves in order to make some tentative decisions about where the "best fit" between these two occurs (Denues, 1972). For the students who terminate their education, however, these decisions are much more pressing and are complicated by the necessity of immediately earning an income. Ideally, students should have individualized instructional materials available as they seek information about how to make career decisions. These self-help units should provide them the opportunity to personalize the occupational information that is made available to them. A first attempt at providing such units has been described in the Santa Clara Educational-Vocational Guidance Program (n.d.).

2. *Assessment.* Despite much criticism of the testing approach, the use of tests and other assessment techniques continues to increase. There are currently a great many tests which purport to measure factors of aptitude, achievement, interests, vocational maturity, and work values. Unfortunately, many of these are overlapping categories which make it difficult for the counselor to use in a way that is clear and helpful for the student. With all of its faults, however, the use of assessment instruments can be a very helpful tool in assisting the student to make some important career decisions (Tarczan, 1972).

3. *Simulation Techniques.* The use of simulation and gaming techniques has already been discussed in great detail throughout this book. Those of special importance to the area were discussed under the part of Chapter 6 entitled "Making Comprehensive Career Decisions."

4. *Contractual Approach.* A new approach developed from behavior therapy technology (see the next section) is the use of a

contract (usually short-term) designed to help students work on the psychological problems that are involved in a career decision. Because there are so many variables impinging on the students as they make such a choice, it is important that they enter into a contract which they not only want to fulfill but are capable of fulfilling. This is part of the movement toward being more specific in helping students to select goals for themselves which are given in behavioral terms. Specifying goals behaviorally makes it much easier to verify whether or not the contractual goals have been attained (Montgomery, 1975).

5. *Using Groups.* Students making career decisions can often be placed into groups where a wide range of gaming and counseling techniques can be used to help the participants evaluate and understand themselves. One approach, called the "Future Group," uses a series of techniques to help the participants start with the past and project themselves into the future (through the use of fantasy) with exercises to help them stop and ask questions about what these changes mean for them. Another model, the "Life Planning Workshop," uses similar techniques and involves some aspects of self-exploration and intrapersonal growth which are designed to have an impact in the student's educational/career development and decision making.

6. *Occupational Exploration Interviews.* A technique which has proven to be of value is to bring in recent graduates of a school and conduct occupational interviews with them, especially with those students who are having difficulty in this area. The struggles, successes, and failures of students who sat in the same classrooms just a short time before are often helpful in getting other students to face more realistically their need for occupational planning and preparation.

PROBLEMS IN PLANNING FOR THE FUTURE. There are obviously other concerns about the future than just the one of making a career decision, as important as that one is. Some of the techniques which have been adapted from behavior modification and social learning have seemed to be especially powerful in the development of a counseling approach which is most helpful in assisting students to make plans for their future.

1. *Behavioral Counseling.* Krumboltz (1966), probably the chief proponent for this approach, has suggested that the goals of any counseling procedure should meet the following criteria. They should be:

a. *Desired by the Student.* The goals of counseling should be able to be stated differently for each individual student. (The common goals that society holds for all individuals are met primarily through the regular instructional program; counseling should be flexible enough to help individuals meet their unique goals.)

b. *Compatible with Society's Goals.* The goals of counseling should be compatible with, though not necessarily identical to, the predominant goals of the society in which the counseling is performed. (Although the student has the right to set his/her own goals, counselors must decide whether or not they would be willing to help a client attain a goal that was not approved by society.)

c. *Externally Observable.* The degree to which the goals of counseling are attained by each student should be observable. (In an attempt to sharpen what behavioral counselors consider the "fuzzy thinking" of those who work with the "vague" concepts of self-understanding and self-concept, the emphasis should be on identifying specific observable behaviors which the student could be helped to achieve and which would help them to know that they had achieved their goal.) It can be seen from these statements that this approach would have merit in helping students decide what they want to do as well as the specific behavioral steps which are required in order for them to attain their goals. Many of the techniques associated with this approach have already been described in this chapter, including contracting, desensitization, and training in assertiveness. Token economies, the reinforcement of successive approximations to the goal, and operant techniques were described in Chapter 5. As in some of the closely related therapies, it has been modified for use as a self-help technique (Watson and Tharp, 1972) and for groups (Keat, 1974; Lazarus, 1971). It is a rapidly growing field which is demonstrating its effectiveness in a variety of problem areas (Liberman, 1972).

EFFECTIVE LIAISON WITH COMMUNITY AGENCIES

Corrective/Therapeutic Interventions which are done *on behalf of* the student will often involve working with community agencies or services. A comprehensive treatment of how these other agencies work with the student would be beyond the scope of this book. It seems appropriate, however, to remind the reader that students have physical, mental, and social aspects of their lives which take place outside the school and which frequently interplay with their learning. There seems to be a tendency on the part of the staffs of many agencies or programs serving children and youth to assume that they are the *only* ones that are really getting the job done, the only ones that really care. Since all are obviously serving the same youth, the most effective intervention in some cases is to bring before the students the wide range of services available to them in other community agencies. In some instances the school will have to reach out and actively involve personnel from the other agency. Some students, for example, will need full-time specialized treatment centers. More frequently students will need specialized services that the outside agency or private practitioner can perform, but that are outside the range of school services.

In certain instances the request for service will be initiated by the outside agency. For example, an agency may try to place students in particular schools or programs within the school. They may seek information about students who are under their supervision and/or care. In some cases the outside agencies are openly critical of the schools and are actively working toward helping schools change. The whole process of exchanging information with these agencies is greatly complicated by the new emphasis on the students' and/or their parents' rights.

The major areas of interface between schools and four major agencies will be briefly described in this section as a logical extension of the Corrective/Therapeutic Interventions. This topic was saved for last however, not because it is least important or because there is no need for agency involvement in some of the areas discussed in other sections of the book; this discussion has been placed here because the liaison with other agencies is most appropriate under a section which concerns helping students with the most severe life-skill deficits. It is obvious that in order for the schools to make available to these students a full range of strategies, educators must build more effective liaisons with other community agencies and services, including those performed by public agencies and by private practitioners.

EFFECTIVE LIAISON WITH HEALTH AGENCIES/SERVICES

Under this category would come all of the agencies and services that are serving the medical and physical needs of students.

1. *Exchanging Information.* In the course of working with students, both the school and agency personnel will often seek information from the other as a means of getting a more complete picture of the student. As in all formal exchanges of information it is essential that informed, parental consent be obtained (with the possible exception of pregnant girls) before seeking information from the agency or releasing it to them. Many medical problems affect school learning and behavior, even though there may be no apparent, direct relationship. On the other hand, knowledge of how a student is functioning in school will affect the kind of medical service given to some students especially in learning, vision, hearing, and other related problems. Many such problems should be referred as another means of working with the student in all spheres of life.

2. *Medical Input Into the School Curriculum.* In many cases educators will want to invite medical agency personnel, doctors, and other health specialists into the school to make a contribution either to regular classes or to work with specialized groups of students. These specialists can be extremely helpful with many aspects of the developmental, life-skills curriculum, especially in the area of family-life education. Health units all the way through the curriculum would have more impact on the student if at some point a public health nurse, hospital technician, or a physician would be invited to discuss topics in their specialty. Many publicly supported health agencies have as part of their responsibility either the prevention and/or the early detection of specific medical/physical problems and would welcome the invitation. Medi-

cal specialists in private practice would also often be willing to make this contribution to their profession if they knew that they were going to be used effectively and if they thought that their efforts would have sufficient impact. The need for medical specialists on "career days" or in career exploration units is also obvious. With such a large percentage of students indicating that they would like to become doctors and nurses it would be helpful to large segments of the student population to study the full range of medically related occupations.

3. *School Initiated Requests for Medical Services.* In working with a specific student, a need for certain kinds of medical information and/or services will often be identified. There may be a need for a general physical check-up or for some sort of specific health service such as testing for vision or hearing. Obviously schools have to make provisions for getting medical attention for students who have accidents on the school property. In the midst of the hurry to get these students to the appropriate medical facility it is essential that the parents be informed and kept involved. The need for liaison with medical agencies and services has already been referred to where problems of venereal disease, suicide, or pregnancy are encountered. In many instances, of course, the students or their parents will initiate the medical intervention and the school's role will often be minimal; in other situations, school personnel must initiate and encourage the student and/or the family to seek outside help. This is greatly complicated both by the fact that medical service is not always available as needed and that some families cannot afford it. In the later case the school personnel must seek other agencies or sources of money in order to get the necessary help for the student. Referral to private physicians and health care providers raises special problems. Whenever possible the school referral of the student and/or his/her parents should include several sources (preferably at least three) where services can be obtained. If possible, one of them should be publicly supported where there is either no fee or a sliding fee. It is appropriate to inform the student and the parent about the kinds of services they can, in general, expect from the various agencies.

Physical examinations and medical supervision are often required for students who are being considered for special education programs, i.e. the visually handicapped, hard-of-hearing, and (increasingly) the learning disabled. In some cases the medical report on these students is needed to establish eligibility for these programs; in other cases the school's concern is to determine whether or not the students are receiving all of the help they need to facilitate their learning. When parents (for religious or other reasons) have strong feelings about the kinds of health services or advisors to use (or whether or not to use any) their wishes should be respected, except for life and death emergencies.

4. *Jointly Sponsored Medical/Educational Programs.* Many schools require preschool physicals that are typically done either in a health agency or in the doctor's office. Schools often cooperate with health agencies in conducting routine immunization programs for students. Vision and hearing screening can be done either by the school nurse or by outside specialists. Even when school personnel do the screening (sometimes with the help of parent volunteers), there is a need for a follow-up on those students who were identified as in the need of referral for more complete medical service. Physical examinations are usually required before students can enter into competitive sports. Direct medical supervision is often required at competitive sport activities such as football games.

For some students, teachers have to be sent from the school to provide an educational program for the home- and hospital-bound. There has been some experimentation with telephone connections between the student's regular class and the home or medical facility, usually in addition to the home teacher. For those students with major medical problems, especially for those in classes or schools for the physically handicapped, a joint effort provides both the educational and the physical/medical services in the same setting. Where the physical problems are less severe, the trend is to assign the student to a regular school and provide him/her with "outpatient" help with physical or medical problems, i.e. physical and occupational therapy, fitting of braces, etc. In some instances there is a need for joint efforts in Easter Seal-type programs, which

are sometimes year-round operations and at other times just summer activities. Certainly there is a great deal of need for effective
liaison between schools and medical agencies on a continuing
basis for severely handicapped students for as long as they attend
school.

5. *Student Involvement with Health Agencies.* Many students
should be encouraged to volunteer time to health agencies both
for the service they can give and for what they can learn. Certainly, schools need to provide a great many more work experience
opportunities in health agencies, both to help specific students get
directed work experience and/or to obtain some income. Another
group of students should be helped to enter into professional exploration experiences with medical specialists of various types as a
means of discovering more about that particular profession or
specialty.

The Candy Striper has long been the prototype of almost all
student volunteer activity; recently, there has been an increased
interest in the use of student volunteers in nursing homes. The
health service agencies cannot possibly afford to give all of the
service that their patients need without some help of this type;
students, on the other hand, often need to identify with older
people and to provide them with needed services. It would appear that educators would do well to bring these two needs together by encouraging both the agencies and the students to make
provisions for meaningful volunteer activities.

6. *Full-time Medical Agency Programs for Students.* There
is of course a wide range of circumstances when the health and
physical needs of the student are paramount and where the medical
agency must establish full-time programs. Even in the hospital
some of the students will be staying long enough to make it advisable to set up an instructional program. Traditionally there have
also been "schools" for children with asthma or tuberculosis;
fortunately modern medical advances have greatly reduced the
need for this type of medical intervention. There are still a great
many full-time medical/educational programs for physically handicapped children under the direct supervision of the health agency.
Almost all states have schools for the deaf and blind which can be

operated either by the schools or the health agencies. These programs are being urged to provide these specialized medical/physical services for the students in a normal setting. This will increase the need for effective liaison between the schools and these health agencies. As has already been pointed out, there is also a strong movement toward requiring that *all* children and youth of school age, no matter how severe the physical or mental problem, be provided with an educational program. This will require closer liaison between the schools and staffs of the institutions that, until now, have been primarily concerned with the medical/physical care of severely handicapped youngsters.

7. *Health Agency Requests for Educational Service.* For the children who have been out of school for a long period of time for physical reasons, the time comes when it is necessary to get them back into a school. Many of the students who have been in these full-time, medically oriented facilities are now being returned to their communities. With these and similar cases, the medical agency personnel will normally approach the school and will seek the cooperation of the school staff in finding an appropriate educational program. The students who are being transferred, the students in the receiving class, and their teachers will often have to be briefed in order to smooth the transition into the school program. Sometimes special adaptations will have to be made to the physical facilities to accommodate such things as wheelchairs or to provide needed medical support in the transitional phase. The fact that so many schools have been built without bathroom and ramp facilities for the handicapped indicates how educators traditionally have not planned for these needs in the mainstream of education.

8. *School Personnel Input Into the Medical Agencies.* Communication is a two-way process; educators need help from the medical agencies and they in turn, need help from educators. Educators need to communicate with them about the full range of strategies and interventions which the school is able and willing to provide to students. Educators also need to communicate with health agency personnel about the areas where students need more (or a different kind of) medical help than they have been receiv-

ing in order to facilitate long-range planning. Americans tend to think that they have the best medical services in the world; unfortunately many of these services are only available to those who can afford them. Such sensitive indicators as our high infant mortality rate remind us that the highly specialized, effective medical services displayed so glamorously on television are not generally available, especially to the poor. Although the schools do not have the responsibility of solving all of the problems facing society, educators do have the responsibility to communicate with other agencies about the unmet health needs of students.

EFFECTIVE LIAISON WITH SOCIAL AGENCIES

Under this heading would be included all of the social welfare and the recreational agencies.

1. *Exchanging Information.* There are times when school personnel want to know whether or not a student is being provided help from a given social welfare agency, and times when agencies need to know whether or not a particular child is attending school. In this regard, there is a fine line between that information which is a public record and presumably available to all, and that information which should be exchanged only with the parent's permission. In general, it is still advisable to require informed, parental permission both before giving or asking for information on a given student, although this would obviously slow down and in some cases stop the flow of potentially helpful information.

2. *Social Agency Input Into the School Curriculum.* There has been reasonably good effort by recreational agencies to work with the schools to inform students of their schedules. There has not, however, been much use of social agency personnel by the schools to assist with life-skills or social studies curricula. This condition may exist because they have been unable or unwilling to take the time, but more likely than not educators have neglected to identify the areas of expertise where these agencies could contribute to the curriculum, and they have not been personally invited to do so. It is little wonder that students get bored with schools and fail to see their relevance as they are required to read books that may or may not apply and where the material is fre-

quently not related to the social problems within the student's community. This process could be materially improved by field trips within the community, or barring that, by bringing in the people who have the expertise and who spend all of their working hours trying to solve social problems. Student-made films or slide shows of social agency activities would also be another way of bringing this information into the school. Many of the social workers in social agencies also have highly developed skills in working with students and their families who are having difficulties; that expertise should be made available to the life-skills curriculum.

3. *School-Initiated Requests for Social Service.* Although the majority of the students whose families qualify for welfare services have been identified and are already getting some help, there are always new students moving into an attendance area who need this kind of service. Application is often complicated by the fact that there are sometimes residency requirements before the family becomes eligible. The schools will often attempt to find some temporary help for the family until more permanent aid can be obtained. A much more frequent problem is for the school personnel to identify students who are on welfare and need clothing or health services, and this is the basis for their contact with the agency. Families living on a very small income, who frequently are unable to manage money effectively, are often unable to meet even the smallest amount of extra expense for their children. Families on marginal incomes, but who are not eligible for welfare, also have difficulty in providing for these extras. In some cases, this help is readily available and reasonably easy to obtain, e.g. the willingness of the Lion's Club to provide money for glasses, but in other cases it is extremely difficult. Often other service clubs and PTAs are quite helpful in this regard.

There has recently been a tremendous increase in interest in cases of child abuse. Because of the potential conflict with the parent's right, this has traditionally been a sensitive area. Many states have recently passed legislation which requires anyone, including school personnel, to report even a suspected incident of child abuse. In this legislative model, it is the responsibility of the agency to do the investigation and carry out the appropriate action. Occasionally school personnel also initiate contacts with social agencies to explore the need for a change in home placement, with either a foster child or a child who is having major difficulty in his/her home setting. A modification would be to seek a "big brother" or "big sister" for a boy or girl through a volunteer social agency.

4. *Jointly Sponsored Social Agency/Educational Programs.* Although just beginning, the efforts to evaluate systematically all children and youth who are on welfare to determine if they have unmet educational, medical, or emotional needs will create the need for closer cooperation between mental health, social, and educational personnel. It will essentially be the responsibility of the welfare programs to find these children. There has usually been good cooperation between schools and welfare agencies in finding those students who need and are eligible (for example) for free summer camping programs. These programs are helpful and are reasonably easy to obtain financial support for, but they do not begin to satisfy the real needs of these students. There are instances of schools and social agencies working together on a youth employment service project which is certainly needed. The economy, with its continuing unemployment factor, makes it extremely difficult for students to find jobs, especially those who are inexperienced and/or who come from lower socioeconomic backgrounds. There are, of course, good examples of cooperative action between schools and recreational agencies, but even this could be improved. There are still times when the programs or the use of facilities conflict with each other and there will likely be a continuing conflict between educational programs and Little League programs which want raised pitching mounds. Although cooperation with recreational programs is certainly not without problems and undoubtedly increases the wear and tear on school buildings, it would appear that an even greater liaison between schools and these agencies would be desirable. Better utilization of the school facilities would probably be made.

5. *Student Involvement with Social Agencies.* Although there are probably fewer jobs in social agencies which could be used for work experience placements than there are in health agencies,

there is still the possibility of using these settings for professional exploration programs. With a larger number of students turning to human service activities, it would appear necessary to improve this kind of liaison. Similarly, there seems to have been less use of student volunteers in social agencies than in some other areas. Exceptions have already been referred to in such programs as the "hot line," "coffee houses," drug centers, and runaway houses. Recreation programs have, of course, made extensive use of students in after-school, Saturday, and summer programs.

6. *Full-Time Social Agency Programs for Students.* In a sense, social agencies which are responsible for placing students in foster homes have full responsibility for them. Foster home placement generally does not require taking students out of public schools, although frequently such a placement does necessitate a change in school. In many communities some residential facilities for non-delinquent children and youth operated by other agencies use the public schools; in others, teachers are provided by the public schools, and in still others, the educational program is under the direct supervision of the social agency. These liaison arrangements have usually been successful.

7. *Social Agency Requests for Educational Service.* When social agencies place students into foster homes, they usually try to coordinate their activities with the local school personnel to ensure that the student is given the extra help he/she needs. Similarly, when students are taken out of institutions before they are returned to the schools, good case work practice recommends careful preplanning with the school personnel. Although these children have not been much of a problem over the years, some do have behavioral difficulties and learning deficits which make them more difficult to place and which constitute another reason for good liaison between these two agencies. This task will be more difficult in direct proportion to the extent that the educational personnel have predetermined that the incoming student will be a problem.

8. *School Personnel Input into Social Agencies.* There is, of course, a need for school personnel to explain the educational program—what it can and cannot do—to these social case work person-

nel. Some of the "temporary" holding facilities do not have educational programs even though, in reality, the students often stay
for relatively long periods of time. With the increased emphasis
on education for such youth, cooperative planning is needed in order to provide this service. As a generalization, personnel from
these agencies are more sophisticated about the school program
than are personnel from the other community agencies.

EFFECTIVE LIAISON WITH LAW AGENCIES

Although traditionally the schools have had little direct contact
with lawyers and the courts, they are involved frequently with extensions of the courts in the form of probation officers, juvenile
workers, youth commission personnel, and general-duty law enforcement officers. Since the areas of overlap are generally small
with fire department personnel, liaison with them will also be considered here.

1. *Exchanging Information.* For most children and youth who
come into contact/conflict with the law, it is highly desirable to
obtain information on their school record. Unfortunately, the
"big stick" quality of many law agency personnel outweighs the
image of their being helpers, and this complicates the exchange of
information with them. It is even more essential that parental
permission be obtained. Requests from the courts for information
about a specific student are usually accompanied with a court
order (often as part of a civil action) which subpoenas either
the records or specific school personnel, or both. While this
clarifies the legal responsibility of the school, it may, at the same
time, complicate the feelings of the school personnel as to what
would be best for the student in question. Juvenile authorities
and probation personnel often work very hard to establish a good
liaison with school people. Although law enforcement personnel
often appraise school personnel of problems encountered by specific students, they do not, as a rule, have occasion to request information from the schools as often as is true of the reverse. Even
so, when information is sought by school personnel, parental permission is required.

2. *Law Agency Input Into the School Curriculum.* For ele-

mentary aged children, law agency personnel have traditionally provided bicycle safety programs. Fire department personnel have also provided fire-prevention programs with school students. Some agencies have worked on drug prevention programs, but these have too often focused on the physiological effects of the drugs and have not usually been effective. Law enforcement personnel and, occasionally, judges have been used in primary school community helper units and career day programs. There has not been good use of these people in social studies classes, although the class that is frequently required for seniors concerning "problems in our democracy" would be a natural place to use them effectively. In high school driver education courses the liaison between school and law agency personnel has generally been good.

3. *School-initiated Requests for Law Enforcement Service.* Schools will often request help in cases of school vandalism or major cases of such things as stealing. Similarly, in cases of major fights or school riots, requests will be made of law enforcement personnel. Otherwise, schools have been reluctant to turn students over to law enforcement officers even though, in some instances, juvenile officers are working essentially on delinquency prevention. It is much more common, once a student has been put on probation or is in school after having been in an institution, that school personnel will contact the student's parole or probation officer if it is felt that they need some help. Occasionally one still hears of juvenile officers being called upon to "read the riot act" or "scare" a student or group of students (such as those who are being truant), but, fortunately this misuse of probation officers is diminishing. Schools will often initiate a request for information about the school records of juveniles who have been educated in a residential facility, even though the responsibility for providing this kind of informaton to the schools should be that of the law enforcement personnel.

4. *Jointly Sponsored Law Agency/Educational Programs.* Reference has been made to the bicycle safety programs which are also sometimes coordinated with bicycle registration procedures. In some settings, juvenile officers and police personnel have started club activities for delinquent-prone young students (mostly boys)

such as the Police Athletic League program, which is technically a law agency program but frequently requires cooperative efforts with school personnel. Some police departments have also sponsored "drag racing" activities in appropriate places and under adequate supervision. As more resources are allocated (both financial and human) to delinquency prevention programs, there should be opportunities for school and law enforcement agencies jointly to sponsor valuable programs. Certainly schools have the need for a more viable program for working with acting-out, aggressive youths before their behaviors go so far that they become acclimated to a criminal/institutional way of life. Some progressive youth commission programs make smooth and effective transitions into the regular schools. As with any program of transferring people out of an institutional setting and into a normal setting, the chances of those persons succeeding are extremely low unless they receive considerable assistance. Once a young person begins to be viewed as someone from "that reform school" there are many factors (some of which are in the youth and some of which are in the environment to which they have to return) which make it very difficult for them to remain in school.

5. *Student Involvement with Law Agencies.* There has been little use of either volunteer or job experience placements in these types of agencies. Some clubs have adopted training programs much like the one that police officers complete; they are sometimes coordinated by police personnel. In some districts opportunities have been made available to older, high school boys to accompany police officers in their cruisers for a short period of time. This is often the first opportunity for many (even those who are model students in school) to see these officers doing something other than handing out speeding tickets or going through the roles one traditionally sees in the media.

6. *Full-Time Law Agency Programs for Students.* Although institutions for children from broken homes are usually operated by social agencies, in some less populated areas they are operated by the law enforcement agencies. As extensions of the Juvenile Court System, the probation departments and youth commissions have a whole range of programs for youths who have been in

trouble or have been judged to be "delinquent prone." For pre-adolescents and early teens, these are typically school-based programs with, of course, other cottage-based and recreational programs which attempt to rehabilitate the young people involved. Typically, these programs will involve boys three times more often than they do girls. As the youth get older, the educational program typically moves heavily into vocational training. Usually both of these types of programs try to get the young people back to their home, school, and community as soon as possible with an average stay from six to twelve months. The emphasis on these programs is traditionally rehabilitative. Unfortunately the rehabilitation takes place in what is often a highly structured situation, a situation that frequently is strongly contrasted with the lives the young persons led (and will have to lead again) in the community.

As students reach their middle and late teens (and as their offenses become more severe in the eyes of the law), some who would ordinarily still be in school are assigned to reformatory-type programs where the emphasis is one of punishment. Here work is done to support the institution's operational program (growing the food, doing the laundry, etc.), with less and less emphasis on educational programming. Although such institutions keep these youths off the street (and in a sense protect society in the short run) the confusion of the purpose of these institutions over whether or not they are trying to punish these people or to rehabilitate them results in these institutions frequently doing neither job very well. If the kinds of punishment given in typical secondary schools are ineffective (especially over the long run), they are even less effective as a long-range rehabilitation for these youthful offenders. One major reason why this is true is that there is little opportunity to carry out the discipline within a framework of warmth and respect for the individual's dignity. Although adult prison reform is clearly outside the scope of this book, these issues are very central to any discussion of corrective/therapeutic interventions in the schools and in the community at large. No simple solution is proposed, but the one that implies that all that has to be done is to increase the rate of sending offenders (be they young or old) to institutions, to keep them locked up for increasingly long periods of time, is definitely questionable.

7. *Law Enforcement Agency Requests for Educational Service.* Unless they are close to or over the age for compulsory attendance, with rare exceptions youthful offenders are returned to the schools. Unfortunately many of those coming back were the ones with which the school personnel had experienced a great deal of difficulty. Even if they were not school problems before they left, they are now labeled as "youthful offenders" (or worse) and have the stigma of having been so incorrigible that they had to be institutionalized. Unfortunately, many of them were originally sent to the special program because of the home or school situation rather than because of anything the young person had done. It would be frightening to calculate how many young people now have a "record" for no more serious offense than smoking in school or nonconformity to a school program (for which conformity was of questionable validity or utility). There is the reality that while they are incarcerated in these "educational programs," the real education has been (no matter how hard the staff had tried to prevent it) one of learning how to get into more trouble. For these and a number of other reasons, it is extremely difficult to find a school placement which will provide a student such as this with a reasonable chance to succeed. A combination of the factors which took them out of the community in the first place plus the new factors which they have to encounter in the home, school, and community to which they have returned, prevent a large percentage of these students from succeeding. The main intervention at the school's disposal is to make certain that those conditions over which it has some control—the receptivity of the school staff—is as open to these young people and as conducive to success as possible. A special problem exists in transferring from vocational programs because many local schools do not offer them and those that do are often full or have a training pattern, i.e. a two-year sequence, that does not permit out-of-sequence entry of a new student.

8. *School Personnel Input into Law Enforcement Agencies.* There is a need for improved communication between the schools

and the personnel in law enforcement agencies. Educators need to communicate and to cooperate with them to find better ways to work with delinquency-prone youth. Educators need to tell the law agencies what intervention strategies they can expect from them. Educators need to work with them to find ways of helping students move in and out of correctional institutions as smoothly as possible. Because so many reforms these days are coming through the courts (rather than from educators or legislators), educators must also learn to "rattle the cage" as advocates for students who need a wide range of human services not currently available to them.

EFFECTIVE LIAISON WITH MENTAL HEALTH AGENCIES

Under this category would be classified all community counseling and therapeutic services, both inpatient and outpatient, including schools and institutions for the retarded and/or emotionally disturbed.

1. *Exchanging Information.* The requesting or giving of information to any mental health agencies should be preceded by obtaining informed parental consent. Typically there has not been much need for the transfer of information unless one of the agencies or the schools directly request service from the other.

2. *Mental Health Input Into the School Curriculum.* Because the life-skills curriculum has not been well developed in the past (see Chapter 6), there has been little use of mental health personnel in the school curriculum. With the increased interest in this area and because students are expressing more interest in human service activities, hopefully this will change. Most of the professionals in mental health are interested in the prevention of mental health problems and would welcome the opportunity to become involved in a developmental/preventative curriculum in the life-skill areas. Since so many students in college are majoring in psychology and sociology, there is a need for more effective use of mental health specialists and behavioral science specialists in Career Day programs for older youth. There is need for professional exploration programs which are sponsored by the school. Students should be helped to understand the social implications

of the identification and care of the severely retarded.

3. *School-Initiated Requests for Mental Health Services.*
Schools make many referrals of students and/or their parents to
community mental health agencies for counseling and therapy.
When these referrals are made it is best, whenever possible, to list
several equally good sources for counseling or therapy when working with the student and/or family. School referrals have been
very ineffective for many reasons. For every referral made, only
a small percentage of the parents and students followed through.
Some did not believe the problem was "bad enough." Some
decided to wait and see if the situation would get better. Some
openly feared what they thought was implied by seeking counseling or therapy. Some undoubtedly questioned the value of such
an approach. Of those who actually did follow through, many
found a long waiting period, especially in the publicly supported
mental health agencies. Of those who did enter into counseling
or therapy, there has traditionally been little feedback to the
school and little observed change in the student's behavior in the
school setting.

Remediation of these problems must be multifaceted. Schools
need to make more effective use of a broad range of developmental
and corrective strategies and interventions in the life-skills area.
Personnel on the Learning Facilitation Team must become more
precise in deciding which students and/or their parents need to be
referred. Improved communication between the agency and school
personnel at the time of referral would be helpful. School personnel need to help these agencies conduct an education program
about what can reasonably be expected of their agencies and help
to reduce the stigma of seeking such help. People within the culture
seek help from medical specialists at the slightest sign of physical
pain but wait until untold months of mental anguish have passed
before they seek the help of mental health professionals. The
school personnel need to improve their ability to refer and to follow through once they have referred so that a larger percentage of
those who really need the mental health services actually receive
them. Educators need to work cooperatively with the agency
personnel to help them improve their services to school-related

problems. Promising trends in this regard include more powerful use of short-term therapy, more effective use of working with the whole family, more precision in the goals and objectives of therapy, more use of the social learning and reinforcement available in groups, and better use of specific "homework" exercise to take place between the counseling/therapy sessions. School personnel will need to encourage more mental health services in the community and learn to keep the avenue of communication open, providing the therapists with feedback about changes in student behavior and learning. Although it happens with a great deal less frequency, it is occasionally necessary to refer a student in some of the special classes to institutions for the retarded.

4. *Jointly Sponsored Mental/Educational Programs.* Agency mental health personnel have for some time attempted to provide mental health consultation to school personnel. The traditional model was for a consultant to work with a teacher (or other educator) who in turn worked directly with the student. Although it has obviously done some good, this process has probably lacked sufficient precision to make it possible for much improvement to take place. There is unquestionably a need for more mental health support and assistance to teachers in their roles as the primary sources of mental health services to large groups of students. Some models of group counseling and systematic human relations training show promise for providing help to teachers. Anyone who works as closely with large groups of students over long periods of time as teachers do needs occasional supportive help and an opportunity to revitalize him/herself.

There has been an increase in the number of mental health professionals approaching the schools to collaborate with school personnel in providing direct counseling services to students. There is, as has been noted, a decrease in interest and support in the efforts of these professionals to treat students in segregated schools and institutions for the emotionally disturbed and, to some extent, for the mentally retarded. School personnel cannot handle all mental health needs of all students. It is also doubtful if the mental health agencies can either, especially with the present models of service and staffing loads. There is a much better chance that these two groups can accomplish this task if they work at it together.

5. *Student Involvement with Mental Health Agencies.* Students have served as volunteers in agencies for the mentally retarded in mental health agencies, especially those serving institutionalized patients. Many older students have volunteered to serve in coffee houses, drop-in centers, crisis centers, or on "switchboards," all of which could be broadly classified as mental health agencies. The use of mental health programs for work experience or professional exploration placements has not progressed very far. More needs to be done to train students to volunteer some of their time to provide helping relationships to others who are having problems. This is another major societal problem which somehow seldom seems to come into sharp focus in the curriculum of the schools.

6. *Full-time Mental Health Agency Programs for Students.* The major mental health programs which involve student-age populations and which are not under the administration of the schools are the residential treatment centers for the emotionally disturbed and the mentally retarded. Some of these are privately operated schools or treatment centers; some are extensions of medical centers; some are attached to mental hospitals for the adult mentally ill, and some are full-time, tax-supported institutions for this purpose.

7. *Mental Health Agency Requests for Educational Service.* Although there is a great deal of overlap in the kinds of young people who are in institutions run by law enforcement agencies and those run by mental health agencies, there does seem to be a difference in the attitude of school personnel about students who have been in these various programs when it comes time to return them to the schools. There is a great tendency to react (overreact?) to the label rather than to attend to the real factors in the individual student who is trying to make it back. It would be extremely helpful to these young people if educators could increase the ability of the regular classroom to accommodate borderline behaviors which may be unusual or strange but which are not harmful. This would allow these students to remain in the main-

stream. It is always amazing how much abnormal behavior one sees outside of the institutions and how much normal behavior one can see inside them. Institutions are being pressured to return more of these young people to the community where they will be returned to the mainstream of education.

8. *School Personnel Input into Mental Health Agencies.* Many theories of personality development and most systems of therapy were devised by people who work only with the abnormal. Although educators are not quite ready to do so, they have the opportunity to help build a theory of personality development based on a much more representative, essentially normally functioning, school-age population. In the meantime they can help other agency personnel remember what normal developmental problems are like. They can also give them information about some of the interventions used in the schools which involve therapeutic components from social interaction and which seem to have such great strength. In general, educators and mental health agency personnel have much to learn from each other and too little opportunity to share.

REFERENCES

Agoston, T. *Insight therapy: Methodology, psychosystematics and differential dynamics.* Columbus: Ohio State Department of Mental Hygiene and Correction, 1969.

Arnstein, H. S. *Billy and our new baby.* New York: Behavioral Publications, 1974.

Banas, N., & Wills, I. H. *Success begins with understanding.* San Rafael: Academy Therapy, 1972.

Bandler, R., & Grinder, J. *The structure of magic: A book about language and therapy.* Palo Alto: Science & Behavior, 1975.

Barclay, J. R. *Foundations of counseling strategies.* New York: Wiley. 1971.

Bates, M. Themes in group counseling with adolescents. In I. M. Berkovitz, (Ed.). *When schools care: Creative use of groups in secondary schools.* New York: Brunner/Mazel, 1975a.

Bates, M. Confrontation in the group process. In I. M. Berkovitz. (Ed.). *When schools care: Creative use of groups in secondary schools.* New York: Brunner/Mazel, 1975b.

Bates, M. M., & Johnson, C. D. *Group leadership: A manual for group counseling leaders.* Denver: Love, 1972.

Berkovitz, I. H. (Ed.). *Adolescents grow in groups: Clinical experiences in adolescent group psychotherapy.* New York: Brunner/Mazel, 1972.

Berkovitz, I. M. (Ed.). *When schools care: Creative use of groups in secondary schools.* New York: Brunner/Mazel, 1975.

Berne, E. *Games people play.* New York: Grove Press, 1964.

Blain, G. B. Jr., & McArthur, C. C. *Emotional problems of the student* (2nd ed.). West Nyack, N.Y.: Prentice-Hall, 1971.

Blatner, H. *Acting in: Practical application of psychodramatic methods.* New York: Springer, 1973.

Bower, E. M. *Early identification of emotionally disturbed children in school,* (2nd ed.). Springfield: Charles C Thomas, 1974.

Bugg, C. A. Systematic desensitization: A technique worth trying. In W. M. Walsh (Ed.). *Counseling children and adolescents: An anthology of contemporary techniques.* Berkeley: McCutchan, 1976.

Carek, D. J. *Principles of child psychotherapy.* Springfield: Charles C Thomas, 1972.

Carkhuff, R. R. *Helping and human relations: A primer for lay and professional helpers,* Vol. 1, *Selection and training.* New York: Holt, Rhinehart, & Winston, 1969.

Clarizio, H. F., & McCoy, G. M. *Behavior disorders in school aged children.* Scranton, Pa.: Chandler, 1970.

Daniels, L. K. *The management of childhood behavior problems in school and at home.* Springfield: Charles C Thomas, 1974.

Denues, C. *Career perspective: Your choice of work.* Worthington, Oh.: Charles A. Jones, 1972.

Downing, L., N. *Counseling theories and techniques: Summarized and critiqued.* Chicago: Nelson Hall, 1975.

Eiseman, J. W. *The deciders.* Menlo Park: Institute for Staff Development, 1969.

Ellis, A. *Growth through reason.* Palo Alto: Science & Behavior, 1971.

Ellis, A. Rational-emotive therapy. In G. M. Gazda, (Ed.). *Basic approaches to group psychotherapy and group counseling* (2nd ed.). Springfield: Charles C Thomas, 1975.

Ellis, A., & Harper, R. A. *A guide to rational living.* Hollywood: Wilshire Books, 1972.

Fassier, J. F. *My grandpa died today.* New York: Behavioral Publications, 1971.

Gang, B. *An adjustment to get a clear image: Focus—Runaway Hotel.* Washington, D. C.: Department of Health, Education, and Welfare, United States Government Printing Office (n.d.).

Gardner, W. I. *Children with learning and behavior problems: A behavioral management approach.* Rockleigh, N. J.: Allyn & Bacon, 1975.

Gazda, G. M. *Group counseling: A developmental approach.* Boston: Allyn & Bacon, 1971.

Gazda, G .M. (Ed.). *Basic approaches to group psychotherapy and group counseling (2nd ed.)*. Springfield: Charles C Thomas, 1975.

Gazda, G. M., Asbury, F. R., Balzar, F. J., Childres, W. C., Desselle, R. C., & Walters, R. P. *Human relations development: A manual for educators*. Boston: Allyn & Bacon, 1973.

Gazda, G. M., & Folds, J. H. *Group guidance: A critical incidents approach*. Chicago: Parkinson Division, Follett Education Corp., 1968.

Gazda, G. M., Walters, R. P., & Childers, W. C. *Realtalk: Exercises in friendship and helping skills*. Authors, 1976.

Glasser, W. *Reality therapy*. New York: Harper, 1965.

Goodman, D. S. *Emotional well-being through rational behavior training*. Springfield: Charles C Thomas, 1975.

Golembiewski, R. T., & Blumberg, A. (Eds.). *Sensitivity training and the laboratory approach: Readings about concepts and applications*. Itasca, Il.: Peacock, 1970.

Gordon, T. R. *Parent effectiveness training: The tested new way to raise responsible children*. New York: Wyden, 1970.

Goulding, R. L. The formation and beginning process of transactional analysis groups. In G. M. Gazda, (Ed.). *Basic approaches to group psychotherapy and group counseling* (2nd ed.). Springfield: Charles C Thomas, 1975.

Greenburg, I. A. *Psychodrama: Theory and therapy*. New York: Behavioral Publications, 1974.

Haas, K. *Growth encounter: A guide for groups*. Chicago: Nelson Hall, 1975.

Hackney, H., & Nye, S. *Counseling strategies and objectives*. Englewood Cliffs: Prentice-Hall, 1973.

Hamburg, B., & Varenhorst, B. B. Peer counseling in the secondary schools: A community mental health project for youth. *American Journal of Orthopsychiatry*, 1972, *42*, 566-581.

Haring, N. G., & Phillips, E. L. *Analysis and modification of classroom behavior*. Englewood Cliffs: Prentice-Hall, 1972.

Harris, T. A. *I'm OK, you're OK: A practical guide to transactional analysis*. New York: Harper & Row, 1967.

Hawes, R. M. Reality therapy: An approach to encourage the individual and social responsibility in the elementary school. In W. M. Walsh, (Ed.). *Counseling children and adolescents: An anthology of contemporary techniques*. Berkeley: McCutchan, 1976.

Hechlik, J. E., & Lee, J .L. (Eds.). *CAPS current resources series: Small group work and group dynamics*. Ann Arbor: ERIC Counseling and Personnel Services Information Center, 1968.

Hewett, F. M. *The emotionally disturbed child in the classroom*. Rockleigh, N. J.: Allyn & Bacon, 1975.

Hora, T. Existential psychiatry and group psychotherapy: Basic principles. In G. M. Gazda, (Ed.). *Basic approaches to group psychotherapy and group counseling* (2nd ed). Springfield: Charles C Thomas, 1975.

Kaltenbach, R. F., & Gazda, G. M. Reality therapy in groups. In G. M.

Gazda (Ed.). *Basic approaches to group psychotherapy and group counseling* (2nd ed.). Springfield: Charles C Thomas, 1975.

Keat, D. *Fundamentals of child counseling*. Boston: Houghton-Mifflin, 1974.

Kozloff, M. A. *Educating children with learning and behavior problems*. New York: Wiley-Interscience, 1974.

Krumboltz, J. D. *Stating the goals of counseling*. Fullerton: California Personnel and Guidance Association, 1966.

Lazarus, A. A. *Behavior therapy and beyond*. New York: McGraw-Hill, 1971.

Landefeld, J. Speaking therapeutically. *Human Behavior*, 1975, *4* (9), 56-59.

Liberman, R. P. *A guide to behavioral analysis and therapy*. New York: Pergamon, 1972.

Lieberman, M. A., Yalom, I. D., & Miles, M. B. *Encounter groups: First facts*. New York: Basic Books, 1973.

Luft, J. *Group processes: An introduction to group dynamics* (2nd ed.). Palo Alto: National, 1970.

Mattson, J. (Ed). Peer counseling. *ERIC Caps Capsule*, 1970, *3*, 1-15.

Maultsby, M. C., Jr. *More personal happiness through rational self-counseling*. Lexington, Ky.: Author, 1974.

Maultsby, M. C., Jr. *Help yourself to happiness*. Lexington, Ky.: University of Kentucky Medical Center, 1975.

McFall, R. M., & Lillesand, D. B. Behavioral rehearsal with modeling and coaching in assertion training. *Journal of Abnormal Psychology*, 1971, *77*, 313-323.

Meador, B. D. Client-centered therapy. In G. M. Gazda, (Ed.). *Basic approaches to group psychotherapy and group counseling* (2nd ed.). Springfield: Charles C Thomas, 1975.

Meyer, J. B., & Meyer, J. K. *Counseling psychology: Theories and case studies*. Boston: Allyn & Bacon, 1975.

Montgomery, D. A short term contractual approach to career counseling. In R. C. Reardon, & H. D. Burck, (Eds.). *Facilitating career development: Strategies for counselors*. Springfield: Charles C Thomas, 1975.

Morris, K. T., & Cinnamon, K. M. *A handbook of verbal group exercises*. Springfield: Charles C Thomas, 1974.

Morris, K. T., & Cinnamon, K. M. *A handbook of non-verbal exercises*. Springfield: Charles C Thomas, 1975.

Nielson, G. E. *Helping children behave: A handbook of applied learning principles*. Chicago: Nelson Hall, 1974.

Pfeiffer, J. W., & Jones, J. E. (Eds.). *A handbook of structured experiences for human relations training*, Vol. 1. Iowa City: University Associates Press, 1974.

Pine, G. J. The existential counselor. In W. M. Walsh, (Ed.). *Counseling children and adolescents: An anthology of contemporary techniques*. Berkeley, Ca.: McCutchan, 1976.

Project TRIAD: Road notes. Flint, Mi.: Genosee Intermediate School District, 1974 (mimeographed).

Purkey, W. W. *Self-concept and school achievement.* Englewood Cliffs: Prentice-Hall, 1970.

Reardon, R. C., & Burck, H. D. (Eds.). *Facilitating career development.* Springfield: Charles C Thomas, 1975.

Redl, F. *When we deal with children.* New York: Free Press, 1966.

Rhodes, W. C., & Tracy, M. L. *A study of child variance: Conceptual project in emotional disturbance.* Ann Arbor: Institute for the Study of Mental Retardation and Related Disabilities, University of Michigan, 1972.

Rogers, C. R. *Counseling psychotherapy.* Boston: Houghton-Mifflin, 1942.

Rogers, C. R. *Carl Rogers on encounter groups.* New York: Harper & Row, 1970.

Rose, S. D. *Treating children in groups.* San Francisco: Jossey-Bass, 1972.

Santa Clara Educational-Vocational Guidance Program. Santa Clara, Ca.: Santa Clara Unified School District (n.d., out of print).

Sarason, I. G., & Sarason, B. R. *Constructive classroom behavior: A teacher's guide to modeling and role-playing techniques.* New York: Behavioral Publications, 1974.

Schein, E. H., & Bennis, W. G. (Eds.). *Personalized organizational change through group methods: The laboratory approach.* New York: Wiley, 1965.

Slavson, S. R., & Schiffer, M. *Group psychotherapies for children: A textbook.* New York: International University, 1975.

Stanford, G., & Stanford, B. D. *Learning discussion skills through games.* New York: Citation Press, 1969.

Sugar, M. (Ed.). *The adolescent group and family therapy.* New York: Brunner/Mazel, 1975.

Tarczan, C. *An educator's guide to psychological tests: Descriptions and classroom implications.* Springfield: Charles C Thomas, 1972.

Walsh, W. M. (Ed.). *Counseling children and adolescents: An anthology of contemporary techniques.* Berkeley: McCutchan, 1976.

Watson, D., & Tharp, R. *Self-directed behavior: Self modification for personal adjustment.* Monterey: Brooks/Cole, 1972.

Wickramasekera, I. *Biofeedback, behavior therapy, and hypnosis: Potentiating the verbal control of behavior for clinicians.* Chicago: Nelson-Hall, 1976.

Widerman, J. L., & Widerman, E. L. Counseling non-verbal students. In W. M. Walsh (Ed.). *Counseling children and adolescents: An anthology of contemporary techniques.* Berkeley: McCutchan, 1976.

Wiseman, J. *People as partners: Individual and family relationships in today's world.* San Francisco: Canfield, 1971.

Zeligs, R. *Children's experience with death.* Springfield: Charles C Thomas, 1974.

Zifferblatt, S. *Improving study and homework behaviors.* Champaign: Research Press, 1970.

Chapter 8

CHOOSING THE BEST STRATEGIES

INTRODUCTION

Strategies for Helping Students is intended to be used both in a developmental/preventative and a corrective/remedial (or therapeutic) way. When used developmentally, it will provide school personnel a compendium of strategies for helping students from which to choose, and hopefully, it will facilitate their initiating some of those that have not previously been available. In this sense, it is conceived as a process of helping educators to conceptualize and to improve on all of the strategies they have at their disposal for helping students. In actuality it is often difficult to make a differentiation between a preventive approach and one which is corrective in nature and is utilized directly to help a student. The primary emphasis of this, the last chapter, is to help those educators who have identified one or more students with discrepant behaviors to decide what can be done, both directly and indirectly, to help them. It is designed to help educators, preferably through a Learning Facilitation Team, to choose and implement that combination of strategies which is most likely to facilitate change in specific students.

In earlier sections of this book, the word *strategies* has been used primarily to define those things which can be done of a developmental/preventative nature and *interventions* has been used to describe those things which are corrective/remedial or therapeutic in nature. Since those using this book are encouraged to look at the full range of ways of helping students, and since the word *strategies* represents the broader term describing ways of helping students, the title of "Choosing the Best Strategies" has been used for this chapter. The emphasis is, or should be, on choosing ways to help students rather than finding "causes" for the problem. Although the process of choosing strategies would probably be facilitated if the "cause" of a given behavior were known, in real life this becomes extremely complicated, time consuming, and not very productive. The concept of finding "interventions" has been stressed in the sense of introducing a service into the life space of a student in order to help him/her function more effectively. Although "adequate performance" is defined to a large extent by the larger society, educators must continuously seek to find ways to involve students in the process of defining what this specifically means in their own lives. In a society such as ours, there should be enough room for individual differences to make it possible for almost every student to find some unique way to satisfy his/her needs without being placed in conflict with the demands of the larger society. It is fervently hoped that the strategies will not be used to force students to conform to artificial, rigid, or harmful standards of behavior.

In discussing strategies for helping specific students, there is much pressure to try to write a "cookbook," i.e. "if a student does this, then use strategy number 12." Everyone is surrounded by complex human problems for which they would like simple, effective solutions. Unfortunately, the state of the art currently does not support this kind of approach, if indeed it ever will. Such an approach is based on several very questionable assumptions. First of all, it assumes that all behaviors that look alike have essentially the same cause (and that raises the whole question of trying to classify behavior into similar categories). There is very little evidence to support this and a lot of evidence that such an approach just does not work. Stealing, for example, may be caused by a wide range of factors, e.g. showing off to one's friends, being hungry, being taught to steal by an older youth, or spite, to mention only a few. The "cookbook approach" also assumes that there is a strategy which will work with almost all students showing the same problem, which does not appear to be true. The Maryland Study Program, introduced many years ago, stressed the fact that "behavior is related, its causes are multiple, dynamic, and interrelated." As previously pointed out, however, educators are frequently forced to try to help children without really knowing what it is that has caused them to need special help.

Choosing a strategy to help one or more students is still much more of an art than it is a science. This chapter is an attempt to make it somewhat more precise; there would be a danger, however, to imply at this time that there is a definite step-by-step procedure to follow. Out of the total range of ways of helping students, the detailed process described in this chapter will ordinarily be reserved for those relatively complex, major problems which have not been helped by more simplistic solutions. For extremely divergent behavior, there is usually no simple solution. Further complicating the process is the fact that for almost every force there is a counterforce. If one tries just one approach to help a student, other factors will often come into play which will negate the effects of what one is trying to do. It has been helpful to remember that for even such a simple task as moving one's arm, one has to not only tighten the muscles on one side of the arm, but also to relax the muscles on the other side. It is best to try to find strategies that work with or complement each other in a natural, stereo fashion. For example, when someone is trying to get a student to stop some particular behavior, he/she should encourage the student to engage in a substitute activity which is in compatible with the thing that the student is trying to stop. This approach is related to the concept of involving students as much as possible in the process of choosing goals which are meaningful and desirable in their own lives. It should be pointed out once again that educators should be seeking several strategies which lead to possible solutions.

As indicated in Chapter 5, it is strongly encouraged that a Learning Facilitation Team be formed in each school, both to work on the process of helping specific students and to work developmentally by helping the school to evaluate and improve its full range of strategies for helping all students. At the elementary level, this team will be made up of the student's teacher (who usually knows the student best), the principal (who has the broadest view of the school's resources to help), the school psychologist (who frequently has the highest level of training in the behavioral assessment of anyone on the team), the elementary counselor (who is in the best position to assist in implementing most strategies), the school social worker (who is the resource person when outside agency help is needed), the school nurse (who has the best grasp of physical deficits of the student and is in the best position to make appropriate referrals in the medical area), all sitting in and contributing as available and as needed (Kaczkowski and Patterson, 1975). Since the team will be considering the total social setting in which the student with special needs will be helped, there will often be need for some measure of the social climate or learning-climate of the classroom (Barclay, 1973). At the secondary level, the teacher who referred the student would be involved but the counselor (who ordinarily takes a major part in scheduling and in providing the carry-through for the Learning Facilitation Team) would often be responsible for collecting the information from the student's other teachers. Typically, the vice-principal (sometimes with and sometimes without the principal) should be involved as one way of helping him/her to become aware of the total process of helping students, rather than restricting him/her to the narrow role of disciplinarian which he/she is frequently expected to fulfill (Chamberlin and Carnot, 1974). Once on the team, all members should drop their traditional professional roles and try to contribute as openly, creatively, and productively as possible.

Since there is so much overlap between the role of the parent and that of the school in the process of trying to help students, educators should strive to find more and more ways to involve the parent in the team process. Whereas parental involvement has been traditionally carried out more at the elementary level than it has at the secondary level, parents of older students should be asked to be involved equally as frequently as parents of elementary school children. The parents are needed for both their valuable input, i.e. what is the student's behavior like at home as contrasted with his/her behavior at school, etc. (Dinkmeyer and McCay, 1973; Moore, 1972), and because they can be a key part of the team that implements the plan which evolves from the process (Friedman, 1973). Educators will also want to involve older students in the process of finding appropriate strategies to assist themselves in overcoming their deficits and achieving their goals. These students have much to contribute and more to gain or lose by the process than anyone else.

Before rushing into the process of choosing the best strategies to "fix up" the student, it is, as always, wise to stop and look at the setting in which the process is taking place. It is hard to imagine any bit of behavior that could be identified as a "problem" in one setting which would not be either extremely normal and perhaps even exemplary in still another. This helps to remind us that it is the social setting which largely determines what is going to be called "normal" as opposed to that which is "abnormal" or "crazy" or "strange" (or any other label). This should remind everyone that part of the process of the Learning Facilitation Team is to help involve the total school faculty and community in the larger process of choosing strategies for helping all students. Although an expanded description of total school/community involvement would be beyond the scope of this book, the questions listed below under the four major processes for helping students should help at least to broach the topic. These questions could also be labeled "Questions to Encourage Total School Growth."

Questions Concerning the Development of Academic/Intellectual Skills, i.e. Strategies That Can be Done Around the Student

1. How narrowly has the school defined what constitutes a "good student"?

2. How flexible is the school system in meeting individual needs?

3. Are there alternate ways for helping students learn what they need to know, both inside and outside the classroom?

4. How relevant is what goes on in the schools in the everyday lives of the students? How relevant will it be in their future?

5. How open is the school to effective change?

6. How much attention is given to the rights of students; of parents?

7. How carefully is the development of each student followed to see if his/her academic/intellectual needs are being met?

8. Is there a problem-solving approach prevailing among the staff, or does it tend to "sweep problems under the rug"?

Questions Concerning the Utilization of Corrective/Remedial Interventions, i.e. Strategies That Can be Done to the Student

1. How full is the range of corrective/remedial interventions available to students?

2. How many resources outside the school are being used to help students (volunteers, parents, agencies, real-life experiences, etc.)?

3. How much of a "person-to-person" climate has been created throughout the school?

4. What alternatives to the standard, formal education have been developed?

5. Is there a climate of administrative/total-faculty support for going out of one's way to help students?

6. What helping specialists (psychologists, counselors, social workers, etc.) have been employed; are they available in sufficient quantity to be useful?

7. Are students/parents informed as problems develop?

8. Are special needs provided for in as normal a setting as possible?

Questions Concerning the Development of Life Skills, i.e. Strategies That Can be Done With the Student

1. Do students and teachers feel as though they should "check their emotions at the door" as they enter the school?

2. Is there systematic thought and effort given to the *affective* growth of each child?

3. What is the "gripe level" of the school coming from both teachers and students? Is there more focus on the negative than on the positive?

4. What effort is being made to help both teachers and students find ways to renew themselves? (The need for nurture is critically important to everyone.)

5. Are there sound provisions for a solidly based human skill-development program?

6. Is there some program/activity/person within the school

with which every student can become identified; i.e. to become "turned on to"?

7. Is there a reasonable balance between the teaching of "facts" of the culture (cognitive) with the personal realities that make those "facts" important (humanistic education)?

8. Is the school making use of the students' "real-life" feelings and situations to help them to develop and to practice the use of life skills?

Questions Concerning the Utilization of Corrective/Therapeutic Interventions, i.e. Strategies That Can be Done in Behalf of the Student

1. Is there an "active sense of outrage" at the system's or society's inhumanity to students?

2. Is everyone working to make the path of "normalcy" so wide that almost everyone can walk down it?

3. Is everyone trying to de-emphasize the fancy labels that so often tend to cut students out and emphasize the human understanding that keeps them involved?

4. Is everyone using a full range of people, i.e., other students, volunteers, aides, or professionals, in the task of helping students with unique personal growth problems?

5. Are the specialists who have been brought into the school integrated into the total program, or are they peripheral window-dressing?

6. Is there a functional child advocate or ombudsman concept, i.e. someone who has the responsibility to see that the child gets a fair chance?

7. Is there a prevailing atmosphere of "people helping people" in which everyone is valued and prized according to their attempts and their ability to help?

8. Is there an effective utilization of the total school climate to help students/teachers grow, as opposed to the pull-them-out, one-to-one approach?

These questions will, in many instances, help to identify the need for a plan of action. Whereas different schools will obviously need different plans, some things which need to be considered are listed below:

Factors Affecting the Formulation of the School Plan

1. Take the "pulse" of the school. Identify specific problems that need solutions. Be especially alert to the types of students who have been "rejected" (both academically and socially) by the school. Establish a climate of bringing the problems out into the open and working on them.

2. Help to identify in the plan the role of every person in the school. Work closely with the principal but do not expect him/her to engineer the climate that makes this possible; that has to come from all the members of the faculty. Try to find some ways to make the necessary "administrativia" of the school less cumbersome and time consuming so more people (but especially the principal) will have more energy left over to work on the creative, problem-solving approach.

3. Build a bulletin board or other visual center which will help to bring into the program long-range, developmental academic/intellectual and life-skill activities. Be alert to the problems that currently exist and to the holes that will appear in the developing plan. Encourage everyone to use the problem-solving approach to find solutions to these problems.

4. Build a plan that involves everyone in the local school unit. Although one can use good ideas wherever they are, do not wait for leadership from other schools or the District Office. Change at this level has to come essentially from the working unit of the local school.

Factors Affecting Interpersonal Relationships of the Staff

1. Encourage all staff members to take stock of themselves. Help them to assess whether or not they are doing all they can to help students. Identify the "blind spots" which are keeping everyone from reaching certain kinds of students.

2. Look at the interrelatedness of the faculty. Are there cliques? If so, is there respect shown by members of each group for other group members, or is there an active one-upmanship going on? Encourage the staff to be aware of how they handle disagreement, hostility, or individual differences etc., with each other.

3. Plan to develop some activities/projects which will help to

build a working team. All members do not need to be alike or even to socialize together, but when working as a team to help students, they should have sufficient respect for each other and a sufficient feeling of relatedness that they are able to work for the common good.

4. It will be essential that some method be used to educate parents, central administration, school board members, and others about what is being done and to enlist their help and support. The job is too big to be done alone; it will require the understanding and support of many others.

Marshalling the Manpower to Get the Job Done

1. A process should be initiated of helping students to become more responsible for their own activities, where they may freely offer to help other students who need it, and to seek help freely when they need it themselves.

2. As part of the regular curriculum process in the school, every student should be involved in the process of systematically using and sharing what they have learned. In this process of "cycle teaching," every student will help one or more other students learn in one or more areas the things they themselves have previously learned. This will provide a ready source of individualized assistance for students learning something for the first time and will tend to help the student who has served as a tutor to forget less rapidly because they now have a practical application for the material.

3. Use a wide spectrum of people in the process of helping, both in the implementation of the regular curriculum and also in the tutoring process (other students, parents, agency personnel, residents from the community, business people, college students, and personnel).

4. Demand the support of student service specialists (counselors, psychologists, social workers, nurses, etc.) in sufficient strength that they can do more than provide for the "student trivia." Demand that they not become isolated and that in addition to their work with individuals that they use their specialized training to work with teachers on the total learning process. Encourage them

to utilize a broader range of strategies for helping students than their professional role usually dictates.

Consideration About Working with Students with Specialized Needs

1. Develop a procedure which keeps track of all students to make sure that there is some part of the school experience that is essentially meaningful for them. Identify and do something about those students who have specialized needs before they develop such enormous problems that they are easily recognized by others as being "different."

2. Develop and utilize a Learning Facilitation Team to plan appropriate strategies for the total school and for students with special needs. Seek out multiple strategies which can be used to intervene in the life space of these students in the most effective way possible. Provide specialized services as close to the mainstream as possible.

3. Encourage each staff member to "adopt" one or more of these special-need students (they may or may not have been assigned to that teacher for academic work), to seek out and provide positive acceptance to them, and to organize their teaching in such a way as to free them (as much as possible) for more individual work with these students.

4. Actively seek the support of all in the plan. Find and use techniques for recognizing/praising effort and progress, both for those who are helping and for those who are being helped. Assume that there will be resistance to change and problems in the plan, but keep the problem-solving process going.

FLOW DIAGRAM AND THE STRATEGY SELECTION CHART

The process that is suggested for the Learning Facilitation Team when it is identifying strategies for a specific student is graphically summarized in the flow diagram seen in Figure 8-1. This process is described in more detail in the strategy selection charts which follow. (The creative work of Mager and Pipe, 1970 has been helpful in providing a visual approach to this complex problem.)

Flow Diagram

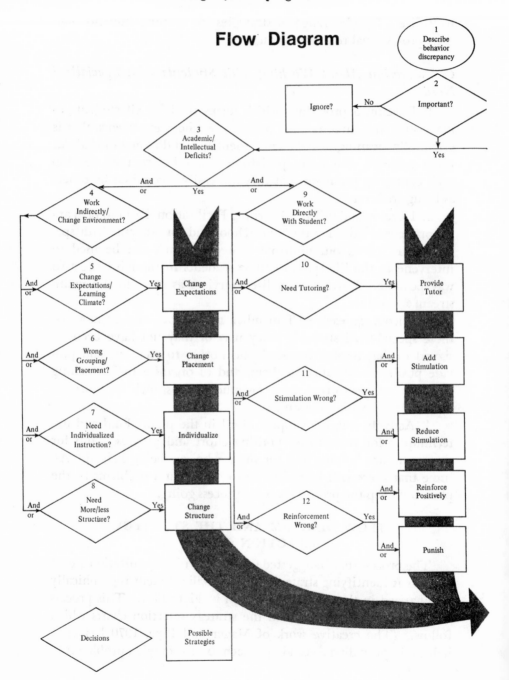

For Choosing Strategies

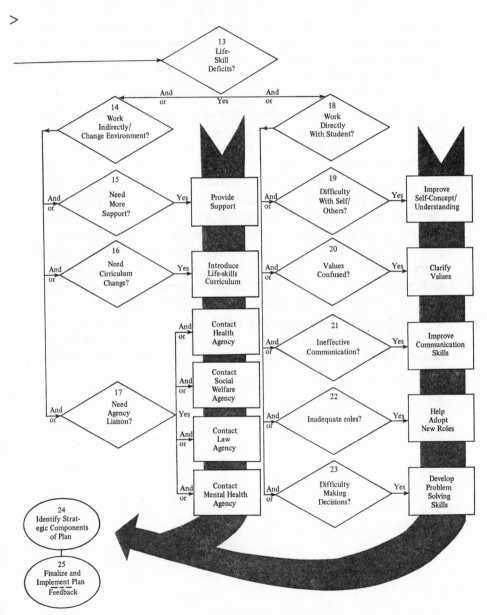

Figure 8-1.

Looking at the flow diagram and the strategy selection chart makes the process look deceptively clear-cut and organized. In real life it will seldom happen this way. One can theoretically start at almost any point in the process. Some problems will lend themselves better than others to this kind of analysis. The steps are shown in a sequence because it is the only way that the task can be approached, one step at a time. The process forces everyone to look for many more possible strategies for helping students than is typically the case. Members of the Learning Facilitation Team are encouraged to appoint one member to be the rotating leader who is responsible for ensuring that the whole range of possible strategies is explored. This will leave the other members free to work at a much more intuitive level. The group process should help each member to grow, both through describing and "selling" the strategies with which they are already familiar, and through hearing about and weighing the value of strategies proposed by others. It is usually helpful if every member takes notes on possible strategies as the process moves along. At the end, each will use the notes to make his/her contribution to the final plan of action. The team decision would also help to weed out the less productive and the high risk solutions which might be suggested. Like learning to drive, the process will seem awkward and cumbersome at first, but should become more natural with practice.

TABLE 8-I
STRATEGY SELECTION CHART: STEP 1

It Has Been Determined:	The Next Step — To Determine:	Ask Questions Such As:	For More Information:
That there is a problem/concern about a specific student.	Step 1. How to describe the behavior discrepancy in the most effective way?	Specifically, what is the student doing? Describe his/her actions as much as possible in behavioral/ observable terms. Specifically, what should he/she be doing? (Describe also in behavioral terms.) What is the behavior discrepancy between the "is" and the "should be"? (Describe precisely.) Who is concerned? Why? Is the behavior you are expecting of the student appropriate for him or her? Needed by him/her? If there are several behavioral deficits, which one should be worked on first?	
			If there is a behavior discrepancy, proceed to Step 2.

TABLE 8-II
STRATEGY SELECTION CHART : STEP 2

It Has Been Determined:	The Next Step — To Determine:	Ask Questions Such As:	For More Information:
That there is a behavior discrepancy (Step 1).	Step 2. Is the discrepancy important?	Why is the behavior discrepancy important? What would happen if it were left alone? What are the possible negative consequences of trying to do something to help, i.e. student feels different, peers tease, etc.? Does the student share your concern about the "problem" or is it primarily in the "eye of the beholder"? What are the chances of being successful in alleviating the problem?	If it is not important, ignore,
			If it is important, proceed to Step 3.

TABLE 8-III
STRATEGY SELECTION CHART. STEP 3

It Has Been Determined:	The Next Step — To Determine:	Ask Questions Such As:	For More Information:
That there is an important behavior discrepancy (Steps 1 and 2).	Step 3. Whether or not there is an academic/intellectual skill deficit?	Is the problem primarily in the student's difficulty to do the work assigned to him/her? Can the student do the work assigned but doesn't do it? (Could it be a lack of motivation or lack of reinforcement, and if so, how can he/she be motivated?)	For background information, refer to Chapter 4.
		Is the academic/intellectual problem associated with a major life-skill deficit or emotional problem? If the academic/intellectual behavior does occur occasionally, under what conditions is it most likely to occur? Is the problem an academic/intellectual skill deficit or a response deficit? If the student could not perform the task even if his/her life depended upon it, how can he/she develop the skill? Are there ways of working with the academic/intellectual problem without making the student feel too "different"?	To explore the possibility that the problem is essentially in the life skills area, proceed to Step 13.
		Should the work be done indirectly with the student, by changing the school environment?	To explore the need to work indirectly, proceed to Step 4.
		Or is it best to work directly with the student?	If it is best to work directly, move to Step 9.

TABLE 8-IV
STRATEGY SELECTION CHART: STEP 4

It Has Been Determined:	*The Next Step — To Determine:*	*Ask Questions Such As:*	*For More Information:*
That this is an academic/ intellectual skill deficit (in Step 3).	Step 4. Whether or not it is best to work indirectly on the student's environment to develop the academic skill?	Is the total school staff working together to help students like this achieve? Is the student's total learning climate conducive to helping him/her achieve? Is too much being expected of the student? Are there specific factors in the student's environment which "trigger" the discrepant behavior? Can they be altered? What roles do the student's classmates play in this behavior? Do they trigger it? Do they reinforce it? Are there ways in which the environment could be restructured which would be more likely to bring out the desired behavior? Is the student in a wrong program placement? Does the curriculum of the student need to be individualized to provide for specific interests/needs? Does the student need more/less structure from his/her environment?	For background information, refer to Chapter 4. To explore changing expectations and learning climate, proceed to Step 5. To explore changes in grouping/ placement, move to Step 6. To explore the need for more individualization, move to Step 7 To explore the need for a change in structure, move to Step 8.

TABLE 8-V
STRATEGY SELECTION CHART: STEP 5

It Has Been Determined:	*The Next Step — To Determine:*	*Ask Questions Such As:*	*For More Information:*
That it is best to work indirectly on the student's environment to correct the academic/ intellectual deficits (Step 4).	Step 5. Whether or not the expectations and learning climate surrounding the student need to be changed?	Are teachers expecting too much of this student? Are teachers expecting too little? What role do the student's peers play in setting a climate that is conducive to learning for this student? Is nonlearning or misbehavior rewarded by the student's peers? Does the faculty generally have a problem-solving approach to helping students such as this? Are students encouraged and willing to help other students? Do most of the students in the school have a feeling that they are contributing positively to the learning climate of the school? Is the attitude of the students essentially one of learning just what is "required" of them?	For suggestions on how to develop the "Facilitation Process," refer to Chapters 1-3. Background information on societal expectations is included in the section "Who Shall Be Educated", in Chapter 4. Explore Step 6 for possible strategies.

TABLE 8-VI
STRATEGY SELECTION CHART: STEP 6

It Has Been Determined:	*The Next Step— To Determine:*	*Ask Questions Such As:*	*For More Information:*
That it is best to work indirectly on the student's environment to correct the academic intellectual deficits (Step 4).	Step 6. Whether or not the student's grouping/ placement needs to be changed?	Is the student's current placement requiring too much of the student? Is the placement requiring too low a level of academic/intellectual excellence for this student? Are the social demands too great for this student? Not demanding enough? What academic/intellectual factors are missing in the student's placement that he/she needs? Are there ways that these factors can be supplied to the student in the present environment? What are the positive factors about the student's current placement? How can the effects of negative "labeling" that this student might be exposed to be minimized? If the grouping/placement is changed, will the possibility of the advantages outweigh the possible disruption caused by the change? If the decision is to change, how can the transition be made as smooth as possible? Does the student need to be screened for a special class or program?	For background information, refer to the "Grouping/ Placement" section in Chapter 4.
			Explore Step 7 for possible strategies.

TABLE 8-VII
STRATEGY SELECTION CHART: STEP 7

It Has Been Determined:	The Next Step— To Determine:	Ask Questions Such As:	For More Information:
That it is best to work indirectly in the student's environment to correct the academic/ intellectual deficits (Step 4).	Step 7. Whether or not the student needs an instructional program more tailored to his/her individualized needs?	Does the student have unique learning needs not being met by the current curriculum? Is the student's level of academic achievement markedly below the level of the curriculum that he/she is currently getting? Markedly above? Does the student have unique interests that should be reflected in his/her personal curriculum? Is the material the student is being asked to learn relevant to his/her interests and lifestyle? Has the student established goals for him/herself, and does he/she see a relationship between what he/she is doing in school and these goals? Is the material being presented to the student too rapidly? Too slowly? Is the student having difficulty forming the separate facts being learned into meaningful concepts? Does the student know how he/she is progressing? Does he/she know how he/she is being evaluated?	For background information, refer to the "Individualizing the Curriculum" section in Chapter 4.
			Explore Step 8 for possible strategies.

TABLE 8-VIII
STRATEGY SELECTION CHART: STEP 8

It Has Been Determined:	*The Next Step — To Determine:*	*Ask Questions Such As:*	*For More Information:*
That it is best to work indirectly in the student's environment to correct the academic/ intellectual deficits (Step 4).	Step 8. Whether or not the student needs a change of structure in his/her environment?	Is the student confused by the rules? Has the student been involved in helping to establish the rules? Is the student confused by the inconsistency with which the rules are being enforced? Does the student generally need more structure within which to operate? Does the student generally need less structure? Is the structuring provided for the student in his/her best interests, or is it provided primarily to meet the needs of others?	For background information, refer to the "Structuring" section in Chapter 4.
			Explore Step 9 for possible strategies.

TABLE 8-IX
STRATEGY SELECTION CHART: STEP 9

It Has Been Determined:	*The Next Step — To Determine:*	*Ask Questions Such As:*	*For More Information:*
That there is an academic/ intellectual skill deficit (Step 3).	Step 9. Whether or not it is best to work on the academic/ intellectual deficits directly with the student?	Is the severity of the academic/ intellectual problem so great that the direct approach is the only one practical? Is the student sufficiently con- cerned that he/she has asked for direct help or would will- ingly accept it if offered?	For background information, refer to Chapter 5, "Corrective/ Remedial Interventions."
		Can the student profit from being tutored?	To explore the need for tutoring, pro- ceed to Step 10.
		Does the student need more or less stimulation?	To explore the need for changes in the amount of stimula- tion, move on to Step 11.
		Does the student need positive reinforcement or punishment?	To explore the need for changes in reinforcement, move on to Step 12.

TABLE 8-X
STRATEGY SELECTION CHART: STEP 10

It Has Been Determined:	*The Next Step — To Determine:*	*Ask Questions Such As:*	*For More Information:*
That it is best to work directly with the student on academic/ intellectual deficits (Step 9).	Step 10. Whether or not the student needs special tutoring?	Would an extra five or ten minutes a day from the teacher help? Does the student need the academic/intellectual facts that can be brought to him/her by a tutor? Would the student's academic/ intellectual learnings be strengthened by the personal encouragement and emotional support from a tutor? Does the student need more immediate knowledge of his/her results, that can be provided by a tutor? Who would be available to tutor the student, i.e. other students, professional staff, other adults, parents, etc.? Who would train and supervise the tutor? Is there any way that the student who is being helped can also tutor still another youngster so he/she will not feel "out of it"? Have all students been encouraged to use and to share with others what they have learned?	For background information, refer to the "Tutoring" section of Chapter 5.
			Explore Step 11 for possible strategies.

TABLE 8-XI
STRATEGY SELECTION CHART: STEP 11

It Has Been Determined:	The Next Step — To Determine:	Ask Questions Such As:	For More Information:
That it is best to work directly with the student on academic/ intellectual deficits (Step 9).	Step 11. Whether or not the student would profit from more or less stimulation?	Has the student had inadequate sensory experiences or does he/she have difficulty integrating them? Has the student such limited experiences that it has affected his/her ability to learn? Are inadequate language development or speech problems cutting into the student's ability to learn? Is the student having difficulty forming the needed concepts? Does the student need an intellectual/academic adjustment to adapt to his/her high academic potential in one or more subjects? Is the student bored? Would the student profit from more competition? Does the student need physical/medical stimulation?	For background information, refer to the "Adding Stimulation" section of Chapter 5.
		Does the student seem overstimulated much of the time? When the student is overextended, would he/she profit from a "time out" procedure to regain his/her composure? Would a small "office" help to cut down on the distraction? Would the student be better off spending less time each day in school? If so, who would supervise? Should a moratorium be declared in some aspect of the student's life, i.e. nagging, homework, etc.? Is he/she getting too many services at once? Does the student need some form of medical destimulation?	For background information, refer to the "Reducing Stimulation" section of Chapter 5.
			Explore Step 12 for possible strategies.

TABLE 8-XII
STRATEGY SELECTION CHART: STEP 12

It Has Been Determined:	The Next Step — To Determine:	Ask Questions Such As:	For More Information:
That it is best to work directly with the student on academic/ intellectual deficits (Step 9).	Step 12. Whether or not changes in the type or schedule of reinforcement of the student would help?	Is the student getting any rewards or satisfactions from not achieving? Is there anything inherently rewarding to the student in the task he/she is being asked to learn? Has the student learned to respond to the normal social reinforcements, i.e. praise, smiles, grades, etc. which keep most students motivated? What kinds of things or events are reinforcing to the student? How can these be used to facilitate the learning process? If primary reinforcers, i.e. money, candy, toys, etc. are going to be used, how can they be paired with appropriate social reinforcers? Does he/she know the rules but has overstepped them? Is he/she emotionally healthy but testing the limits? Has someone carefully listened to the student's story? Is the punishment a natural consequence of his/her behavior? Will the punishment make the student hostile to the school? If the student is punished, does he/she know the desirable behavior, and will he/she be reinforced for displaying it? Will the punishment come close enough to the undesirable behavior so the student understands the relationship? If punishment is to be administered, are the student's rights (and those of the parents) properly observed?	For background information, refer to the "Reinforcement" section of Chapter 5. For general information, refer to the "Punishment" section of Chapter 5. Explore Step 13 for possible strategies.

TABLE 8-XIII
STRATEGY SELECTION CHART: STEP 13

It Has Been Determined:	The Next Step — To Determine:	Ask Questions Such As:	For More Information:
That the skill deficit is not essentially academic/ intellectual in nature (Steps 3 through 12).	Step 13. Whether or not The skill deficit is essentially in the life-skill area?	Are there social/emotional/behavioral problems which strongly contribute to the behavior discrepancy? Has the behavior discrepancy created major secondary behavioral problems which should be dealt with? Is the student able to demonstrate the life skills appropriate for his/her age-level and for the demands placed upon him/her? Are the social demands too great for the student to handle at this time?	For background information, refer to Chapter 6.
		If the student does not have the appropriate life skill, is it best to work indirectly through changes in his/her environment?	To explore the need for environmental changes, proceed to Step 14.
		Or should the work be done directly with the student to help him/her to develop the necessary life skills?	To explore the need for working directly with the student, move to Step 18.

TABLE 8-XIV
STRATEGY SELECTION CHART: STEP 14

It Has Been Determined:	*The Next Step — To Determine:*	*Ask Questions Such As:*	*For More Information:*
That there is a life-skill deficit (Step 13).	Step 14. Whether or not it is best to work indirectly on the student's environment to help to develop the needed life skill?	Has the student's educational environment facilitated the development of the needed life skill?	For background information, refer to Chapter 6.
		Is the social climate of the school conducive to helping this student grow and mature?	Also see the "Environmental Supports" section of Chapter 7.
		Is the school making too many life-skill demands on the student?	
		Does the student need additional emotional support from his/her educational environment?	To explore the need for environmental support, proceed to Step 15.
		What role do the student's peers play in the undesirable/inappropriate behavior?	
		Are there life skill curriculum changes that should be made which would help this and other students to develop/ use appropriate life skills?	To explore the need for curriculum change, move on to Step 16.
		How can the conditions of learning be arranged in such a way as to facilitate life-skill development/usage?	For more information on working with agencies, refer to Chapter 8.
		Is there a need for liaison with outside community agencies, i.e. health, social welfare, law, mental health, etc.?	
			To explore the need for liaison with these agencies, move on to Step 17.

TABLE 8-XV
STRATEGY SELECTION CHART: STEP 15

It Has Been Determined:	*The Next Step — To Determine:*	*Ask Questions Such As:*	*For More Information:*
That it is best to work on the life-skill deficits indirectly (Step 14).	Step 15. Whether or not the student needs more support from his/her environment?	Does the student have the life skill but is not able to use it or maintain control under a stressful situation?	For background information, refer to "Environmental Supports" section of Chapter 6.
		Under these circumstances, should the student be left alone for a given period of time to reorganize him/herself (perhaps at the same time trying to reduce the demands of the environment)?	
		Would a change in situation, i.e. new seat, new class, new school, etc. help the student get a new start? Would such a change destroy some positive factors working for the student in his/her current environment?	
		Would a club activity help the student develop/use the needed life skill?	
		Does he/she need to be placed in a special program/class? Would the potential gains make the risk of a disruption worthwhile?	
		Does the student need more structure, i.e. help with the rules, more consistent application of the rules, clearer understanding of what is expected of him/her?	See the "Structure" section in Chapter 4.
		Is there an appropriate punishment which would deter the student from displaying inappropriate life skills?	See the Punishment" section of Chapter 5.
		Can the punishment be administered without alienating the student?	
			Explore Step 16 for possible strategies.

TABLE 8-XVI
STRATEGY SELECTION CHART: STEP 16

It Has Been Determined:	*The Next Step — To Determine:*	*Ask Questions Such As:*	*For More Information:*
That it is best to work on the life-skill deficits indirectly (Step 14).	Step 16. Whether or not the student would be helped by the introduction of a life-skills curriculum	Has the student been systematically taught to use the life skill? Is there adequate opportunity for practice and use of the life skill in the student's educational environment? Are there other students who have a need for help to develop the life skill in question? Can this student be grouped for instruction with them? Would the student be helped to gain more information about the acquisition of the life skill through reading or other educational resources? Can the student perform the life skill adequately under certain circumstances but not under others? Can the learning conditions be so arranged that the appropriate life skill will be brought out in almost all instances?	The six-strand, nine-cycle life-skills curriculum is described in Chapter 6.
			Explore Step 17 for possible strategies.

TABLE 8-XVII
STRATEGY SELECTION CHART: STEP 17

It Has Been Determined:	The Next Step — To Determine:	Ask Questions Such As:	For More Information:
That it is best to work on the life-skill deficits indirectly (Step 14).	Step 17. Whether or not there is a need to establish a liaison with a community agency in order to help the student?	Is the student known by or already under the care, supervision, or responsibility of another agency? Does another agency have a service currently needed by this student? Is this student likely to need the services or supervision of an agency at some date in the forseeable future?	For background information, refer to Chapter 7.
		Is there a need for a specific liaison with outside health agencies? Does the student have a history of health problems? Does the student have physical/health factors that currently need attention?	See the "Effective Liaison with Health Agencies/Services" section in Chapter 7.
		Is there a need for a specific liaison with outside social welfare agencies? Has the student or his/her family been on welfare, or are they on welfare now? Is it likely that the student will subsequently need welfare services? Has he/she been physically abused? Does he/she need recreational services?	See the "Effective Liaison with Social Agencies" section in Chapter 7.
		Is there a need for specific liaison with law agencies? Has the student been brought to the attention of the police? Has the student been placed on probation either for protective custody or delinquency?	See the "Effective Liaison with Law Agencies" section in Chapter 7.
		Is there need for a special liaison with mental health agencies? Does the student have a history of major mental health problems? Has he/she received service from any of	See the "Effective Liaison with Mental Health Agencies" section in Chapter 7.

TABLE 8-XVII — (Continued)

It Has Been Determined:	The Next Step — To Determine:	Ask Questions Such As:	For More Information:
		these agencies? Does he/she need mental health service at this time? Is it likely that he/she will need such service in the near future? If liaison is to be implemented, has adequate attention been given to the protection of the student and/or his/her parents' rights?	
			Explore Step 18 for possible strategies.

TABLE 8-XVIII
STRATEGY SELECTION CHART: STEP 18

It Has Been Determined:	The Next Step — To Determine:	Ask Questions Such As:	For More Information:
That there is a life-skill deficit (Step 13).	Step 18. Whether or not it would be best to work on the life-skill deficit directly with the student?	Is the behavior discrepancy in the life-skill area so great that changes in the environment will in all likelihood not bring about the desired change?	For background information, see "Corrective Therapeutic Interventions," Chapter 7.
		Is the student under such pressure that he/she has asked for direct help?	
		Is the discrepancy so severe that a great deal of very specific, direct service is needed to help the student?	
		Is the student's problem so unique for his/her age level that it is impractical to try to use indirect methods?	
		Is the time pressure such that one cannot wait until the indirect methods can operate?	
		Is the problem so personal that involving other jeople would be embarrassing to the student and/or counter-productive in helping him/her?	
		Is there a danger to the student's health or life so great that immediate, direct interventions are needed?	
		If direct corrective therapeutic interventions are used, will they be supplemented with other environmental supports as needed?	
		Does the student have difficulty with self or others?	Move to Step 19.
		Does the student need values clarification techniques?	Move to Step 20.
		Does the student need help with communication skills?	Move to Step 21.
		Does the student need help to adopt more satisfying roles?	Move to Step 22.
		Does the student have difficulty making decisions?	Move to Step 23.

TABLE 8-XIX
STRATEGY SELECTION CHART: STEP 19

It Has Been Determined:	*The Next Step — To Determine:*	*Ask Questions Such As:*	*For More Information:*
That it is best to work directly with the student on the correction of life-skill deficits (Step 18).	Step 19. Whether or not the student needs help in understanding him/herself and/or others?	Does the student have an adequate concept of self? Is the student aware of his/her feelings? Does he/she understand him/herself? Does the student have difficulty understanding/relating to others? Does he/she have adequate control over his/her emotions and feelings? Does he/she prejudge people on the basis of superficial characteristics? Does he/she tend to "look down" on large groups of people? Is the student too sensitive to others: not sensitive enough? Is the student in frequent conflict with others? Has the student attempted to harm him/herself or to commit suicide? Does the student have difficulty making and keeping close friends?	For background information, refer to "Strand 1—Understanding and Valuing Self and Others," Chapter 6. See also the sections on "Difficulty in Understanding/Accepting Self and Others" and "Problems Relating with Others' in Chapter 7. Explore Step 20 for possible strategies.

TABLE 8-XX
STRATEGY SELECTION CHART: STEP 20

It Has Been Determined:	The Next Step — To Determine:	Ask Questions Such As:	For More Information:
That it is best to work directly with the student on the correction of life-skill deficits (Step 18).	Step 20. Whether or not the student needs help in clarifying their values?	Does the student act under what appears to be one set of values at one time and another conflicting set at another time? Is the student in major conflict because his/her values differ markedly from those of his/her peers? His/her parents? With the school and/or society? Does the student have difficulty in identifying things that are of major interest (value) to him/her? Does the student have difficulty in expressing values (both verbally and nonverbally) in a way that enables others to relate to him/her effectively? Is the student having difficulty in shifting from values which are appropriate at one level of development to those which are more appropriate for a later stage? Is the student prejudiced in such a way as to affect his/her relationships to a major extent?	For background information, refer to "Strand II— Clarifying One's Values" in Chapter 6. See also the "Value Conflicts" section in Chapter 7. Explore Step 21 for possible strategies.

TABLE 8-XXI
STRATEGY SELECTION CHART: STEP 21

It Has Been Determined:	*The Next Step— To Determine:*	*Ask Questions Such As:*	*For More Information:*
That it is best to work directly with the student on the correction of life-skill deficits (Step 18).	Step 21. Whether or not the student needs help in communicating with others?	Is the student having a great deal of difficulty in understanding others? Is the student having difficulty communicating with others because of articulation problems? Is the student having difficulty communicating with others because of difficulty in expressing him/herself? Is the student having difficulty synthesizing the verbal and nonverbal communication of others? In the messages that he/she sends? Is there a language problem, i.e. does the student primarily think in or use a foreign language or some form of non-standard English, which is affecting his/her ability to communicate? Does the student have difficulty in speaking with specific groups or classes of people, i.e. older people, members of the opposite sex, people in authority, etc.?	For background information, refer to "Strand III— Improving Communication Skills" in Chapter 6. See also, "Communication Problems" section in Chapter 7. Explore Step 22 for possible strategies.

TABLE XXII
STRATEGY SELECTION CHART: STEP 22

It Has Been Determined:	*The Next Step — To Determine:*	*Ask Questions Such As:*	*For More Information:*
That it is best to work directly with the student on the correction of life-skill deficits (Step 18).	Step 22. Whether or not the student is having difficulty in developing and using more satisfying roles?	Does the student seem so indefinite or indecisive that he/she does not appear to be "anybody"? Does the student always play the same role regardless of how appropriate it is? Does the student have difficulty in putting him/herself in the place of others? Is the student using a role that once was appropriate but no longer is? Is the major role that the student is playing causing problems with his/her peers? Home? School? Is the student having difficulty with his/her sex-role identity? Are the sex roles that he/she is playing placing him/her in conflict with society?	For background information, refer to "Strand V— Adopting More Satisfying Roles" in Chapter 6. See also "Need for More Satisfying Roles" and "Sex and Sex/Role Problems" sections in Chapter 7. Explore Step 23 for possible strategies.

TABLE XXIII
STRATEGY SELECTION CHART: STEP 23

It Has Been Determined:	*The Next Step — To Determine:*	*Ask Questions Such As:*	*For More Information:*
That it is best to work directly with the student on the correction of life-skill deficits (Step 18).	Step 23. Whether or not the student is having difficulty making decisions?	Is the student very indecisive and unable to decide what he/she wants to do? Does the student know generally what he/she wants to do but is unable to identify the steps in how to get there? Does the student have difficulty finding and using the information necessary to make good decisions? Does the student keep shifting indiscriminantly from one goal to another? Is the student frequently making unwise decisions that get him/her into trouble? Does he/she have difficulty learning from his/her mistakes? Is the student too easily influenced by his/her peers? Is the student worried about not being able to make a decision about what to do with his/her life? Does the student seem generally apprehensive about the future? Does the student have problems with some form of substance abuse? Is the student in some sort of crisis which temporarily has made it difficult for him/her to make appropriate decisions?	For backgound information, refer to "Srand IV—Solving Life's Problems" and "Srand VI—Making Creative Decisions," both in Chapter 6. See also the "Drug Related Problems," "Difficulty in Making Decisions," and "Difficulty in Planning for the Future" sections of Chapter 7.
			Proceed to Step 24.

TABLE XXIV
STRATEGY SELECTION CHART: STEP 24

It Has Been Determined:	*The Next Step — To Determine:*	*Ask Questions Such As:*	*For More Information:*
That there are a number of possible ways of helping the student (Steps 3 through 23).	Step 24 Which combination of strategies is it best to use in a plan for helping the student?	Do some of the strategies require more resources than are currently available? Is the behavior discrepancy great enough to warrant the cost in time, energy, expense, etc., required to bring about the change? What combination of strategies is most cost-efficient, i.e. most likely to bring about the desired results with the least amount of resources/effort? What combination of strategies is most likely to help the student to grow and develop as a person? What combination of strategies are most under the control of the school and the ones most likely to draw upon the expertise available in the school? Which combination of strategies are of most interest (and hence the ones which are most likely to be used in appropriate follow-through)? What combination of strategies is most likely to supplement each other and work together in a stereo fashion to produce the desired results?	For background information, refer to "'Effective Liaison with Community Agencies" in Chapter 7.
			Proceed to finalizing/implementing the plan: Step 25.

TABLE 8-XXV
STRATEGY SELECTION CHART: STEP 25

It Has Been Determined:	*The Next Step — To Determine:*	*Ask Questions Such As:*	*For More Information:*
What combinations of strategies to use in a plan (Step 24).	Step 25. How to implement/finalize the Plan of Action?	What is the flow of the plan? Who will do what, to and with whom, by what time, etc.? What are the checkpoints to show that the plan is being implemented? Who reports what to whom? Whose responsibility is it to remind/reinforce people to activate the various components of the plan? What behavior on the part of of the student will indicate that the plan is succeeding? Failing? Who will be responsible to reconvene the Learning Facilitation Team to draw up a new plan or to revise the old one?	Watch the progress of the student to get feedback as to whether or not the plan is working.

REFERENCES

Barclay, J. R. Multiple input assessment and preventive intervention. *School Psychology Digest*, 1973, *2*, 13-18.

Chamberlin, L. J., & Carnot, J. B. *Improving school discipline*. Springfield, Il.: Charles C Thomas, 1974.

Dinkmeyer, D., & McKay, G. D. *Raising a responsible child: Practical steps to successful family relationships*. New York: Simon & Schuster, 1973.

Friedman, R. (Ed.). *Family roots of school learning and behavior disorders*. Springfield, Il.: Charles C Thomas, 1973.

Kaczkowski, H., & Patterson, C. H. *Counseling and psychology in elementary schools*. Springfield, Il.: Charles C Thomas, 1975.

Mager, R. F., & Pipe, P. *Analyzing performance problems or "you really oughta wanna."* Belmont, Ca.: Fearon Publishers, 1970.

Moore, D. J. *Preventing misbehavior in children*. Springfield, Il.: Charles C Thomas, 1972.

AUTHOR INDEX

SUBJECT INDEX